GW00771086

PSYCHE AND MATTER

A C. G. JUNG FOUNDATION BOOK

Published in association with Daimon Verlag,
Einsiedeln, Switzerland

The C. G. Jung Foundation for Analytical Psychology is
dedicated to helping men and women grow in conscious
awareness of the psychological realities in themselves and
society, find healing and meaning in their lives and greater
depth in their relationships, and live in response to their discovered sense of purpose. It welcomes the public to attend
its lectures, seminars, films, symposia, and workshops and
offers a wide selection of books for sale through its book-
store. The Foundation also publishes *Quadrant,* a semian-
nual journal, and books on Analytical Psychology and related subjects. For information about Foundation programs
or membership, please write to the C. G. Jung Foundation,
28 East 39th Street, New York, NY 10016.

PSYCHE AND MATTER

MARIE-LOUISE
VON FRANZ

Foreword by Robert Hinshaw

SHAMBHALA
Boston & London
1992

Shambhala Publications, Inc.
Horticultural Hall
300 Massachusetts Avenue
Boston, Massachusetts 02115

Shambhala Publications, Inc.
Random Century House
20 Vauxhall Bridge Road
London SW1V 2SA

Originally published by Daimon Verlag, Einsiedeln, Switzerland, under
the title *Psyche und Materie,* © 1988 by Daimon Verlag.
Pages ix–xi constitute a continuation of the copyright page.

All rights reserved. No part of this book may be reproduced in any form
or by any means, electronic or mechanical, including photocopying,
recording, or by any information storage and retrieval system, without
permission in writing from the publisher.

9 8 7 6 5 4 3 2 1

First Edition
Printed in the United States of America on acid-free paper ♾

ISBN 1-57062-620-0

Library of Congress Cataloging-in-Publication Data

Franz, Marie-Louise von, 1915–
    [Psyche und Materie. English]
    Psyche and matter / Marie-Louise von Franz.—1st ed.
        p. cm.
    Translation of: Psyche und Materie.
    "C. G. Jung Foundation book."
    Includes bibliographical references.

    1. Coincidence. 2. Jung, C. G. (Carl Gustav), 1875–1961.
3. Time perception. I. Title.
BF175.5.C65F7313 1992   91-53229
150.19′54—dc20   CIP

CONTENTS

vi · *Contents*

FOREWORD

This is the second volume in a series collecting the essays and lectures of Marie-Louise von Franz by subject for the first time. On the heels of the first volume (*Dreams,* published in spring 1991), which is devoted to the phenomenon of dreams, we are pleased now to present the second volume, with its theme of "Psyche and Matter." Included are lengthy presentations on synchronicity, the nearly simultaneous occurrence of two or more events that are not "causally" connected but are a meaningful coincidence. The concept of time is also investigated, as are contemporary potentials of rapprochement between the natural sciences and analytical psychology, in particular with regard to the relationship of mind and matter.

This last question is among the most crucial today for fields of research as varied as microphysics, quantum physics, psychosomatic medicine, biology, and depth psychology. Marie-Louise von Franz has concerned herself for more than thirty years with the issues, new discoveries, and hypotheses connected with this theme, from both psychological and natural science points of view. Her own observations, hypotheses, and conclusions have been presented in numerous articles, essays, and lectures over the years, but many of them were unavailable in English until now. Thus the urgency of this series, bringing together the fruits of her labors in standardized single-language volumes.

All of the articles have been revised and updated, and some were completely reworked by the author. They appeared originally in the years from 1960 to 1986 and are now, as then, of great relevance for contemporary holistic thought.

With the agreement of the author, we have structured each volume according to the general degree of complexity and the thematic affinity of the individual articles rather than placing them in chronological order. Bibliographic data concerning the place and date of original publication are given on page ix, and a bibliography appears at the end of the book.

Because the articles included here were originally written for a wide variety of interest groups or publication vehicles rather than conceived as successive chapters of a book, there is a small amount of overlapping of content; completely eliminating such repetitions would have detracted from the continuity of certain sections, so a looser editorial policy was adopted in this respect.

We would like to thank the author and all who helped to bring together these papers from many a journal or filing cabinet, and also to thank the previous publishers who agreed to their publication in this new and unified form.

Robert Hinshaw
Daimon Verlag
Einsiedeln, Switzerland

SOURCES

"Matter and Psyche from the Point of View of the Psychology of C. G. Jung" ("Materie und Psyche in der Sicht der Psychologie C. G. Jungs") was originally delivered as a lecture at the Conference of the Evangelical Academy of Baden Baden in Herrenalb, October 11–13, 1974. The German version of the recorded proceedings of the conference was checked and reworked by the author. The English translation is by Michael H. Kohn. Copyright © 1992 by Shambhala Publications, Inc.

"Symbols of the *Unus Mundus*" ("Symbole des Unus Mundus") first appeared in *Dialog über den Menschen: Eine Festschrift zum 75. Geburtstag von Wilhelm Bitter* (Stuttgart: Ernst Klett Verlag, 1968). An English translation appeared in *The Reality of the Psyche: Proceedings of the Third International Congress for Analytical Psychology*, edited by Joseph Wheelwright (New York: G. P. Putnam's Sons/C. G. Jung Foundation for Analytical Psychology, 1968). That translation has been expanded here. Copyright © 1992 by Marie-Louise von Franz.

"Time: Rhythm and Repose" was published as a book by Thames and Hudson, Inc., in 1978. Copyright © 1978 by Marie-Louise von Franz. Reprinted by permission of Thames and Hudson.

"The Psychological Experience of Time" first appeared in English in the *Eranos Yearbook 1978,* vol. 47 (Frankfurt am Main: Insel Verlag, 1979), containing lectures given at the Eranos Conference in Ascona, August 23–31, 1978. Copyright © 1979 by Marie-Louise von Franz.

"Psyche and Matter in Alchemy and Modern Science" was a paper delivered at the opening of the Jung Centennial Pro Helvetia Exhibit in Zurich in 1975 and subsequently in New York. It appeared in *Quadrant* 8, no. 1 (Spring 1975). Copyright © 1975 by Marie-Louise von Franz.

"The Idea of the Macro- and Microcosmos in the Light of Jungian Psychology" ("Die alchemistische Makrokosmos-mikrokosmosidee im Lichte der Jungschen Psychologie") first appeared in *Symbolon: Jahrbuch für Symbolforschung,* vol. 1 (Basel: Schwabe Verlag, 1960). In English it appeared in *Ambix* 13 (1965): 22–34. Reprinted by permission of the Society for the History of Alchemy and Chemistry, Sussex. Copyright © 1965 by SHAC.

"Some Historical Aspects of C. G. Jung's Synchronicity Hypothesis" ("Einige historische Aspekte zu C. G. Jungs Synchronizitätshypothese") is an abridgment of a lecture given at a conference on the space-time problem in Garmisch Partenkirchen. Participants at the conference, which was organized by the Dianus Triakont Verlag, included Carl Friedrich von Weizsäcker, the Dalai Lama, and Joseph Needham. The English translation is by Michael H. Kohn. Copyright © 1992 by Shambhala Publications, Inc.

"The Synchronicity Principle of C. G. Jung" ("Das Synchronizitätsprinzip C. G. Jungs") was originally published in the encyclopedia *Die Psychologie des 20. Jahrhunderts,* vol. 15 (Zurich: Kindler Verlag, 1979). The English translation is by Michael H. Kohn. Copyright © 1992 by Shambhala Publications, Inc.

"A Contribution to the Discussion of C. G. Jung's Synchronicity Hypothesis" ("Ein Beitrag zur Diskussion der Synchronizitätshypothese C. G. Jungs") first appeared in *Spektrum der Par-*

apsychologie: Festschrift zum 75. Geburtstag von Hans Bender (Freiburg im Breisgau: Aurum Verlag, 1983). The English translation is by Michael H. Kohn. Copyright © 1992 by Shambhala Publications, Inc.

"Some Reflections on Synchronicity" appeared in French as "Quelques réflexions sur la synchronicité" in *La Synchronicité, l'âme et la science,* edited by Michel Cazenave (Paris: Editions Poiesis, 1984). The English translation is by Michael H. Kohn. Copyright © 1992 by Shambhala Publications, Inc.

"Meaning and Order: Concerning Meeting Points and Differences between Depth Psychology and Physics" appeared in *Quadrant* 4, no. 1 (Spring 1981) and in *Jung in Modern Perspective,* edited by Remos K. Papadopoulos and Graham S. Saayman (Hounslow: Wildwood House, 1984; Dorset: Prism Press, 1991). Copyright © 1981 by Marie-Louise von Franz.

"Time and Synchronicity in Analytic Psychology" appeared in *The Voices of Time,* edited by J. T. Fraser (New York: Braziller, 1966; Amherst: University of Massachusetts Press, 1981). Copyright © 1981 by Marie-Louise von Franz.

PSYCHE AND MATTER

Matter and Psyche from the Point of View of the Psychology of C. G. Jung

The Archetype as a Category of Experience

As is generally known, there were two discoverers of the unconscious, Sigmund Freud and C. G. Jung. They rediscovered a fact that had long been under discussion but had not been empirically investigated, namely, that there is a psychic reality beyond ego consciousness. Freud primarily saw the unconscious as a realm where repressed sexual drives exist. For Jung, however, the unconscious is, in addition, a realm in which subliminal perceptions, incipient processes of psychic development—that is, anticipations of future conscious processes—and in general all *creative* contents are constellated. Actually, there was also a third independent discoverer of the unconscious, the French mathematician Henri Poincaré, who found the unconscious in himself through a personal experience. He was looking for an explanation for the so-called automorphic functions but was unable to find the formula. Then he intuitively glimpsed the solution to this problem in a kind of half-awake, half-asleep vision. On the basis of this, he came to the conclusion that there must exist in man a second unconscious personality, which, to his great astonishment, was even capable of valid mathematical judgments.

In directing his primary attention to the drive aspect of the unconscious, Freud sought to link up with the medical knowledge of his day, with brain physiology, endocrinology, and research on general biological processes altogether. In contrast, Jung from the beginning had consciously avoided creating any such premature equivalences between the unconscious and physical and material processes. Indeed this was not because he did not believe in such relationships, but rather because he was convinced that the phenomena should first be investigated much more in the psychic realm per se before connections to somatic processes were established. In this way, he was also seeking to counter the materialistic prejudice of his time, which was inclined to draw the hasty conclusion that the psyche was an epiphenomenon of physiological processes. Jung was convinced that a link with physiology would manifest itself naturally when both fields had gone far enough in their research. This link now seems little by little to be peeking through in a very unexpected place, where no one had anticipated it—in microphysics. In my view, this shows how wise Jung's restraint was.

As is well known, Jung developed and changed the so-called association experiment of Wilhelm Wundt. In this test, a list of a hundred words is put together, one part of which is composed of words to which the test persons are expected to be relatively indifferent (like *table, chair, water, glass,* and so on); the rest of the list are words that might well hit some kind of emotionalized content. The test person must associate something to each word as rapidly as possible, as for example: *table—chair, glass—water, light—dark.* As soon as a complex is touched, the response time slows down extraordinarily. When an important complex is touched, even the answers to the following words slow down, which is called a "perseverance phenomenon." Later this test was combined with the psychogalvanic experiment. The breathing curve or the electrical permeability of the skin can then be measured, and here a similar phenomenon is encountered: at the moment when a perseverance—a delayed answer—shows up, curve deviations also occur. These are measures not of the psychic phenomenon, but rather of the physiological phenomena resulting from emotional excitement. Dr. F. Riklin, Sr., who brought the association experiment of Dr. Aschaffenburg in Germany to Burghölzli, where Jung was employed as a junior assistant, at first, under the influence of Aschaffenburg, tried primarily to derive data on brain physiology from the test. He hoped in this way that brain lesions could be detected. Jung took over the same experiment and gave it an entirely different application by entirely disregarding its possible application to the physiology of the brain. He concentrated instead on illuminating the purely psychic context of delayed responses. In this way, he discovered that in the psyche there exist "complexes"—a word well known by now—that is, emotionally intensified content clusters that form associations around a nuclear element and tend to draw ever more associative material to themselves. They behave like unconscious fragmentary personalities. Whenever these complexes are touched off, as I have indicated, physical changes also take place. Here it was shown that Jung had done well not to rush into establishing connections with processes in the brain, for it later became clear that these complexes affect the whole bodily sphere rather than just the brain. Today this is taken for granted. We might speak of the psychosomatic aspect of heart neuroses, and so on. There are neuroses that typically affect the functioning of the heart, neurotic complexes that typically affect the digestive function, the liver function, the gallbladder function. If the unconscious psyche appears to be connected with the body, then it is natural to think that it is connected with the *whole* body and not just especially with processes in the brain. In more recent views, the brain appears to be just *one* of a number of sophisticated apparatuses, which is specialized in ordering our perceptions of the external world.

Intuitive medicine, especially that of the Far East, has always associated certain complexes with specific focal points in the body. In China, there are 365 deities of the body. Every body part, every bodily function, every inner organ, every nerve center has its "deity." It could be said that these body deities symbolize intuitive inner perception of certain endosomatic sensations. That there is a relationship between complexes and bodily processes is beyond doubt. But we ought not draw any hasty conclusions from this.

Jung went on to concentrate his attention on closer investigation of the effect of unconscious complexes on the personality as a whole and on their role as strongly determinative components of the individual human personality.

In this connection, a definition of what Jung understood by "psyche" is necessary. It is first of all everything that is conscious, that is, everything in us that is associated with the so-called ego complex. If I know something, then I say, "I know it." The moment a content has become associated with the ego complex, we say, "I am conscious of it." In addition, the psyche consists of the so-called unconscious, that is, that which in the psyche is unknown but which, when it crosses the threshold of consciousness, immediately assimilates itself to the conscious contents. This includes, for example, many phenomena that we can observe during sleep. There psychic imaginative processes called dreams take place, which (when they are properly interpreted) can enter into consciousness in accordance with their meaning. I can dream about something and then afterward I can understand the dream. At that point, that which was previously a content of an unconscious dream process crosses the threshold and becomes a content of my consciousness. The third element in the makeup of the psyche is what Jung called the psychoid system. By this he meant that which in the psyche is *completely* unknown or, we might also say, unconscious material that never comes in contact with the threshold of consciousness, the really absolutely unconscious, that which is by its nature unknown. But Jung uses the expression in a specific sense. In his view, the psychoid system is the part of the psychic realm where the psychic element appears to mix with inorganic matter.

Although the complexes, as contents of the unconscious, are unconscious, they can nevertheless behave in us like additional "consciousnesses" or "personalities." This fact was first discovered by Pierre Janet, through whose efforts a very fragmented female hysteria patient of his was able to recount her conscious processes orally to her doctor, while simultaneously writing down with her left hand what her unconscious was saying. She could also to some extent enable a second unconscious person, a complex, to express itself. And here it became clear that the manifestations of this second person (in this case it was simply a complex that was very strongly repressed) *also* possessed a certain consciousness, a certain ability to reason and to calculate, and had affects, etc., as well. In order to distinguish this phenomenon from ego consciousness, Jung referred to the "consciousness" of the unconscious complex as a "luminosity." Complexes possess something resembling a rather diffuse, unclear consciousness. This is clearest in cases in which an unconscious complex makes an "arrangement," which is something that can be observed in strongly fragmented personalities. Jung published a case in which a lady had fallen in love with her best friend's husband. On understandable moral grounds, she absolutely refused even to consider the possibility of a liaison with her friend's husband—nevertheless she persuaded her friend to take a vacation by herself. Then the next day it happened that she was struck by a horsedrawn wagon right in front of the grass widower's house and as a result of the accident was carried into the house. Analysis then of course brought to light that a complex had quite deliberately "arranged" this situation; at the same time, one had to believe that the woman had no conscious idea of it. The whole thing was not associated with the ego complex in any way. Nonetheless, the complex was able to behave itself relatively consciously (if we define consciousness as something that, among other things, is capable of availing itself of appropriate ways and means).

Now, Jung's second great discovery lay in not seeing the complexes as something purely pathological, as the psychiatry of his time was inclined to do and as Freudian psychology did as well. Rather he assumed the existence of normal complexes. In other words, our psychic system is composed of various complexes, of which the ego complex is only one among various others, and this is normal. Every human being has complexes, and these are not in themselves the cause of psychological illness—only under certain circumstances. They are part of the normal psychic makeup. These normal complexes that everyone has are what Jung called archetypes. The archetypes are more or less the inborn normal complexes that we all have. Thus Jung understood archetypes to be inborn dispositions or unobservable psychic structures that in recurring typical situations produce similarly structured ideas, thoughts, emotions, and fantasy motifs. The Jungian archetypes have often been compared with the Platonic ideas. In this regard, it should be said that the difference between an archetypal representation and a Platonic idea is that the Platonic idea is conceived of as a purely cognitive content, whereas an archetype might as easily manifest as a feeling, an emotion, or a mythological fantasy. Thus the Jungian archetype is a somewhat broader concept that the Platonic idea. We must also distinguish between the archetype in itself and the archetypal image, representation, idea, or fantasy. In other words, archetypes are in themselves completely unobservable structures; only when they are stimulated by some inner or outer state of need (either inner compensation processes or outer stimuli) do they, at crucial moments, produce an archetypal image, an archetypal fantasy, a thought, an intuition, or an emotion. These can be recognized as archetypal, because they are similar in all cultures and among all peoples. At this point that may seem a bit abstractly formulated, but if we read a collection of love songs or war songs from all over the world, we will see that people in such archetypal situations ever and again express similar feelings, ideas, and fantasies. There is no doubt that the archetypal *structures* are inherited; this is not, however, the case with the *images*. Jung was repeatedly reproached with the idea that mental images could not be hereditary. But he never claimed that. The *disposition* is passed down, the structures are passed on, and they then always produce the same or similar images afresh. When an inborn archetypal structure passes into the manifest form of an archetypal fantasy or image, the psyche makes use of impressions from the external surroundings for its means of expression; therefore, the individual images are not entirely identical but only similar in structure. For example, an African child, when an image of something overwhelmingly terrifying needs to take shape in him, will perhaps fantasize about a crocodile or a lion, and a European child in the same situation will imagine a truck that is barreling toward him, threatening to run him over. Only the structure of something overpoweringly threatening will be the same in this case. The image is of course enriched by impressions from the external world.

There is a further distinction that must be made. The archetype must be distinguished from an instinctive behavior pattern. We could say that what the student of behavior principally determines in his studies of animal behavior today is to a great extent typical forms of reaction—for example, typical forms of offspring care or typical forms of mate greeting. These are well known to be definite patterns that are species-wide and are inherited from generation to generation. Irenäus Eibl-Eibesfeld in his book *Liebe und Hass* ("Love and Hate") extends this to human beings by establishing through the use of many photographs a common standard for all human forms of greeting.[1] Thus he shows that the same thing goes for us humans—we greet each other with certain gestures that are very similar to those of other primates. We must note, however, that behavioral researchers take an extraverted approach; that is, they observe people from the outside, as does American behaviorism as a whole. By considering people statistically from the outside, they have been able to determine that human beings, just like animals, have certain behavior patterns, though these seem to be somewhat more flexible among human beings than among apes, for example. Nevertheless, they do still remain relatively flexible among the primates, whereas when we go further back in the evolutionary sequence, on the whole they become increasingly mechanical and automatic. With the increase in ability to learn in higher animals, a certain mixture of types of behavior patterns appears.

Jung to some extent took the opposite approach to that of the behaviorists, that is, he did not observe people from the outside, did not ask how we behave, how we greet one another, how we mate, how we take care of our young. Instead he studied what we feel and what we fantasize while we are doing those things. This is something we cannot investigate in animals—we have no idea if a blackbird building her nest has a creative fantasy about nest structure. We simply have to leave open whether an idea-

tional process takes place within her or not, whether she thinks
or imagines anything about it or is aesthetically satisfied when
she has built her nest in thus-and-such a way. For now, as we
observe animals in their behavior, we can say nothing about their
inner processes, unless the latest attempts being made in America to learn the language of the higher apes or dolphins should
yield new results.

All of this, however, is still in the early stages. I am convinced
that in the higher warm-blooded life forms also, corresponding
inner processes—perhaps of a more diffuse nature than ours—
are present. However, that has not been proven.

With people, on the other hand, just because they can communicate, we can ascertain, for example, that whenever the feeling of falling in love appears, inner mental representations are
also present—fantasies, feelings, emotions, and fantasy images—and that, just like outer behavior, these can be categorized
as belonging to different types. We can see that in these situations, our reactions all exhibit similarity of structure, and it
would even be disturbing if this were not the case. The archetypal disposition shows itself most clearly in man in the fact, to
which Jung therefore referred the most often, that all of his religious systems and myths and mythological customs and folk
tales, with all their individual differences, show structural similarity.

This, as we know, had already been noticed by the ethnologist
Adolf Bastian, who had also already distinguished between elementary ideas and tribal ideas. Elementary ideas are basic structures that can be shown to exist in people throughout the world,
and tribal ideas are those that appear only in certain groups of
peoples. Jung was able to declare himself completely in agreement with Bastian, with this single distinction—that Bastian
spoke of *thought* forms. For Jung, archetypes are not only elementary ideas, but just as much elementary feelings, elementary
fantasies, elementary visions.

Today we must go even further and in addition look into the
relationship between the Jungian concept of the archetype and
the various concepts of structuralism. Based on my perusal of
this literature so far, the authors we should mainly consider are

Claude Lévi-Strauss[2] and Gilbert Durand.[3] However, for one particular reason, I do not find their presentations fully convincing. This reason is related to a point that is also of concern to us in psychology: the fact that the archetypes are contaminated with one another. They merge one into the other; they are not like separate particles, as electrons were formerly viewed as little particles, but are more like an "electron smear," in the language of the physicists. They are like a blurred cloud; at their edges they run over into parallel phenomena. For example, it often cannot be said of an archetypal image exactly which archetype it belongs to. Let us take the following image as an example. In the tomb of King Sethos I, there is a representation of a tamarisk tree with a breast, and the king is sucking on it. Now, is this an image of the archetype of the Great Mother or the archetype of the Tree of Life? Both. We cannot separate the archetypes from each other. However, that is what the structuralists do. Lévi-Strauss, for example, distinguishes the cooked from the raw, life from death, and on the basis of this apparently sets up outright absolute categories. But one might just as easily pick others. The archetypes do not swim around in the collective unconscious like pieces of bread in a soup, but rather they are the whole soup at every point and therefore always appear in specific mixtures. That is also why they are so hard to describe clearly outside of an individual psychological context.

Jung once formulated the relationship between the archetype and the instinctive mode of behavior in a diagrammatic model:

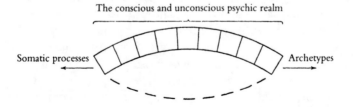

To the right is the "ultraviolet" end, and to the left is the "infrared" end, naturally used only metaphorically or as a model for thought. The sphere of the psyche is the entire spectral band. At the infrared pole, the psychic processes flow or merge into the physical processes; how and where are still unclear in many respects.

However, we know quite definitely that there is a relationship of exchange between these two factors. At the archetypal pole, the modes of psychological reaction appear. There would be the place of the unobservable structures that impose themselves on the psyche as archetypal images, representations, and thoughts. That would be the pole from which spiritual inspirations emanate—much as in the case of Henri Poincaré who, after he had drunk lots of black coffee and lain down in bed, glimpsed the entire structure of the automorphic functions. He recounts: "I saw the thoughts playing around like atoms on the ceiling, making various combinations, and suddenly I saw the right combination." It took him a half-hour to write down in logical sequence the argument that he had seen in a single glimpse in a structural form. That is an example of the type of insights that arise from the ultraviolet archetypal pole. The two poles may be characterized as mind versus matter.

We see that there is such a polarity when we imagine a person possessed by a drive—for example, a nymphomaniac who is possessed by sexuality, or someone possessed by the craving for food or some other such drive. On the other hand, people can also fall under the domination of the spiritual pole—for example, someone who is possessed by an idea. At either pole, there is no freedom, but rather a certain automatism. The more the psychic processes merge with the behavior patterns and the physiological processes, the less freedom remains. Reactions become automatic and compulsive. The same thing happens at the ultraviolet, or mind, pole. People who are possessed by an idea are no longer capable of discussing it from the standpoint of critical evaluation. The extreme case is represented by the psychologically ill person who thinks, for example, that he is the savior of the world. We cannot bring his weak ego complex to criticize this conviction that once came over him in a vision. Naturally, we can say to him sanely, "Yes, yes, but listen; you are surely Mr. Jones; and in that case, where is the savior?" and so on. Every psychotherapist knows that this is no argument, nothing can be done here. If, however, one has studied the archetype of the savior through myths, it becomes possible to predict what the ill person may now do or say. He is more or less caught in an archetypal automatism, which is accompanied by a feeling of fanaticism and absolute conviction. Only in the middle region of the psychic spectrum, in the sphere of ego consciousness, is a certain freedom available. Only there do we have voluntary motivation, which Jung defined as psychic energy that is available to the ego complex. At the edges, the psychic energy is appropriated by the other unconscious complexes.

But where in this model is the relationship of psyche and matter represented? It is at the "infrared" pole or so it would seem. There the psychic functions merge into the physiological processes of the body. But matter also sometimes shows up at the other "ultraviolet" pole—in the form of parapsychological phenomena. Thus it is to be suspected that our division into material versus mental, that which is observable from the outside versus that which is perceivable from the inside, is only a subjectively valid separation, only a limited polarization that our structure of consciousness imposes on us but that actually does not correspond to the wholeness of reality. In fact it is rather to be suspected that these two poles actually constitute a unitary reality. I have represented this with the dotted line completing the ring to the rear. It is there that we might posit a potential unitary reality of psyche and matter. This sphere cannot, however, be observed directly.

The archetypes not only underlie those of mankind's religious and mythical conceptions that are similar throughout the world, and they are not only the basic categories of human fantasy; they of course also underlie science in its intellectual premises. S. Samburesky, in his outstanding book *Die physikalische Weltbild in der Antike* ("The Image of the Physical World in Antiquity"), demonstrates in a detailed fashion that all the basic themes of modern Western physics are derived from the intuitive primal symbolic images of Greek natural philosophy.[4] From there comes the idea of a single prime matter out of which the entire visible cosmos is somehow constituted, as well as the idea of the conservation of this prime matter, in other words, the concept of a universal energy. For example, we have the fiery *pneuma* of the Stoics or the logos-fire in the philosophy of Heraclitus. There also we find the idea of the transformability of material substances into one another (for example, in Aristotle). And the concept of continuum and discontinuum, for example in the paradoxes of Zeno, also already existed. In the Stoic idea of the *pneuma*, we already have the basic intuition for the modern idea of a force field or a stationary wave. As we know, the Stoics thought that the whole world is borne up by a kind of energic tension, the *tonos*, or wave, which, however, is stationary.

Also the idea of the uncertainty principle has its germ in the view of the Greek atomist Leucippus, who taught that atoms had a certain free will. Most interesting are the conceptions of space-time, for they all derive from the archetypal image of the omnipresence of a deity or the omnipresence of the divine *pneuma*. This was already implicitly formulated by Plato, then explicitly by Plotinus: "God is an intelligible sphere whose center is everywhere and whose periphery is nowhere." Here we also already have the modern conception of the omnipresent point. A further idea, one of the most important of contemporary ideas and one that is becoming ever more important, perhaps one of the fundamental philosophical models for modern physics, is the idea that ultimately what we are dealing with is a mathematical structure. This idea was already anticipated by the Pythagoreans, who regarded the natural numbers and certain relationships among the natural numbers as actual constants of nature. Up to 95 percent of these ideas that constitute the basic themes of modern natural science (I have yet to find an exception but say 95 percent out of prudence) are images of the divine. And that is why they are argued over so passionately.

The paradoxes of the uncertainty principle have now forced the physicists to turn their attention to the processes taking place within the observer, because it is impossible to carry out an observation that is independent of the influence of the means of observation on the object. As a result, modern physicists must now once again consider the question: What are we really doing? We are forcing Nature with our means of observation into a particular mode of response. We are forcing her to give an answer that she would not give if we were not observing her in this fashion. This had proved a powerful stimulus for pure research in modern physics. Wolfgang Pauli has gone so far as to define physical knowledge as the coming-to-meet of inner psychological images and outer facts.[5] Rudolf Carnap prefers to narrow this even further and say that the knowledge of physics consists of images that have been purified into mathematical formulae.[6] The psychological images have all become abstract formulae. The ultimate goal of physics in this mold according to Carnap is the *predictability* of outer events on the basis of particular mathematical formulae. Max Jammer formulates this as follows: "What physics is about is an isomorphism of structures."[7] This means that the mental structures of the physicists stand in some relationship of isomorphism with the structures of matter. Even practical experiments are prejudiced by the mental representations of the observer. Now, the mathematical formulae of today, in contrast to those of the ancient Pythagoreans, are all algebraic formulations and, in the great majority of cases, a refined and corrected further development of the probability calculus. However, calculation of probabilities can only give information about averages and relative regularities. It can give no information about the *random and unique*. This is grounded in the structure of the probability calculus. Therefore most physicists say that that which is random and unique does not enter the sphere of physical research. They simply exclude the random from the domain of investigation, because it cannot be grasped by the mathematical instruments that have been developed over the course of time. Any unique-experience information is simply ruled out.

At this point, if we wish to delve deeper into this matter, we must gain a more profound understanding of the foundations of mathematics, because it is after all mathematics (i.e., algebra) that is the main tool of modern physics. In this area, we quickly come to a fact that every mathematician dislikes but does not deny, which is that the whole edifice of mathematics ultimately rests on an irrational foundation, namely, on the natural whole number series. At this point opinions differ sharply. Some mathematicians say that the numbers are no more than conventional names: I just make marks one after the other and conventionally call them 1, 2, 3, 4. I could also call them X, Y, Z, or something else. The name has no effect on the matter; it is a purely conventional designation of units devised by our consciousness, units that follow one another in sequence. This is not accurate, however, and for a very simple reason. Let us take the case of such a rational formalist, who takes some peas and says: "This one I call 1 and the next 2, and the next 3. We now have something completely transparent and simple that we ourselves, or our minds, have created." But what happens now? When we study this series of pea-numbers, terrible things begin to happen. Odd and even numbers appear, and prime numbers, the distribution of which has remained undeterminable to this day. The mathematician Goldbach, who lived in Leibniz's time, postulated a theory to the effect that every even number is the sum of two prime numbers. This has now been checked through with computers up to the number 10,000. It is accurate, however, that the law (i.e., the reason that this is the case) remains unformulable up to the present. Now, how does it come about, if we really devised something so completely transparent (simple units set one after another and then named), that we end up with things that we do not understand to this day and that entail complications that remain completely enigmatic for modern mathematicians? In addition, we find that the natural integers suddenly have individual properties. They are triangular or quadratic or have specific relations with each other, and all of this had to be discovered *afterward*, since we did not intentionally create it. If we had created this intentionally ourselves, then surely we would know all about it. When we build a machine, we still know all about it once it is built. Nothing irrational can happen in it. But with the numbers, we just set something up for ourselves but afterward were confronted by total enigmas. This fact (which is at the base of Kurt Gödel's discovery of 1931) leads, as Hermann Weyl says, to *all the hopes of mathematicians to elucidate rationally the foundations of mathematics* being dashed once and for all.[8] To my disappointment, I have discovered that mathematicians living today, when pressed on this problem, for the most part say: "Yes, that is true, but that does not interest us now." As Weyl says, out of resignation, they have simply directed their interest away from this point, because there we are confronted by an inexplicable enigma. Weyl, who is a solid realist, says interestingly, "It is surprising that something created by the mind itself" (he is of the opinion that once upon a time we simply invented numbers), "namely, the whole number series, as simple and transparent as it is for the constructive intelligence, takes on such an unfathomable and unmanagable quality when considered from the axiomatic perspective."

In another passage, he adds: "As simple as the method of arithmeticizing a formalism may be (that is, an algebraic formalism or any other kind), it nevertheless leads to an insight of considerable philosophical interest, namely, that the natural numbers with their law-conforming relationships constitute such a broad field that any kind of theory at all, once fully formalized, can be expressed in terms of it."⁹ In other words, whatever mathematical formalisms have been found up till now—and formalisms are constructions of the human mind—can be expressed in terms of the field of natural numbers, but also there is, endlessly, much more to discover.

Thus we have now to return—as Werner Heisenberg urged—to a kind of revived Pythagoreanism. What is essential for us for the moment is that there is not a single important scientific paradigm that is not based on a primal archetypal intuition. An archetypal structure pre-existing ego consciousness has generated the themes of Western natural science. They manifested as primal intuitions out of the unconscious; they simply appeared to investigators as thoughts and took hold of mankind. In this sense, the concept of matter is also only one archetypal representation among many others; indeed the concept of matter derives from the archetype of the Great Mother. The most important aspects of the Great Mother archetype were summarized by Jung in the following typical images: On the personal level, she is the mother, the grandmother, the stepmother, the wetnurse, the nanny, the ancestress, the goddess, the Virgin Mary, Sophia. She is the goal of the longing for salvation, paradise, the kingdom of God, the church, a piece of land, heaven, earth, the forest, the sea and nonflowing bodies of water, matter, the underworld, the moon, the tilled field, the garden, the boulder, the cave, the tree, the springhole, the baptismal font, the flower, the mandala, the oven, the stove, the cow, the hare, and, in a quite general way, the helpful animal. Psychologically, it is whatever is kindly, sheltering, bearing, growth-fostering, fertility-bringing, nourishment-providing; places of transformation; rebirth; that which is secret, hidden, dark; the world of the dead; that which devours, seduces, poisons, arouses fear; that which is inescapable. All these images belong to the archetype of the Great Mother.

The archetype of the Father, that is, of the mind, is the polar opposite. It is connected with the following mythological associations: moving air, wind, spirit breath, that which provokes possession, apparitions of the spirits of the dead; things like *pneuma,* the psyche, sprites, spirits, devils, demons, angels, the helpful old man. On the personal level: the father, the wise professor, the authority figure, the priest. The mind is the active, winged, moving, alive, stimulating, provocative, arousing, inspiring, dynamic element of the psyche, that which produces enthusiasm and inspiration. Therefore Jung defined the mind as a spontaneous principle of movement and activity, in which inheres the faculty of free generation of symbolic images beyond the sense perceptions and the capacity for sovereign, autonomous manipulation of these images. As can easily be seen, these two archetypes overlap—as all archetypes do—in certain areas. That is why Jung stressed that mind and matter are nothing graspable in and of themselves, but are ultimately forms of appearance of essentially transcendent (that is, transpsychic) being. Whereas many in the West would like to derive everything from matter, conversely, in the East, for instance, the Tantrics say that matter is nothing other than the definiteness of God's thought. However, these are merely metaphysical assertions that cannot be proven empirically. The only directly investigatable reality is the psychic reality, i.e., the immediate contents of our consciousness, which we then, ex post facto, ascribe to either a material or a mental-spiritual origin.

In sum, that which we designate as matter or energy in the external world is an archetypal image, just as the mind is. The latter consists of an inspired cluster of thoughts and meanings, based on an archetypal structure. Thus what is interesting for psychologists is the question of how these two archetypal powers show themselves in our consciousness, what processes occur in us that require us to become conscious of their existence—for it seems as though, like all other opposites of nature, they wish to unite in a *mysterium coniunctionis* in man. The greatest mystery for us psychologists is therefore not matter and not mind, neither of which we can actually investigate in its being-in-itself, but rather these strange psychic processes through which these powers actualize themselves as an experience of meaning in man and seek to attain consciousness in the mirror of his psyche. In this connection, Jung spoke of the cosmogonic meaning of human consciousness.

At this point, however, a further difficulty must be mentioned. It is related to the problem of basic research in depth psychology. Jung considered his psychology to be empirical in method and therefore part and parcel of natural science. However, what is problematical about this method is that psychology describes psychic contents with psychic means. Its knowledge or process of explanation does take place in the same medium. Physics has an advantage in this respect, because it represents physical processes in a mental (that is, psychic) medium. The physicist mirrors matter in his psychic processes; he reconstructs the matter of the external world in his mind. Psychology cannot do this. It is in the situation of Münchhausen, who had to pull himself out of the bog by his own pigtail. It lacks an Archimedean point outside of itself, and in this respect it is critically limited. As physics experienced a limitation of its knowledge potential through the discovery of the uncertainty principle, psychology also acquired knowledge of its limits through this factor. Here microphysics and Jungian depth psychology come together. And at this point the wisdom of restraint with regard to hasty conclusions concerning the connection of matter and psyche becomes clear; for today it is neither molecular biology, nor psychology—nor brain research to be sure—but rather quantum physics that has turned up insights whose relationship with the psyche of the observer has made an impression on physicists. In this area of research, according to Jung, we find hints of a possibility of reconstructing psychological processes in another medium, that is, in the microphysics of matter. We do not, however, know today, Jung goes on to say, what this might turn out to be like. *This reconstruction can only be carried out by nature itself. It can be supposed to be going on as constantly as the psyche perceives the physical world.* In other words, in the science of physics, the psyche mirrors matter, but that leads to the question: Can matter also mirror the psyche? In China it has always been thought so. The Chinese, when they wanted information about their unconscious psychological processes, simply observed what was happening around them physically, and that was regarded as a mirror of their inner psychic processes. For them, this was self-evident.

Once when I was giving a lecture at the Jung Institute on synchronicity and causality, a Japanese man came up to me and said, "Now I understand what casuality is! When I was reading about Western physics, I always thought that it was all synchronistic. And now that you have taken so much trouble to show the differences, I am able to understand for the first time what casuality is!" In the East people think so differently that they cannot even understand what we mean by casuality. Many Oriental peoples seem to understand physical happenings as a synchronistic reflection of the psychic realm. There is a beautiful story about this from the annals of the Tang period. Once a volcano erupted. First a crater lake formed and then in the middle of it a volcanic cone arose. The empress of the time was a very domineering woman who had entirely deprived her husband of power. This empress visited the mountain and called it Fortunate Mountain. A servitor wrote her a polite letter. "Your Majesty, I have learned that the world is destroyed when the breath of Heaven is destroyed. When the breath of earth is destroyed, the human soul is destroyed. Your Majesty has set herself in masculine fashion above the feminine. I would advise Your Majesty to take the path of remorse and repentance, so that no misfortune falls upon the empire." The empress had a fit of anger and banished the outspoken citizen from the court. Now, *kên,* "mountain" in Chinese, is a masculine principle. "Lake" is called *tui* and is a feminine principle. A mountain having formed over the lake, synchronistically reflected the psychic state of the empress or of the royal court. Thus the external occurrence was seen as a representation of a psychic situation. While we cannot return to such a way of thinking, we have somewhat overdone our rejection of it. There is more than a grain of truth hidden in this Oriental way of looking at things.

Fringe Phenomena of the Archetypal Realm and the Unity of Being

The following remarks concern something extraordinarily difficult, which cannot be completely simplified even with the best of intentions. We shall be dealing with a complex phenomenon and with entirely new ideas, the full implications of which we ourselves do not yet grasp.

In the previous section I have tried to explain that the foundations of nearly all our essential knowledge are structurally predetermined by the archetypes of the collective unconscious. The archetypes are in some sense the psychic preconditions of our entire human existence, and we can go neither over nor around them. We can, however, develop them further or refine them. Thus we are not trapped in the sense that no evolution is possible.

Jung for the most part investigated the archetypes only in their psychological forms of manifestation, that is, in terms of how they manifested in dreams and spontaneous unconscious fantasies of his patients and in terms of how such fantasies affected the lives and behavior of his patients. Images and archetypal (i.e., "revealed") thoughts appear on the ultraviolet end of our scale, while emotions and impulses to action appear at the infrared end of the scale of psychic processes, where they merge with physiological (i.e., material) processes. The influenceability of the psyche and the body is mutual. The psychic state can be altered with chemicals, but the chemical processes of the body can also be influenced by psychic alterations.

However, we have seen that at the ultraviolet pole of the schema depicted above, there likewise occur certain material

phenomena. Here we encounter so-called ghost or spirit phenomena, as they are called in parapsychology. I do not wish to
go into the phenomenology of these things but shall merely indicate that from our vantage point in therapeutic practice we can
also observe parapsychological phenomena often enough to be
convinced that such phenomena exist, even though for the moment we can still find no consistent scientific explanation for
them. Among these "ghost" phenomena, in which to a certain
extent something psychic simultaneously expresses itself materially, there is a special category of parapsychological phenomena that Jung called synchronistic phenomena. In our historical
example from the Chinese Tang period, the appearance of a
mountain out of a lake was taken to be a synchronistic event that
somehow coincided with the psychological situation in the im-
perial family. That is synchronicity. Other parapsychological
phenomena are interpreted today as telepathic. In relation to telepathy, most people imagine something like an electric or electromagnetic current or wave being the cause of telepathy. Experiments up till now (putting a medium in a lead chamber and
asking him or her to suggest something to other people, etc.)
have at least shown that we are not justified in associating the
cause of telepathy with any known material energy or radiation
phenomena. There is no provable connection. What we can observe is rather a coincidence, for example, that something arises
in somebody's mind that takes place in external reality ten miles
away or even somewhat later, without there being any possibility of a causal connection. The most frequent type, which probably everyone has experienced, is, for example, that we dream
of a contact with someone whom we have neither seen nor
thought of in ten years, and the next day we find a letter from
this person in the mailbox. We think, "This is a strange coincidence! The whole night I was having a conversation with this
person, and while this was going on the letter was already in the
mail." Because we are so caught up in the notion of causality,
we generally would think that most likely the other person was
thinking intensely about us, which somehow set off waves in
our own unconscious and in that way brought about the dream.
But, as already mentioned, no such material currents or waves

can be proven to be involved. Moreover, in cases where the "telepathic" perception takes place *before* the event, they are extremely unlikely. In Rhine's experiments,[10] for example, a medium in New York was asked to guess what playing cards a card-dealing machine would deal out two days later in Budapest and was able to achieve a noteworthy score. Now, cards that have not yet been dealt certainly cannot give out waves that let the medium know how they lie. Here a causal connection is not only not provable or still unknown, but *it is logically inconceivable*. It is difficult to give an account of synchronistic phenomena, since in our practice we always see them embedded in the problem situation of the person involved. If we want to explain a synchronistic phenomenon, each time we have to elucidate the entire current case history in order to show how the meaning of the external events fits into it. Therefore I must ask readers to make their own observations and reflect on them. Such things happen fairly often, and anyone who puts his attention to it can perceive synchronistic phenomena. Primitive peoples still think synchronistically today; that is, for them there is no such thing as a meaningless accident. If, for example, a woman is pulled underwater by a crocodile, then they question the meaning of it. That it was mere accident that *just* this woman was pulled underwater in *just* that moment as she was fetching water is inconceivable for them. In the primitive picture of the world, there are no accidents. That which the modern scientist evaluates strictly as an accident, the primitive will always try to fathom the meaning of. So it would be possible for us, by slipping back a bit into our primitive side, to revive this way of seeing in ourselves and say to ourselves: "What happened just now was hardly an accident—why did that happen to me today of all times?" If we do this, we very often find that meaningful connections indeed exist. Naturally, we could exaggerate this procedure and see synchronicities where none exist. The men of ancient times always interpreted synchronistic events as a sign from the gods—a *numen*. The word *numinosum* comes from the verb *nuere,* which means "to nod" or "give a sign." Thus when Zeus gives a sign with his eyebrows, something numinous occurs. Throughout the world, this kind of coincidence was regarded as a sign of destiny or a signal from the divine principle. It provided the foundation for the magical sciences that sought to interpret it, whether by means of the flight of birds, the structure of the liver of a sacrificed animal, or something else. Nothing unusual was regarded as accidental; rather, the visible arrangement of a flock of birds or the configuration of the liver of a sacrificed animal was experienced as communicating a message. Through such means, people tried to find the meaning of the moment, primarily in order to make a prediction about the future.

However, we do not simply want to regress to the level of primitive magical thought, which believed in a kind of magical causality. Modern science has slowly struggled free of this magical approach only with the greatest of efforts, and it is by no means Jung's intention that we should now fall back into this kind of magical-causal thinking. But we should realize that causality as an explanatory principle (or as a probability) is only *one* possible category of thought for describing the connection between events. It leaves the entire realm of the accidental or contingent outside its framework of consideration, since this realm is excluded as not being susceptible of investigation. Now the question arises: Is that which is contingent really only just an amorphous clump of seemingly senseless accidents? Or is it worthwhile to make distinctions between meaningful and meaningless coincidences? For example, what if, at an airport, when I blew my nose, an airplane crashed? Something like this is only a meaningless coincidence, an accident that does not call for us to look for anything behind it. However, if the night before I have a dramatic dream about a plane crash and then, while I am waiting for the arrival of an acquaintance at the airport, the crash happens just as I dreamed it, then I have no alternative but to say to myself, "This cannot be a meaningless coincidence."

What is interesting here is that, even though synchronistic events, being almost all one-time experiences and therefore not confirmable, nevertheless possess great informational value. Even a one-time experience, if it falls into an archetypal context, can reveal most important insights for us. This concerns precisely those synchronistic elements that are known never to repeat themselves or never repeat themselves as part of arranged experiments.

What distinguishes synchronistic events from synchronous elements is not an absolute but a relative simultaneity. For example, if I dream one night about a plane crash and then see it take place the next day just as I dreamed it, a few hours fall between the two. In general, there is a small time interval between the two events; thus we have only relative simultaneity. What is essential, however, is *equivalence of meaning*. The connection between the two elements is based on their equivalent meanings and not on some causal relationship. For example, I go into a shop and buy a blue dress and have it sent to me. Three days later, the package comes, I unpack it, and the dress is black. The dresses were mixed up at the shop. At this moment, I get a telegram saying that a close relative has died, for whose sake I will have to wear black. Naturally, my reaction to this is that it is not just an accident, but it is extremely "odd." In this example, the relationship in meaning is only the blackness of the dress. We associate black with mourning, and that connects it with the external event. In our view, this too would be a case of synchronicity, although the image is not the same—I did not see the image of the death, but something happened that in its meaning is connected with death. In his essay on synchronicity, Jung gives the example of a woman who sees birds gathering on the roof of her house, which on the basis of a previous similar experience, she immediately reads as a message of coming death.[11] And in fact, shortly thereafter her husband, who has dropped dead completely unexpectedly on the street from a heart attack, is carried into the house. Here, too, a connection of meaning is present—a gathering of birds means mythologically that souls are coming to take someone away. This corresponds to a belief found throughout the world, and in this example something of like meaning in fact takes place externally.

If we formulate this scientifically in a more precise manner, it is not an inner and outer state that coincide, since any outer state or external event cannot be perceived per se. We can perceive it only through the filter of our psychic reality. Therefore, in formulating the situation scientifically, we have to say: synchronicity is constituted by the coincidence or simultaneity of two psychic states, that is, a normal psychic state that can be adequately explained causally and another, not derivable from it, that is the critical experience which is not causally connected with the first and the objectivity of which can only be verified later.[12]

I would like to make that clearer with the help of a further example. I had a female analysand who was extremely suicidal. When I went off on my summer vacation, I was concerned over how she would get through this period without analysis. I did, however, take my vacation. I had made her solemnly promise that she would write to me if she had any kind of trouble.

One morning, I was chopping wood and had these thoughts (I was able to reconstruct my thought process precisely later): This wood is still wet; I'll pile it up at the rear so that it won't be used first and will still have a chance to dry out. This was a rather long thought process that could be completely causally connected with my activity. Then suddenly I saw this patient before me and thought about her. This completely disrupted the flow of my thoughts. I felt directly how this other thing broke in on my thoughts. I thought: What could that woman suddenly want from me? Why am I thinking about her? Then I asked myself if I could have somehow gotten to the thought of her from my preoccupation with the wood. There was no associational path from the wood to her. I went back to the wood chopping and again her image was there—this time with a feeling of urgent danger. At that point, I put aside my ax, closed my eyes, and thought: Should I take my car and drive to her immediately? Then I got the quite definite feeling: No, it would be too late. Then I sent a telegram: "Don't do anything foolish," with my signature. Later it came out that the telegram reached her two hours later. At that moment she had just gone into the kitchen and turned on the gas valve. At that point the doorbell rang, the postman delivered the telegram, and she was naturally so struck by this coincidence that she turned the gas valve back off and is now—thank God—still among us. I mention this only as an illustration of the two states, to show the simultaneity of two psychic states, one normal, adequately explainable by causal means—my thoughts about the wood—and the critical experience not derivable from the first state, the objectivity of which can only be verified later, and which manifested by forcing an image through. Only two days later was I able to find out what had actually happened. For this reason, Jung did not consider these phenomena to be synchronous, that is, precisely coinciding in time, but rather *synchronistic,* since a certain time lapse is present. In such moments the customary space-time continuum or the causal network of events seems to be suspended. It seems that the flow of causal events should be regarded as constant factors only if they can be measured independently of psychic states.

Bound up with the archetypes that underlie synchronistic events is the presence of something like a *knowledge* in the form of symbolic images. This is a kind of luminosity or partial consciousness on the part of the archetypes, a knowledge that is conscious only in the archetypal realm, *but not conscious for the ego;* it is something that makes a sudden appearance in ego consciousness. We might therefore say that something archetypal in me knew about this suicide attempt, and this suddenly broke in on my conscious thought process.

Jung described synchronicity as follows. First, an unconscious image crops up, directly or indirectly, as a dream image or a waking idea or presentiment; second, an objective state of similar meaning coincides temporally with this content. Jung showed in his work on synchronicity that the Chinese notion of the Tao actually reflects synchronistic thinking. As I mentioned, I have learned from experience that the Asians clearly—and this must have something to do with their languages—do not understand connections between events *causally,* but rather as synchronicities. Thus we could say that man can pose two legitimate questions to nature. He can ask: Why does this happen when I do that? This question leads to the establishment of the causality principle, which has now been relativized to the level of probability. Or he can ask: What in nature tends to coincide in the same moment? That is also a legitimate question, the one that the Oriental peoples have asked. This idea was implicit in their idea of Tao. The Tao is more or less the cosmic meaning at each moment. Thus we should say: the total meaningful moment of time that lies behind all appearances is the Tao. For instance, Lao-tzu says:

> Because the eye gazes but can catch no glimpse of it,
> It is called elusive.
> Because the ear listens, but cannot hear it,
> It is called the rarefied.
> Because the hand feels for it but cannot find it,
> It is called the infinitesimal. . . .
> These are called the shapeless shapes,
> Forms without form,
> Vague semblances.
> Go towards them, and you can see no front;
> Go after them, and you see no rear. [Chap. 14]

> Heaven's net is wide;
> Coarse are its meshes, but nothing slips through. [Chap. 73][13]

Chinese thought presumes that the whole of nature is a psychophysical unity or has a unitary wholeness, which, however, escapes observation that concentrates on details.

In the West we find the beginnings of a similar outlook in antiquity and the Middle Ages, primarily in the doctrine of the sympathy of all things and in astrology. This element can also still be found in the philosophy of the Renaissance, where a symbolic and psychophysical wholeness of all cosmic existence is referred to. This wholeness is based on the postulated existence of a world soul or on the sympathy principle.

The idea of synchronicity that comes closest to Jung's is Leibniz's concept of a prestabilized harmony.[14] In his view, God as the author of things, as the first Monad, "flashed" the other monads or essences out of Himself. There is no causal relationship among the monads. Human souls are monads, and as human beings we cannot causally affect one another, for the monads are "windowless." The fact that we can communicate with one another and that apparent connections do develop rests on all monads being like synchronized watches. They all experience the same thing at the same time because they are in harmony; thus seemingly causal contacts take place. The only difference between Jung's concept of synchronicity and Leibniz's prestabilized harmony is that the latter assumes that synchronistic phenomena are general and regular phenomena, while the Jungian view is that this does not appear empirically to be the case. For example, we are not able to predict synchronistic phenomena. They elude all predictability. If they took place regularly, then we would be able to predict them. However, the most we can say is that something synchronistic might happen when an archetype is constellated; and if something does happen, then it will have the same meaning as the archetype. But we cannot predict this with certainty—it might happen, it might not.

In other words, synchronistic phenomena, to the extent we have so far been able to observe and learn about them, happen only sporadically, and this speaks against the idea of "pre-established harmony."

Jung tells us, moreover, that the contingent element in nature, that is, all events that do not follow from causal connections, when considered from the outside—that is, physically—appear to be a formless chaos, but they reveal themselves to psychic introspection as a pattern of events that is apparently based not only on psychic but also on psychophysical existence. The only law-conforming factor that can be detected in these synchronistic events is that they tend to take place when an archetype is intensively constellated in and around the observer. This is generally the case in prepsychotic states, those hyperexcited states that people exhibit before a psychotic explosion. At such times, powerful basic archetypal levels of the psyche are always intensively constellated. Synchronistic events also take place in life's critical moments. We know from parapsychological literature how frequently these phenomena surround the deaths of close friends and relatives. Thus in moments of death, birth, the first big love experience, and so forth—that is, in all those profound and stirring situations shared by all humanity in which an archetype or the archetypal level of the unconscious is constellated— synchronistic events tend to occur. They need not necessarily occur, but they "tend" often to do so. They happen much more often than is generally thought, and when they do happen we have always until now, if in a position to investigate the situation, been able to discover a constellated archetype behind them. Thus it seems that in contingent events, something manifests that is conditioned by, or based upon, not only the psychic but also the psychophysical flow of events. But when I use the expression "based upon" here, it should under no circumstances be interpreted causally. Arthur Koestler accused Jung of expressing himself in a terribly complicated manner in his essay on synchronicity. Unfortunately, he failed to notice that it is impossible to do otherwise, because our language is completely causally structured, entirely oriented toward cause and effect. We are so bound to the idea of a cause and its effect that, linguistically and intellectually, we cannot get away from it. We should rather see synchronistic phenomena in terms of the simple actuality or suchness of a contingence that cannot be reduced any further, that is, in terms of an acausal modality.

When we examine this concept more closely, we see that it must be expanded further. Jung noted that in nature there is also something that he called acausal orderedness, for instance all *a priori* facts in physics, such as half-lives and the speed of light. These also cannot be causally explained; they can only be observed, but we can give no cause for them. In the psychic sphere, an acausal orderedness can be found in the properties of the natural integers. The natural integers are a psychic content that just simply is the way it is. Five, for example, is a prime number. That is just the way it is. We cannot ask why five is a prime number. It is one, and everyone can see that it is. In other words, our psychic, intellectual processes are ordered in such a way that this strikes us as evident. We are so structured that we must see it this way. Perhaps on other stars there is another psychic structure for which this is not the case. But for us it is, though we cannot account for this causally. The question "Why?" or "Where does that come from?" or "What makes it that way?" appears to be meaningless. The properties of the natural integers are thus a psychic orderedness, as half-lives are a physical orderedness. Both are phenomena that Jung characterized by the concept "acausal orderedness," by which he meant an *a priori* "just so" order that we cannot account for in terms of cause and effect or probability.

Thus we have *two* phenomena: on the one hand, something like an acausal orderedness seems to exist in the domain of both psychic and material reality; and on the other hand, sporadic, irregular synchronistic events occur. The acausal orderedness is regular, generally determinable, universally valid, and observable at all times. By contrast, none of this is true for the sporadic cases of synchronicity. They are primarily characterized by their unexpected, irregular, unpredictable occurrence. But they also manifest acausal orderedness. In this regard, Jung considered a hypothesis according to which synchronistic events, being sporadic "miracles," were only a special case of the more general principle of acausal orderedness. In fact, they are those special cases in which the observer is in a position to know the *tertium comparationis,* the meaning in the simultaneity of the psychic and physical events. It may well be the case, however, that we are often not in a position to recognize a meaning in what happened and therefore cannot understand it as a psychophysical synchronistic event.

On no account should we regard the archetype as the cause of synchronistic events. To do so would be once again to think causally. It would be better to say that synchronicity is a special case of a causal orderedness. Acausal orderedness appears or manifests itself in these phenomena; it does not bring them about. Therefore, our next definition would be: The archetype is the structure, which can be perceived through introspection, of an a priori psychic orderedness. If a synchronistic event associates itself with that archetype, Jung goes on—that is, if something happens externally that fits in with its meaning—then that event follows the same basic pattern; that is, in this case it is ordered in the same way. This kind of synchronistic orderedness, however, is distinct from the general acausal orderedness (of whole numbers or the discontinuities of physics) in that the latter happens with regularity, but the former does not. Rather, the former represents unique *acts of creation in time.* Here we come to the question of whether these archetypal structures have always existed and were in some way already present in the prime matter of the universe, or whether they only developed later. In Jung's view, the basic structures were always there, but within them ever-new acts of creation are taking place. Jung came to the view that the archetype is something we can never get beyond; it is *the* ultimate, *the* most fundamental structure of our psychic being, which we cannot transcend. However, within these archetypal patterns, acts of creation can take place in the sense of a *creatio continua*. This expression refers to the Augustinian view that God is eternally outside time, and therefore in His mind everything that happens in the world is timelessly coincident, and only we humans experience the movement of time within temporal creation as a successive sequence. But God intervenes as the creator now and again within temporal creation. In this connection, if we may make a short digression into theology, we must recall that the principle of causality corresponds to a God image. The father of causality, Descartes, justified the absolute determinism of all natural processes by saying that God would never alter His established laws. Now, we know from the Bible that He sometimes did change them, and it is hard to see why man should forbid God to be creative! But this did not occur to Descartes. God once established a rule and now has to stick to it for all times. We could also say: God was permitted to publish up to the year A.D. 120, but after that all further publications were forbidden!

Synchronistic phenomena are thus *acts of creation in time,* of which Jung says in conclusion:

> We must of course guard against thinking of every event whose cause is unknown as "acausal." This, as I have already stressed, is admissible only when a cause is not even thinkable. But thinkability is itself an idea that needs the most rigorous criticism. Had the atom corresponded to the original philosophical conception of it, its fissionability would be unthinkable. But once it proved to be a measurable quantity, its nonfissionability became unthinkable. Meaningful coincidences are thinkable as pure chance. But the more they multiply and the greater and more exact the correspondence of the events is, the more their probability sinks and their unthinkability increases, until they can no longer be regarded as pure chance but, for lack of a causal explanation, have to be thought of as meaningful arrangements. As I have already said, however, their "inexplicability" is due not to the fact

that the cause is unknown, but to the fact that a cause cannot even be postulated in intellectual terms. This is necessarily the case when space and time lose their meaning or have become relative, for under those circumstances a causality which presupposes space and time for its continuance can no longer be said to exist and becomes altogether unthinkable.

For these reasons it seemed to me necessary to introduce, alongside space, time, and causality, a fourth category which not only enables us to understand synchronistic phenomena as a special class of natural events, but also takes the contingent partly as a universal factor existing from all eternity, and partly as the sum of countless individual acts of creation occurring in time.[15]

At this point we are confronted with a major problem: How can we do further research on synchronicity without being confined to merely heaping up accounts of experiences? This is in fact the tragedy of parapsychology. There is an unending supply of anecdotal documentation, which to some extent is absolutely trustworthy and seems to have been composed by honest people; but it is not clear how a properly set-up or repeatable methodical procedure for gaining further understanding of these things might come about out of this. I consider it very improbable that sporadically occurring synchronistic phenomena will ever become predictable and thus to any degree become part of the realm of ordinary scientific research. They are after all acts of creation, and acts of creation are not predictable. We cannot even predict the creativity of an individual, let alone that of nature. I would never be able to predict what image a painter I am analyzing will paint next. After he has painted it, I can say, "Yes, yes, of course, that had to come—because of the archetypal configuration." But I can never say this beforehand. Thus we must pretty nearly exclude the possibility of ever methodically predicting synchronistic events. It is another matter, on the other hand, with the acausal orderedness that Jung speaks of as a regular phenomenon. Would it not be possible to investigate this more closely? The means employed until now to investigate configurations of psychophysical meaning have been the mantic or divinatory methods of primitive peoples—liver auspices, bird-flight auspices, and so on. If we look at nonmathematical divinatory methods, the common denominator is that one starts always with a chaotic pattern. Then one chooses a point, and according to where the point lies, we say: this means something. That is the basic principle, whether we are looking at how birds fly or how a spider walks. In Africa, the following method of divination is widespread: The diviner throws some sand on the ground, makes a big spider walk across it, and then consults the pattern it has made. Or, for example, in Switzerland in Uri Canton, there is a little bridge that the people of a village have to cross in order to get to the graveyard. It is a path with clayish soil, and when the weather is dry, it cracks up in a pattern of fracture lines. When the people go to a burial, they always read this pattern to see who will be the next to be carried across the bridge in a coffin. They read this in the configuration of fracture lines in the soil.

The development of divination in China is interesting. There chaos was gradually developed into a matrix that was reflected in the pattern on a tortoise's back. An attempt was made to enumerate its fields, that is, to connect them with number. That was the original form of the divination method. From this was later derived the celebrated divinatory text known as the *I Ching*.[16] This next step was the introduction of number, which in other mantic methods also always comes as the next higher cultural step. One casts a number grid over the chaos and then asks: when the point of incidence is in the field of the number 2, or when the "sign" is in field 4 or 5, then does this have this or that meaning? The great discovery and in my view the best arithmetical tool that has arisen for investigating synchronicity is the famous *I Ching,* the Book of Changes, which goes back to historically indefinite ancient times, but which developed in the twelfth century into what it now is, a detailed and psychologically profound philosophical system that claims to provide an explanation of the universe. Before that, it was simply a system of ordinary divination.

We must now go back and look at how our causal way of thinking, to which we are so attached, was further developed in modern physics, in the probability calculus, and in their various offshoots, and how it is founded on the law of large numbers. A probability calculus becomes more precise the more repetitions of an experiment or an observation can be made. The intention here is to eliminate chance to the greatest extent possible. The individual case is not considered in the probability concept, and therefore the physicist D. Rivière, for example, says: "According to quantum mechanics, two kinds of changes take place in a system. The first is classical and obeys the Schrödinger equation; the second is essentially contingent, outside of time if not even reversible. This special kind of change completely eludes theory. This is a bit like the way the circumstances that cause an honest card dealer to draw one card rather than another out of a deck elude the probability calculus, the rules of which nevertheless apply to card-drawing as a whole."[17] On the basis of the probability rules we can say: In such-and-such a percentage of cases, the six card must be drawn out of a deck, even if there are a billion repetitions. But if we draw a card out of a deck just once, we cannot say that it will be the six rather than any other card. The probability theory cannot provide this kind of data. The one-time chance occurrence is pushed away by this kind of mathematics onto the fringes of the observable.

Now, the Chinese had an entirely different interesting idea, in which mathematics, or at least numbers, are also used to find laws, but in just the opposite way from the probability calculus. They asked this question: If at this moment *one particular* number comes up, what does that mean? Our probability theory pushes chance occurrences as much as possible onto the fringes of observation and by repetition eliminates the chance factor to a great extent. The Chinese make chance the focal point of their observation and attempt to see something law-conformable precisely in the chance occurrence. This of course presupposes a holistic view of nature. It presupposes that psychic and physical nature—outer and inner nature, cosmic nature as a whole—constitute an ultimate unity of meaning, which the questioner finds himself face to face with. By just flipping a coin with the question heads or tails, yes or no, he poses a unique, one-time question to nature, and chance is what gives the answer. Not regularity but chance gives the answer. King Wen and the Duke of Chou were shut up by a tyrant for ten years in a dark hole, and every morning they had announced to them: "Today you will be executed." The nearness of death caused these two outstanding Chinese scholars to work out an interpretation of the *I Ching*. Evidently they tossed the coins every day or divided up the yarrow stalks and then tried to conclude from chance what the current overall situation of the Tao was. They presumed that the same sense or meaning would express itself simultaneously in the psychic and the physical state of affairs. In this method of divination, only one condition is placed on Nature; that is, she must answer in either odd or even numbers. It is interesting that odd and even numbers are chosen, since they correspond to the father and mother archetypes. In China, the odd and even numbers mean "mind and matter," and the *tertium comparationis* is their combination; it is out of that that they try to read a meaning. This is obviously produced intuitively from the unconscious. What is fascinating is that the arithmetic of the *I Ching* is exactly the same as the genetic code.[18] The same relationships of numbers are involved, even in detail. We find ourselves confronted with the strange fact that the Chinese, through intuitive introspection alone in experimenting with their own psychic state, came upon a numeric system that signified information for them and that they then expanded philosophically; and now the same numeric system is discovered by Western science as the physical basis of all information.

But here we encounter, as is inevitable with synchronicity, the problem of time. The Chinese formulation of the question is more or less: "What is the constellation in just this moment?" Jung once said that to investigate synchronicity would mean looking at the cosmic clock and asking, "What cosmic moment is it now?" And if the answer is, for example, the cosmic moment is now strife or decline or love or something else again, then it is not only me that is that way but the whole cosmic moment, and therefore everything that is happening outside me is in agreement with what is happening inside me. This is the premise underlying the *I Ching*. Tossing the coins amounts more or less to looking at the cosmic clock and finding out the cosmic moment. This brings the factor of time into the picture in quite a special way. In Western physics, time is conceived of as an empty framework within which inner and outer happenings take place, whereas the Chinese view, which is oriented toward synchronicity, attributes quality to time. The stream of events in time has a particular quality at each moment. This was formerly "proven" by astrology, when people believed that the moment in time at which a person is born determines his qualities. Thus the astrologers looked at the heavenly constellations—all of which are projections of the collective unconscious—and tried to deduce the qualities of a newborn individual. Even if this perhaps represents an overload for our rationalistic outlook, it is nevertheless interesting to note that numbers, throughout the world—except in recent Western number theory—always have a relationship to time ascribed to them. In the great mythologies of China, among the Aztecs, and among the ancient Babylonians, all the gods were also time-numbers. Every god was a calendrical number. The Aztecs have the "One-Hunter," the "Seven-Hunter," and so on. This establishes a relationship between numbers and archetypal representations. Or to put it more precisely: The archetypes of the collective unconscious are ordered successively in time in accordance with certain temporal relationships. There are certain sequences of events that make a certain predictability possible. This is something that I believe can be substantiated empirically. To do this is, I think, even somewhat simple. When one knows many myths or fairy tales, then one knows, for example, that when the fairy tale or myth begins, "For a long time, a married couple had no children," then usually a child who will be a hero is born. Thus we could say in this regard that archetypal proposition A strictly calls for archetypal proposition B. The archetypes would thus not only be structures of necessary associations but also of a necessary sequence of images that will prevail. I am now attempting to observe this in my patients, and I believe that proving it will not be at all difficult. This would of course greatly modify our notion of time.

Now, what is number from this point of view? I have tried to show that the rationalist view, as for instance represented by Hermann Weyl, implies that number is simply a creation of the human intellect. We name some units in a conventional manner and can arbitrarily construct various arithmetical systems, since it is all just a matter of naming. However, this is not accurate. The natural numbers, as mentioned earlier, have irrational properties that we did not put there, but which we only discovered after the fact. This has also lately been stressed by Gerd Müller in the *Studium Generale*. He said that "the realm of the natural numbers is a realm of reality that we should do research on,"[19] that is, in much the same way that we should do research on matter or the psyche. Jung tells us that when we take away all properties such as size, consistency, and color from an outer or inner object, what remains as what we might call its most elementary property is its number. The primary means for ordering something in the chaotic multiplicity of appearance is therefore number. It is the precondition of all knowledge, for knowledge, as Jung specifies elsewhere, comes about through the reactions of the psychic system that flow into consciousness being brought into an order that corresponds to the behavior of metapsychic things, that is, things that are real in themselves. The given instrument for establishing such an order, or for the formulation of an already existing order, perhaps a still unknown state of regularity, or of an orderedness, is number. *It is the most basic element of order in the human mind.* Jung defines number simply as *an archetype of order that has become conscious.* Interestingly, number appears in the most essential realm in the psyche, that is to say, in mandala structures, which are images of the divine. In them we always encounter numerical structures. In these numerical orders an *a priori* meaning of existence reveals itself. This is why the ancient mathematicians always emphasized the divine nature of number.

Jung suspected that the place to look for breakthroughs connecting the physical and psychological sciences would be more or less here, in this area related with the archetype of number and the concept of time. It seems to me that the strange numerical isomorphism of the genetic code and the *I Ching,* which both use the same number systems, is a strong pointer in this direction. But of course, in my view, these are not the only possible number systems. Today we have the widespread school of Hans Kaiser, represented principally by Professor Haase in Vienna, that studies "harmonic symbolism." As I see it, these scientists are groping along the same path as we are. However, they are of the opinion that everything can be explained through the Pythagorean schema of pitch intervals. I do not believe this. That would be like my now postulating that everything must be explained according to the schema of the *I Ching* or genetic code. There are probably many different numerical structures that repeatedly make a parallel appearance in the psychic and physical realms. I do not think that this can be reduced at this point to a universal formula. That would be too speculative and would not do justice to the multiplicity of possibilities. This is, however, where further research must be encouraged. When Jung came to this point, he said the following: "Now I have the feeling that I've hit my head against the ceiling. I can't get any farther than this." This was shortly before his death. Now, I have not tried to produce any creative new ideas, but rather, in my book *Number and Time* I have tried to take this idea that Jung hinted at somewhat further and to show that the natural numbers in fact do possess in exactly the same way in the world of psychic representations all the qualities that they possess mathematically and that they have in physics and in the hereditary code.[20] Thus a real, absolute isomorphism is present. I was able to take this up to the number four. Then it became too complicated, and at that point I also hit my head on the ceiling.

In my view, investigators should proceed to a complete overhaul of mathematics. It should place the emphasis on number theory, which has been so very neglected, because in regard to it—as Poincaré once put it—we always keep running into annoying exceptions rather than rules. But these exceptions are what is so fascinating. Moreover, we need a complete revision of the whole probability calculus; that is, we must develop a greater awareness of the relativity of its propositions.

Notes

1. Irenäus Eibl-Eibesfeld, *Liebe und Hass: Zur Naturgeschichte elementarer Verhaltensweisen* (Munich, 1970).
2. Claude Lévi-Strauss, *The Savage Mind* (Chicago: University of Chicago Press, 1966).

3. Gilbert Durand, *Les structures anthropologiques de l'imaginaire* (Paris: Presses Universitaires de France, 1960).

4. S. Sambursky, *Die physikalische Weltbild in der Antike* (Zurich & Stuttgart: Artemis, 1965).

5. C. G. Jung and Wolfgang Pauli, *The Interpretation of Nature and the Psyche* (New York: Pantheon Books, 1955).

6. Rudolf Carnap, *Physikalische Bergriffsbildung* (Darmstadt, 1966).

7. Max Jammer, "Die Entwicklung des Modellbegriffs in den physikalischen Wissenschaften," *Studium Generale* 18, no. 3 (1963).

8. Hermann Weyl, "Über den Symbolismus in der Mathematik und mathematischen Physik," *Studium Generale* 6 (1953).

9. Ibid.

10. Cf. C. G. Jung, "Synchronicity: An Acausal Connecting Principle," in *The Structure and Dynamics of the Psyche,* vol. 8 of the *Collected Works* (cw), pp. 432ff.

11. Ibid., cw 8, p. 417.

12. Ibid., cw 8, p. 445.

13. Arthur Waley's translation of the *Tao Te Ching,* cited in Jung, "Synchronicity," cw 8, pp. 487–88.

14. G. W. Leibniz, *Kleinere philosophische Schriften,* VI (Leipzig, 1883); cf. also G. W. Leibniz, *Grundwahrheiten der Philosophie und Monadologie,* ed. J. C. Horn (Frankfurt, 1962).

15. Jung, "Synchronicity," cw 8, pp. 518–19.

16. Richard Wilhelm, *The I Ching or Book of Changes,* trans. Cary F. Baynes (Princeton, N.J.: Princeton University Press, 1967).

17. D. Rivière, *La Physique et le temps,* Proceedings of the Schweizerische Naturforschende Gesellschaft, 1965.

18. See Marie-Louise von Franz, *Number and Time: Reflections toward a Unification of Depth Psychology and Physics* (Evanston, Ill.: Northwestern University Press, 1974), pp. 105, 106.

19. Gerd Müller, "Der Modellbegriff in der Mathematik," *Studium Generale* 18, no. 3 (1963).

20. Von Franz, *Number and Time.*

Symbols of
the Unus Mundus

Today, increasingly, we are faced with the question: In what form is that vital domain we call the human unconscious psyche joined with matter? As C. G. Jung often stressed, it seems that we have not yet acquired enough knowledge of the two domains to build a reliable bridge between them. Nonetheless many conceptual parallels have emerged that appear to suggest a close relationship between the two. Moreover, as Jung discovered, we are increasingly beset by the question of whether or not the archetype of the natural numbers is connected in an essential manner with the relationship of mind and matter. We shall investigate this question in the pages that follow.

The point of departure for my reflections is the so-called synchronicity principle of C. G. Jung. In his observations of the deeper levels of the unconscious psyche of individual persons, Jung encountered the frequently observed fact that when there is a constellation (an excited state) of archetypal contents, events with the same meaning tend to occur in the outer world. These so-called coincidences are "more than just a coincidence" to the extent that they exhibit a meaning equivalent to the inner psychic, unconscious content that has been activated. Jung termed this class of events "synchronicity phenomena," since the connection between them does not seem to be causal, but is indicated by their meaning and relative simultaneity. It gives the impression of a synchronicity that Jung began to observe this phenomenon just at the time he was becoming acquainted with Richard Wilhelm and was introduced by him to the mysteries of the *I Ching,* which seems to be based entirely on the synchronicity principle.

This discovery of Jung's—more than many another clue—leads to the postulation that that reality which we seek introspectively to describe as the collective unconscious might be the same unknown and uncognizable reality that atomic physics seeks to describe from the outside as "material" reality. Therefore Jung even asserted that he would have no objection to regarding the psyche as a quality of matter and matter as a concrete aspect of the psyche, provided that the psyche was understood to be the collective unconscious.[1] This is just simply nature, "nature that contains *everything,* therefore also unknown things . . . including matter."[2]

When he created the concept of synchronicity, Jung laid a foundation which might lead us to see the complementary realms of psyche and matter as *one* reality.[3] For in each synchronistic event it is the same meaning which manifests in the psyche and also in the arrangement of outer events that occur simultaneously. Also, *a priori* knowledge of facts which could not be known at that moment often becomes manifest. Jung has called this "absolute knowledge." The latter consists of something like an "immediate existence" of images or "a 'perceiving' which consists . . . of subjectless 'simulacra.' "[4] Synchronistic events thus seem to point towards a *unitary aspect of existence* which transcends our conscious grasp and which Jung has called the *unus mundus.*[5] In the natural philosophy of the Middle Ages this word served to denote a transcendental *oneness* of the world which was personified in the *Sapienta Dei* ("Through which God knows Himself") or as the Soul of Christ, Mary, or preexisting Logos (Word). It was the model *(exemplar)* or potential *archetypus mundus* or the sum of all *typi* or *primordiales causae* dwelling in God's mind before He created the universe according to their pattern.[6] Later the alchemist Gerhard Dorn identi-

fied this "*unus mundus* idea" of the Middle Ages with the *lapis* as
well as with the ultimate goal of the alchemical *coniunctio*.[7] But
while the term denotes a metaphysical concept in these medieval
speculations, Jung discovered that the synchronistic phenomena
provide *empirical* evidence for the existence of such an *unus mundus*. He then added the most important statement that the mandala is the psychological equivalent and synchronicity the parapsychological equivalent of the *unus mundus*.[8]

Since this oneness of all existence transcends our conscious
comprehension, it is expressed—as always in such cases—by
many symbols. In the historical traditions of many nations we
find attempts to unite simultaneously the above-mentioned two
aspects (mandala and synchronicity) and thus to invent a sort of
cybernetic device by which people hoped to contact the *absolute
knowledge*. The best-known symbol of this kind is the astrological horoscope. From the very beginnings of alchemy the horoscope's circular structure was identified with the *prima materia*
and with the goal substance of the alchemical process. In the
treatise of Komarios[9] (probably first century A.D.) it is said that
the *prima materia* is an analogy of the firmament and its twelve
sections, that it is shaped like a wheel or whirl and consists of an
all-pervading substance. God put this "rotating" circular order
of heaven into matter at the very beginning of creation and, in
the mystery of his resurrection after death, man becomes one
with this whirling circular substance.[10]

Not only in alchemy but also in other areas of the antique
sciences there were such circular horoscope-like structural models, drawn down, as it were, from heaven into matter or into
some special situation. For instance, in geomancy or in the so-
called "spheres" (of Ps. Demokritos or Petosiris), there were
mandalas which served as methods of divination to learn things
which normally could not be known except through the "absolute knowledge" (for example, where an escaped slave was
hiding or whether a patient would die or live).[11]

In her fascinating book *Giordano Bruno and the Hermetic Tradition*, Frances Yates has shown that in the Renaissance there was
an enormous revival of just this symbolism.[12] It began with Marsilio Ficino and his book *De vita coelitus comparanda*. According

to Ficino's theory, the whole universe was one living being (=
unus mundus!). It consisted of the cosmos as its body, the world
soul (linked with the body by an all-pervading life principle),
and the divine Nous. The body contained the *species* of all
things, the world soul their *rationes seminales,* and the Nous their
ideae. These three *(species, rationes,* and *ideae)* are all connected
by *magical "links";* therefore, one can influence and constellate
or even transform the *ideae* by putting together their corresponding earthly substances. The best of all such magical com-
pounds, according to Ficino, would be a mandala shaped like a
cosmic clock—an image of the whole universe. One should (he
says) make such an image when the sun rises in Aries (i.e., at the
beginning of cosmic time) and use three metals (gold, silver, and
brass) and three colors (gold, blue, and green), corresponding
to Sol, Jupiter, and Venus-Ceres. One can either wear such a
mandala as a medallion or hang it up in one's bedroom and med-
itate on it, for when one has to go out and be overwhelmed by
the ten thousand outer things, one can *make them into one*
through the image of that mandala which one has imprinted on
one's mind through meditation.

Pico della Mirandola held very similar ideas, and his cosmic
mandala also served primarily as an aid to inner recollection and
for making a connection with God. It was like that of Ficino—
triadic in structure, for both Ficino and Pico remained essentially Christian in their basic attitude toward life.

In contrast, Giordano Bruno adopted a pagan *Weltanschauung*
and worshiped mainly the Egyptian gods. Accordingly he postulated the construction of a quaternarian cosmic mandala. Like
Ficino's model it served primarily to re-form and reconstellate
"the inner man," but it also aimed at turning one into an effi-
cient religious "magician" who could produce parapsychological effects in the outer world.

Bruno's mandala was also thought of as a mnemotechnical
system (to which I will return later). Frances Yates goes so far as
to affirm that Bruno supported the Copernican world system
and died for it as a martyr, not for scientific reasons but only
because he saw it as a parallel to his own mandala, which had
moved him so much.[13]

The antique use of mandalas, as instruments of divination serving to tap absolute knowledge, remained alive in other forms as well throughout the Middle Ages. First of all there was the famous *Ars magna* of Ramon Lull of Majorca, who constructed a "machine of logics" by drawing different circles into and upon each other. For instance, one circle of sixteen sections had the word *God* in the center and sixteen qualities of God, such as *greatness, benevolence,* etc., in the sections; another circle had the *anima rationalis* in the center and corresponding qualities all around it. If one turned these circles within one another, they were supposed to give the "logical" answer concerning the central themes. According to legend, Lull had received this "art" as a direct inspiration from the unconscious, a fact which won him the title of a *doctor illuminatus*.[14] Probably he was influenced by certain antique mnemotechnical methods. Many ancient orators, such as Cicero, learned their speeches by heart, connecting each section with a part of the room in which they were to speak. When they looked around during the speech, the memorized parts came back to their mind. An orator, Methodius of Skepsis, invented a trick in which, instead of parts of the room, he used the zodiacal houses of the horoscope. He thus invented a sort of mnemotechnical mandala. Giordano Bruno also thought that his cosmic mandala would serve as an aid to memory. Probably the idea behind these queer speculations was to establish an archetypal structure which would order one's thoughts and thus help one to memorize them. This idea is quite sound.[15] But Lull's magical logic-machine, with which he even hoped to convert the Arabs to Christianity, was soon shown up as pure nonsense. The hopeful dream of certain cyberneticians to replace the human brain by a giant computer is a modern variation— and probably just as unreal!

Interestingly, biological research has now encountered facts that cause Lull's absurd construction to seem like an anticipation of facts now at hand. For example, it has now been discovered that the storage and transmission of "information" in the cells of our bodies, and particularly in those that make up the physical base of our memory processes, occur through the RNA and messenger RNA (ribonucleic acid). In 1968 I published the discovery that these acids, as well as DNA (desoxyribonucleic acid), which are the basis of all hereditary material, make use of a mathematical code whose fundamental numerical structure precisely corresponds to that of the *I Ching* hexagrams.[16] As we know, there are sixty-four of them. And also there are $4^3 = 64$ possible combinations of code signs for the structure of the twenty amino acids in the RNA and DNA codes.[17] The transmission of information occurs by means of a tripartite code, just as each *I Ching* hexagram is composed of two trigrams. The divination technique of geomancy is also based on the same numerical combinations in reverse order. Thus Lull's anticipation of a possible basic numerical structure behind our memory processes was not all that senseless, even though newly discovered facts have nothing in common with his absurd construction.

The important points for us are the following: the above-mentioned mandalas are attempts to combine the psychic equivalent of the *unus mundus* (i.e., mandala) with an attempt to tap the "absolute knowledge" (i.e., synchronicity). Some of them are triadic, and these seem more explicitly intended to put the inner man in order, whereas others can be turned, and these have the additional purpose of obtaining ESP knowledge or of producing magical effects. Some of these cosmic models, such as the calendar of Guillaume de Digulleville, which Jung describes in *Psychology and Religion* and *Psychology and Alchemy*, have a double structure of two circles. The same holds true for the mysterious modern vision of a world clock which Jung published in *Psychology and Alchemy*. Jung suggests that this world clock might represent the essence of the time-space union or rather its origin, a point to which we will return. The double-structured models definitely all go back directly or indirectly to Plato's *Timaeus*. According to Plato, there was a massive simultaneity of mathematical forms present in the "body of ideas" following the example of which the visible world was created. Since these could not be translated into actual reality all at once, the demiurge created a revolving model so that the individual forms could manifest in a temporal succession, and in fact in accordance with the sequential arrangement of the natural numbers.[18]

I presume that the famous "illumination" of Descartes, which he himself praises as the discovery of a "miraculous science" *(scientia mirabilis),* was also the vision of such a cosmic model. Afterward, Descartes believed that every field—such as geometry, mathematics, arithmetic, astronomy, and music—was founded on some "universal mathematics" whose basic principles were the serial character of numbers and their proportional relations. The creation of analytical geometry—that is, the Cartesian coordinates (a clear mandala!)[19]—was somehow inspired by this illumination. Actually the whole metric methods of classical physics, which fix all events into such a system of coordinates, were born from this and remained valid until Einstein went deeper into the question of time, when the relative artificiality and thus only the relative usefulness of this system were discovered.[20] The structural model of Descartes again was only triadic-static and thus left the fourth factor aside.

The dual structure of many of the models I have mentioned can also be found in certain Chinese parallels. From earliest times the Chinese theory of numbers was founded on certain numerical basic "plans" which they thought to be cosmic *patterns.*[21] They were—as Marcel Granet explains[22]—mirror images of certain ultimate, mathematical, basic patterns of the whole cosmos. The latter thus gives us (by means of these patterns) number-symbols by which we can order all things. Thus the numbers serve to make us aware of the circumstantial single appearances of the great Oneness or of the Whole. One such pattern is the so-called Lo-shou model, which was purportedly revealed to the culture hero Yu by the god of the Yellow River in the form of a tortoise.

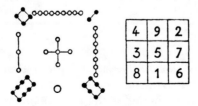

4	9	2
3	5	7
8	1	6

Another pattern is called Ho-t'ou. According to legend it appeared on the back of a dragon-horse.

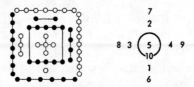

The Lo-shou was also represented as a man who is in the position of the 5 in the center. He has a number 9 on his hat, the numbers 3 and 7 are right and left of him, the numbers 2 and 4 are on his shoulders, and the numbers 8 and 6 are his legs, which stand on the number 1. Through the movements of this figure, the operations of addition, subtraction, and multiplication originated, whereas the geometry of triangles was derived from the Ho-t'ou.[23] From earliest times, the trigrams of the *I Ching* have also been combined with these number patterns. The founder of this system of secret knowledge was the legendary Fu-shi, whose body ends in a snake's tail.[24] We thus have again two patterns. One is the "pre-cosmic" or "older" heavenly order and is connected with the numbers of the Ho-t'ou. It looks like this:

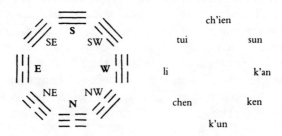

In this pre-cosmic order the opposites are vis-à-vis each other, but—as the texts point out—they do not fight each other.

The second pattern, the "inner-cosmic order" or "order of King Wen," was connected with the Lo-shou (see p. 47).

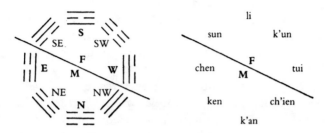

These two cosmic patterns were also drawn on two boards (planchettes), the inner-cosmic on a quadrangular board below, which represented the earth, and the pre-cosmic on an upper round board, which represented heaven. If one turned these two boards around a stick through their common center, one could get divinatory answers to questions. Probably this technique was already known in the oldest Chinese shamanism.[25]

These numerical matrices in China are not the same as those of our modern Western mathematics and physics, for they are not quantitative "sets" or structures but, as Granet has pointed out,[26] qualitative, hierarchical, numerical orders which also serve to grasp *des ensembles d'objets*. One could call them qualitative "fields" or lists of expectation values for probable synchronistic events.

These are probably the presuppositions which underlie the remarkable "*unus mundus* theory" of Wang Fu Ch'ih (1619–1692),[27] a theory in which he tried to explain the functioning of the *I Ching*. According to his point of view, the whole of existence is ultimately a continuum which, in itself, is ordered according to definite rules. It has no visible shape which could be grasped by our senses. However, through its inherent dynamic, images are differentiated out of it which, through their structure and position, participate in the rules of the continuum. Since they are ordered according to rules, they also participate in the world of number and can thus be grasped by a numerical procedure.[28]

According to Wang Fu Ch'ih the invisible continuum in the

background of the universe can be approached in two ways: either directly through (qualitative) experience which is mediated by images or through theoretical speculation which is mediated by numbers. Both ways can give us information about the momentary constellation of the psychophysical background of the universe.

It seems to me that there is a striking frequency of *dualistic unus mundus* symbols in all the examples which I have mentioned and that, in their double structures, one tends to be a timeless "absolute," the other a rotating time-bound structure. This could be connected with the two aspects of reality which Jung mentioned in his paper on synchronicity: namely, first the phenomenon of "acausal orderedness" as we have it in the discontinuities of physics or in the *a priori* properties of the natural numbers, and second the actual individual synchronistic events.[29] In the first, a timeless formal just-so existence appears, and in the second, time-bound acts of creation, a fact which implies the idea of a *creatio continua*. Jung stresses, however, that this *creatio continua* should be seen not only as a successive series of creative acts but equally as the eternal presence of the *one* creative act.[30]

The mandala structure of a static timeless nature seems to point more toward the "acausal orderedness" of the unitary reality, whereas the rotating divination methods aim rather at grasping the parapsychological aspect of the specific synchronistic events. They can, however, only establish qualitative "fields" within which such synchronistic events could happen but not the specific event itself, for as a *creatio* they remain by definition unpredictable.

Certain developments in modern theories in physics seem also to grope toward some tentative symbolic formulations of the *unus mundus* and the "absolute knowledge." The French physicist Olivier Costa de Beauregard,[31] for instance, while studying the problem of entropy, came to the conclusion that the universe which the physicist studies is not the whole but rather the *avers* of a much more primordial psychic universe, of which the physical cosmos is only a passive double. This psychic universe he calls an *infrapsychisme* or a *subconscient*, which he claims should be regarded as coextensive with the four-dimensional Minkowski-Einsteinian "block universe." According to the relativists, everything which appears to us in the space-time continuum is ultimately the realization of the mathematical properties of an irrepresentable "world" in which not only space and time but also dynamisms and substances are translated into mathematical formulations.[32] Space is formed by the distribution of matter and energy, and thus matter itself becomes graspable by its mathematical imprint on the Reimann continuum,[33] and thus matter can be conceptually identified—as Hermann Weyl[34] puts it—by number.[35] In this four-dimensional continuous "block universe," however, time becomes questionable, and therefore the relativistic theory, with its deterministic view of things, is in opposition to quantum physics, because the adherents of its points of view allow for a certain freedom in all events on account of the Heisenberg uncertainty principle. It is because of this that the problem of time has come so much to the fore today in scientific discussion. In order to reconcile the two schools— the static-mathematical Einsteinian world model with the flow of undetermined events which is reality according to quantum physics—the physicist Aloys Wenzl of Munich proposes that we should regard the Einsteinian model as only potentially real, as only a potential mathematical framework, so to speak, within which the events that quantum physics describes actually take place. As from our point of view the *unus mundus* also has only potential reality, this form of relativistic world model approaches very closely to an *unus mundus* symbol, especially if, as Costa de Beauregard boldly speculates (without knowing Jung!), the unconscious should be coextensive with this potential continuum of a "block universe."

In order to solve the above-mentioned problem of time within the framework of the relativistic theory, certain physicists such as A. S. Eddington, Wheeler, and Richard Feynman proposed to postulate two time dimensions, one for ordinary "directed" time (time arrow) and a second in which time should be regarded as "arrowless" so that micro-events could happen in it "backward and forward." This dimension should be "imaginary" (i.e., its values should be multiplied by $\sqrt{-1}$). This second time dimension without an intrinsic "arrow" reminds the psychologist of the *illud-tempus* or *Aljira* idea of certain primitives and probably goes back to the same archetype. But again this new theory of a second time dimension seems to spring from a tentative effort to grasp that double aspect of reality which Jung has called "acausal-orderedness" and "synchronicity." According to Eddington micro-events, which happen in an imaginary time dimension, could sometimes have micro-effects on events in the ordinary time dimension, just as synchronistic events, according to Jung, sporadically interrupt and interfere with the "ordinary" flow of events which are observed in our normal state of consciousness.

The phenomenon of "absolute knowledge" is also beginning to interest modern physicists, who naturally approach it from a quite different angle. Cybernetics is the science of technical "information" (computers, signals, codes, etc.),[36] and its mathematical foundation has inevitably encountered the problem of the psyche. Certain of its theoretical investigators, such as M. Ruyer, L. Brillouin, D. Gabor, J. Rothstein, and others, came to the conclusion that cybernetics could not ignore the fact of "psychic resonance" within their field of investigation. In connection with this, Costa de Beauregard comes to the following conclusions: Predictions in modern physics are based nowadays on mathematical probability, i.e., calculations which allow predictions but not retrodictions (because many natural processes cannot be reversed on account of the principle of entropy). Each act of measuring is also—as John von Neumann pointed out—irreversible; that is, each detail of information we acquire is bought by an increase of entropy in the universe. Information, however, means also a possibility of diminishing entropy by our "ordering" interference into single systems. (Information consists in itself of image-like representations which are present in our minds.) In order to make such an "ordering interference" (= decrease of entropy or negentropy) our psyche need only switch from a passively contemplating state into an active volitional attitude. In the former state information consists of an acquisition of knowledge; in the latter it is a power to organize (i.e., negentropy). During the time that the order-sustaining energy which opposes entropy disappears more and more out of the universe, it must circulate in a psychic "elsewhere" *(ailleurs)* in its potential form of information. This psychic "elsewhere" of physical energy Costa de Beauregard calls *infrapsychisme*. He obviously means something similar to what Jung has called the psychoid aspect of the archetypes and the collective unconscious. Costa de Beauregard also assumes that this *infrapsychisme* contains a sort of *supraconscience*—something very akin to Jung's "absolute knowledge." (Ruyer calls it an absolute *survol*, a bird's-eye view of the universe as a whole.) This cosmic *infrapsychisme* is, according to Costa de Beauregard, an antiphysical world (anti-Carnot!) ruled by final instead of causal laws. It coexists with matter and crystallizes itself out into the individual psychisms of animals and men. The knowledge which it contains can move faster than light and thus "synchronizes" all single beings because their psychisms all come from the same "storehouse of telecommunication." Thus the whole material universe is like a gigantic cybernetic machine which serves the growth of consciousness in all individuals.[37]

As Roland Weitzenböck has shown in a most amusing way in his book *Der vierdimensionale Raum,*[38] there have always been a lot of fantasies smuggled into the ungraspable concepts of modern physics, fantasies which we can easily recognize as projections of the collective unconscious. But in my opinion Costa de Beauregard's ideas seem more logical and serious and might lead us closer to a unitary scientific view of physics and psychology than many of the other attempts, because he recognizes that the "hidden" parameters point to something nonphysical.

In the field of biological investigation, facts have also been discovered which seem to me to throw new light on the problem of "absolute knowledge" and on Jung's idea of the archetype. In his paper on synchronicity Jung has pointed out that the "absolute knowledge" in man should not be associated with cerebral processes. We get rather closer, he says, to the formal factor in nature when we observe the "intelligent" behavior of primitive brainless animals.[39] Since Jung wrote this, the investigations of McConnell and his group at the University of Michigan have shown that flatworms are capable of "learning" and of storing what they have learned in a sort of memory (probably with the help of the ribonucleic acid in the nerve cells). If an "uneducated" flatworm eats a "learned" comrade of his own species, he afterward produces the "learned behavior" of his victim.[40] (Probably that is why primitives ate missionaries: to integrate the holy doctrine!) This fact not only gives further support to Jung's idea quoted above but also throws new light on how inborn patterns of behavior could originate—that it adds a more solid foundation to Jung's hypothesis of the archetype. Beyond this, perhaps it suggests that certain microphysical processes in the living cell might be the first primitive instruments which serve to fix certain aspects of the "absolute knowledge" materially.

Naturally, this "intelligent" behavior of the flatworm is *not* the same as "absolute knowledge," but perhaps it will enable us soon to find a material, numerically structured foundation which serves to record statistical and formal regularities in nature (while "absolute knowledge" can also foresee unique events, as Jung's example of the prophetic dream of a misprint shows). As Jung said, we only come *closer* here to the formal factor in nature, but it is *not* this factor itself. However, it seems remarkable to me that here again, as in the fantastic memory-systems of antiquity and of the Renaissance, a connection appears to exist between the phenomenon of memory and "absolute knowledge," although we cannot yet grasp it in any more accurate form.

As Jung pointed out in his paper on synchronicity, the natural numbers play an important role in most of the divination procedures of humanity. Toward the end of his life, Jung was even planning to undertake a work on the archetypal aspects of numbers so that he could further pursue the trail pointing to his *unus mundus* idea. As he once asserted in a discussion, for Jung number was the most primitive expression of mind. By "mind" he meant an active, dynamic ordering factor that operates in and behind the unconscious psyche. To the extent, however, that number, as a result of the quantization of all energy, also represents an inalienable property of matter (we have only to think, for example, of the so-called nucleonic numbers), number also appears as that objective-mental element which jointly orders psyche and matter.

As we learn from the reports of mathematicians—for example, Henri Poincaré, Friedrich Gauss, Felix Klein, Jacques Hadamard, and others—numbers and complex numerical arrangements can "reveal" themselves directly out of the unconscious psyche.[41] The fact that the Chinese claim that their Ho-t'ou and Lo-shou were revealed by a tortoise and a dragon-horse, for us, symbolically expresses the same thing. In this light, number is not only "enacted" by an act of consciousness but is something found in nature. It is a dynamic structure or, more precisely, a rhythm configuration of energy that appears isomorphically in the psychic and physical domains of reality.[42]

Interestingly, whenever numbers are used as instruments of divination, they do not have that quantitative aspect (a multitude of units) which is their chief characteristic in the Western theory of number (Gottlob Frege and Bertrand Russell), but *they have a field aspect of—rather, their series appears as—a continuum.* They appear like "excited points" of a field. In other words, one could conceive of the natural numbers as specifically distributed virtual centers of a continuous numerical field. This would make it possible to construe an isomorphism of the microstructure of matter and the structure of the collective unconscious. Indeed, it has lately been discovered that the so-called elementary particles are further divisible. That is why Wheeler says that fundamentally there only exist something like continually fluctuating electrodynamic fields, and the particles are the "energically charged fragments of the basic geometry of space,"[43] that is, they are like excited points in a continuum. Lancelot Whyte had already pointed out that the idea of the field was coming more and more to dominate today's science when understood as "the pattern of relationship operative in every situation."[44] This is particularly valid for the elementary particles, which exhibit the tendency to take on regular configurations, and even when damaged, like crystals, to form themselves anew. Whyte even defines "life" as such as the self-diffusion of a pulsating pattern.[45]

Ernst Anrich stresses that physical reality is essentially connected with number as a whole oneness.[46] And concerning the proportional or "magic" numbers, which frequently recur in atomic structures and were discovered by P. J. Jensen and Maria Goeppert Mayer, he proposes calling them hierarchical numbers because they are not just "counting" units but have the qualitative property of creating proportional order.[47] I would suggest that we go even one step further and say that number is a quantity *and* an active specific qualitative manifestation of the one-continuum, i.e., the *unus mundus*. Each natural number (positive integer) would then possess four basic aspects: (1) relationship to space-time and geometrizability, (2) quantity, (3) positional ratio, and (4) quality, i.e., a specific retrograde *Gestalt* relation to the one-continuum.

Now it can actually be empirically proven that the whole psychic domain called by Jung the collective unconscious, which is the deepest level of the psychic unconscious in man, possesses a field structure whose excited points correspond to the archetypes. Energic processes in this field in part follow a linear sequence, thus becoming temporally determinative. Also, the so-called progression of the natural number series is probably nothing other than a sequence of typical procedures of this kind created by ordering rhythms. Our feeling of time is based on these and possibly also, as Wolfgang Pauli speculated, the possibility of parapsychological precognition. Interestingly, in the earliest times in China, mathematics was regarded as nothing other than the science of predicting the future! (Unfortunately, this aspect of Chinese number theory has not been researched even by Chinese science itself; to Westerners, it is entirely inaccessible.) In this way, the concept of time would be based on the concept of numerically structured rhythms, a view that jibes with the facts observed from an entirely different angle by Jean Piaget and Paul Fraisse. Instead of following Thomas Aquinas (following Aristotle) in defining time simply as *numerus movens,* we should perhaps, speaking in a more detailed fashion, say that the common movement patterns of the psychophysical energy are numbers. These, with their rhythms of progression, form the basis of the idea of time, and in their field nature, the basis of a timeless order. This explains why mythological personifications of time—like the god Aion in Rome, Zurvān in Persia,

Kāla in India—are emphatic embodiments of the polyvalent psychic energy.

The "field" of the collective unconscious, conceived of as iso-morphic with the field of natural numbers, is, however, not ran-domly or chaotically/partially organized, but seems to be or-dered by a higher energic center, which Jung called the archetype of the Self. This, when represented statically (as in the mandala), seems to exhibit quaternary structures; however, looked at more closely, it is rather, as Jung explained in his book *Aion,* a dynamic sequential structure of the following character:

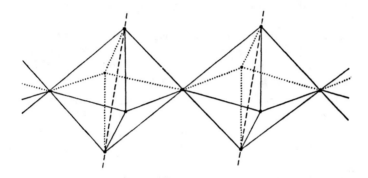

which in turn is connected with a similar structure found in the *I Ching,* in geomancy, and also, last but not least, in the DNA and RNA code. I cannot refrain at this point from mentioning the dream of a modern physicist that also seems to refer to this structure.

The evening before the dream, the dreamer had been occu-pied in drawing certain key factors for his (we would say) com-plexes in the corners of a Star of David. Then he dreamed:

> A Chinese woman (elevated to the rank of a Sophia) is present with two men. I myself was the fourth. She told me: "You must let us all play chess as much as possible in all possible combina-tions."

In a hypnagogic vision, the dreamer heard her further remark:

> "There is something quite right in your drawings and something transitory and wrong. What is right is that there the number of lines is six, but what is wrong is that the number of points is six.

Look here"—and I saw a square with clearly traced diagonals.

"Do you now at least see the four and the six? Spatially four points and six lines or six pairs based on four points. They are the same six lines that are in the *I Ching*. Look again at the square: four of the lines are the same length; the two others longer in an irrational proportion. There is no figure based on four points with six lines of the same length. Therefore the symmetry cannot be statically produced, and a dance is generated. *Coniunctio* means changing places in this dance. One could also speak of a game or of rhythms and turns. Therefore, three must be dynamically expressed, which is latently already contained in the square."

This dream and the fantasy that followed it are obviously also connected with a similar fundamental rhythm of life as intuited by the Chinese. Such a dance rhythm with its trinary and quaternary structures is contained in almost all the *unus mundus* models of mankind and also in special mandalic models for divination. In this connection, it is striking that the method of calculating in most divination techniques runs conceptually retrograde, taking the form of repeated recursion to the One. The qualitative number sequence could thus perhaps be the foundation of "timeless orderedness."

In the vision of a cosmic clock, described by Jung in his *Psychology and Alchemy*, two heterogeneous systems are combined. Jung says about this that it might perhaps be a graphic hint of the origin of space-time, but he did not want to lay too much weight on this interpretation, because he lacked proofs for it.[48] His humility did not permit him to put further emphasis on this important statement. However, it seems to me that science has come somewhat nearer to the developments of this problem just presented and that this double mandala structure in fact represents a kind of primordial symbol of the *unus mundus* with space-time generated out of it as a heterogeneous system. The dovetailing of the two systems in the vision is periodic; perhaps this should be taken literally. In any case, it seems that the "dove-tailing" of the two systems is conditioned by the structuring power of number.

This complementary double aspect of number (quantity and quality) is in my opinion the thing which makes it possible for the world of quantity (matter) and of quality (psyche) to inter-lock with each other in a periodical manner (world clock!), but there is still *one* fact which remains different and is outside this schema: the specific synchronistic event itself. If, for instance, I should throw an *I Ching* oracle and by numerical procedure get hexagram 52, *chên* ("Shock," "Thunder"), it would give a qual-itative "list of expectation values" about events within which inner shocks could coincide with outer shock-events—a quali-tative "field" of such possibilities, so to speak. But if once a real earthquake should actually occur on top of it—*that* would re-main a spontaneous event, which (though it fits into the quali-tative "field" indicated by the *I Ching*) was in itself not *expressis verbis* predictable. In such an event the meaning, the absolute knowledge, and the real event become completely one, and that is the *unus mundus*. It is like a "happening information."

Perhaps I should complete this paper, which has been mainly formulated with the thinking function, with a hint as to what this could mean from the standpoint of feeling experience. The old alchemical text of Komarios, which goes back to the Egyp-tian liturgy of the dead, seems to me to speak most clearly. Ac-cording to Komarios the *unus mundus* is a transcendental expe-rience of wholeness which occurs in the mystery of resurrection after death.[49] "Then," the text runs, "the soul says to the body: Awake from Hades, rise up from the grave and stay away from darkness. Clothe thyself in Spirituality and Divinity." Then spirit, soul, and body become "the One, in which the whole mystery lies hidden." This "One" is also described as a stone statue which is born out of the fire. It unites spirit, soul, and body and contains all four elements. "And thus the *one* nature is created, which hunts and overcomes all natures, and it is the One which conquers all natures, that of the fire and of moisture, and which changes them all in their essence. And, behold, I will tell you further what comes later when this is completed. As it has (now) reached its own body (the stone), it now pervades the other bodies in a deadly manner. In putrefaction and warmth this *pharmakon* is born which goes without hindrance through all other bodies." This deadly aspect of the Self arises, if I understand the text rightly, at the moment when the One (the Self) has reached its "own" body, namely the *corpus glorificationis* in resurrection. *Then* it kills its former body and pervades all other bodies. That would probably mean—translated into our language—that when the Self, after having grown within the earthly man, has completely reached its goal, i.e., the mandala of the *unus mundus,* then it has a deadly effect on the earthly body because it has reached a form of definite oneness with the all-pervading cosmic One-continuum, which seems to be hostile to separated existence. If it happens this way, death seems to be the "right" thing, i.e., something naturally connected with the goal. That is why the abode of the dead in primitive mythologies is often described as being identical with the *unus mundus*.[50] The spirit which rules and pervades the *unus mundus* would be the alchemical Mercurius, as Jung says, "the original non-differentiated unity of the world or of Being; . . . the primordial unconsciousness which contains all opposites."[51]

The experiential experience of the *unus mundus* seems to be a transcendent one. The West Nigerians say, "Only when a man dies does he discover the mystery of life."[52] Thus in many archaic cultures, numeric divination is also used as a means of communicating with the spirit world. According to Carl Hentze, the Chinese sign for *lung* ("playing with something") also means *hiang* (the major offering to the ancestral spirits).[53] What the two hands are playing with is a jade rhombus (according to others, a counting stick) as a symbol of the cosmic whole. The Chinese word *suan shu* (counting) is the same sign but with four hands:

or it consists of a doubling of the radical *shih,* which, according to Joseph Needham, means "to show, demonstrate, inform, reveal as, in a numinous demonstration of the divine."

While the technology of the West is intruding more and more destructively into the spiritual tradition of the East, a strange conversion seems to be beginning in Western science. If a tunnel breakthrough between psychology and atomic physics were to take place, confirming Jung's intuition of the archetype of the natural number as the joint ordering principle of the domains of psyche and matter, we would thus emerge at a place where lie the most ancient knowledge and traditions of the East, which in part have even long been forgotten there. This would empirically prove an ancient conviction of the Buddhists that the deepest, most profound level of human nature, at the place where our psyche fuses with the unknown of the cosmic whole, remains the same everywhere.

The paradox of the interlocking of the two heterogeneous mandala systems—as long as life in this space-time still lasts— has been wonderfully described by Zen Master Ma. When he was eighty years old and had fallen seriously ill, only twenty-four hours before his death the supervisor of his monastery went to Ma and asked, "O venerable Master, how is your state of health these last days?" The Master answered, "Buddha with the sun-face, Buddha with the moon-face." As Wilhelm Gundert explains, this refers to a passage in the so-called third *Sutra of the Names of Buddha,* where it is said in the ceremony of the twelfth month of the year: "There I saw a Buddha with the name of Moon-face. The duration of the life of this Buddha with the moon-face is one day and one night. Looking past the Buddha with the moon-face I saw again a Buddha. He has the name of Sun-face. The duration of the life of this Buddha with the sun-face is a whole one thousand, eight hundred years."[54] Therefore, one could understand the words of Master Ma as an allusion to these two heterogeneous systems—one limited in space-time, the other of infinite duration. But both are called "Buddha," i.e., both are facets of that great Oneness[55] of which the Zen master, Ma, became conscious on his deathbed.

Notes

1. C. G. Jung, "Ein Brief zur Frage der Synchronizität," *Zeit-schrift für Parapsychologie und Grenzgebiete der Psychologie* (Bern & Munich, 1961), vol. 5, no. 1, pp. 1ff.
2. Ibid., p. 4.
3. C. G. Jung, "Synchronicity: An Acausal Connecting Principle," in *The Structure and Dynamics of the Psyche,* vol. 8 of the *Collected Works* (cw).
4. Absolute, i.e., detached from any ego-consciousness; ibid., paras. 912, 923, 931.
5. C. G. Jung, *Mysterium Coniunctionis,* cw 14, paras. 659ff, 767.
6. Cf. John Scotus Erigena, *De divisione naturae,* II, 18 and 31; Hugh of St. Victor, "Annotationes elucidariae in Evangelium Joannis" in *Allegoriae,* quoted in W. Preger, *Geschichte der Mystik im Mittelalter* (Munich, 1874), vol. 1, p. 238.
7. Jung, *Mysterium Coniunctionis,* cw 14, para. 767.
8. Ibid., para. 662.
9. Cf. M. Berthelot, *Collection des anciens alchimistes grecs* (Paris, 1887–1888), vol. 1, p. 298; and Zosimos, ibid., p. 112.
10. This probably comes from the Egyptian death ritual in which one becomes a star at the end, rotating in heaven with the never-setting circumpolar stars.
11. Cf. Lynn Thorndike, *History of Magic and Experimental Science* (New York, 1923), vol. 1, p. 676f.
12. Frances Yates, *Giordano Bruno and the Hermetic Tradition* (London: Routledge & Kegan Paul, 1964).
13. He also loved Mordent's compass for the same reason.
14. Cf. Thorndike, *History of Magic and Experimental Science,* vol. 2, p. 862f.
15. It has been found that our memory is not just something mechanical but that certain structures *(schemata)* and the intensity of our interests play a role. G. J. Whitrow, *The Natural Philosophy of Time* (London & Edinburgh: Nelson, 1961), pp. 89ff. and 95ff.
16. *Dialog über den Menschen: Eine Festschrift zum 75. Geburtstag von Wilhelm Bitter* (Klett. Stuttgart, 1968). Joseph Needham had already compared the binary arithmetical foundation of the *I Ching* with its modern electronic application. Cf. J. Needham and Ling Wang, *Science and Civilization in China* (Cambridge, 1954), vol. 2, p. 340f; cf. also A. Rump, "Das

Problem des Bösen im I Ging," unpublished thesis, pp. 22–23.

17. For more detail, see G. Beadle and M. Beadle, *The Language of Life* (New York: Doubleday, 1966), p. 204f.
18. Cf. Whitrow, *The Natural Philosophy of Time*, p. 28f.
19. Cf. "The Dream of Descartes" in Marie-Louise von Franz, *Dreams* (Boston & London: Shambhala Publications, 1991).
20. Cf. Albert Einstein, *Über die spezielle und allgemeine Relativitätstheorie*, 3rd ed. (Brunswick, 1918).
21. These are matrices, but of a different nature than the matrices of Western mathematics.
22. Marcel Granet, *La Pensée chinoise* (Paris, 1948), pp. 154ff., 175ff., and 284.
23. Cf. D. Chin-te Cheng, "On the Mathematical Significance of the Chinese Ho-t'u and Lo-shu," *American Mathematical Monthly* (1925), pp. 499ff. I am grateful for the kindness of Arnold Mindell in bringing this article to my attention.
24. Ibid., p. 182ff.
25. Ibid., pp. 200–201.
26. Granet, *La Pensée chinoise,* pp. 205ff.
27. Helmut Wilhelm discovered this remarkable philosopher and described his theory in an Eranos lecture, "The Concept of Time in the Book of Changes," in *Man and Time* (New York: Pantheon, Bollingen Series XXX, 1957).
28. By adding the value of heads or tails on a coin or by counting sticks.
29. Jung, "Synchronicity," cw 8, para. 965.
30. Ibid., para. 967.
31. Olivier Costa de Beauregard, *Le Second Principe et la science du temps* (Paris, 1963), pp. 14ff.
32. Cf. Aloys Wenzl, *Die philosophischen Grenzfragen der modernen Naturwissenschaft*, 3rd ed. (Stuttgart, 1960), p. 127ff.
33. Ibid., p. 32.
34. H. Weyl, *Raum, Zeit, Materie* (Darmstadt, 1961), p. 9.
35. Ibid., passim.
36. Cf. J. B. Pierce, *Symbols, Signals, and Noise: The Nature of and Process of Communication* (New York, 1961), passim.
37. Beauregard, *Le Second Principe,* pp. 95, 101ff., 112, 123, 141ff.
38. Roland Weitzenböck, *Der vierdimensionale Raum* (Basel & Stuttgart, 1958).

39. Jung, cw 8, para. 947.
40. Cf. the current publications in *The Worm Runners Digest* (Ann Arbor: Mental Health Research Institute of the University of Michigan). Jean Rosenberg has shown that if one injects the RNA of an educated animal into an uneducated animal, the latter shows vestiges of the memory of the former.
41. J. Hadamard, *The Psychology of Invention in the Mathematical Field* (New York: Dover, 1954), passim.
42. The Greek word *arithmos* is etymologically related to *rhythmos*. Both are derived from *rhein* = "flow." Cf. Withrow, *The Natural Philosophy of Time*, p. 115.
43. According to the report of W. Sullivan in *New York Times*, Sunday, February 5, 1967.
44. L. Whyte, *Accent on Form* (New York: Harper, 1954), pp. 27–28.
45. Ibid., p. 118.
46. Ernst Anrich, *Moderne Physik und Tiefenpsychologie* (Stuttgart, 1963), p. 8. Anrich practically ignores the synchronicity problem.
47. Ibid., pp. 130, 142. Anrich strangely enough denies the fact that number is an archetypal image.
48. Jung, *Psychology and Alchemy,* cw 12, para. 307. p. 280f.
49. Cf. Berthelot, *Collection,* vol. 1, p. 297f.
50. Unfortunately I cannot comment further on this aspect here.
51. C. G. Jung, *Mysterium Coniunctionis,* cw 14, para. 660.
52. Cf. B. Maupoil, *La Géomancie à l'ancienne Côte des Esclaves* (Paris, 1943), p. 34.
53. C. Hentze, *Tod, Auferstehung, Weltordnung* (Zurich, 1955), vol. 1, pp. 15ff; cf. also Needham and Wang, *Science and Civilization in China,* vol. 3, pp. 4ff.
54. Bi-yän-Lu, *Niederschrift von der smaragdenen Felswand,* ed. Wilhelm Gundert (Munich, 1960), p. 97.
55. Gundert stresses that there are many other Buddhas mentioned in this sutra who are all only facets of the *one luminous body.*

Time:
Rhythm and Repose

Time as a Deity and the Stream of Events

Time is one of the great archetypal experiences of man, and has eluded all our attempts towards a completely rational explanation.[1] No wonder that it was originally looked upon as a Deity, even as a form of manifestation of the Supreme Deity, from which it flows like a river of life. Only in modern Western physics has time become part of a mathematical framework, which we use with our conscious mind to describe physical events. The mind of primitive man made less distinction than ours between outer and inner, material and psychic, experiences. Primitive man lived in a stream of inner and outer events which brought along a different cluster of coexisting events at every moment, and thus constantly changed, quantitatively and qualitatively.

Even our seemingly self-evident concepts of past, present, and future do not seem to be universal. The Hopi Indians, for instance, do not possess them in their language. Their universe has two basic aspects: that which is manifest and thus more "objective" and that which is beginning to manifest and is more "subjective." Concrete objects are manifest and in this way already belong to the past; inner images, representations, expectations and feelings are "subjective," on their way to manifestation, and thus bend more towards the future. The present is that razor's-edge where something stops beginning to manifest (is already past) or is on the verge of beginning to manifest. There is no continuing flow of time for the Hopi, but a multiplicity of subtly distinguished moments. The creator of all this is *'a'ne himu,* a "Powerful Something" which is a kind of cosmic breath.[2] Children, too, do not at once live in our communal clock time. They have been shown to perceive rhythm, velocity, and frequency long before they begin to adapt to our ordinary notion of time.[3]

In man's original point of view time was life itself and its divine mystery. This remains so in the ancient Greek notion of time. The Greeks actually identified time with the divine river Oceanos, which surrounded the earth in a circle and which also encompassed the universe in the form of a circular stream or a tail-eating serpent with the Zodiac on its back. It was also called Chronos (Time) and later identified with Kronos, the father of Zeus, and also with the god Aion.

Aion originally denoted the vital fluid in living beings, and thus their life span and allotted fate. This fluid continued to exist after death in the form of a snake.[4] It was a "generative substance," as was all water on earth and especially Oceanos-Chronos, the creator and destroyer of everything. The philosopher Pherekydes taught that the basic substance of the universe was time (Chronos), from which fire, air, and water were produced.[5] Oceanos was also a kind of primal World Soul.[6]

In Hellenistic times, Aion Chronos was identified with the old Persian time-god Zurvān.[7] The ancient Persians discerned two aspects of this supreme deity: Zurvān akarana, Infinite Time, and Zurvān dareghō-chvadhātā, Time of a Long Dominion. The latter was the cause of decay and death, and was sometimes even identified with Ahriman, the principle of evil. The Orphic and Mithraic circles of late antiquity identified Zurvān, in both his opposed aspects at once, with their Aion.[8] A text invokes Aion with the following words:

> I greet thee, thou that fillest the whole structure of the air, spirit that stretchest from heaven to earth . . . and to the confines of the

abyss . . . spirit that also penetratest myself and leavest me again.
Thou, the servant of the rays of the sun, that enlightenest the
world . . . a great circular mysterious form of the universe, heavenly spirit, ethereal spirit, earthy, fiery, windy, light . . . dark
spirit, that shinest like a star. . . . Lord, god of the Aions. . . .
Ruler of everything.[9]

Aion, the god of time, is here clearly an image of the dynamic
aspect of existence, of what we might call today a principle of
psychophysical energy. All opposites—change and duration,
even good and evil, life and death—are included in this cosmic
principle.

This Aion was also sometimes identified with the sun god,
who is obviously the great indicator of time measures. The ini-
tiate prays to him: "O Lord, who with thy spirit bindest the
fiery keys of the fourfold belt . . . fire-walker, creator of light,
fire-breather, with fiery courage . . . Aion, lord of light, . . .
open the doors to me."[10]

This god inherited many aspects of the Egyptian sun god, Ra,
who was the ruler of time. Every hour of the day and night this
supreme deity changed his shape: he rose, for instance, as a
scarab, and descended into the underworld as a crocodile; in the
moment of his resurrection after midnight he assumed the shape
of a double lion, Routi, "Yesterday and Tomorrow."[11] Osiris,
the resurrected human being who became a god, also says of
himself: "I am Yesterday, Today and Tomorrow."[12] He lives in
the "House of Eternity" or a "House of Millions of Years."

Besides the sun god, the ancient Egyptians personified
unending time also as a separate god, Ḥeḥ, who has the Ankh,
the symbol of life, suspended at his right arm. As in Greece, the
snake in Egypt was also connected with time. It symbolized life
and health, and each individual was protected by a "lifetime
snake," which was a daemon of time and of survival after
death.[13]

This same archetypal symbolism of time, as the godhead and
also as an unending stream of life and death, can be found in
India. In the *Bhagavad Gītā* (3rd or 4th century B.C.) the god
Krishna reveals himself to Arjuna in his terrible form. He sees in
him all other gods together: "I see a figure infinite, wherein all

figures blend to countless bodies, arms and eyes." In a great stream they disappear into his jaws of flaming fire, entering them with hurried step.[14] Then Vishnu says: "Know I am Time that makes the worlds perish, when ripe and come to bring them destruction." Not only Vishnu but also Shiva represents time. He symbolizes "the energy of the universe increasingly creating and sustaining the forms in which he manifests himself."[15] Shiva is called Mahā Kāla, "Great Time," or Kāla Rudra, "All-Devouring Time." His Shakti, or active energy, appears in its destructive form personified in the terrible goddess Kālī, who is Time, for Kālī was interpreted as the feminine form of Kāla, which means Time, the black-blue color, and death.

The mystical philosophy of Hinduism looks upon this world as unreal; time is especially what deceives the unenlightened soul into believing exclusively in his own self-conscious being and the reality of outer things. But in fact this perishable, changing world is a kind of illusion: "Verily for him who knows this [for the enlightened man] . . . the sun never rises nor sets. For him it is day forever" (*Chandogya Unpanishad* III, 11.3).

This "eternal day" is God himself. Similarly, a North American Delaware Indian described a vision he had of God: He saw "a great man clothed with the day, the most radiant day he had ever seen, a day of many years, even of eternal duration. The whole world was spread over Him, so that one could see the earth and all things on earth in Him."[16]

In China the supreme deity had not always been personified, but here too time is seen as an aspect of the dynamic, creative basic principle of the universe. Time thus belongs to the masculine Yang principle, which is symbolized by three straight lines; its female counterpart, Yin (symbolized by three broken lines), is associated with space. These two together manifest the Tao, the secret law which governs the cosmos. Yang, the Creative, "acts in the world of the invisible with Spirit and Time for its field; Yin the Receptive acts upon Matter in Space and brings material things to completion."[17] Time, seen in this way, is "the means of making actual what is potential." The group of lines which symbolizes Yang when doubled is called Ch'ien (Heaven) and denotes the movement of heaven which is unending. This duration in time is the image of the power inherent in the creative principle; it is symbolized by the dragon. It produces quality, while the receptive produces quantity.[18]

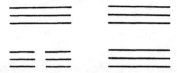

As Marcel Granet has shown, Yang and Yin are not static cosmic principles but alternating cosmic *rhythms*.[19] Time has never been considered in China as an abstract parameter or as an "empty" time period. The word for time, *che,* means rather a circumstance favorable or unfavorable for action. Time and space, says Granet, "were considered as an *ensemble* [grouping, cluster] of occasions and places,"[20] a bundle of coinciding events. What "bundles" such occasions together is called *chin,* "duration": "Former times, the present time, the morning and the evening are combined together to form duration. . . . Time however sometimes has no duration, for the beginning point of time has no duration."[21] As long as they are "germs," situations are still outside time and can be influenced by men; only when they have entered duration-time do they become fixed entities.

A close relationship of time with the cosmic creative energy emanating from the godhead can also be found in the Maya and Aztec notions of time. The most frequently used word for time in the Mayan language, *kin,* is most often represented by the hieroglyph drawing shown below, which means "sun" and "day."[22] It consists of a four-petaled flower, a species of plumeria. The emanating lines below are the "sun's beard" or "cords of the sun" or "arrowshafts of the sun"; in my opinion, they represent the creative vital energy of the sun. The snake is also not missing in this connection: the Maya worshiped a double-headed snake whose one head meant life, the other death.[23]

In the Aztec civilization time was associated with the supreme deity, with the creator-god Omotéotl, mother and father of all things, who was called "mirror that illumines all things," Lord of Fire and Lord of Time. This god first created four other gods: the red Tezcatlipoca, placed in the east; the black one, who lives in the north; the white one in the west; and the blue one in the south. To these four gods belong certain plants, animals, and qualitatively different years. In the middle dwells the god of fire. The four Tetzcatlipocas, then, created all other things. Only with them did space and time fully enter the world. The idea of time contains in the Aztec idea something abrupt. At one time east and positive forces dominate, at another the north and austerity; today we live in good times, tomorrow perhaps in unfavorable days. "Is there perchance any truth in our words here?" says a wise man and poet; "all seems so like a dream." Only after death, says another, shall we "know His face," namely that of the supreme god whose name is "Night and Wind," and "who is an inscrutable mystery."[24]

In contrast to these myths in which God Himself *is* time (and also not-time) itself, our own Judaeo-Christian tradition sees God as purely outside time, as having created time together with the universe. After God separated the waters above the firmament from the waters below, and created the sun and moon, day and night came into existence and time began. And though we believe that material nature obeys laws, which make certain events recur in time, there are also recurrent miracles, magical and parapsychological phenomena, which are caused by the direct intervention of the creator God, a constant dramatic confrontation with His creation and with man. The most radical of these events, which disrupted time into a completely different Before and After, is the incarnation of Christ. According to I Peter 3:18, Christ died but once for our sins, once and for all *(hapax, semel)*. Thus the development of history is governed and oriented by a unique fact which can never be repeated. On account of Christ's promise to return, the early Christian congregations were oriented much more to the future than to the past, hoping for Christ's return in glory.[25] In a similar way the Jews expect the coming of the Messiah at the end of time.

With Saint Augustine a new aspect of this idea of time entered into our tradition: the idea that God is present not only in the cosmos but also in man's innermost soul. Thus time too, being a "working" of God, acquires a psychological nuance. The present is nothing if not an experience in the soul; the past is a memory image in the soul; and the future exists only as our psychic expectations. But ordinary time is transient and meaningless: it disappears when the soul unites with God.[26]

Later I will discuss the partial return to a cyclic notion of time in Christian civilization; what never disappeared was the association of time with the idea of God's direct interference in the world. Even for Isaac Newton there still existed an absolute space and an absolute flux of time, which were both emanations from God, though in practical physics they had become parameters, time being measurable through moving bodies. This incipient separation of "divine time" from measurable time is not unrelated to the development of the clock, our instrument of time measurement.[27]

The original image or intuition of time as a river or flow underlies those time-measuring devices which were based on the flow of some substance, a liquid—in water clocks and mercury clocks—or sand.

Either the Chaldaeans or the Egyptians seem to have first invented the clepsydra or water clock. Water flowed from an upper receptacle into a lower one which was graduated. (This measurement was based on an error, because in fact when the upper pressure diminishes the water flows more slowly.) In classical antiquity clepsydras were in widespread use. Around the year 100 B.C. there was one installed in the market in Athens to indicate time officially. In Athens and Rome the courts of justice used them to time and limit speeches. Water clocks were in use in Europe and Asia throughout the Middle Ages. The hourglass or sand clock, which is based on the same idea of time as a flux, was always less accurate. It seems to have been in use only since the fourteenth century.

The other symbol of cosmic energy, in addition to water, is fire, as we saw in the many divine images mentioned above. Thus fire too was used to measure time. The Arab Al-Yazari, in a treatise of A.D. 1206, describes a light clock, a candle which burned for thirteen hours. It contained little balls in holes on different levels. Each hour a ball fell down and activated a little mechanical figure, which trimmed the wick. It was the Chinese who made the most use of fire to measure time. This was done by spreading a combustible powder round a generally circular labyrinth and igniting it at one end, so that its burning crept slowly forward like a fuse. Conventional phrases, such as "long life" or "double good fortune," were often placed in the center, and pebbles attached with a thread at certain places fell down when the thread burned up and were used, by their fall, to awaken the sleeper.

These systems which measure time by the flux of a substance or the burning of a powder imply that time is a linear flow, and similarly Western classical physics used a line to represent time, alongside the three parameters of Euclidian space, for all its measurements and descriptions of physical events. The great change came through Albert Einstein, who realized that temporal indications were always relative to the position of the observer. Only because the velocity of light is so high—186,000 miles per second—can we ignore this in the practical macrophysical realm; as soon as the observer also moves with a high velocity, the time span between the event and its observation becomes a problem for establishing a sequence of events. Two events which are seen as occurring simultaneously by one observer may occur as different temporal sequences for others. In high-energy physics, where we observe interactions between nuclear particles that move almost at the speed of light, time is completely relative. The idea of the space-time coordinate system as something objective is no longer valid. It is only a tool used by an observer to describe his special environment.[28]

Einstein further realized that the requirement that the laws of nature be formulated in such a way that they have the same form in all coordinate systems, that is, for all observers in whatever positions and motions, can be satisfied in the description of electromagnetic phenomena only if all spatial and temporal specifications are relative. Every change of coordinate systems mixes space and time in a mathematically defined way. Space and time are thus inseparably connected and form a four-dimensional continuum—which is generally called the Minkowski-Einsteinian block universe. This insight of Einstein's appears to be a return, on a higher level and with mathematical precision, to the age-old primitive intuition whereby, for instance, the Aztec god Omotéotl, with the four Tetzcatlipocas in the four corners of space, created space and time simultaneously. Fritjof Capra quotes the *Avatamsaka Sutra* of Mahayana Buddhism,[29] which asserts that in a state of illumined dissolution we lose the distinction between mind and body, subject and object, and realize that every object is related to every other object, not only spatially but also temporally: "As a fact of pure experience, there is no space without time, no time without space. They are interpenetrating."

Einstein went one step further in his special theory of relativity, a step which in a strange way revives the primitive intuition of time as a flow of inner and outer events, now grasped in a precise mathematical formalism. This step means including gravity within the picture of space-time, for it makes space-time curved.[30] This is caused by the gravitational fields of massive bodies filling it. In a curved space-time the curvature affects not only the geometry of space but also the lengths of time intervals: "Time does not flow at the same rate as in a 'flat space-time' and as the curvature varies from place to place according to the distribution of massive bodies, so does the flow of time."[31]

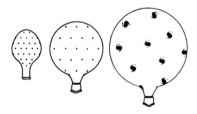

Block universe in three-dimensional approximation

Mass produces a curvature in space.

It is a remarkable coincidence that, at approximately the same time as physicists discovered the relativity of time in their field, C. G. Jung came across the same fact in his exploration of the human unconscious. In the world of dreams, time also appears as relative and the categories of "before" and "after" seem to lose their meaning. If we go as deep as the archetypal layer of the unconscious, time even seems to disappear completely. Man has always known this, in a way: all over the world stories are told in which a person goes into a fairy hill, into paradise, into the realm of death, or into the kingdom of dwarfs, and when he returns, thinking that he has spent only one evening or night there, finds all his contemporaries dead; his village has vanished, and he hears that only a vague rumor has survived of a man having disappeared hundreds of years before. Washington Irving's *Rip van Winkle* is just one example of this type of story.

Whenever we touch the deeper archetypal reality of the psyche, it permeates us with a feeling of being in contact with something infinite. And, as Jung pointed out, this is the telling question of our life: whether we are related to something infinite or not. "Only if we know that what truly matters is the infinite can we avoid fixing our interests on futilities. In the final analysis we count for something only because of the essential we embody, and if we do not embody that life is wasted."[32]

The most exciting application of Einstein's new notion of

space-time can be found in its application in astrophysics. As astronomers and astrophysicists have to deal with very large distances, even light takes a long time to travel from the observed object to the observer. Thus the astronomer never looks at an object in its present state, but in its past. With our telescopes we can see galaxies which in fact existed millions of years ago. We can look at stars and clusters of stars at all stages of their evolution, looking at them, so to speak, backward in time.[33]

The same applies to the effects of gravity. Because stars and galaxies are extremely massive bodies, the curvature of space-time becomes a relevant phenomenon. Its most extreme effects become manifest during a so-called gravitational collapse of a massive body—as happens, so we assume today, in the black holes. Due to the mutual gravitational attraction of its particles, which increases as the distance between the particles decreases, the star becomes more and more dense and thus space-time more and more curved, until finally even light can no longer escape from its surface. Thus a so-called "event horizon" forms around the star, beyond which nothing is any longer observable and no clock signals can reach us;—in a way, the star walks out of time for us. It seems to me that something analogous might happen to us in death. When C. G. Jung died, on 6 June 1961, a patient of mine who did not know him dreamed: There were many people on a sunny day on a meadow; Jung was among them. He wore a suit which was green in front, black on the back. There was a black wall with a hole cut out exactly matching the outlines of Jung. He stepped into it, and so one saw now only a black wall, but she knew that he was still there, although invisible. She looked at herself and saw that she wore an identical green-black frock. In dying we may only step outside the "event horizon" of the living, but still exist in an unobservable state.

Cyclical and Linear Time

Two aspects which belong to the primordial archetypal idea of time have already been touched upon in our mythological examples: the irreversible linear character of time and its cyclical aspect. The latter, which seems to predominate in most primitive civilizations, is probably based on the observation of the regular motion of the heavenly luminaries, and of the recurring seasonal changes. The circular river Oceanos and the tail-eating Zodiac snake imply this idea. Chronos-Kronos was directly called the "round element" and also the "giver of measures." Macrobius writes: "Insofar as time is a fixed measure it is derived from the revolutions of the sky. Time begins there, and from this is believed to have been born Kronos who is Chronos. This Kronos-Saturn is the creator of time."[34]

In India a completely cyclical notion of time was predominant. The primary unit of time was the yuga, or age (1,080,000 years). A complete cycle, or mahāyuga, consists of four such yugas, the number four signifying totality or perfection.[35] The first yuga of each cycle is a kind of Golden Age; then each yuga is worse than the last until at the end comes the "great dissolution," and then the process begins again. The names of the yugas are taken from throws of dice. One mahāyuga or great year consists of 12,000 "divine years," each comprising 360 ordinary years—a total of 4,320,000 years. Thousands of such mahāyugas constitute a kalpa ("form"), which is equivalent to a day in the life of Brahma. In this way time consists of a cosmic rhythm, a periodic destruction and re-creation of the universe.

For man, this cyclical aspect of time, viewed negatively, gives rise to Samsara, the ever-rotating wheel of birth and death, of endless reincarnations. Only the enlightened yogi or Buddhist who has understood Brahman or the Buddha-Mind in himself "in a lightning flash of truth" is delivered in this life and can escape rebirth.[36] He has transcended the play of opposites and arrested all memory processes for ever.[37]

Mircea Eliade has shown that in many other civilizations there exists a slightly different myth of Eternal Return. The idea is that at the (extratemporal) moment of creation (which he calls *illud tempus,* "that time") the archetypal models of all things and all human actions on earth came into existence.[38] However, the earthly replicas of these archetypes show a tendency toward deterioration and decay. Through retelling the myths of creation and by re-enacting the original rituals, man can renew the archetypal patterns and restore his own life forms. Similarly, with us Easter is considered the festival not only of Christ's resurrection, but of a total renewal of creation.[39] In Christianity the idea of *illud tempus* has become partly internalized: paradise or the Kingdom of Heaven is within ourselves and can be reached at any time by metanoia: by a basic change of attitude.[40]

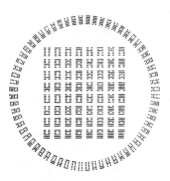

The Chinese, too, knew a primordial time *(illud tempus)* when the culture heroes set all the patterns of life. They had a cyclical time concept (along with a linear one, which will be discussed later). At the bottom of the Chinese idea of time, as it underlies the *I Ching (The Book of Changes),* there were two circular time-models or time-mandalas. One was the so-called Sequence of Earlier Heaven, or Primal Arrangement, a circle built by the eight Kuas, the basic principles of all existence. Yang, the Creative or Heaven (Ch'ien), was placed in the south; Yin, the Receptive or Earth (K'un), was in the north. The whole sequence was arranged as shown here. This system is in a way timeless, though not without motion.

> Within the Primal Arrangement, the forces always take effect as pairs of opposites. Thunder . . . awakens the seeds of the old year. Its opposite, the wind, dissolves the rigidity of the winter ice. The rain moistens the seeds . . . while its opposite, the sun, provides the necessary warmth. Hence the saying: "Water and fire do not combat each other." . . . Keeping still stops further expansion. . . . Its opposite, the Joyous, bring about the joys of the harvest. Finally . . . the Creative, representing the great law of existence,

and the Receptive, representing shelter in the womb, into which everything returns after completing the cycle of life.[41]

Thus the opposites do not conflict: on the contrary they balance each other. This Primal Arrangement was associated with an arithmetical mandala called the Ho-t'ou:

$$
\begin{array}{ccccc}
 & & 7 & & \\
 & & 2 & & \\
8 & 3 & 5 & 4 & 9 \\
 & & 1 & & \\
 & & 6 & &
\end{array}
$$

This movement repeats itself externally inside the arrangement.

According to Chinese tradition, King Wen and the Duke of Chou discovered, while they were imprisoned by the tyrant Chou Hsin (about 1150 B.C.), a new time mandala called the Later Heaven or Inner World Arrangement. In it Li (Fire) is in the south instead of Ch'ien (Heaven), K'an (Water) in the north instead of K'un (the Receptive). The trigrams are no longer grouped in pairs of opposites, but are shown in a *temporal progression* in which they manifest themselves in the phenomenal world through the cycle of years.

It shows "God's activity in nature." The Earlier Heaven emphasizes Duration, the Later emphasizes motion, but both are circular in form. The Later Heaven was also associated with a number mandala, the so-called Lo-shou (pattern of the river Lo), which was considered *the* basic numerical pattern of the universe.

$$
\begin{array}{ccc}
4 & 9 & 2 \\
3 & 5 & 7 \\
8 & 1 & 6
\end{array}
$$

This is a so-called magic square, in which all columns, rows, and diagonals add up to 15. This square was regarded in China as a basic pattern of the universe, according to which architecture, music, and even menus were arranged.[42]

Of course the Chinese had also an astrological system of time which resembles our own tradition.[43] However, its solar zodiac contains different animals and figures from ours; and our signs are monthly, whereas the Chinese are annual symbols.

Close resemblances to the astrological systems of China are visible in the Mayan and Aztec calendars. Not only did the Maya consider time as a deity (the sun god) but every year, month, day and even hour was identical with a number and was at the same time a god. The same holds true for the Aztecs, who also had such a time mandala. Though time existed potentially from the beginning as a principle connected with the supreme Lord of Time, it actually became manifest only after the creation of the four Tetzcatlipocas. After a period of equilibrium, which resembles the balance of opposites in the Chinese Sequence of Earlier Heaven, each of these Tetzcatlipocas wanted to become the sun. Thus strife and change came into existence. This led to a linear view of time which unfolds in five successive aeons or Suns. The sun "4 Tiger" lasted 676 years; then the people were eaten by ocelots and the sun destroyed. Then followed the Sun called "4 Wind," which ended with everything being carried away by the wind and the people becoming monkeys. Then came the Sun "4 Rain," at the end of which everything was burned up and the people became turkeys. Finally came the Sun of our time, called "4 Movement." In its reign there will be earthquakes and hunger, "and thus our end shall come," as the *Leyenda de los Soles* says.[44]

In the view of the Aztecs the days all "work" while they move across the sky. Pictorially the time gods are represented as figures carrying a sum of days, months, or years on their backs, following each other in an immense circular sequence. (Interestingly, the ancient Greek poet Hesiod speaks of the hours also as *daimones*—gods.)

Our own astrological system consists also of a circular procession of divine images. It stems from Mesopotamia, about the sixth century B.C., and also shows some later Egyptian influences. The zodiacal signs originally varied greatly; they were originally earthly, tribal gods which got projected onto the celestial constellations when the Babylonians began to observe the motion of the stars and gather arithmetical information about their movements. Thus the Babylonians began to realize the existence of a *lawful order* in this procession of gods or archetypes over the sky; this order they expressed by numbers. Jung has defined number as *an archetype of order which has become conscious*. The time gods of the Maya and Aztec were also numbers; no wonder that the Chinese too associated the stellar order in the sky with numbers. The word for reckoning, *shih*, is written 叄 , the upper horizontal lines representing heaven and the three vertical lines denoting the influence of the sun, moon, and stars on the earth. Reckoning was thus closely associated with the prediction of the future.[45] The new Babylonian science-religion spread into Persia and Egypt, where the Babylonian gods were partly renamed and associated with the gods who were known there. The Babylonians also believed in the eternity of the world,[46] and that a certain destiny, Heimarmene, rules in the cosmos.[47] All things on earth correspond to what happens in the skies. In the vast period of 4,320,000 years the whole heavens return to their initial configuration—the Indian myth of the Eternal Return.

These ideas influenced the Greeks from the time of Thales of Miletus onward, and largely stand behind Plato's famous cosmological model of time: above and outside the universe exist the Platonic Ideas, forming one unit around the Idea of the Good. But when the creator god (Demiurge) created the world he could not transfer this model as a whole into the world of transient reality:

> So as that pattern is the Living Being that is forever existent, he sought to make the universe also like it. . . . Now the nature of the Living Being was eternal, and it was impossible to confer this character in full completeness on the generated thing. But he took thought to make, as it were, *a moving likeness of eternity*: and, at the same time that he ordered the Heaven, he made of eternity that abides in unity an everlasting likeness *moving according to number*—that to which we have given the name Time [Aion].[48]

Aion here means an "aeonic" time[49] which exists in between the timeless world of ideas and the time-bound perishable world of our reality; it consists of long historical aeons. Aion is an everlasting being, the heavenly sphere of the fixed stars, which were thought to be eternal, not subject to suffering and change.

It moves in an eternal circle.[50] Only below the moon does the world of Chronos begin, the futile transient 'sublunary' sphere of decay.

The cyclical idea of time is still discussed by physicists, in the form of the so-called ergodic theorem, according to which "no matter in what state the finite universe may be at a given moment, it will go through all other possible states in a given sequence and come back eventually to the starting state."[51] Present-day theories about the life of the universe vary widely, however. The most widely accepted is the idea that the universe started with one "big bang," an explosion, and is expanding towards one end-point of "heat death." Other scientists believe rather in a steady-state universe, in which matter is continuously created and destroyed with no beginning or end in sight.

It is certainly not for rational reasons, but on account of the archetypal intuition of a cyclical time (as distinct from the flux aspect) that our invention of clocks made them circular. The faces of clocks today are still mostly fashioned in a circle in order to simulate the heavens.[52]

To the oldest forms of clocks belong the gnomon and sundial, both of which make use of the seeming rotation of the sun around the earth by measuring the shadow of a rod, column, or obelisk, and (in the sundial) by tracking its changes of position. The gnomon was probably introduced to the Greeks in the beginning of the sixth century B.C.[53] It had the great disadvantage of being able only to indicate local time. Its usefulness was also impaired by the complexity of apparent motion of the sun around the earth. By inclining the rod so as to put it parallel with the axis of the rotation of the earth this was simplified. Now the direction of the shadow was identical for identical hours at a certain place regardless of which day of the year it was; only the length of the shadow continued to vary.[54] This is the sundial which one finds in Egypt from the thirteenth century B.C. onward, but probably the Babylonians knew it first. Until the seventeenth century such sundials were more accurate than any mechanical clock.

The invention of the latter goes back to one essential step, to the invention of the toothed gear-wheel in the days of Archimedes, which probably arose from modelling the calendar cycles. Very little is known of it until the ninth century, when in Islamic countries gear-wheels in complicated ratios were in use in astrolabe mechanisms "recognizable as clockwork ancestors of all modern machinery."[55]

From such beginnings the mechanical clock slowly evolved. All the widely varying mechanisms that exist contain four basic components, not all of which were discovered at the same time: a motor, first in the form of a weight (later a spring); an oscillating regulator (a pendulum or, as mostly nowadays, an electromagnet),[56] which counterbalances differences of temperature, pressure, and shock; an escapement, which compensates for the loss of energy through friction; and a face, indicating the hours, minutes, etc.

But in addition to all the above-mentioned manifestations of a circular idea of time, there also exists from the beginning the idea of a linear and irreversible succession of time, probably based on the observation of the aging of all living beings and of permanent changes brought forth by historical events. Despite their circular models of time, the Chinese, for instance, accumulated a body of historical facts extending over a period of more than three thousand years. They did it in order to study "how to conduct oneself in the present and the future, how love *(yen)* and righteousness *(i)* may result in favorable, evil deeds in unfavorable social results. Thus they believed in a possible moral improvement and social evolution."[57]

In a similar way the doctrine of the aeons of the five suns of the Aztecs also gives history a linear course, though not leading to evolution but final destruction. Long before man knew about the reasons for aging (because certain cells in our body are not replaced and others are replaced much more slowly), time was in many mythological systems associated with decay and death and even with evil. The Hellenistic Aion was, as we know, also Kronos, the god who eats his children, the former supreme god supplanted by Zeus. This figure of time as devourer even survived into the Christian era, in the symbolic image of Father Time, which unites in itself the attributes of Kronos-Saturn and death. The sixteenth and seventeenth centuries revelled in such macabre representations of the destructive aspect of time.

The Judaeo-Christian tradition believed primarily in a linear model of time, due to the intervention of God and to His Providence, His plan to lead mankind step by step to perfection and finally to the destruction of the world. However, the older Christian notion of time was far from being a purely mathematical parameter. It included certain cyclic elements, as well as the idea of a Divine design—a teleological linearity of time—periodized in terms of the seven days of creation.[58] In the Old Testament there are *typoi*—images or prefigurations of events and things which were later revealed more fully in the New Testament. The Tree of Knowledge, in Genesis, for instance, is the same wood from which the rod of Moses was made and also served as a beam in the Temple of Solomon and as the cross of Christ's crucifixion. Thus an eternal pattern interacted with the linear course of history.

Besides stressing that Christ died once and for all, certain Church Fathers, believing in astral influences, accepted in part a cyclical view of history.[59] Such views existed side by side until the seventeenth century. The *illud tempus* model of an extratemporal existence of all patterns is also to be found in Christianity in the notion of an *unus mundus,* which was the plan of the cosmos in God's mind before creation. This plan was also called the *Sapientia Dei,* the personified Wisdom of God. Certain primal forms, ideas, prototypes constitute together the *archetypus mundus* or "exemplar" of the universe in God's mind. It contains a mathematical order which is closely related to the Trinity: number belonging to the Son, measure to the Father and weight to the Holy Spirit.[60] The *unus mundus* is thought of as an infinite sphere, like God Himself.[61] In spite of a repetitive manifestation of the *typoi,* they follow a linear course of evolution in that they make the Godhead and His purpose increasingly manifest: "What shone forth in the Old Testament, radiates in the New Testament."

One of the most famous creators of such a pattern of Divine Providence in history is the Abbot Gioacchino da Fiori (twelfth century), who announced that history was divided into three great aeons: the period of the Old Testament, which was the time of the Father, and in which the law and its literal understanding dominated; the first Christian millennium, which was the time of the Son, and in which obedience to the Church and wisdom dominate; and finally the present age of the Holy Ghost in which spiritual men will live in poverty but in complete freedom following the inspiration of the Holy Ghost.[62]

The idea that God had a timeless plan of the world in His mind before its realization in matter is consistent with what has been called the Christian sacramental view of history; it is related to Plato's idea of all things developing out of seeds or primordial archetypes (Ideas). As C. Haber has pointed out, the clock was looked upon in the fifteenth century, as a model of such a divine plan.[63] In 1453, in his *Vision of God*, Nicolas Cusanus writes: "Let then the concept of the clock represent eternity's self; then motion in the clock representeth succession. Eternity therefore both enfoldeth and unfoldeth succession, since the concept of the clock which is eternity doth alike enfold and unfold things."[64] Only gradually did this idea of a clockwork universe become desacramentalized—in the eighteenth century the clock became an automaton that had no connection with God.[65]

In physics a breakthrough towards a purely mathematical idea of linear time occurred with Newton, who used a geometrical line to describe measurable time: but its dominant role in physics really came only with the discovery of the Second Law of Thermodynamics, formulated by Carnot and Boltzmann. This theorem says that in every physical process a certain amount of energy becomes irretrievably lost in the form of heat, and that the consequent loss of order—the process known as entropy—will lead to the death of our universe. This led to the idea of the "arrow of time" in physics, i.e., its irreversible directedness.

However, some physicists believe that mind, in contrast to matter, is a negentropic factor: that it is able, in other words, to recreate order from disorder and build up systems of a higher energy level. This led Olivier Costa de Beauregard even to postulate a cosmic underlying soul or *infrapsychisme*, coexistent with the Einsteinian block universe, as a cosmic source of negentropy.[66] But in modern physics the "arrow of time" idea still largely predominates.

Besides these developments in physics it was mainly the breakthrough of Charles Darwin's ideas which reinforced the already existing Western predilection for a purely linear model of time.[67] Darwin asserted that all modification of life on earth was mechanical and ultimately due to mere chance. Time thus became a purely mathematical time—a line was sufficient to explain it. Though some "vitalistic" thinkers have continued to object to this view, it is still a dominant idea in science. Finally, the undeniable subjective psychological changes which man experiences during his life in aging also support the idea of a linearity of time.[68]

Many attempts have been made to bring forth a reconciliation of the linear and cyclic views of time. Thus Saint Augustine's view of time and eternity is in many ways a combination of both models, just as in another form of the Chinese idea cyclical time was combined with a moral evolution of man through historical experiences.

The image for such a combination is the idea of the spiral or helix. Jung has tried to bring evidence for such a spiralic process within the inner psychic God-image in man, the Self.[69] In the development of this God-man image, as viewed by the Book of Enoch, the Gnostics, and certain Western alchemists, the Self was conceived first as a divine Adam figure and then as a lower earthly Adam figure (after the Fall).[70]

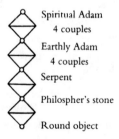

Spiritual Adam
4 couples
Earthly Adam
4 couples
Serpent
Philospher's stone
Round object

If we find this chain up in a spiral, we get the diagram shown here (but one must think that at the upper point the *rotundum* symbolizes a slightly higher level of consciousness than the first Anthropos). This model is, as Jung points out,[71] in line with the main historical development of our idea of God. The still lower counterpart is the serpent which brought about Adam's fall. This corresponds to the "primary matter" and main concern of the alchemists. When it has been worked through the four elements, it becomes the Philosophers' Stone—another God-man symbol. The latter was finally conceived as the "round thing" *(rotundum),* the most basic structure of the universe. In between are four times four centers, which form an upper and a lower marriage-quaternion, the four rivers of Paradise, and the four elements. These quaternions were regarded as revealing the structure of each center above.

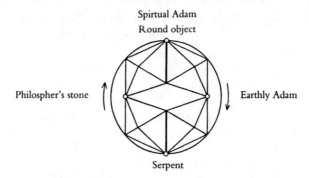

Man was first like a child, dependent on the "pneumatic" (spiritual) sphere. The latter was threatened by Satan, the dark side of reality, and by man's own instincts (man's own shadow). Christ broke the gates of hell but did not return as He had promised. The ideas of a quaternion and of the Philosophers' Stone coincide with the beginnings of natural science. Alchemical speculations led to the idea of four states of aggregation, to the model of a space-time quaternion of four dimensions, and finally to different modern quaternarian models of the subatomic world. The series ends with the *rotundum,* the archetypal image of rotation (which goes beyond the static models of quaternity). This coincides again with the pneumatic Anthropos.

In the form of an equation, this model of the Self could be expressed in the formula shown here:

> *A* stands for the initial state (in this case the Anthropos), *A1* for the end state, and *B C D* for intermediate states. The formations that split off from them are denoted in each case by the small letters *a b c d*. With regard to the construction of the formula, we must bear in mind that we are concerned with the continual process of transformation of one and same substance. This substance, and its respective state of transformation, will always bring forth its like; thus *A* will produce *a* and *B b*; equally, *b* produces *B* and *c C*. It is also assumed that *a* is followed by *b* and that the formula runs from left to right. These assumptions are legitimate in a psychological formula. . . .
>
> What the formula can only hint at is the higher plane that is reached through the process of transformation. . . . The change consists in an unfolding of totality into four parts four times, which means nothing less than its becoming conscious.[72]

$$
\begin{array}{ccc}
b_3 & & d \\
\diagup \diagdown & & \diagup \diagdown \\
c_3 \quad a_3 = A = a & & c \\
\diagdown \diagup & & \diagdown \diagup \\
d_3 & & b \\
\| & & \| \\
D & & B \\
\| & & \| \\
d_2 & & b_1 \\
\diagup \diagdown & & \diagup \diagdown \\
a_2 \quad c_2 = C = c_1 & & a_1 \\
\diagdown \diagup & & \diagdown \diagup \\
b_2 & & d_1
\end{array}
$$

Jung compares this spiralic process in the Self with the self-rejuvenation of the carbon nucleus in the carbon–nitrogen cycle, where the carbon nucleus captures four protons and emits them again as an alpha-particle at the end of the cycle in order to return to its original structure.[73]

> The analogy with physics is not a digression since the symbolical schema itself represents the descent into matter and requires the identity of the outside with the inside. Psyche cannot be totally different from matter, for how otherwise could it move matter? And matter cannot be alien to psyche, for how else could matter produce psyche? Psyche and matter exist in one and the same

world, and each partakes of the other, otherwise any reciprocal action would be impossible. If research could only advance far enough, therefore, we should arrive at an ultimate agreement between physical and psychological concepts. Our present attempts may be bold, but I believe they are on the right lines. Mathematics, for instance, has more than once proved that its purely logical constructions which transcend all experience subsequently coincided with the behaviour of things. This, like the events I call synchronistic, points to a profound harmony between all forms of existence.[74]

This symbolic model of Jung's seems to represent *a basic structure of physical and psychic life*. Interestingly enough, the Melanesian marriage system which attempts to perpetuate the flow of life by a system of marriage exchange between two clans (one matrilinear, one patrilinear) also produces as a result two types of spiral, a closed spiral representing the matrilineal lifeline, and an interrupted spiral the virile power.

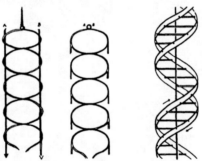

And last but not least, the genetic substance, as has been discovered by Watson, Crick, and Wilkins, is a double helix. Perhaps this model represents a biological analogy to the archetypal idea of time as a spiral, which reconciles the linear and cyclic aspects of time.

Rhythm and Periodicity

It was not only Plato who associated time with number. For Aristotle, too, time was a kind of number: "Time is the number of motion with respect to earlier and later." But he had only *one* motion in mind; this was the revolving motion of heaven, because it is everlasting and uniform.[75] On the other hand, time for Aristotle does not exist without change:[76] "Time is a kind of number, in fact the number of continuous movement." This remark obviously refers to the periodicity of celestial events. This point of view of Aristotle's has been criticized as being only a definition of measurable time but not of time itself. However, it seems to me that the relationship of time and number is in fact a much deeper one. If Alexander Marshack is right, one of the oldest games of palaeolithic man was to make numerical marks on stones and bones as a "time factoring" occupation.[77] This, according to Marshack, was *the* beginning of our civilization. These marks served from the beginning to keep count of calendrical dates.

The relation of time and number was also a fundamental assertion in China, but with a different nuance. Numbers, in their aspect of quantity, were unimportant to the Chinese; for them number, as Granet points out, was much more a qualitative emblem or symbol, which however, as with us, also denotes regular relations among things.[78] These emblems mirror within a hierarchical order certain basic patterns of the universe; thus they make visible "the circumstantial individual aspects of the cosmic unity as a whole." This is where time comes in—because these circumstantial aspects appear in a temporal order. They vary in the course of time, being each a qualitative moment.[79] Time in China was therefore a concrete continuum containing qualities or fundamental conditions which can be manifested relatively simultaneously in different places. The famous book of divination, the *I Ching,* is built upon this premise. *Time consists in its view in certain time-ordered phases of transformation of the cosmic whole.*[80] According to the philosopher Wang Fu Ch'ih (1619–1692), all existence is a cosmic continuum which is in itself without perceptual manifestation. But on account of its immanent dynamics it differentiates in itself certain images or structures, which follow each other in time, and which can be explained by arithmetical procedures. Thus all numbers in China are also time indicators which tell us something about the quality of each moment. In China, therefore, time never became an abstract parameter or empty frame of reference but was always qualified by the coincidence of the events which all meet at certain of its moments. The whole universe had, in this way, a temporal rhythmic structure. The most basic rhythm is the alternating one of Yang and Yin. Chinese music as a whole was created in accordance with the rhythmical patterns of the universe. An essential idea connected with rhythm was that of enantiodromia: whenever a line of the *I Ching* oracle (see page 99) or a symbol reached its extreme state of fullness, it jumped over into its opposite. This idea has also been formulated by the Greek philosopher Heraclitus, who called fate "the world order *[logos]* stemming from enantiodromia, the creator of all things."[81] Jung took the term "enantiodromia" up again, showing that it was a psychological law; all extreme psychological states tend to tip over into their opposite: goodness into evil, happiness into unhappiness, exaggerated spirituality into surrender to instincts, etc.

The close relation of time with rhythm has contributed to our clockmaking in the form of the pendulum, which was invented by Galileo and perfected for time measurement by Christiaan Huyghens. A simple rhythmic pendulum movement is still used to mark time for music in the form of the metronome. Recently electricity has conquered the field of clockmaking in serving to produce synchronous oscillations.[82] An alternating current keeps up the vibrations and a device regulates the period of the current. Nowadays we have gone even one step further in using piezoelectric quartz or ammonia molecules to produce exceedingly regular and imperturbable oscillations. Compressing a band of quartz produces a migration of some of its electrons towards one of its sides; the process can then be reversed. If the quartz is then connected to an alternating current, the impulses of the electrons are converted into mechanical oscillations of several thousand alternations per second, of such regularity that they even correct the slight inequalities of an alternating electric current.[83] But quartz ages; it is now being supplanted by ammonia molecules of the formula NH_3, the N atoms constantly oscillating towards the opposite pole above a plane of 3H in a frequency of 24,000 megacycles or 24 million vibrations per second. Clocks based on this atomic movement inaugurated the technique of *masers* (*microwave amplification by stimulated emission of radiations*). *None of these clocks could exist without the basic rhythmicity of energy, i.e., matter.* "All matter," says Capra, "is involved in a continual cosmic dance."[84] All particles "sing their song, producing rhythmic patterns of energy."[85] Modern physics has revealed that "every subatomic particle not only performs an energy dance but also *is* an energy dance, a pulsating process of creation and destruction."[86]

Returning to the macrophysical plane and to the bodies of living beings, we still come across the same phenomenon. They all follow certain rhythms, which are now called biological clocks. Plants as well as animals are adapted not only to their spatial environment but also to time: to the solar day through what are called the circadian rhythms, to the cycles of the moon, to the tides of the sea, and even to the solar year. Certain activities, such as looking for food, are not activated by the outer stimulus of sunrise but by an inner rhythm which enables the animal to "plan ahead."[87] Plants also "have something resembling a time memory," for some (not all) begin to open their buds a few hours before sunrise, "as if they knew that the sun will rise soon"; and if one plunges them artificially into darkness, they still open their buds at the same time of day.[88] The physiological clock in animals seems to work by oscillations.[89] It also works like a master clock from which several other temporarily regulated physiological processes depend. Periods of activity and rest, and quantitative changes in metabolism, temperature, and other processes, are regulated in this way. Such rhythms seem to be inherited and are probably endogenous, not produced by outer conditions.[90] In unicellular animals or plants the whole unit is bound to the rhythm. Lowered temperatures (for plants differences of only 5°–10° C) slow down the biological clocks.

In more complex beings it is still a matter of discussion how far these rhythms are unified by a regulating organ or spread over different tissues and organs; both seem to be the case.[91] In higher animals there might be a central regulator located in the brain.[92] There also seems to be, as G. Schaltenbrand formulates it, a standardized rhythmic chronological organization in the brain, which functions as a whole.[93]

This basically rhythmic structure of our physiological life is not its only relation to time. As Adolf Portmann has shown, whole patterns of behavior in plants and animals show a relation to time: "Every form of life appears to us as a *Gestalt* with a specific development in time as well as space."[94] The social year of the Samoans and Fijians is calculated according to the cycle of the palolo worm *(Eunice viridis)*. Each year this worm sloughs off a part of its body charged with sexual substances, and reproduction takes place in the open sea, where the worm reconstitutes itself. This rhythm is related to the phases of the moon; at exactly the same time a certain tree *(Erythrina indica)* blossoms too. Certain sea urchins of the Mediterranean off Egypt, and the oyster and scallop in temperate seas, follow similar rhythms in their reproduction. The migration of birds is also related to the diurnal cycle. The development of animals is

> more than a mere undergoing of the temporal process; it is a resistance to [entropic] time, a mode of formation provided in the protoplasm of the particular species. . . . Just as in a well-planned display of fireworks one set piece may bear the next latent within it, so in the life of many insects we find at each stage a prefiguration of new organs, which subsequently unfold in an exactly regulated temporal process.[95]

Man too seems to possess a biological clock or clocks (which get upset by long-distance flights), although his clock-time consciousness predominates.[96]

In the field of emotion, which is a phenomenon very much on the border between physiological and psychological reality, rhythm is essential. In states of strong emotion we make rhythmical movements (stamping our feet, for instance) and tend to repeat endlessly the same thoughts and utterances. This led Jung to suspect that unconscious complexes might have a periodical rhythmic nature, a fact which is now under observation through the study of the periodic recurrences of themes in dream series.[97] The great common complexes of mankind, which Jung called the archetypes, manifest as physical and psychic patterns of behavior and were in the past experienced as gods or mythic images. The astrological systems discussed above are in fact attempts on mankind's part to express a temporal procession and recurrent order or "play of the archetypes," constituting an aeonic time rhythm. That such a play exists may well be true, but we are far from understanding it. The relation of gods to moments and to chance, which I discuss in the following sections, also points to a partly timeless and partly timebound nature of the archetypes.

What has been much more studied lately by psychologists is the immense variety of man's subjective time. Thus, for instance, young people live more in expectation of the future, old people look more at the past. Aging people generally feel that time goes faster, probably due to their own slowing down.[98] "Subjective" time differences might be based largely on physiological factors (for instance temperature), which have been shown to interfere with the speed of our intake of sensory information and our estimate of time. Intoxication with hashish, opium, mescaline, etc., also expands or condenses our subjective experience of time.[99]

Subjective time varies not only from one individual to another, but also between different social, ethnic, and psychological groups. Adaptation to clock-time remains (in my experience) difficult for intuitive people, while people whose sensation function is dominant get so stuck in what is now that they are often incapable of imagining a change tomorrow. Because time is connected with our whole "rhythm of life," the adaptation to it is generally disturbed in neuroses (and even more in psychoses). Some people, for instance, live "faster" than they can afford, or they lag behind in their own inner development. Then they feel "haunted by time."

If it is true, as I have tried to show, that time is closely related to the rhythm of the inner God-image, the Self (i.e., the conscious-unconscious totality of the psyche), then it is obvious that every neurotic deviation from the rhythm of the Self entails also a disturbed relation to time.

Besides the biological rhythms, memory processes play a role in our subjective time experience. Their complex nature has not yet been elucidated. Many scientists think that "the brain or the mind retains a complete record of the stream of consciousness, that is of all details which were recorded mentally (including infraconscious awareness) at the time of occurrence, although later most of it is entirely lost to voluntary recall."[100] Many things we can recall "are only generalizations and summaries," that is, most memories seem to become part of a more or less extensive organization, called by Bartlett "schemata,"[101] and which Susanne Langer called "man's symbolic transformation of experience."[102] From a Jungian point of view this organization would be produced by the archetypes, which are inborn psycho-physical ordering principles of human experience. Whatever role memory plays in it, our mind, says Whitrow, "is certainly temporal in its very nature. It manifests in our consciousness as a 'train of thoughts.' "[103] Here we return to the primitive notion of time as a quantitative and qualitative stream of simultaneous outer and inner events. In his *Experiment with Time*, J. W. Dunne has tried to formulate a model of multidimensional time, mirroring psychic states and their coincidental "times." This model has not been generally accepted; but it seems to me that Dunne is basically correct, in seeing time as a multidimensional phenomenon which is characterized by the simultaneity of different psychological conditions.

Necessity, Chance, and Synchronicity

Causality has been accepted in some form in all civilizations. In the Far East its basic form is the concept of *karma*. Throughout all the innumerable reincarnations of a person, a certain identity goes on, in a chain of causation carried by *karma:* "If we see an identity of being in events in the course of time, it is due to the causal chain that connects them."[104]

What we call causality in the West has its roots in the Greek images of Ananke (Necessity), Dike (Justice), Heimarmene (Allotted Fate), and Nemesis (Retribution)—all goddesses which were feared and respected. They were responsible for the balanced play of opposites in the universe: "The source of generation for all things is that into which their destruction also leads . . . according to Necessity, for they pay penalty and retribution to each other for their injustices according to the order of Time," says Anaximander.[105] And Heraclitus stressed that "all things happen by strife and necessity."[106] Later, in the philosophy of the Stoics, Ananke or Heimarmene became *the* all-ruling world principle, which even rules over the gods. According to the Orphics, Chronos (Time) was mated to Ananke (Necessity), which holds the universe in powerful fetters, surrounding it in the form of a serpent.[107] Our word *necessity* itself is related to the Latin *necto* ("I bind") and *nexus* ("bound"). This inexorable goddess personified also the fetters of death, our destiny (*destino* also means "I bind"). Ananke spins the thread of our life and cuts it at its fated end.

In the Christian era the concept of Necessity did not disappear but was projected on to the lawful order of nature, created by God Himself (Who also, however, sometimes interfered with it through miracles). Only with René Descartes (1596–1650) did the principle of determinism, in the form of general natural laws, become absolute, excluding any possible new creative divine interference." And generally we can assert that God does all that we can understand, but not that He cannot do what we cannot understand." He *could* act differently but He does not want to do so. *God's activity coincides completely with the principle of causality.*[108] Much the same is true for Isaac Newton. According to him God created in the beginning the material particles, the forces between them and the fundamental laws of motion, and it has continued to run ever since like a machine governed by immutable laws.[109] It was an easy next step to exclude the idea of God altogether and thus, in the age of materialism, the universe became an immense mechanical clock which ticks on stupidly into all eternity.

From that time on, the belief in the absolute validity of causality lasted until the beginnings of quantum physics, where the study of elementary particles forced the physicists to replace it with the concept of mathematical probability. Certain prediction is no longer possible for the behavior of single particles, but only for very large sets of particles. However, this does not simply reflect our ignorance of the physical situation, as does the use of probabilities by insurance companies. As Capra formulates it: "In quantum theory we have come to recognize probability as a fundamental feature of the atomic reality. . . . Subatomic particles do not exist with certainty at objective places, but rather show 'tendencies to exist,' and atomic events do not occur with certainty at definite times and in definite ways, but rather show 'tendencies to occur.' "[110] There thus exists a certain margin of uncertainty.[111] Einstein could not at first accept this and uttered to Niels Bohr his famous words: "God does not play with dice!"

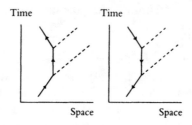

Quantum physics came across another fact which concerns the problem of time even more directly, namely, the so-called symmetry concerning the direction of time. In the space-time diagram here, this can be read either as an electron-photon collision or scattering (the electron being depicted by an upward arrow, the photon by a broken line) or as a positron-photon scattering (the positron being depicted by a downward arrow). "The mathematical formalism of field theory suggests that these lines can be interpreted in two ways, either as positrons moving forward in time or as electrons moving backwards in time."[112] This feature of the world of subatomic particles can also be sketched like the third diagram: an electron (solid line) and a photon (broken line) approach each other. At point A the photon creates an electron–positron pair, the electron moving on to the right, the positron to the left. At point B the positron collides with the initial electron and they annihilate each other, creating a photon which flies off to the left. "We may," however, "also interpret the process as the interaction of the two photons with a single electron travelling first forwards in time, then backwards and then forwards again."[113] We can therefore interpret the process as a four-dimensional pattern of interrelated events which does not have any definite direction of time attached to it.[114]

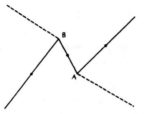

In spite of this, the "arrow of time" and causality are still valid in many areas of the world of matter. In order to find a more general framework for the description of the protons and neutrons (the most basic form of particles) one approach is to use a so-called S-matrix, first proposed by Werner Heisenberg.[115] The circle represents simply the area where complicated single observed processes might take place. A and B are two particles (of any kind) which undergo in this circle a collision-process and emerge as C and D, two different particles.[116] This S-matrix theory bypasses the problem of specifying precisely the position of individual particles.

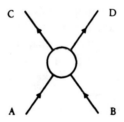

The use of the S-matrix involves a number of basic principles.[117] The first is that the reaction probabilities must be independent of displacements of the apparatus in space and time, and independent of the state of motion of the observer. The second is that the outcome of a particular reaction can only be predicted in terms of probabilities. The third principle is related to causality: it states that energy and momentum are "transferred over spatial distances only by particles and this occurs in such a way that a particle can be created in one reaction and destroyed in another only if the latter reaction occurs *after* the former."[118] There is a fourth factor (Capra includes it in the third): it concerns the values at which the creation of new particles becomes possible (although not predictable). At those values the mathematical structure of the S-matrix changes abruptly: "it encounters what mathematicians call a 'singularity.' " The fact that the S-matrix exhibits singularities is a consequence of the causality principle, but the location of the singularities is not determined by it.' (See page 100.)

The logical opposite of the concept of causality (and its historically older form, Necessity) is *chance*. The latter seems to reach back to older religious ideas and habits of life than the former. As Hermann Usener has shown, the Romans and Greeks possessed in their pantheon many time-gods, in the sense that certain gods personified specific instants in time.[119] There was a god of the moment when the horses panic, of the right moment to pull up weeds, to take the honey out of the hive, etc. Hermes was, among other things, the god of that moment when a sudden silence fell upon a social gathering. One god, Kairos, who was iconographically related to Hermes, was especially important: he personified a lucky coincidence of circumstances, favorable for action; one had to "grasp Kairos" (one's chance) by the hair, otherwise he escaped. Another "lucky-chance" deity was Nike (Victory). She represented that mysterious agent or moment when the scales tip in favor of one or the other combatant in war or competitive games. Nike was the daughter of Styx, the circular river in the Underworld, closely related to Oceanos, the time-river god. Still another time-goddess was Fortuna; she was depicted with another time symbol, the wheel.

The great pre-scientific attempts to explore the numinous quality of a moment were the astrological systems, mentioned earlier. Every day, month, year, and aeon had its own "god" or divine symbol, lending man's essence, action, and life a definite quality. The astrological time-gods, however, were no longer pure chance-gods, for they moved *in an ordered temporal succession* over the skies in the course of that time-ordered play of arche-types, the laws of which we do not know.

These gods do not really belong to the sky: they have been projected on to it by man. However, they *do* belong to time. This is made evident by the fact that Chinese, Aztec, Mayan, and Western astrological doctrines developed a technique *by which one could make the same predictions as does astrology by an earthly numerical oracle.* Today one of them, the *I Ching,* has become famous. According to it one can determine the meaning of a given moment by counting off by fours a randomly picked bun-dle of 49 yarrow stalks. The remainders constitute four types of line, two masculine (—) and two feminine (--). Six such lines (two trigrams or *Kua*) constitute an oracle answer. There are 64 double-trigrams, depicting basic symbolic life situations within the moving on of Tao. In the West there exists a similar tech-nique called geomancy, whose symbolic configurations of four lines, each of either two or one dot, is constituted by counting off in pairs a randomly picked cluster of pebbles or dots. While the *I Ching* oracles have been elaborated into a deep philosophy of existence, Western geomancy has largely remained a primi-tive divination technique. But not so in West Africa, where it is also connected with a differentiated religious system.[120] Its effi-ciency is based on the workings of a divinity called Fa, who has no collective cult but only talks "individually to the individual." He is the god of truth, but he uncovers his whole secret to us only in the after-life. He is not a force of nature but symbolizes God's solicitude for his creation. He is the "Lord of Life" and "the hole that calls us over to the Beyond." Through the geo-mantic oracle he communicates to the medicine-man, who finds by it the inner truth of every situation.

Looked at from a mathematical point of view these divination techniques form a complementary opposite to the calculus of probability. The latter becomes more accurate as more cases are considered; its answer is never yes or no but a fraction between 0 and 1 (no and yes). Chance is implied but eliminated as much as possible. On the other hand, the divinatory oracles of the *I Ching* and of geomancy operate with whole (natural) numbers.

Their answer is based on a just-so absolute numerical result. Chance is taken *into the center of attention; repetition and averages are set aside.*[121]

By studying the *I Ching* over many years, Jung was inspired by it to seek for a new principle complementing our Western concept of causality, a new principle which he called synchronicity. In his Introduction to the *I Ching* he writes:

> The Chinese mind, as I see it at work in the *I Ching,* seems to be exclusively preoccupied with the chance aspect of events. What we call coincidence seems to be the chief concern of this peculiar mind, and what we worship as causality passes almost unnoticed. We must admit that there is something to be said for the immense importance of chance. An incalculable amount of human effort is directed to combating and restricting the nuisance or danger represented by chance. Theoretical considerations of cause and effect often look pale and dusty in comparison to the practical results of chance. It is all very well to say that the crystal of quartz is a hexagonal prism. The statement is quite true in so far as an ideal crystal is envisaged. But in nature one finds no two crystals exactly alike, although all are unmistakably hexagonal. The actual form, however, seems to appeal more to the Chinese sage than the ideal one. The jumble of natural laws constituting empirical reality holds more significance for him than a causal explanation of events. . . . The manner in which the *I Ching* tends to look upon reality seems to disfavour our causalistic procedures. The moment under actual observation appears to the ancient Chinese view more of a chance hit than a clearly defined result of causal chain processes. *The matter of interest seems to be the configuration formed by chance events in the moment of observation* . . . synchronicity takes the coincidence of events in space and time as meaning something more than mere chance, namely, a peculiar interdependence of objective events among themselves as well as with the subjective (psychic) states of the observer or observers.

> The ancient Chinese mind contemplates the cosmos in a way comparable to that of the modern physicist, who cannot deny that his model of the world is a decidedly psycho-physical structure. The microphysical event includes the observer just as much as the reality underlying the *I Ching* comprises subjective, i.e., psychic conditions in the totality of the momentary situation. Just as causality describes the sequence of events, so synchronicity to

the Chinese mind deals with the coincidence of events. The causal point of view tells us a dramatic story about how *D* came into existence; it took its origin from *C*, which existed before *D*, and *C* in its turn had a father, *B*, etc. The synchronistic view on the other hand tries to produce an equally meaningful picture of coincidence. How does it happen that *A'*, *B'*, *C'*, *D'*, etc., appear all in the same moment and in the same place? It happens in the first place because the physical events *A'* and *B'* are of the same quality as the psychic events *C'* and *D'*, and further because all are the exponents of one and the same momentary situation. The situation is assumed to represent a legible or understandable picture.[122]

Besides experimenting with the *I Ching* Jung observed that frequently a patient would dream of symbolic images which then in a strange way coincided with outer events. If one looked at the latter as if they were symbols, they had *the same meaning* as the dream images.[123] This seems mostly to happen when an archetype is activated in the observer's unconscious, producing a state of high emotional tension. In such moments psyche and matter seem no longer to be separate entities but arrange themselves into an identical, meaningful symbolic situation.[124] It looks at such times as if *physical and psychic worlds are two facets of the same reality*.

This unitary reality Jung called the *unus mundus* (the one world).[125] Synchronistic events are, according to Jung, sporadically and irregularly occurring parapsychological phenomena. But they seem to be only special incidences of a more general principle which Jung termed *acausal orderedness*.[126] The latter means that certain factors in nature are ordered without its being possible to find a cause for such an order. Within the realm of matter this would be such facts as the time rate of radioactive decay, or the fact that the speed of light is 186,000 miles per second and not more or less.[127] In the realm of the mind or psyche acausal orderedness is manifest in such examples as the fact that 6 is a perfect number; the addition of its factors, $1 + 2 + 3$, and their multiplication, $1 \times 2 \times 3$, both yield 6. We are mentally forced to accept this as true without being able to indicate a cause for 6 having just this quality. These orders can be studied and underlie the above-mentioned divination techniques. As opposed to them, synchronistic events form only momentary special instances in which the observer stands in a position to recognize the third, connecting element, namely *the similarity of meaning* in the inner and outer events. Their orderedness "differs from that of the properties of natural numbers or the discontinuities of physics in that the latter have existed from eternity and occur regularly, whereas synchronistic events are *acts of creation in time*."[128] In this sense the world of chance "would be taken partly as a universal factor existing from all eternity and partly as the sum of countless individual acts of creation occurring in time."[129]

These creative acts in time, however, do not occur completely outside recognizable means of prediction, but on the contrary take place within certain fields of probability within the acausal orderedness.[130] It is these fields of psycho-physical probabilities which the divination techniques try to explore by means of *numerical* procedures.

Since Jung published his discovery, some recent developments in nuclear physics seem to me to have come closer to similar ideas. In the S-matrix theory, mentioned above, it is held that within the causal and predictable chain of events observed in the channel of sensation there happens also the *unpredictable* creation of the new particles which are called "singularities." There is, however, a difference between the observation of meaningful synchronistic events and the physical "singularities" for which we cannot detect any *psychological* meaning. Jung has proposed referring to the synchronistic events in which no observer can state the meaning as similarity or "equivalence."[131] This coincides with L. L. Whyte's investigations,[132] according to which in nature "incomplete patterns are trying to become complete." The mathematical symbolism of patterns displays a tendency and movement of its own: towards completion. This is true not only for crystalline forms but also for microphysical patterns. All incomplete structures are in some degree unstable and tend either to complete themselves or to disintegrate.[133] Thus Whyte defines life as a spreading of a pattern as it pulsates.[134] One could interpret this "spreading" as being based on "similarity." But only the human mind can see meaning in this and can consciously experience the oneness of mind and matter. Modern physicists have come independently to a similar idea of a basic oneness of the cosmos (realizing simultaneously that all the things we can say about it are constructs of our own mind). In this "one world," as Fritjof Capra puts it, "every particle consists of all other particles,"[135] and at the same time they also all "self-interact" by emitting and reabsorbing virtual particles.[136] "Particles are not isolated grains of matter but are probability patterns, interconnections in an inseparable cosmic web."[137] They are various parts of a unified whole.[138]

What is different in this physicist's "one world" from Jung's *unus mundus* is that the latter also includes psychic reality, or rather that it *transcends both psyche (mind) and matter*. The ultimate nature of both, the *unus mundus* itself, is transcendental; it cannot be grasped directly by our consciousness.[139] Synchronistic events are "singularities" in which the oneness of psyche and matter, the *unus mundus,* becomes sporadically manifest. Number too seems to be in an exact relation to both realms, being an aspect of all energy manifestations and of the reasoning working of our mind. Number, according to Jung, is the most basic or primitive form of the archetypes, which are the "arrangers" of our conscious ratiocinations;[140] "it is quantity as well as meaning."

But where is time in all this? Let us return briefly to the two Chinese time-mandalas, the Sequences of Earlier Heaven and Later Heaven. The Chinese shaman drew their equivalents, the Ho-t'ou and the Lo-shou number patterns, on two boards, round and square respectively, ran a stick through the center of both, and spun them around it. Where they stopped, one above the other, he "read" out the symbolic situation in time. The interplay of the two boards was understood as a sacred marriage between Heaven and Earth, the coming together of the eternal order of time with the actual just-so moment, indicating "fields of probability" within which synchronistic events could occur.[141] The Earlier Heaven corresponds to what Jung called acausal orderedness; it is timeless. The Later Heaven deals with the lapse of time. Time in it is a "field" which imparts to all things which coincide within it a definite quality. It mediates, as the Hopi see so clearly, between the possible and the actual meaningful chance-event. Between the two realms stands man, who sets the boards in motion. Here chance or freedom enters the game and the laws which govern it, though man is naturally also part of the whole coinciding situation. The Chinese saw the wise man's relationship to the cosmos as a ritual play. His "superiority and freedom is founded in rites which are wholeheartedly played by the player. . . . It is expected that a deeply serious and straightforward game will mediate clarity or wisdom and bring about liberation. The rites call for sincerity; the game requires fixed rules, or at least the prototypes of rules."[142] This means that the rules are not absolute laws, for they preserve room for play.

Interestingly, the Nobel Prize winner Manfred Eigen has recently also made an attempt to explain evolution and biological processes by comparing them with number games.[143] However, he does not yet believe in a meaning in chance, only in "blind" chance. But this notion of "blind" chance is a remnant of the age of a deterministic view of reality; it is perhaps only "blind" when *we* are blind to its meaning.

Transcending Time

We have seen that the image or notion of time nearly always contains several pairs of opposites, or even triads. In China we have a timeless order, a cyclic time-order, and a linear historical time. In India Brahma is time and not-time. The Maya draw time, *kin,* as an image which contains a static element, the flower, and a flowing element, the arrows of the sun. The Aztecs know of a cyclical time and a linear historical time of five sun-periods. Plato's system contains a timeless world of Ideas, a cyclic aeonic time, and a perishable world of ordinary time. The old Persians had two Zurvān figures: Infinite Time and Time of Long Dominion (aeonic time). In his excellent survey of the different philosophical notions of time, G. J. Whitrow states that basically some always tend to eliminate time, others to take it as a basic objectively existing factor. Time is seen as life and death, good and evil. Basing himself on these facts (and others) J. T. Fraser attempted to define time in terms of conflict. I would prefer to apply Nicolas Cusanus's definition of God also to time, that it is a coincidence of opposites: *coincidentia oppositorum.*

Let us briefly turn to the extremest of all complementary opposites: to the contrast of time and not-time. The greatest efforts to transcend time have been made by the Eastern sages, for instance in the practices of Indian yoga. However, when a yogi seeks to transcend time he does not do so with a jump. Through his breathing exercises he tries initially only to overcome ordinary time and "burns up" all his karmic personal inheritances. Then he begins to breathe according to the rhythm of the great cosmic time.[144] His inspiration corresponds to the course of the sun, his expiration to that of the moon: "The yogi lives a cosmic Time, but he nevertheless continues to live in time." Later he attempts to unify even these two rhythms and thus abolishes the cosmos and unites all opposites. He breaks the shell of the microcosm and transcends the contingent world, which exists in time. The ultimate foundation of reality, into which he breaks through, is both time and eternity; what we have in fact to overcome is only our wrong assumption that there is nothing outside ordinary time.

In Taoist mysticism, and in Buddhism, we find very similar ideas. The *Lankavatara Sutra,* for instance, says:

> Why are all things neither departing nor coming? Because though they are characterized with the masks of individuality and generality, these masks coming and departing neither come nor depart. . . . Why are all things permanent? Because though they take forms . . . they take really no such forms and in reality there is nothing born, nothing passing away.[145]

> Being and non-being—between these two limits the mind moves; with the disappearance of this field the mind properly ceases to operate. When an objective world is no more grasped there is neither disappearance or non-being, except something absolute known as Suchness *(tàthatàvastū)* which realm belongs to the wise.[146]

The ancient *Treatises of Seng-Chao* elucidate this Buddhist idea in even more detail concerning time:[147]

> When [the Sutras] say that [things] pass, they say so with a mental reservation. For they wish to contradict people's belief in permanence. When they say that things are lost, they say so with a mental reservation, in order to express disapproval of what people understand by "passing." . . . Their wording may be contradictory, but not their aim. It follows that with the sages: "Permanence" has not the meaning of staying behind [while the Wheel of Time, or Karma, moves on]; "Impermanence" has not the meaning of outpassing [the Wheel]. . . . People who seek in vain ancient events in our time conclude that things are impermanent; I who seek in vain present events in ancient times know that things are permanent. . . . [Therefore] the Buddha is like the Void, neither going nor coming. He appears at the proper moment but has no fixed place [among beings].[148]

How one can exist both in ordinary time and in aeonic time together can best be illustrated by the story of the death of the great Zen Master Ma. When he reached the end of his life and was lying very sick in his room, the warden of the monastery visited him and asked reverently: "How has the Venerable One's state of health been recently?" Ma replied: "Buddha with the sun visage, Buddha with the moon visage." As Wilhelm Gundert explains, these words hint at a passage in the Third Sutra of the Name of Buddha, where it is explained that the life span of the Buddha with the moon visage is only one day and one night. The life span of the Buddha with the sun visage is one thousand eight hundred years. Both Buddhas, however, are only facets of the Great One.[149] After one day and one night Ma died. His mortal part (his moon visage) lasted only that long, but another, more archetypal part of himself was to last much longer; and beyond it there would even be an eternal kernel; but of this Ma did not speak, because it is ineffable.

In a certain way—and this has been visible in earlier sections of this essay—one could clarify the problem of time and not-time as shown in the diagram on the opposite page.

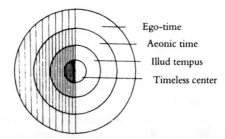

One could compare time to a rotating wheel: our ordinary communal time, which we are aware of in our ego-consciousness, would be the outermost ring which moves more quickly than the others. The next inner ring would represent aeonic time, moving progressively more slowly as the center is approached. This aeonic time is represented in the idea of the Platonic Year or the Aztec ages or Suns—a time which lasts infinitely longer than our ordinary time. The next and smallest would represent Eliade's *illud tempus,* which is right on the razor's edge between time and no-time, representing, as he says, an "extratemporal moment of creation." It is right between unutterable eternity and the beginnings of aeonic time, the latter being the slow-moving life of the archetypes. And finally there is the hole, the non-rotating empty center of the wheel, which remains permanently quiet, outside movement and time. This is, for instance, the Chinese Tao, which lies beyond the rhythms of Yang and Yin:

> There was something formlessly fashioned
> That existed before Heaven and Earth,
> Without sound, without substance,
> Dependent on nothing, unchanging,
> All-pervading, unfailing.[150]

It is completely void and still:

> Push far towards the Void,
> Hold fast enough to Quietness.
> . . .
> This return to the root is called Quietness,
> Tao is forever and who possesses it,
> Though his body ceases, is not destroyed.[151]

Western mysticism also knows of this step of completely transcending time at the moment of union with the extratemporal
Godhead. One of the great masters who stressed this point often
is Meister Eckhart. He says:

> St. Paul says: "In the fullness of time God sent his Son." . . . It is
> the fullness (or end) of the day when the day is done. . . . Certain
> it is that there is no time when this birth befalls, for nothing hin-
> ders this birth so much as time and creature. It is an obvious fact
> that time affects neither God nor the soul. Did time touch the soul
> she would not be the soul. If God were affected by time he would
> not be God. Further, if time could touch the soul, then God could
> not be born in her. The soul wherein God is born must have es-
> caped from time, and time must have dropped away from her.[152]

> Suppose that someone had the knowledge and the power to sum
> up in the present now, all the time and the happenings in that time
> of six thousand years, including everything that comes until the
> end, that would be the fullness of time. That is the now of eter-
> nity, where the soul in God knows all things new and fresh.[153]

But from the timeless God flows the "flow of grace" which creates an ever-present now—so that God is simultaneously stillness and an everlasting flux.

Notes

1. Cf. J. T. Fraser (ed.), *The Voices of Time* (New York: Bra-
ziller, 1966), and J. T. Fraser and N. Lawrence (eds.), *The
Study of Time: Proceedings of the First (Second, Third) Confer-
ence of the International Society for the Study of Time*, 3 vols.
(Heidelberg & New York, 1972, 1975, 1979). Cf. also J. T.
Fraser (ed.), *Of Time, Passion and Knowledge* (New York:
Braziller, 1975); G. J. Whitrow, *The Natural Philosophy of
Time* (London & Edinburgh, 1961); J. B. Priestley in *Man
and Time* (London: Aldus, 1964); F. Le Lionnais, "Le
Temps," Série Science no. 2 de *l'Encyclopédie essentielle*
(Paris, 1959).
2. Cf. B. L. Whorf, *Sprache, Denken, Wirklichkeit* (Hamburg,
1963), p. 80.
3. Cf. Jean Piaget, *Le Développement de la notion du temps chez
l'enfant* (Paris, 1964).

4. Cf. R. B. Onians, *The Origins of European Thought* (Cambridge, 1954), p. 206.
5. Ibid., p. 248.
6. Ibid., p. 249.
7. Cf. S. G. F. Brandon, *History, Time and Deity* (Manchester, 1965), and "The Deification of Time," in *The Study of Time I.* p. 376.
8. Cf. C. A. Campbell, *Mithraic Iconography* (New York, 1968).
9. K. Preisendanz, *Papyri graecae magicae* (Stuttgart: Teubner, 1973), vol. 1, p. 111.
10. Ibid., p. 93.
11. Cf. C. de Wit, *Le Rôle et le sens du lion dans l'Egypte ancienne* (Leiden, 1951), p. 72; Marie-Louise von Franz, *Number and Time* (Evanston, Ill., 1974), pp. 92ff.
12. Cf. Brandon, "The Deification of Time," in *The Study of Time I*, p. 372.
13. Cf. H. Bonnet, *Reallexikon der ägyptischen Religionsgeschichte* (Berlin, 1952), pp. 682, 257ff, 833–34.
14. *The Bhagavad Gita* trans. A. W. Ryder (Chicago: University of Chicago Press, 1929), chap. 11.
15. Cf. Heinrich Zimmer, *Myths and Symbols in Indian Art and Civilization* (New York, 1962), pp. 148–51.
16. W. Müller, *Indianische Welterfahrung* (Stuttgart, 1976).
17. Cf. Richard Wilhelm, *The I Ching or Book of Changes,* trans. Cary F. Baynes (London, 1968), vol. 1, p. 307.
18. Ibid., pp. 324, 367.
19. M. Granet, *La Pensée chinoise* (Paris, 1963), p. 79.
20. Ibid.
21. Cf. Joseph Needham, *Time and Eastern Man,* The Henry Myers Lecture (London, 1964); J. Needham and Wang Ling, *Science and Civilization in China,* 7 vols. (Cambridge, 1954–1959).
22. Cf. S. G. Morley, *An Introduction to the Study of Mayan Hieroglyphs* (Washington, D.C., 1915), p. 72. For the picture, see J. E. S. Thompson, *Maya Hieroglyph Writing* (Washington, D.C., 1950), pp. 142ff. I owe this information to the kindness of Dr. med. José Zavala.
23. Cf. W. Krickeberg, et al., *Pre-Columbian American Religions* (London, 1968), p. 65.
24. M. Léon-Portilla, *Aztec Thought and Culture* (Norman, Okla., 1963; 2nd ed., 1970), p. 73.

25. Cf. G. Quispel, "Time and History in Patristic Literature," in *Man and Time*, p. 89.
26. Ibid., pp. 99–104.
27. Cf. Le Lionnais, "Le Temps," p. 22.
28. Cf. Fritjof Capra, *The Tao of Physics: An Exploration of the Parallels between Modern Physics and Eastern Mysticism* (Berkeley, 1975), p. 105 and elsewhere.
29. Ibid., pp. 98, 172n.
30. For this and the following, see Capra, *The Tao of Physics*, pp. 173ff.
31. Ibid., p. 77.
32. C. G. Jung, *Memories, Dreams, Reflections* (New York & London, 1961, 1962, 1963), pp. 325ff.
33. Capra, *The Tao of Physics*, p. 169.
34. Macrobius, *Saturnalia* I, 22, pp. 6–8.
35. Cf. Mircea Eliade, *The Myth of the Eternal Return* (London, 1949); *Patañjali et le yoga* (Paris, 1962); "Time and Eternity in Indian Thought," in *Man and Time*, pp. 177ff.
36. *Kausitaki Upanishad*, IV, 2, quoted in *Man and Time*, p. 187, and in Eliade, *The Myth of the Eternal Return*, p. 113.
37. Eliade, *The Myth of the Eternal Return*, p. 113.
38. Ibid., p. 105.
39. Ibid., p. 59.
40. Ibid., p. 129.
41. Wilhelm, *I Ching*, vol. 1, p. 287.
42. For details, see Granet, *La Pensée chinoise*.
43. Cf. L. de Saussure, *Les Origines de l'astrologie chinoise* (Paris: Maison Neuve, 1930), and *Origine babylonienne de l'astronomie chinoise, Archives de Sciences Physiques et Naturelles, 5th series, 198, 5 (1923)*; Needham and Wang, *Science and Civilization*, III and elsewhere.
44. Cf. León-Portilla, *Aztec Thought and Culture*, pp. 37–39.
45. Needham and Wang, *Science and Civilization*, p. 4.
46. Cf. F. Cumont, *Astrology and Religion among the Greeks and Romans* (New York, 1912), pp. 30ff.
47. Ibid., p. 28.
48. *Timaeus*, 37 C, D. See F. M. Cornford, *Plato's Cosmology* (London, 1948), pp. 97–100.
49. I use this term following H. Conrad-Martius.
50. Cf. G. Böhme, *Zeit und Zahl: Studien zur Zeittheorie bei Platon, Aristoteles, Leibnitz und Kant* (Frankfurt, 1974).

51. D. W. Dauer, "Nietzsche and the Concept of Time," in Fraser and Lawrence (eds.) *The Study of Time II*, p. 91.
52. Cf. D. J. De Solla Price, "Automata and the Origins of Mechanism and Mechanistic Philosophy," *Technology and Culture* 5 (1964). Quoted in D. J. De Solla Price, "Clockwork before the Clock and Timekeepers before Timekeeping," in Fraser and Lawrence (eds.), *The Study of Time II*. Quoted in C. Haber, "The Darwinian Revolution in the Concept of Time," in Fraser and Lawrence (eds.), *The Study of Time I*, p. 388.
53. Cf. Le Lionnais, "Le Temps," p. 13.
54. Ibid., pp. 14, 19.
55. De Solla Price, "Clockwork before the Clock," p. 370.
56. Le Lionnais, "Le Temps," p. 26.
57. Needham, *Time and Eastern Man*, pp. 52–53.
58. Cf. Haber, "The Darwinian Revolution," pp. 385ff.
59. Cf. Eliade, *The Myth of the Eternal Return*, pp. 143–44.
60. Wisdom 11.21. Cf. von Franz, *Number and Time*, pp. 171–73.
61. Cf. D. Mahnke, *Unendliche Sphäre und Allmittelpunkt* (Stuttgart, 1939, 1966).
62. Cf. G. Da Fiori, *Tractatus super quattour Evangelia*, ed. E. Bonaiuti, pp. xli, lii–liii, 23, and elsewhere.
63. Haber, "The Darwinian Revolution," pp. 387ff.
64. Quoted in ibid., p. 390.
65. Cf. ibid., pp. 392ff.
66. Olivier Costa de Beauregard, *Le Second Principe et la science du temps* (Paris, 1963).
67. Cf. Haber, "The Darwinian Revolution," pp. 383, 384, 385.
68. Cf. K. G. Denbigh, "In Defense of the Direction of Time," in Fraser and Lawrence (eds.), *The Study of Time I*, p. 148.
69. C. G. Jung, *Collected Works* (CW), vol. 9/ii, paras. 248–49.
70. Cf. Jill Purce, *The Mystic Spiral* (New York: Avon, 1974).
71. Jung, CW 9/ii, paras. 404, 406ff.
72. Ibid., para. 408.
73. Ibid., paras. 410–11. See also G. Gamov, *Atomic Energy* (Cambridge, 1947), p. 72.
74. Jung, CW 9/ii, para. 413.
75. Cf. G. J. Whitrow, *The Natural Philosophy of Time* (London & Edinburgh, 1961), pp. 29, 30, and "Reflections on the

History of the Concept of Time," in Fraser and Lawrence
(eds.), *The Study of Time I*, pp. 4–5.

76. Cf. P. E. Ariotti, "The Concept of Time in Western Antiquity," *Study 2*, p. 75.
77. Alexander Marshack, *The Roots of Civilization* (New York: McGraw-Hill, 1972).
78. Cf. Granet, *La Pensée chinoise*, pp. 154ff., 171ff.
79. Cf. von Franz, *Number and Time*, p. 26.
80. Ibid., p. 77.
81. Aetius, *Placita Philosophorum*, I, 7.22.
82. Cf. Le Lionnais, "Le Temps," p. 71.
83. Ibid.
84. Capra, *The Tao of Physics*, p. 241.
85. Ibid., p. 242.
86. Ibid., p. 244.
87. Cf. E. Bünning, *Die physiologische Uhr*, 2nd ed. (Berlin & New York, 1963), p. 2.
88. Ibid., p. 4.
89. Cf. E. Pöppel, "Oscillations as a Possible Basis for Time-Perception," in Fraser and Lawrence (eds.), *The Study of Time I*, p. 221.
90. Though also partly working in connection with outer stimuli.
91. Cf. E. Bünning, *Die physiologische Uhr*, pp. 40–41, 52.
92. Cf. C. P. Richter, "Astronomical References in Biological Rhythms," in Fraser and Lawrence (eds.), *The Study of Time II*, p. 52.
93. G. Schaltenbrand, "Cyclic States as Biological Space-Time Fields," in Fraser and Lawrence (eds.), *The Study of Time II*, p. 59.
94. Adolf Portmann, "Time in the Life of the Organism," in *Man and Time*, p. 312.
95. Ibid., pp. 313–14.
96. Cf. Richter, "Astronomical References," pp. 39 and 52 and the literature cited there.
97. By Paul Walder, C. G. Jung Institute, Zurich. Cf. also, on the periodicity in the behavior of schizophrenics, B. S. Aaronson, "Time, Stance and Existence," in Fraser and Lawrence (eds.), *The Study of Time I*, p. 308.
98. Cf. R. Kastenbaum, "Time, Death and Old Age," in Fraser and Lawrence (eds.), *The Study of Time II*, pp. 20ff., and

esp. H. B. Green, "Temporal Stages in the Development of the Self," ibid., pp. 1ff.

99. Cf. Le Lionnais, "Le Temps," pp. 103, 107ff.
100. Whitrow, *The Natural Philosophy of Time*, p. 105.
101. Ibid., p. 107.
102. Quoted ibid., p. 111.
103. Ibid., p. 11.
104. M. S. Watanabe, "Causality and Time," in Fraser and Lawrence (eds.), *The Study of Time II*, pp. 267ff.
105. Anaximander, "Simplicius in Aristotelis physicorun libros Commentarius, translated by Marie-Louise von Franz. Quoted in H. Diels, Doxographi Graeci (Berlin & Leipzig, 1929), p. 476.
106. Frgm. 80, from Clement of Alexandria, Stromata IV, 17.2. Cf for this P. E. Ariotti, "The Concept of Time," in Fraser and Lawrence (eds.), *The Study of Time I*, p. 171.
107. Cf. Onians, *The Origins*, pp. 251, 332.
108. Cf. Karl Barth, "Descartes Begründung der Erkenntnis," dissertation, (Bern, 1913).
109. Adapted from Capra, *The Tao of Physics*, p. 56.
110. Ibid., p. 68.
111. Ibid., p. 184.
112. Ibid., pp. 182–83.
113. Ibid., p. 184.
114. Ibid., p. 185.
115. Ibid., pp. 262ff.
116. Ibid., pp. 262–63.
117. Ibid., p. 274–75.
118. Ibid., p. 275.
119. Hermann Usener, *Götternamen* (Frankfurt, 1948), pp. 279ff.
120. Cf. von Franz, *Number and Time*, pp. 265ff. From B. Maupoil, *La Géomancie à l'ancienne Côte des Esclaves* (Paris, 1943).
121. Von Franz, *Number and Time*, pp. 220, 223.
122. Jung, cw 1, pp. iiiff. (my emphasis).
123. Jung, cw 8, paras. 870, 902ff, 915; von Franz, *Number and Time*, pp. 6ff.
124. Cf. also von Franz, *Number and Time*, p. 7.
125. Ibid., p. 9.
126. Jung, cw 8, paras. 964–65.
127. Naturally one could use another measure, but the just-soness would remain.

128. Jung, cw 8, para. 964.
129. Ibid., paras. 964ff.
130. Von Franz, *Number and Time*, p. 12.
131. Jung, cw 8, pp. 513, 516.
132. Whyte, *Accent on Form*, pp. 97–98.
133. Ibid., p. 101.
134. Ibid., pp. 104ff.
135. Capra, *The Tao of Physics*, p. 295.
136. Ibid., p. 244.
137. Ibid., p. 203.
138. Ibid., p. 159; cf. also pp. 137–38.
139. Cf. Jung, cw 8, paras. 420, 439.
140. Von Franz, *Number and Time*, pp. 9, 15.
141. Ibid., pp. 241ff.
142. Granet, *La Pensée chinoise*, pp. 316, 321.
143. M. Eigen and R. Winkler, *Das Spiel: Naturgesetze steuern den Zufall* (Munich & Zurich, 1975).
144. For this cf. Eliade, "Time and Eternity in Indian Thought," in *Man and Time*, pp. 197–198.
145. D. T. Suzuki, *Studies in the Lankavatara Sutra* (London, 1930, 1957, 1968), p. 304.
146. Ibid., p. 306.
147. Chao-lun, *The Treatises of Seng-Chao*, trans. Walter Liebenthal (Hong Kong, 1968), p. 49. Seng-Chao belongs to the period of Buddhism before the T'ang period.
148. Ibid., p. 110.
149. Bi-Yän-Lu, *Niederschrift von der smaragdenen Felswand*, ed. W. Gundert (Munich, 1960), p. 97.
150. Arthur Waley, *The Way and Its Power: A Study of the Tao Te Ching* (London, 1942, 1949), chap. 25.
151. Ibid., chap. 16.
152. Pfeiffer (ed.), *Meister Eckhart* (1857) (London, 1956), I, pp. 80–81. Cf. also p. 227.
153. Ibid., II, p. 152; also pp. 144, 155, 186, and I, p. 399.

The Psychological
Experience of Time

As G. J. Whitrow has shown in his lucid survey, time has been a problematic and contradictory theme in philosophy from Plato and Aristotle to Saint Augustine, Saint Thomas Aquinas, to Kant, Leibniz, Bergson, Einstein, and many others.[1] And all their attempts to define time have mostly dealt with man's conscious experience of it. Through the discovery of the unconscious it has become even more complicated. C. G. Jung found early in his work that in the unconscious, time becomes more and more relative, the more we penetrate into the deeper layers, and that in certain realms of the unconscious there even seems to be no time at all. In our dreams we can shift from the remotest past to the present and even to the future. The dream itself, which seems to occur in a nick of time, is in some ways nearly timeless, for we can often remember it as a cluster of simultaneous scenes which we have to sort out in their time sequence when telling or writing them down, and in innumerable instances people say: "And then there was somehow another scene, but I do not know where it belongs in the sequence."

The relativity of time in the unconscious has been often expressed in folklore. Especially in Celtic countries we find innumerable stories in which a man goes into a fairy hill or into the ghostland and when he returns—thinking that he has stayed there only one night or one day—he finds that all his relations are gone, his village has disappeared; in fact, he had been away many hundreds of years. Generally when he realizes this he drops dead and dissolves into dust. In other countries, hell, paradise, or the land of the dead is described in a similar manner. A Slavonian story, for instance, tells how God once wandered as a beggar on earth, riding in a carriage with a donkey. He comes to a poor man who gives Him shelter. The next day God asks His host to visit Him in *His* house. "You will find it easily if you follow the tracks of my carriage, which are broader than usual and never grow together." The two stepbrothers of the poor man first try to follow these tracks, but they misbehave and suffer misfortune. Then the poor man sets himself to the journey. He first comes to an iron bridge. Nearby two goats are engaged in a bloody fight. The tracks begin to glitter like silver. The next bridge is of copper. There he sees two black bitches fighting. The next bridge is of silver, "as beautiful as in a dream." There is a man who is attacked by ravens, and oxen who pull out his hair. The last bridge is of gold. Finally the man comes to a circular wall made of precious stones, with a many-colored entrance. Inside it is a beautiful garden, full of flowers and singing birds. "He felt neither hunger nor thirst and shed tears of joy." There God appears and explains to him that the different animals and tortured people which he saw were people who had committed different sins on earth. Then God leads him back to the entrance and says with a smile: "Come again. I await you this evening." The man suddenly finds himself at home, but he cannot recognize either his village or his people. He asks about them, but people only stare at him in bewilderment. "What can he do? He can only return on the tracks and ask that beggar what it is all about. The beggar received him kindly and thus he never left again but stayed with him in paradise."[2]

This type of story can be found all over Europe.[3] Seen psychologically it describes the deeper layers of the collective unconscious, where "a thousand years seem to be like a day." The silvery tracks are especially interesting: they describe the famous controversial axiom of Euclid of the two parallels which meet in infinity.[4]

Another testimony for the relativity of time in the deeper layers of the unconscious are those weird breakthroughs into the past reported by parapsychology. Most famous is the experience of two English ladies, Miss C. A. E. Moberley and Miss E. F. Jourdain, the former a principal of St. Hugh's Women's College at Oxford, the latter her vice-principal and formerly also head of a college. One afternoon in 1901 the two ladies took a walk in Versailles toward the Petit Trianon. They saw a woman shaking a white cloth out of a window and two gardeners dressed in grayish green coats and three-cornered hats. Suddenly Miss Moberley "felt a sudden gloom upon her spirits," but she said nothing and they went on. They came to a circular kiosk. "Everything looked unnatural, even the trees seemed to have become flat and lifeless, *like a wood worked in tapestry.* . . . It was intensely still." They go on a long way and meet several other people in old-fashioned costumes and later return to Paris. Only afterward did they exchange their impressions and then decided to write down exactly what they saw, independently of each other. After years of painstaking research they found out that they had seen the Versailles of Marie Antoinette and that they had not only seen people of that time but buildings which no longer exist, including having passed a little bridge which had disappeared since.[5] J. W. Dunne, author of the famous *An Experiment with Time,* has commented on their report, for it fits his theory of the many-dimensionality of time. C. G. Jung's experience in Ravenna, where he saw, together with a friend, some mosaics which also no longer existed, is a similar instance.[6] It shows that somehow the past can be completely present in the deep unconscious.

In fact one cannot analyze a person deeply without meeting in him or her dream motifs which come from the remote past of their cultural background. Once a Catholic Mexican analysand did not tell me about the latter in his analysis, and in spite of sympathy and efforts on both sides the analysis got stuck. Then he had a dream: He saw in a tree an obsidian stone which jumped down and pursued him. He ran and stood in the center of a dugout square, where the stone became gradually smaller and finally laid itself quietly at his feet. I exclaimed: "What on earth have you to do with Tezcatlipoca?" Then—at last—he told me that he was three-quarters Aztec! I adapted my language to this fact, and the analysis continued well.

Not only the past is preserved and still fully alive in the unconscious but also the future. This is even so much so that the age-old interests of mankind, the studies of dreams in all civilizations up to now, have exclusively circled around the "prognostic" aspect of dreams. Oriental, Middle Eastern, and antique dreambooks testify to this fact. In dreams which deal with the future there are, however, two forms to be distinguished: (1) telepathic dreams, which directly depict a future event, and (2) dreams which anticipate future developments in a symbolic form.

As an example of the first type, let me quote a story which especially interested Schopenhauer.[7] It was originally reported in the *Times of London* of 2 December 1852: A Mr. Marclane had drowned. Before anyone could find his corpse, his brother said that he knew where it was because he had dreamt the night before that he was standing in the river near the gate of Oxenhall, trying to pull him out. A trout was swimming beside the corpse. He sounded the alarm to some people, and indeed they found the corpse exactly in the indicated place. There was a trout swimming just beside the corpse when they found him. As Schopenhauer points out, even such a detail which lasts only a few seconds, that a trout is swimming past, had been foreseen in the dream.

The second type of dream is more difficult to detect in its prognostic function because it needs a symbolic interpretation. Also it can even happen at the same time that it is confirmed in outer reality by a synchronistic event. Such a case is, for instance, the scarab dream which Jung reports in his paper on synchronicity. It could have occurred without the subsequent "miracle" of a beetle appearing in the analytical hour. The scarab of Old Egypt symbolized the agency which every morning brings the new sun up at the eastern horizon. It symbolizes therefore a total renewal of consciousness—just what was preparing to break through in the dreamer. The synchronistic appearance of a scarab-like insect at the moment when the analysand told the dream to Jung was like a numinous confirmation of the importance of that renewal.

Let me illustrate this point also by a little personal experience: When traveling in Canada I stayed with a very nice family in Toronto. The night before flying to Chicago I dreamt that I was sinking deeper and deeper into drifting snow. Suddenly a snow-mobile was moving threateningly toward my head—I woke up with a cry for help. The usual interpretation that snow meant coldness of feeling made no sense. I left Toronto in sunshine, but we came over Chicago into a frightful snowstorm which eventually forced us down in Cleveland. The bustle and brutality of a panicking crowd were terrible, and only after eight hours of waiting and catching a bad cold did I get a very poor room for the night. The telephone was broken, and wind and snow blew in through the window. When I crept into the cold bed I thought: "There is my dream!" However, this was not literally a telepathic dream. It rather sketched *symbolically* what was going to happen to me physically and psychologically as well. The second indirect form of anticipating the future is, in my experience, more frequent than the former. Rarely the future seems preformed as it becomes actually real later, but often it is anticipated symbolically, and in the latter case there seems to still exist a small space of freedom, where we can sometimes choose whether it should become real inwardly or also outwardly. I could, for instance, have canceled my flight after my dream and avoided the whole trouble.

As you know, C. G. Jung has shown that most dreams have the same basic structure as the classical drama: (1) An exposition where time, place, and dramatis personae are shown; (2) a naming of the problem; (3) a peripety or several peripeties; and (4) a lysis-solution or catastrophe. Owing to a dream which he had, Dr. Paul Walder added to this the idea that the first two parts of dreams deal more with the past, the peripeties with the present, and the last part with the future. He was able to confirm this after studying over one hundred dreams, and I myself have also found it to be often true. We could therefore venture the scheme illustrated by the accompanying diagram.

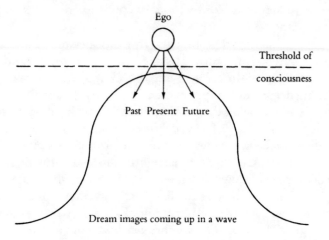

The ego is moving in time from the past to the future. The dream comes up toward it from the unconscious, like a wave containing a cluster of images. The three arrows show the field of perception when we become aware of the dream: first perceiving the past, being hit by the present, and then seeing ahead the solution. All this makes it highly probable that what we nowadays experience as regular clock-time is closely linked with the specific structure of our consciousness. Jung calls it even a mere *modus cogitandi*. Jean Piaget has also shown that children only develop a sense of time slowly, through a learning process, and that they develop a sense of rhythm, frequency, and speed before this, much more readily and to a much more heightened degree.[8] Many civilizations, such as some Africans or many North American Indians, for instance, do not have our sense of time at all. Especially interesting are the Hopi Indians, who do not seem to have in their language any forms at all to designate the present, past, or future.[9] They also have no word for "quick" or "rapidly," but use words which express instead an *intensity*.[10] Their verbs also have no tenses,[11] and their nouns have only two forms: one in which the speaker tells about a fact or event, corresponding to our past and present, and one where he *expects* something, corresponding to our future.

The Hopi's universe has thus only two great temporal forms: the manifest and the manifesting (or not yet manifest).[12] Manifest is everything which we perceive with the senses; it is *objective* and *past*. The manifesting is purely subjective and is a content of our heart. It is simultaneously present in the "Heart of Nature," in the "powerful something" *(a'ne himu)* or Spirit of Breath *(hi' wsn)*; it embraces everything of the future. The razor's edge situation between the subjective and its having become objective is what *we* would call the present. But the Hopi circumscribe it by indicating either that the causation of something has stopped or by an inceptive suffix telling us that the end situation is beginning to manifest. The "subjective" or "futuric" form is the pure realm of hope.[13] The Hopi verb *tunátya* means "think," "wish," and "cause"; it is the word for what is subjective and not yet manifest. The past, on the contrary, is manifest and perceptible until, in its most remote forms, it re-disappears into the realm of the Origins, into the time and place of myths. There it becomes again "subjective" because it is only known to our consciousness after having come to visible forms in this world. It is as if from the original divine "Heart of Nature" a stream of events would flow out, becoming manifest and thus already past, while ever-new events still press forward from the realm of the subjective into actual manifestation. The remote past is, as I said, again "subjective" because no longer perceptible. One is reminded there of the Aljira of the Australian aborigines, who know a mythical Dreamtime (Aljira) where the great mythical figures walked about and created the world and from which the souls of the children still come and to which the souls of the dying return. It is the sphere from which dreams come. This is just another instance of the relative timelessness of what we would now call the collective unconscious.

The Hopi view of time seems to me to have a certain kinship with the Chinese idea of "seeds," which are called the "first signs of the time." "The seeds," we read in the *I Ching*, "are the first imperceptible beginnings of movement, the first trace of good fortune (or misfortune) that shows itself. The superior man perceives the seeds and immediately takes action."[14] The material world arises according to the Chinese in the following way: First there is a preexistent image (trigram); then a copy of this takes shape in corporeal form. What regulates this process of imitation is called a pattern. "What is above form is called tao; what is within form is called tool."[15] "The movements of the lines and images, and of the infinitesimal germs of events symbolized by them, are invisible, but their results manifest themselves in the visible world as good fortune or misfortune."[16] "The lines and images move within, and good fortune and misfortune reveal themselves without."[17] (The Hopi would call these "seeds" subjective and not yet manifest, the fortune and misfortune manifest and thus already past and expanded in time-space.) Here we come across intimations of the fact that the archetypes of the collective unconscious are like these "seeds"; they are imperceptible, invisible in a way, only potentially real; only when they become actualized in the form of an archetypal *image* do they become "real," and only then do they seem to enter our consciousness and with it into our space-time world. What they are in themselves remains, as Jung stressed, forever unknowable.

What the "seeds" are can be felt in us if we are sensitive to it. Toward the end of his life Jung no longer used the *I Ching* because, he said, he always knew anyhow what result he would get. He seems to have followed the advice of Chu Hsi, who wrote:

> We study the changes *[I Ching]* after the lines
>   have been put together.
> Why should we not set our minds on that which was
>   before any line was drawn?
> When we understand that the two forms have originated
>   from the Ultimate
> We can safely say that we can cease to study the
>   *I Ching*.[18]

The greater timelessness of the archetypal "seeds" is also shown by the following fact: In our analytic work, when one has to deal with a dream containing only personal material, one can generally relate its meaning to the immediate present as a reaction to things one did or experienced the day before or which one would meet the day after the dream. If we have to deal with an archetypal dream motif, its meaning is valid for a much longer period of time, for months or even for many years. Archetypal dreams remembered from early childhood even often anticipate the fate of an individual for his whole life, or at least for his first half of life. The Chinese "seeds" thus resemble what we would call an archetypal constellation in the deep unconscious. In interpreting dreams we often try, and sometimes succeed in the effort, to make the individual realize such a "seed" within, so that—if it is negative—it does not become a "misfortune" without.

The archetypes (not the archetypal images) are thus probably per se outside time. They also lie behind synchronistic events, behind so-called "meaningful coincidences," for they tend mainly to occur to us when an archetype is constellated or—the physicists would say—is in an excited state. This can manifest itself in an emotional state or when an objective outer situation of basic importance, such as death or illness, is about to occur.[19] "It looks," Jung writes, "as if the collective character of the archetypes (or the collective unconscious) were not only inside the individual, but also outside, viz. in one's environment, as if sender and percipient were in the same psychic space, or in the same time (in precognition cases). As in the psychic world there are no bodies moving through space, there is also no time. The archetypal world is 'eternal,' i.e., outside time, and it is everywhere, as there is no space under psychic, that is archetypal, conditions. Where an archetype prevails, we can expect synchronistic phenomena, i.e., *acausal correspondences,* which consist in a parallel arrangement of facts in time."[20]

We could thus represent time with the scheme shown in the diagram on page 122, keeping in mind that every schematic model clarifies but also blurs in some ways the facts which one tries to describe by it.

On the outer rim the ego is moving in a stream of outer and inner events—in time. Below it is the psychic sphere of the so-called personal unconscious, which is still relatively closely time-bound. Inside it comes the sphere of archetypal images, which seem still time-bound but exist in a much vaster time, some even moving in aeons of thousands of years. They can

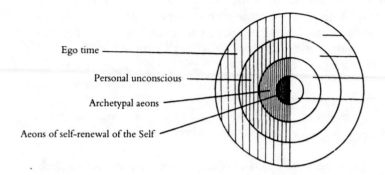

Ego time

Personal unconscious

Archetypal aeons

Aeons of self-renewal of the Self

"constellate" themselves, however, as we call it, an expression which alludes to the existence of time. Further inside is that movement of inner self-renewal within the Self, which Jung has described in his work *Aion,* and still further inside would be the eternal archetypes, their many-oneness, and the Self. In the center is the empty hub of the wheel, a realm of pure not-time.

> Thirty spokes converge upon a single hub;
> It is on the hole in the center that the use of the cart hinges.[21]

The closer we get to the outer ring, the more we come into the realm of time, in that form which is generally known to us. Our clock-time, however, as I said before, is a specific achievement of our civilization, just as is the parameter *t* in modern physics. It is in contrast to all more original archetypal ideas of time a mere concept of *measured* time. This measurability of time is in my view based on its natural relation to number. We generally measure time by some regular motion, and most movements in the universe are oscillations, wave movements, or wavelike phenomena. Most of these show three basic characteristics: rhythmicity (oscillation), seriality (repetitive patterns), and periodicity.[22]

Rhythm, seriality, and periodicity are also basic aspects of the series of natural numbers. This creates the basis for making time a measurable phenomenon. Today we measure time by atomic oscillations.[23] In the past it was measured everywhere by the motions of the heavenly luminaries, most frequently of the sun, but other civilizations, as well as our own cultural forerunners, saw time not only in its regular movements but conceived it more intuitively as a linear flow or stream.

Jung therefore, as I mentioned before, defined time as a mere *modus cogitandi;* what we perceive in fact is a stream of inner and outer experiences; time is the flow of outwardly perceived events and the inwardly experienced train of thoughts, feelings, and emotions. [24] Viewed in this broader way, as being a stream of events, the idea of time is based on an archetypal foundation which is confirmed by the fact that its religious and mythical images show a certain conformity in different cultures.

In the *Bhagavadgita* the god Krishna reveals to Arjuna his true terrifying form: "I see a figure infinite wherein all figures blend to countless bodies, arms, and eyes." In a great stream these figures disappear into his jaws of flaming fire, "entering him with hurried step."[25]

The old Greeks identified their idea of Chronos-Time with the great river Oceanos, which circles around the earth and also again around the universe in the form of a snake which carries the signs of the zodiac on its back. Oceanos is also the world-soul, because the idea of the old Greeks was that the soul was liquid or an exhalation of moisture. The alchemist Zosimos says about this moisture: "The round element of two parts which belongs to the seventh zone of Kronos, that is what it is called in profane language. But what it is in the mystical language this cannot be explained. . . . In the profane language however it is Oceanos, origin and seed of all gods . . . this great and marvellous Ω element that embraces all that has been said about the instruments of the divine water."[26]

The fluid or snake was also, on a smaller scale, a symbol for the "aion," the allotted lifetime of an individual, and we find again the snake in the same connection in old Egypt, where it was thought that everybody had a "lifetime snake" to guard him in his life and after death.

In late antiquity this god, Oceanos-Chronos-Aion, was identified with the Persian god Zurvān in both his aspects as "Infinite Time" and "Time of Long Dominion." Late Mithraic texts praise him as a "spirit that stretches from heaven to earth and the confines of the abyss, that enlightens the world, the great circular mysterious form of the universe. He is earthy, fiery, windy, dark and moist"; that is, he encompasses all opposites and is the "Ruler of Everything."[27] In the famous Aztec Calendar-Stone the outermost ring is formed by two fire snakes which meet at the bottom, head against head. Here we have again the snake and the symbols of opposites related to the idea of Time.

In China time is associated not with the snake but with the dragon. The latter is the symbol of Yang, the light masculine dynamic, creative cosmic principle which has, according to the *I Ching,* spirit and time for its field of action, while Yin, the receptive, acts upon matter in space.[28]

If we sum up, what we have seen until now is that time has been psychologically associated with the image of the Self or the Godhead in its dynamic, creative, active aspect. There is a time element in the Self, so to speak, in its aspect of energy, emanations and motion, or: *Because the Self moves it creates for us the experience of time.*

I want to illustrate this point by quoting a dream of a modern man in his forties. He had trained to become an analyst, and on the day before he was to have seen his first patients, he fell into a panic. He did not feel up to the task and began to puzzle about what analysis and "right" dream interpretation might be altogether. "What happens when we analyze dreams?" With this question in mind he fell asleep and dreamt:

I am sitting in an open square place in an old town. A young man full of vitality and health, with golden blond hair, comes to me and tells me his dreams. He spreads them out, as if they were a sort of material. Each time he tells a dream, a stone falls from heaven onto it and scatters the dream material. When I touch one of these fragments I discover that it is a morsel of bread. What remains from the dream is its inner structure, which consists of bolts and nuts. I say to the youth: One must unwrap a dream till one comes to these bolts. And it is then said: Dream interpretation is the art of knowing what one keeps and what one throws away, just as in life too.

Then the scene changes. We are now both sitting on the shore of a beautiful *broad river*. The structure which has been formed by the dreams is now a whole pyramid of bolts and nuts; it looks like an abstract painting by Braque, but it is three-dimensional *and it lives*. It consists of thousands of little colored triangles and quadrangles, which change constantly. I explain that it is essential always to keep the balance of the whole; if the color of one part is changed, one must compensate it by changing one on the other side. At the top point of the pyramid there is: nothing!—empty space. But when I look at it a light begins to emanate from it.

Again the scene changes: The pyramid is still there but it now consists of shit. The top point is still radiating, and I realize suddenly that the point makes the shit visible and vice versa. I look deep into the shit and realize that I look at the hand of God. And now I understand why the point is invisible: it is the face of God! [Then follows one more little purely personal bit of the dream.][29]

I will interpret that dream as a whole only briefly, but mostly concentrate on the meaning of the river. The dream first tries to tell the dreamer what happens when one interprets dreams: it is an aspect of his own Self, the healthy young man, who produces the dreams, and it is not he, his ego, who interprets them, but they get "hit" by stones falling from heaven. The latter represents the fact that a right intuition about the meaning comes also from the unconscious; it is a *"hit,"* something which "hits the mark." Parts of the dreams then reveal themselves to be "the bread of life," but more important is that pyramid-shaped structure which slowly becomes visible and which would be, according to Jung, a symbol of the Self—the divine nucleus of the psyche. Helmuth Jacobsohn has shown that the pyramid-shaped stone at the top of the Egyptian pyramids was always placed in a way that it was hit by the first sunray in the morning. It represented the immortal kernel of the soul of the dead person which appears in his resurrection and becomes one with the cosmic god Atum, without losing his individual identity.[30]

While the dreamer sees this aspect of the pyramid he is in a square place of a town—in a manmade static surrounding. But now he suddenly sits with his interlocutor *at the bank of a broad river,* and from that moment on he sees that the pyramid is a *living* thing which *changes* incessantly. Time enters the scene. It is as if the dream would say that there is a first phase in the process of individuation in which one realizes the Self by "hitting the mark" in looking for the meaning of dreams. By this, one becomes aware of the existence of the Self. But this is not all, because now the task becomes one of keeping *within time* in contact with the Self in a constantly changing balancing act. That is why we now have the image of the river, and simultaneously the image of the Self, the pyramid, begins moving and being alive. With this the dreamer is confronted with a new paradox: The pyramid is made of shit, most useless matter, and reveals at the same time the "hand of God." The most transient and the most eternal are contained in it. (We are reminded of the alchemistic saying that the philosophers' stone is found in the manure.)

The two places (town and river) and phases of the dream remind me of some Chinese Zen Buddhist's distinction between "substance" and "function." The former means the realization of the Self, but afterward a Zen master develops what is called his "great function," his constantly acting and non-acting from this inner center in the right way, thus causing others to become enlightened too.[31] "Substance" is out of time, so to speak, the speechless awareness of the immaterial body, the *dharmakaya*, but the "great function" is its timebound manifestation during the continuing life of the master.

Something similar applies to what we call the process of individuation. It is not enough to have become aware of the Self's existence, it is necessary to go on living with it, of acting from this center instead of from the ego. That is where the river of time comes in our dream and with it the realization that the Self is alive and ever-changing, as well as solid and still. And both belong to the Self: the "shit" of our transient everyday life and the invisible luminous point which is the "face of God," the resting pivot in all changes.

What this dream symbolizes by the dreamer seeing "the hand of God in the shit" is what Jung called being related during our lifetime to something infinite. "Only if we know that the thing which truly matters is the infinite can we avoid fixing our interest upon futilities and upon all kinds of goals which are not of real importance. . . . If we understand and feel that here in life we already have a link with the infinite, desires and attitudes change. In the final analysis we count for something only because of the essential we embody and if we do not embody that, life is wasted. . . . The feeling of the infinite, however, can be attained only if we are bounded to the utmost. The greatest limitation for man is the 'self,' it is manifested in the experience: 'I am only that!' . . . In such awareness we experience ourselves concurrently as limited and eternal, as both one and the other."[32] For "limited" one could here also say "timebound," for this is one of our many limitations of which we become especially painfully aware when aging.

A second archetypal image of time which we find represented in many myths and religious documents is that of a procession—and in dreams of modern people that of a train. Let me illustrate this by two dreams of a little girl which she had when she was about seven years old. Jung has analyzed them in one of his seminars on children's dreams.[33] The first dream was:

Seven white geese came along the street; all living beings which they pass drop dead.

The second dream says:

A locomotive drives along a street. It does not kill beings by rolling over them but by its pure passing them.

Jung pointed out that seven is a number which is related to the moon, which according to the Greeks rules the world of transience, and to processes in time. The train is something which passes us in a certain rhythm.

The basic idea (like that of the street too) is "passing over," which is the essence of time. The geese are pure nature, animal nature; the locomotive, on the contrary, is a human invention; but both walk or roll by and then all life drops dead—passes over too. According to Jung this child who had the dreams was not abnormal, but she was a bit naive and had difficulty in adapting to this world. The soul comes from the realm of timelessness and it has a tendency to fall back into it, to fall back into that form of life where life is not a short dream but a long one, an eternal one. These two dream-visions mean to give the child a helpful shock, in order to wake her up to *our* cultural time world, to which she now has to adapt when going to school. She has to learn that all goes over rapidly and that she now has to live *in time*. Primitive man has no such time, he lives as if he had eternities to spend; but we are unfortunately no longer in paradise, we have a watch and we are acutely aware of the passing of time.

Probably most of you have had once or more times that typical agonizing dream of having to catch a train, coming across one obstacle after another. This generally indicates that we are not in harmony with time, that we are not "up to the moment" in one way or another, but that we sleepily drift along in life not realizing what is meant to be realized *at that moment*.

We see in psychological practice that young people often have such a neurotic difficulty in entering time completely, while old people, on the contrary, cannot leave its stream and return to the shores of eternity.

Before trains existed, the same aspect of time was expressed, as in the first dream of the seven geese, by a procession. At the Sed festival of the old Egyptians, for instance, there marched behind the king fourteen standard bearers to the sanctuary. The standards represented the *ka*'s, the souls of his fourteen predecessors. Thus the king walked along followed by his whole past, so to speak—he had history backing him up. In many other civilizations, endless lists of dead former chiefs or kings were preserved and recited on important occasions—they had the same function of keeping the past alive. In the procession we have a relation of time to number, for one can count off its rows. This even led A. Seidenberg to assume that processions led to the origin of counting.[34]

The most majestic of all time-processions are the zodiacs of the different civilizations—a "moving image of eternity," as Plato called them.[35] In periods of thousands of years—or sometimes in yearly or monthly periods—divine images march in an ordered sequence over the sky.

Some of our zodiac signs are proved to have been earthly tribal gods before they became projected into the stellar constellations. There must have existed a hunch that the archetypes of the collective unconscious do not constellate themselves randomly but in a mysterious order or "play of the archetypes," as Jung calls it—an ordered play which, however, we do not yet understand at all. Most impressive are the date-symbols of the Mayan and Aztec calendar in that respect: they are pictured as divine figures which carry like bundles, which are signs for periods of days or years, literally on their backs—marching in a row in an arduous walk over the skies. The Indian and Chinese zodiacs are other examples of such a circular time-order of archetypal images. This all has to do with what we often call a psychological "constellation" without knowing exactly what we mean by it.

The relationship of gods to time however has not begun with the birth of astrology. The old Slavonic people, the old Greeks and Romans, for instance, knew gods who literally represented certain numinous moments of time, moments which also had a specific emotional quality. There was, for instance, a god of that moment when the horses panic, or one of the right moment to gather honey. Pan was the god of that moment when panic breaks out in battle. Then there is Kairos—the god of lucky coincidences who was represented in art as a winged youth with little wheels under his feet because he escapes so swiftly; if we do not "seize the moment" it is gone. And there is also Nike, the goddess of that magical moment when the scales tip over to victory in a battle or competitive game. And Fortuna, with her wheel! She is actually an old mother goddess but later became the symbol of that blind force which in the course of time carries some people upward to luck and success, throwing others down into misery. When in Mesopotamia, around the sixth century B.C., some gods became associated with stellar constellations, this seems to be an attempt of mankind to grasp an *order* behind the temporal appearance of certain gods; to order them into a time procession, through which we might calculate the likeliness of their appearance or disappearance. On the contrary, Kairos, Fortuna, Pan, Nike, Eros, and other such gods of the moments (*Augenblicksgötter,* as Hermann Usener called them)[36] are representations of archetypes when they manifest within synchronistic events. These happen randomly, and therefore the appearance of such gods remains unpredictable.

Sometimes synchronistic events are not only irregular but

even seemingly *arbitrary*. For this reason they were in our Christian past called "miracles," which were performed by either God or the Devil. In many medieval images, in Renaissance pictures, and in folk art even until today, we often see in pictures which represent a miracle a hand (of God) pointing down from the clouds. This is the way God interfered with His creation and why in the Christian view the universe was never a pure time-bound mechanism. Miracles and the creation of new things were always possible.

Jung calls synchronistic events "acts of creation in time," and he also speaks of a continuous creation of a "pattern that exists from all eternity, repeats itself sporadically, and is not derivable from any known antecedents."[37] "Continuous creation is to be thought of not only as a series of successive acts of creation, but also as the eternal presence of the *one* creative act. . . ."[38] Synchronistic events, as Jung points out at the end of his work on synchronicity, seem to be only specific instances of a much wider principle in nature, which he calls "acausal orderedness."[39] In the realm of physics such an acausal orderedness manifests, for instance, in the time rate of radioactive decay, which is a just-so fact, for which we cannot indicate a cause. In the realm of the psyche an example of acausal orderedness would be the just-so-ness of individual natural numbers, 1, 2, 3, etc. Nobody can give a "cause," for instance, why just six should be a perfect number (except formulating a tautology!).

This idea of "acausal orderedness" found its expression in the different zodiacs and also in the two Chinese arithmetical world models, which underlie the functioning of the *I Ching*. In the world model which is called the "Sequence of Earlier Heaven" or "Primal Arrangement," the eight universal principles (K'ua) were ordered in pairs of opposites, as seen in the diagram on page 131.[40]

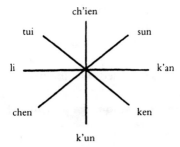

These opposites "do not combat each other," but are kept in a kind of state of dynamic balance. [41] In this way this model is, as a whole, timeless. The so-called "Arrangement of King Wen" or "Sequence of Later Heaven," on the contrary, is revolving in a cycle, as shown in the second diagram.

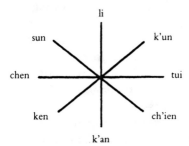

The first model is extratemporal, the second temporal. The former symbolizes the world of "acausal orderedness," the second brings in time and was used as an indicator of possible synchronistic events. These two models are not contrasting, as Richard Wilhelm points out, but it is as if the "Later Sequence of Heaven" were transparent and one could see the earlier order shining through it from below. [42] The Chinese thus have a view of the universe in which temporality and not-time are a complementary Two-Oneness; and synchronistic events would be the sporadic manifestation of their complete oneness. To get an *I Ching* oracle one has to count bundles of yarrow stalks backward (till one has the remainder one or two). This was explained as follows: There is the "normal" forward moving of time from the past to the future, but there is also a backward movement folding up and contracting as time goes on. To know this latter movement is to know the future, for "if we understand how a tree is contracted into a seed, we understand the future unfolding of the seed into a tree."[43] This is why the Chinese used a backward counting technique for guessing the future.

Number altogether in China was closely related to time. Numbers were, as Marcel Granet puts it, classificatory emblems.[44] The universe was thought of as a finite whole and the different numbers, one, two, three, all describe the same whole, but in its different qualitative aspects, which show themselves in successive different time moments. Thus number indicates the various types of organization which are imposed on things when these are manifest in their proper order in the cosmos. Numbers are not only names for quantities but also indicate *qualitative time phases* in the existence of the whole. That is why the *I Ching* works with a *counting system,* using the just-so-ness of numbers to find out the just-so-ness of certain time moments. Numbers, like all other archetypes, have an "eternal" aspect and a temporal aspect as well. They incorporate "acausal orderedness," timebound succession and periodicity and, taken as individuals, "just-so-ness."

The third great symbol of time is the wheel, which I have already used in my own schema. Both Kairos and Fortuna have the wheel as an attribute. The latter was originally one of the great pre-Roman matronae—the mother goddesses of nature.

Our zodiac was also often interpreted as such an heavenly wheel. The most famous images of the Wheel of Time are probably the Indian and Tibetan representations of the Wheel of Samsara (of becoming or rebirth), which visualize the world of *anitya,* the world of impermanence and transiency, from which the Buddhist strives to escape into *nirvana.* In the center are depicted three animals: a pig (desirousness, passion), a cock (hatred), and a snake (stupidity or unconsciousness). They keep the wheel turning forever and ever. In opposition to this negative aspect of the Wheel of Time there existed the "eightfold path" of salvation (Dharma), which was also represented as a wheel (with eight spokes). It rolls through the world bringing salvation to mankind.[45]

The observation of all regular circular recurring of heavenly phenomena led mankind eventually to the invention of the toothed gear, which made it possible to construct first calendars and later clocks and watches. This invention led, however, to a strange development. Originally meant to represent the divine power of time in the universe, it later became *the* model of a mechanical godless world. Nicolaus Cusanus, for instance, still saw in the clock a divine image. He writes in his *Vision of God:* "Let then the concept of the clock represent eternity's self; the motion in the clock representeth succession. Eternity, therefore, both enfoldeth and unfoldeth succession, since the concept of the clock, which is eternity, doth alike enfold and unfold all things."[46] Only in the Age of Enlightenment and until the end of the nineteenth century, man thought of a clock without its divine maker, as a model of a purely mechanical universe. If we look at this psychologically, it means that the ego has put itself into the position of the cosmic clockmaker (because it can make mechanical clocks) and fallen into an inflation. Regularity was confused with mechanical functioning, the elements of chance and creativity in time were definitely excluded from sight. Only now, in modern physics and depth psychology, do we turn to reconsider this erroneous view.

In modern dreams the clock or watch sometimes has the meaning of a reminder of our temporality. Sometime before death people dream, for instance, that their watch is broken beyond repair. Such a dream seems to mean for the dreamer that not he but his temporal existence will soon come to an end. In other dreams, however, clocks have sometimes the meaning of a timebound/not-timebound world order, and are then a symbol of the Self. The reader may recall that vision of a physicist which Jung published in *Psychology and Alchemy,* in which he saw the following:

> a vertical and a horizontal circle, having a common centre. This is the world clock. It is supported by the black bird.

The vertical circle is a blue disc with a white border divided into
4 × 8 = 32 partitions. A pointer rotates upon it.

The horizontal circle consists of four colours. On it stand four
little men with pendulums, and round about it is laid the ring that
was once dark and is now golden. . . .

The "clock" has three rhythms or pulses:

1. The small pulse: the pointer on the blue vertical disc advances
   by ⅓₂.
2. The middle pulse: one complete revolution of the pointer. At
   the same time the horizontal circle advances by ⅓₂.
3. The great pulse: 32 middle pulses are equal to one revolution
   of the golden ring.[47]

Jung comments on this vision by first bringing in different parallels from alchemy and medieval calendars. Then he says:

> . . . if we start . . . from the assumption that the centre and its
> periphery represent the totality of the psyche and consequently
> the self, then the figure tells us that two heterogeneous systems
> intersect in the self, standing to one another in a functional rela-
> tionship that is governed by law and regulated by "three
> rhythms." The self is by definition the centre and circumference
> of the conscious and unconscious systems. . . .[48]

> Since the figure has a cosmic aspect—world clock—we must
> suppose it to be a small-scale model or perhaps even a source of
> space-time, or at any rate an embodiment of it and therefore,
> mathematically speaking, four-dimensional in nature although
> only visible in a three-dimensional projection.[49]

Elsewhere Jung adds:

> If we hark back to the old Pythagorean idea that the soul is a
> square, then the mandala would express the Deity through its
> threefold rhythm and the soul through its static quaternity, the
> circle divided into four colours. And thus its innermost meaning
> would simply be the *union of the soul with God*.[50]

If Jung is correct in interpreting this image of two intersecting
systems as a source of space-time, this would mean no less than
that the conscious realization of time is "engendered" in the in-
tersection of the conscious and unconscious psychic systems.
The dual world model of the old Chinese, the overlapping of the

older and later Heavenly orders, would be another instance which corroborates this idea—where the eternal atemporal order of the Self meets with the time-bound order of our consciously experienced world, time comes into being. This would lead us to the conclusion that our relationship with time can be only "right" if our ego lives in close connection with the Self. That explains why neurotic people are so often "haunted by time"—they do not live in rhythmic correspondence with the Self and thus time becomes for them completely negative. Baudelaire, for instance, in his poem "l'Horloge" calls the clock "ce Dieu effrayant et sinistre." But Baudelaire is only one of the many modern writers who describe time in its terrifying aspect.[51] Whenever an individual fails to live the meaning of his life or loses sight of its "eternal" pattern on account of rationalistic prejudices, it gets at odds with time, and when too many people do this, "time is out of joint." Seen from this angle, we can now better understand why in classical China the calendar reforms undertaken by some emperors were praised as such great events. By reforming "the numbers of the calendar" the emperor did nothing less than restore the social and religious orders of his people and put the whole empire back into Tao.[52]

In his work *Aion,* Jung has tried to show that within the Self there seems to take place a recurring motion of self-renewal. The course of this process is either circular or, more likely, spiral in form and has to do with a slow evolution of man's becoming conscious of the Self.[53] "The self," he writes, "is not a static quantity or constant form, but is also a dynamic process. . . . The . . . transformations represent a process of restoration or rejuvenation taking place, as it were, inside the self, and comparable to the carbon-nitrogen cycle in the sun, when a carbon nucleus captures four protons (two of which immediately become neutrons) and releases them at the end of the cycle in the form of an alpha particle. The carbon nucleus itself comes out of the reaction unchanged, 'like the Phoenix from the ashes.' The secret of existence, i.e., the existence of the atom and its components, may well consist in a continually repeated process of rejuvenation, and one comes to similar conclusions in trying to account for the numinosity of the archetypes."[54] "Psyche cannot be totally different from matter. . . . Psyche and matter exist in one and the same world, and each partakes of the other."[55] Seen in this way, the Self is not only a center of stillness outside time but lives in a dynamic process, as the dream pyramid which I mentioned before also seemed to express.

To the three great archetypal symbols and time, the river (or snake), the procession (or train), and the wheel (or clock), we could add one more archetypal image, the God of Death. In antiquity Chronos-Time was identified with the old man Saturn and his scythe and depicted in this form. He was represented devouring his own children as Saturn did. This figure survived in the Middle Ages and up to the seventeenth century as the image of old "Father Time." Often he is represented together with death (as a skeleton), holding an hourglass. I have never met a similar motif in modern dreams. But in the stern moods and fits of depression from which many aging people suffer and which can even lead to certain old-age psychoses, one might assume that this archetype is at work. It seems to me that the Father Time figure is in fact an autonomously split-off part of the God-image itself, a dark aspect of God which people were loath to attribute to Him directly. In European folktales death is often personified as a not unkind but very earnest, mysterious man who acts directly on God's orders. The only dreams which I have met in my practice referring to the coming of death in a similar vein were dreams in which the dreamer woke up with a start, feeling that an uncanny unknown visitor was knocking at his bedroom door.

In India death and decay are more openly associated with the highest godhead. In the *Bhagavad Gita* (xi) Vishnu says about himself: "Know I am Time, that makes the world perish when ripe and come to bring on them destruction."[56] Shiva too is death; he is called Bhairava, the Terrible Destroyer, or Mahā-Kāla, "Great Time," or Kāla-Rudra, All-Devouring Time. His *shakti* is Kālī, whose name is the feminine of Kāla, Time. She is black and wears a garland of severed heads and holds destructive weapons in her many hands.[57]

More frequently, as the personification of death, one finds in modern dreams an allusion to death in the form of the destruction of animal life or vegetation: a horse is killed, the life tree is felled, a field of wheat is trampled down, etc., which reminds one that death carries in art a sickle or scythe, like the old god Saturn. This seems to mean that not all of our life is destroyed, but only the animal and vegetative life of our body.

Our particular sense of time is certainly also linked up with the functioning of our living body. I only want to remind you of the fact of our having biological clocks in us which regulate times of activity and sleep, hormonal rhythms, etc. Also that our estimation of time lapses varies under drugs or through the influence of cold and fever, youth and old age. Physiological clocks seem to be partly able to function without outer stimuli and thus to be endogenous. It is not yet certain, but likely, that many of these rhythms are synchronized by the brain. Our perception of time is therefore closely linked with the existence of our psyche *in its incarnated form in the brain;* in its non-incarnated aspect, the psyche appears rather to be at least partly outside of time, as I mentioned in the beginning.

In a letter from 1952 Jung has ventured a speculative explanation of this problem.[58] In the beginning Jung expresses his wonder about the fact that we have "so exceedingly little direct information of the body from within, and that . . . the unconscious . . . refers very rarely to the body and, if it does, it is always in the most roundabout (symbolic) way." It is as if there were a "curious gap between mind and body." What Jung means by that, I would say, is that we can have, for instance, a quite advanced cancerous growth in certain places of our body without being aware of it and even needing a specialist to detect it via indirect symptoms.

Then Jung mentions the relativity of space-time in the case of parapsychological psychic phenomena, which I have dealt with before, and finally asks the question: "Shouldn't we give up the time-space categories altogether when we are dealing with psychic existence?" "It might be," he continues, "that psyche should be understood as *unextended intensity* and not as a body moving with time. One might assume the psyche gradually rising from minute extensity to infinite intensity, transcending for instance the velocity of light and thus irrealizing the body. That would account for the 'elasticity' of space under ESP conditions. If there is no body moving in space, there can be no time either and that would account for the 'elasticity' of time."[59]

Let me illustrate this idea a bit further. We know that the nucleus of an atom for instance has a minimal extension in space but contains an enormously intensive compact amount of energy, as one can see in an atomic explosion. Now let this extension in space become still much smaller, right down to the point zero and the intensity of energy still greater—then we would reach that threshold where the psyche "irrealizes" the body and becomes pure intensity. Interestingly enough B. L. Whorf, in his description of the Hopi language, pointed out that they have no word for "quick" or "rapid," but only for intensities.[60] Perhaps, he writes, a new physical term i (intensity) is needed.[61] Also acceleration should be understood in a different way, all things having a factor i regardless of whether they move or are at rest. If Whorf is right, the Hopi word for "intensity" would then stress more the psychic aspect of events than their physical aspect, in the sense of our physical concepts.

Jung continues, after his postulate of psychic intensity, as follows: "You will certainly object to the paradox of 'unextended intensity' as being a *contradictio in adiecto*. I quite agree. Energy is mass and mass is extended. At all events, a body with a speed higher than that of light vanishes from sight and one may have all sorts of doubts about what would happen to such a body otherwise. Surely there would be no means to make sure of its whereabouts or of its existence at all. Its time would be unobservable likewise."[62]

Let me comment again: We know now of such bodies which "vanish from sight" in the so-called "black holes" of the universe. In them any light-signals and thus also space-time become unobservable. Once I came across a telepathic dream of an analysand which seems to allude to something similar, when the psyche leaves the body in death. She dreamt of a party at which she met C. G. Jung, who wore a suit which was green in front and black on the back. There was a wall into which a hole was cut which filled exactly Jung's body. He stepped into the hole and then one saw only a uniform black wall, but the dreamer knew that Jung was still there, though invisible. The morning after the dream she heard over the radio that Jung had actually died the evening before. This dream seems to try to convey that in death the psychic being goes over a threshold of observability, as into a black hole, but actually continues to exist. But we still do not see how the psyche is then connected with the body. Jung continues: "In the light of this view the brain might be a transformer station, in which the relatively infinite tension or intensity of the psyche proper is transformed into perceptible frequencies of 'extensions.' Conversely, the fading of introspective perception of the body explains itself as due to a gradual 'psychification,' i.e., intensification at the expense of extension. Psyche = highest intensity in the smallest space."[63]

Jung stresses that all this is pure speculation. However, it seems to me that the usefulness of an explanatory hypothesis depends on how many hitherto inexplicable facts it can bring into a meaningful connection. And this idea does a lot of this for me. It explains most ESP phenomena, which all testify that the psyche is not absolutely bound to our space-time categories. It fits with the testimonies of Eastern and Western mystics that in certain states of ecstasy time-space is transcended with a simultaneous and enormous *intensification* of psychic awareness. It explains why, when the functioning of the brain is hampered by toxic effects (by drugs or by schizophrenia), there is also an enormous intensification of psychic experience, though in this latter case more disorganized and fragmentary. It also explains why so many schizophrenics assert that their psychotic episode began with "an explosion in the brain"—and as a positive counterpart the assertion of practitioners of yoga that when the Buddha-body is born, their skull opens and it comes out of it with a cry. The assertions of people who have been clinically "dead" for a short while but have come back again also point to similar facts. Jung's own visions, which he had in 1944, described in *Memories, Dreams, Reflections,* are another example.

In everyday life we presuppose a certain dichotomy of mind and matter which is, however, only a way of consciously observing things. In fact, we do not know what matter per se is, nor what mind or psyche per se is. They are, according to Jung, most likely just two facets of the same living mystery which he called the *unus mundus,* the *one* world. By the hypothesis that the psyche and matter are two forms of one and the same manifestation of energy (one in low frequencies and extension in time-space, the other in pure intensity), the world of psyche and matter would indeed be one. If this is true, then the temporal and the atemporal are also only two facets of a mystery which one would have to call Time and Not-Time in one. In other words Time, being an aspect of the God-image or the Self, seems to be a *coincidentia oppositorum.* This is why the symbol of the clock in dreams sometimes signifies our mortal timebound person which stops functioning in death, but at the same time it can also signify the Self in its eternal aspect.

This paradox of time is not difficult to understand, but to live with it—to fulfill the demands of clock time and simultaneously to follow the rhythms of the Self—requires a considerable maturity. It means that one should be able sometimes to drop all plans and duties imposed from the outside when the Self suddenly asks us to do something else and also that one can distinguish whether such a demand comes from the Self or only from some other unconscious complex. Seen in this way, time becomes a touchstone which can show us exactly how much or how little we are in harmony with ourselves.

Notes

1. G. J. Whitrow, *The Natural Philosophy of Time* (London & Edinburgh: Nelson, 1961).
2. "Der Bettler und das Paradies," *Märchen aus dem Balkan,* ed. A. Leskien (Jena: Diederichs, 1919), no. 67.
3. See P. M. Huber, *Die Wanderlegende von den Siebenschläfern* (Leipzig, 1910), on the motif of a "thousand years like a day."
4. This axiom has been shown to be relative by the mathematicians Schläfli and later Riemann, for one can construct geometries in which this axiom is not valid.
5. C. A. E. Moberley and E. F. Jourdain, *An Adventure* (London: Faber & Faber, 1907, 1948). Cf. also Aniela Jaffé, *Geistererscheinungen und Vorzeichen* (Zurich & Stuttgart: Rascher, 1958), p. 149. (Published in English as *Apparitions: An Archetypal Approach to Death Dreams and Ghosts.*)

6. Cf. C. G. Jung, *Memories, Dreams, Reflections,* ed. Aniela Jaffé, trans. Richard and Clara Winston (New York: Vintage Books, 1963), pp. 285–86.

7. Quoted in W. von Scholz, *Der Zufall als Schicksal* (Berlin: Deutsche Buchgemeinschaft, 1924), p. 151.

8. Cf. Jean Piaget, *Le Développement de la notion du temps chez l'enfant* (Paris: Presses Universitaires de France, 1964).

9. Cf. B. L. Whorf, *Sprache, Denken, Wirklichkeit* (Hamburg: Rowohlt, 1963), pp. 15ff.

10. Ibid., p. 17.

11. Ibid., p. 85.

12. Ibid., pp. 104ff.

13. Ibid., pp. 105–106.

14. Richard Wilhelm, *The I Ching or Book of Changes,* trans. Cary F. Baynes, 3rd ed. (Princeton: Princeton University Press, 1967), book I, chap. 16, line 2, p. 70.

15. Ibid., p. 323.

16. Ibid., p. 327.

17. Ibid.

18. Quoted in Chang Chung-yuan, *Creativity and Taoism* (New York: Julian Press, 1963), p. 183.

19. See C. G. Jung, letter to J. R. Smythies, 29 February 1952, *Letters,* vol. 2 (London: Routledge & Kegan Paul, 1976), p. 46.

20. Ibid.

21. Lao Tzu, *Tao Teh Ching,* trans. John C. H. Wu (Boston: Shambhala Publications, 1989), chap. 11, p. 23.

22. Cf. H. Jenny, *Kymatik* (Cymatics) (Basel, 1976), pp. 12 and 176ff.

23. Cf. F. Le Lionnais, "Le Temps," *Encyclopédie essentielle* (Paris: Delpire, 1959), pp. 71ff.

24. Cf. Jung, letter of 29 January 1934, *Letters,* vol. 1, p. 139, and letter of 26 May 1954, p. 176.

25. *The Bhagavad Gita,* trans. A. W. Ryder (Chicago: University of Chicago Press, 1929).

26. M. Berthelot, *Collection des anciens alchimistes grecs,* vol. 1 (Paris: Steinheil, 1887–1888), p. 228.

27. K. Preisendanz, *Papyri Graecae Magicae,* vol. 1 (Stuttgart: Teubner, 1973), p. 111.

28. Cf. Wilhelm, *I Ching,* pp. 285–86.

29. Shortened version. I have interpreted this dream more exten-

sively in *Praxis der Psychotherapie,* ed. J. Schultz, vol. 22 (1977), pp. 193ff.

30. Cf. H. Jacobsohn, "Das göttliche Wort und der göttliche Stein im alten Ägypten," *Eranos* 39 (1970), pp. 217ff.

31. Cf. Lu K'uan Yü, *Ch'an and Zen-teaching,* series 2 (London: Rider, 1961), pp. 61 and 62, n. 5.

32. Jung, *Memories, Dreams, Reflections,* p. 325.

33. C. G. Jung, "Psychologische Interpretation von Kinderträumen," unpublished monograph, ed. Liliane Frey and Rivkah Schärf, Eidgenöss. Techn. Hochschule (Zurich School of Technology), Winter 1938/1939.

34. A. Seidenberg, "The Ritual Origin of Counting," *Archive for History of Exact Sciences* 2, no. 7 (1962–1966): 10.

35. Plato, *Timaeus,* 37 C; cf. F. M. Cornford, *Plato's Cosmology* (London, 1948), pp. 97–100.

36. Hermann Usener, *Götternamen* (Frankfurt: Schulte-Bulmke, 1948), pp. 279ff.

37. C. G. Jung, "Synchronicity: An Acausal Connecting Principle," in *The Structure and Dynamics of the Psyche,* vol. 8 of the *Collected Works* (CW), para. 965.

38. Ibid., CW 8, para. 967 and n. 17.

39. Ibid., CW 8, paras. 965ff.

40. Cf. Marcel Granet, *La Pensée chinoise* (Paris, 1948).

41. Cf. Wilhelm, *I Ching,* book I, p. 266. For more detail see Marie-Louise von Franz, *Number and Time* (Evanston, Ill.: Northwestern University Press, 1974), pp. 236ff.

42. Wilhelm, *I Ching,* p. 271.

43. Ibid., p. 267.

44. Granet, *La Pensée chinoise,* p. 138. Cf. also von Franz, *Number and Time,* pp. 72ff.

45. Rhys Davids, "Zur Geschichte des Radsymbols," *Eranos* 2 (1934): 153ff.

46. Nicolaus Cusanus, *Vision of God,* trans. E. G. Salter (London: Dent & Sons, 1928), p. 52. Cf., on this, F. C. Haber, "The Darwinian Revolution in the Concept of Time," in J. T. Fraser and N. Lawrence, *The Study of Time I,* p. 390.

47. C. G. Jung, *Psychology and Alchemy,* CW 12, para. 307. Cf. also *Psychology and Religion,* CW 11, paras. 111ff.

48. Jung, CW 12, para. 310.

49. Ibid., para. 312.

50. Jung, CW 11, para. 124.

51. Cf. Hans Meyerhoff, *The Broken Center*, cited in T. Ungvar, "Time and the Modern Self: A Change in Dramatic Form," in Fraser and Lawrence (eds.), *The Study of Time I*, p. 475.
52. Cf. Granet, *La Pensée chinoise*, pp. 139ff. and 143ff. For more detail see von Franz, *Number and Time*, pp. 158–59.
53. Cf. Jung, *The Archetypes and the Collective Unconscious*, cw 9/i, para. 260.
54. Jung, *Aion*, cw 9/ii, para. 411.
55. Ibid., para. 413.
56. Quoted in S. G. F. Brandon, "The Deification of Time," in *The Study of Time*, I, edited by J. T. Fraser and N. Lawrence, p. 378.
57. Ibid., p. 379.
58. C. G. Jung, letter of 29 February 1952 to J. R. Smythies, *Letters*, vol. 2, pp. 43ff.
59. Ibid., p. 45.
60. Whorf, *Sprache, Denken, Wirklichkeit*, p. 87.
61. Ibid., p. 17.
62. Jung, *Letters*, vol. 2, p. 45.
63. Ibid.

Psyche and Matter in
Alchemy and Modern Science

Western alchemy originated in Alexandrian times when the philosophical mind of the Greeks encountered the techno-magic of the Orient and the North African cultures. Before this time, that great turn of mind had happened in Greece from the seventh to the fourth centuries B.C., that turn which one could call the birth of Western science. Ultimately it consisted in a change of the God-image. Before this the Greeks venerated a group of anthropomorphic gods. But now a new archetypal image arose from the depths: the idea of one divine basic principle—*arche*, as they called it—of the universe. This one principle was either something spiritual, for instance numbers (one thinks of the Pythagoreans), or a spiritual vortex (Anaxagoras); the infinite, or the sphere of existence; or some kind of primordial matter: water (Thales of Miletos); a mind-endowed fire (Heraclitus); air (all the atoms of Democritus); the four elements; or later, in the times of Stoic philosophy, a fiery all-encompassing divine pneuma—spirit. The older gods—Zeus, Hera, and so on—were either declared to have been an illusion or, more frequently, reinterpreted by a newborn science, the so-called hermeneutics, as symbols of the newly discovered divine world principle. Zeus was interpreted as the universal pneuma, Ares/Mars as the fire, Hera as the air, Demeter as the earth, and so forth.

There was no real contrast between spirit and psyche versus matter, as we know it today. The natural realm was understood by the Greeks as being animated by a World Psyche or World Spirit, and this psychic principle was not separated from matter (except with Parmenides or Plato). But it was a formal principle which coexisted with matter. A great part of what we recognize today as being psychic belonged, in the view of the old Greeks, to a superindividual, objective world soul.

In the view of the Stoic philosophers, Ares/Mars symbolized the angry affect; Aphrodite/Venus, the love passion; Athene, the reasonable mind, etc. These impulses, however, existed in the outer universe and only occasionally seized the individual from outside. Another part of what we call today the psyche existed in different parts of the human body, for instance in the phrenes, which meant originally the lungs and later the diaphragm; in the liver; in the heart; or in the brain. With these body centers Ulysses had conversations, as with another human being. In the later centuries B.C., astrology, which came from Asia Minor, spread widely over the whole area, and the idea that the gods were identical with certain psychological moods increased even more. Saturn meant depression, Venus love, Hermes the flexible intellect, and so on. The constellation of such gods at the moment of an individual's birth—the horoscope—determined the psychic structure of that person.

Through the influence of Eastern astrology, a new idea came into the foreground which had been rather strange to the Greek mind before: namely, the idea that certain basic psychic structures—we would now call them the archetypes—had a relation to time and to certain numinous moments of time. (A numinous time moment is called *kairos* in Greek. *Kairos* means a magical moment in which synchronistic events happen. The Chinese, the Babylonian, and the Mayan civilizations all identified some days of the calendar with certain gods. The gods constellated themselves in a great order of time, in a definite sequence. This represents, like the *I Ching* in China, as Jung once pointed out, a first attempt to grasp an order of the collective unconscious, or a time-ordered interplay of its archetypes.) This basic idea of astrology appears in the writings of Zosimos of Panopolis and continued to play a major or minor role in later alchemy.

What was completely lacking in the development of Greek science, with the exception perhaps of (Pseudo-) Democritus, was the actual practical chemical or physical experiment. The latter developed in another area, in what I called before the techno-magic of Asia Minor and Egypt. (Africa is always bringing something new, as the Romans said.) In the oldest metallurgy of the Mesopotamians, all substances were looked at as being gods. As Eliade has shown, copper, iron, and bronze were divine factors. This was even more so in the view of the old Egyptians. Even at the highest point of the evolution of their culture, they kept a primordial magical relationship to matter. All chemical substances were divine, they even *were* the gods. The statues of stone, for instance, represented directly the living gods themselves. This identity of material substance and the divine shows itself especially clearly in the so-called liturgy of the dead. Each dead person, according to Egyptian belief, becomes the god Osiris, the hidden god of the underworld, not in some invisible way or in the way of an analogy, but through the actual concrete operations of the mummification of the corpse. By the mummification of the corpse, the dead person was turned into a god. So bathing the corpse in natron, or sodium hydrate, oiling the corpse, or wrapping him in the mummy-bands is how he was transformed into the god of the universe, embracing in himself then all other gods. Sodium hydrate, or natron, is in Egyptian *neter*, which simply means "god." The bath in *neter* is a concrete deification in a god-solution. The linen wrappings of the body are concretely the goddesses Isis and Nephthys, who embrace the dead person.

In this Egyptian techno-magic, another, even more important idea was included, though it was probably not conscious to the Egyptians, namely the idea that man can manipulate or handle the gods. For instance, the leader of the mummification process, the Anubis priest, was actually handling god material. Still another idea was involved in these mummification techniques, an idea which dominated throughout alchemy for the next millennium, namely the preoccupation with producing an eternal, indestructible resurrection body for the dead. It is obvious that even today the question of death and life after death is a point where the problem of the relationship of psyche and matter still touches us most personally. In lifetime we identify with our body, so when the body dies and it becomes seemingly inanimate matter, how will we save our individual identity from dissolution in the universe? How can our psyche survive without some kind of a body? Here the question is no longer one of scientific curiosity; it becomes a burning personal problem.

When the speculative mind of the Greeks met with the experimental techno-magical practices and experiences of the Orient, they cross-fertilized each other tremendously. This was the moment of birth of alchemy. One of the oldest texts of the first century A.D., the celebrated instructions of Komarios to Cleopatra, concerns itself exclusively with the production of an immortal resurrection body. The philosopher's stone was thought to be the resurrection body. The secret of the philosopher's stone is represented by a drama in which first psyche, body, and mind lie buried in Hades, tortured by a spirit of darkness. But then after many washing operations, the soul calls to the cleansed body: Awake from the underworld! Arise from the grave! Clothe thyself with spirituality and deification, for the call of resurrection has reached thee! And the soul, the text continues, is now happy in her new house (that is, the resurrection body). First she found him wrapped in darkness; now a statue full of light and divine quality has been erected. The fire has unified them; the womb of fire has borne them; and one image was completed through body, soul, and mind. They all have become one. Thus arises the one nature which overcomes all other natures. This same resurrection body is also called the "secret of the spiritual vortex," the "wheel of the stars" which circles round the north pole. For in old Egypt, the dead person who became Osiris circles with the never-setting stars round the north pole.

Some other old texts of the third century A.D. were written by a Greek living in Egypt, by Zosimos of Panopolis, who is known to many people through Jung's wonderful interpretations. In his search for the basic material of the universe, Zosimos let himself be guided by his dreams and visions, which revealed to him in strange archetypal images a mysterious sacrifice or transformation process. In his writings, a new motif turns up, which comes from Gnostic philosophy, and which became a central theme in later alchemy—namely, the idea of the god-man, the Anthropos, who has fallen down into the cosmic matter. From there he must be redeemed and freed by the alchemists. Jung has explained this motif in *Psychology and Alchemy:* it is the literal representation of a projection. The god-man, or Anthropos, is no longer located, as he was for the Gnostics, in some metaphysical realm, but is now projected, which means literally thrown, into matter. Matter therefore now contains the secret of the incarnated divine man—in our Jungian language, the secret of the Self. It is precisely because matter now seemed to contain the god-man mystery that Zosimos began a new procedure in his chemical experiments, namely to attend to his dreams, visions, and meditative exercises during his work, that is, to let himself be guided by his unconscious. This is an introverted creative method, which most outstanding later alchemists also used. Basically, it is a sort of active imagination, which is performed not by writing or painting, but by mixing chemical substances: substances which were at the same time gods or demons. Lead, for instance, is Saturn, a demon who creates depression and madness. Quicksilver is Hermes, an aspect of the Anthropos, or god-man. Gold is the glorified indestructible final form.

Like the author of the Komarios text, Zosimos also always thought in astrological terms. The numinous moment in time—the so-called *kairos*—was decisively important to him. In his writings, he warns against making so-called *kairikai baphai*—astrologically conditioned transformations. He calls them the work of demons. Only if the alchemist has through meditation established a relationship to his inner self, that is, to the Anthropos in matter, can he produce the right kind of transformations. Here we can see the beginnings of a critical attitude toward the unconscious: a differentiation between *deceiving* synchronistic events, constellated by autonomous complexes (which the ancients called demons), and *positive constructive* synchronistic events, which arise in connection with an appearance of the Self. This is a problem in modern analysis to which I will return later.

This short, sketchy historical survey has shown us that in late antiquity the major part of what we call today the psyche was located outside the individual in the animated matter of the universe; it consisted of a multiplicity of colliding components, or of gods, star-divinities, and demons, or of powers in the organs of the body, or in chemical substances. Jung has shown that what we now call the collective unconscious has never been something psychological; it always was relegated to the outside cosmos, to the extrapsychic cosmic sphere. Man protected himself against it with religious symbols and rituals in order to avoid experiencing it within himself. Only today do we discover the collective unconscious in the area of inner psychic experience. Furthermore, in antiquity, the conscious ego of man was a helpless victim of different moods or divine influences. Only slowly did man develop an ethical, critical attitude toward these powers.

It is the spreading of Christianity which primarily produced an ethical progress, a differentiation of ethical feelings. This happened however at the cost of the antique sciences, which lost their importance for the first millennium A.D. in Europe. In the Christian world, the multiplicity of the soul—so many demons and soul gods in the individual—became suddenly a modern problem.

The church father Origen refers to this problem several times. In 2 Kings 1:4 there is a completely unimportant sentence which runs "and there was one man." (But, as you know, every sentence in the Bible was always taken as having a deeper meaning.) On this sentence, "there was one man," Origen comments, "As long as we still are sinners we cannot earn this name of one man because each of us is not one but many. You can see how that man who is considered to be one person is not at all one, but there seems to be in him as many persons as mores [mores could perhaps translate in this case as patterns of behavior], according to the scripture that the fool changes like the moon." And in a commentary on Leviticus 52, Origen says also: "Realize that you have in yourself herds of cattle, herds of sheep and goats, that the birds of heaven are in thee. Realize that you are a second microcosm containing the sun and moon and the stars." All these different mores—ways of reaction—become only one through the influence of Christ, who was considered to be the One Man—the real *Vir Unus*.

The monotheism of the Old Testament and the idea of Christ being the One Man required from other human beings an ethical decision in their confrontation with the varied inner demons and animal souls. But even then the latter were not regarded as being in man himself, but rather partly extraneous—*attached* to man, so to speak, but not *in* him.

I mentioned in the beginning how the gods of Greece were psychified by their interpretation as psychological powers. The Christian interpretation of the Scriptures continued this art of hermeneutics in exactly the same manner. Following the example of Philo Judaeus, who interpreted the Old Testament in a symbolic way, the great Origen also began to interpret many passages of the New Testament in such a symbolic, psychological form. Many miraculous events described in the Bible were, according to his view, not to be believed literally, but only as symbolic images—*eikones*—which illustrate the actions of God. For, as he says, the visible material world points to something beyond itself, namely to the invisible realm of spiritual truth. Especially, many stories and motifs of the Old Testament were understood as symbolic prefigurations of, or veiled allusions to, the events which are reported in the New Testament in which their secret became unveiled. They point to something spiritual which reveals itself slowly in the course of history. According to Origen, many miracles in the New Testament did not happen concretely, but happened in a sort of subtle-body reality. For Christ, as Origen stresses, appeared in the middle between the created and the uncreated things. This middle realm of subtle-body quality resembles the older Stoic idea of the pneumatic world-soul. What qualifies the Christian miracles is not, according to Origen, their different form, but their *higher ethical effect,* which manifests itself in Christ, and the Christian's more ethical life.

Though Christianity brought a moral progress and a greater unification of the personality, there came along with it, as I mentioned before, a *big loss*. Man no longer experienced the numinosum in nature and in chemical substances: only evil spirits continued to live there. The symbol of Christ had attracted all projections of positive psychic images upon himself and had taken them away from nature. Thus, an early Christian poet, Ephraem Syrus, could even say: "Because the creatures were tired of carrying the prefigurations [the symbols] of Christ's glory, Christ relieved them of their weight, as he relieved the womb which carried him." Or, "Christ clothed himself with the symbols he carried," the archetypal images of himself. They are a hidden treasure which reveals great wonders when one opens it. This relief of nature, as Ephraem puts it, means a partial taking back of projections from outer nature. But with it, man lost all interest in nature.

European alchemy therefore gradually died away. Its traditions moved to the North African realm, which remained pagan, especially to Mesopotamia, where later it flourished under Islamic rule. The Islamic culture has brought forth several important creative alchemists, such as Mohammed ibn Umail (tenth century), who became famous in later Western alchemy under the name of Senior (which is the translation of *sheikh*).

Jung has often pointed out that Islam is a religion of pure eros. Accordingly, *coniunctio* symbolism, the *hierosgamos* of the sun and moon, plays a great role in the writings of Senior. In itself, the motif of the sacred *coniunctio* also springs from the Egyptian ritual of the dead and again comes up in the Komarios text, which I mentioned before. From then on, the motif of the *hierosgamos,* the sacred marriage, remained *the* central theme of alchemy. It denotes on the one hand chemical affinity and on the other the union of psychic opposites in the process of individuation, which Jung has so deeply interpreted in "The Psychology of the Transference" and *Mysterium Coniunctionis.*

Around A.D. 1000 the knowledge of the antique natural sciences began to return from the Islamic land to Europe. This was a result of the Crusades. The Sicilian and Spanish Moors and

Jews were the main translators and intermediaries. The so-called "Liber sextus" of the great Persian philosopher, Ibn Sina, who in Latin is called Avicenna, exerted an especially great influence on some of the prominent scholastic thinkers in the twelfth and thirteenth centuries, such as Albertus Magnus, Thomas Aquinas, and Roger Bacon. This "Liber sextus" spread the essential idea that in the soul of man there is a power of imagination which can produce concrete changes in matter. When the scientist is in a state of great emotional tensions, and is also helped by the astrological constellations, then he can by his own imagination transform matter within the retort; his soul can actually change chemical matter. The introverted aspect of alchemy thus returned into Western science, its essence being a creative active imagination performed with substances. It has to be thought of as a kind of primitive experimenting with nature, on the level described in Carlos Castaneda's books, what the Indian don Juan calls "dreaming after the world has been stopped." You'll remember, if you know those books, how Castaneda has to *learn* dreaming. Don Juan's dreaming is this kind of active imagination, which you do, not as we generally do on paper with words or painting, but in nature, with things of nature. Plants and stones then begin to speak to the experimenter. It is very similarly described by Albertus Magnus and many other medieval alchemists.

This renewal of antique ideas was first neither fully accepted by the Church nor was it rejected. Some authors identified the world-soul with the Holy Ghost or assumed that it had separate existence. Sometimes the Philosopher's Stone was identified with Christ, sometimes rather with the resurrection body. And the strange thought that the alchemist manipulates God, so to speak, and tries to redeem and complete Him, was expressed but, as Jung pointed out, never became quite conscious.

If this fluctuating state of affairs had continued to exist, a great cross-fertilization of ideas between alchemy and Christian theology might have occurred, but there was one psychological trend which prevented this cross-fertilization. And this trend has become especially destructive today. Therefore, I would like to return briefly to the historical beginnings of science, which I described before, to look at this special problem.

I mentioned that some Greek philosophers, the so-called Sophists, did not reinterpret the older gods into the symbols of the new ones—the newfound principles—but declared that they had been illusions. This was the birth-moment of enlightened rationalism, which still haunts us, because it means robbing the world of its divine and psychic qualities. The basic motivation behind this way of thinking is fear. For in a world which is rationally explained, as Jung once said, one feels more at home. The second motivation is the power complex. For wanting to know everything completely and exactly is a power drive, coupled with a wish to protect oneself against everything unexpected and irrational. The antique atheistic rationalism had only a small and short success and was not able to destroy man's religious attitude. But unfortunately it remained alive within one domain, namely in the religious polemics of the Sophists, and later in the Christian Fathers' polemical attitude against all other religions. They called the latter illusions, old wives' tales, etc. According to my view, this was due to the patriarchal element in the Judeo-Christian religion, its intolerance and aggression against all other religious standpoints. Because Christianity did not contain the feminine principle, the latter also became intolerant (as Jung has described in *Answer to Job*) and made itself felt heavily in the hard, concrete, material presence of Mother Church. Because matter was no longer included in the divine symbol of totality, a compensatory materialism came into being, a vengeance, so to speak, of the rejected mother archetype. Whoever reads a book on modern theology or studies the financial activities of the Vatican knows what I mean! This materialism was even more coarse in the Middle Ages, when popes openly fought for land and money. The marital harmony between father-spirit and mother-matter thus fell apart. Spirit became a hard dogmatic intellectualism—scholastic philosophy—and matter seduced man into a concretistic, materialistic outlook. Rationalism and materialism thus belong together— and hold together again in the Marxist doctrine which has dominated a great part of our world. The cabalists would say that God has been separated from his Shekhinah.

According to their idea, this causes all evil in the world. This unfortunate development came into the full light of day in the seventeenth century, which is the time when the hypothesis of a world-soul and of nature being animated was definitely abandoned. This is why in a dream Jung had to return to the seventeenth century in order to rediscover alchemy. In that time Descartes began that "idiotic clockwork fantasy," as Jung calls it, the idea that God once and forever has created the world out of inanimate matter and that it now ticks along in a mechanically determined way. Descartes actually proved his mechanical causal outlook with a statement that "God will keep forever to his own rules which he once set." In other words, God can no longer be creative. It is interesting that this idea is still behind the determinism of the natural sciences—you all know of the famous, desperate cry of Albert Einstein, to Niels Bohr, when he was confronted for the first time with the results of quantum physics: "God does not play with dice!" Now, which god does not play with dice? Certainly a god of *law* does not play with dice. But think, for instance, of the god of whom Heraclitus said:

A boy rules the universe,
A boy who sets the stones on the chessboard,
A playing child . . .

So it is only one god-image which does not allow God to change; there are, in other civilizations, god-images which do allow God to change or to continue to be creative.

Then, when determinism got its death-blow, so to speak, certain physicists, like Wolfgang Pauli, began to believe in *symmetry*. Symmetry was then the form of God—again something very stable, something which does not change. And when Pauli heard by telephone from the States that the principle of parity was broken through in a certain weak interaction, he exclaimed, "But then God is a left-hander!" You see the shock?

In the seventeenth century theology hardened in the Counter Reformation and became even more dogmatic than before, and the rationalism of the scientists also stiffened by clinging to the prejudice that matter is ruled by mechanical laws. Where was the psyche in all this, the world-soul, what Jung calls the collective unconscious, or the objective psyche? Its existence was simply denied. What remained was only the conscious ego. Descartes identified it with his thinking function—*cogito, ergo sum*—others, like Spinoza or Hegel, with their intuition. The gods of body organs also disappeared. Instead, people quibbled about the localization of the subjective psyche, whether it was in the adrenal glands, the heart, the brain, or certain parts of the brain, etc. And when they could not find the psyche there, most scientists gave up looking for it!

The vengeance of the rejected mother archetype went even further. In all scientific matters a coarse concretism of ideas took over, which destroyed even religion. Jung has made evident that religious statements are essentially impossible from a concrete point of view, i.e., paradoxical, in that they testify to the autonomous reality of the psyche. Rationalism, therefore, destroyed one article of faith after another, first in Protestant countries, then more and more in the Catholic realm (supported by Paul VI). Today, Freud, who declared religion a neurotic illusion, seems to have won out. He is often quoted by modern theologians of both denominations. But that world-soul in which many god-powers had become one, containing star-gods, animal demons, where *was* it? People still believed in the possibility of becoming possessed by devils or animal demons. It was the time of witch-hunting. But that was only a negative reminder—that black tide of mud of occultism, against which Freud tried to warn Jung. Against the rise of rationalism, some romantic philosophers—Schubert, von Hartmann—still tried to assert the existence of a night aspect of the soul. So did the Rosicrucians and some German Pietists, but they could not prevail. It is the great achievement of Jung to have rediscovered empirically the objective psyche; through this greatest of his achievements, the germs and groping attempts of the alchemists have led to a new view of reality. As Jung often pointed out, the collective unconscious is not only an identical psychic structure in all human beings, but, as he also stressed, it is additionally an omnipresent continuum, an unextended-everywhere or unextended presence. "That is to say, when something happens here at point *A* which touches upon or affects the collective unconscious, it has happened everywhere." Hence the strange parallelism of the Chinese and European periods of style, or the unfathomable simultaneity of Christ and Krishna, or the fact that the same idea is sometimes produced by two scientists working completely independently of each other. In this view of reality, the problem of spirit-versus-matter, or psyche-versus-matter, assumes a completely new form. Spirit is seen as the dynamic aspect of the objective psyche—that which moves us, inspires us, which spontaneously produces and orders images in the inner field of vision (you could also call it the composer of dreams). The most primitive self-manifestation of this spirit, according to Jung, is natural number.

What spirit is in itself, in its trans-psychic essence, we cannot know. Matter, on the contrary, as the opposite of spirit, manifests itself in the instinctual, or even physiological, processes which touch upon our psyche; we can observe it with our senses, or with their equivalents, instruments, but we cannot define its trans-psychic essence. Thus spirit and matter are two unknown realms of existence which we call inner and outer reality. We have to make such a dualistic distinction because there are two archetypes at work—father-spirit and mother-matter. We do not know these archetypes in their essence; we can only observe their effects on our psychic system. The only immediate reality we know is psychic—psychic experience. That is something the old alchemists already suspected when they approached matter not only from without in chemical experiments, but also from within by active imagination. They knew that the psychological, emotional condition of the observer was involved in their work. As they knew very little about matter and the objective psyche, they naturally ascribed to matter all sorts of qualities which nowadays we know to be psychological projections.

The rationalism of the seventeenth century thus had one advantage after all: it drove father-spirit and mother-matter so far apart that now we can reunite them in a cleaner way. Today physicists have seen that when they penetrate into the micro-physical realm they cannot exclude the mental presuppositions of the observer from the experiment. They have to return to the attitude of the alchemists on a higher level, so to speak. The alchemist, as Jung has put it, experienced in projection, as a quality of outer matter, what really was his own unconscious:

> In an age when there was as yet no empirical psychology such a concretization was bound to be made, because everything unconscious, once it was activated, was projected into matter—that is to say, it approached people from outside. . . . But, just because of this intermingling of the physical and the psychic, it always remains an obscure point whether the ultimate transformations in the alchemical process are to be sought more in the material or more in the spiritual realm. . . . there was no "either-or" for that age, but there did exist an intermediate realm between mind and matter, i.e., a psychic realm of subtle bodies whose characteristic it is to manifest themselves in a mental as well as a material form. . . . Obviously, the existence of this intermediate realm comes to a sudden stop the moment we try to investigate matter in and for itself, apart from all projection; and it remains non-existent as long as we believe we know anything conclusive about matter or the psyche. But the moment when physics touches on the "untrodden, untreadable regions," and when psychology has at the same time to admit that there are other forms of psychic life besides the acquisitions of personal consciousness—in other words, when psychology too touches on an impenetrable darkness— then the intermediate realm of subtle bodies comes to life again, and the physical and the psychic are once more blended in an indissoluble unity. We have come very near to this turning-point today. [*Psychology and Alchemy*, pp. 277–79]

Since Jung wrote this in 1944, this turning point has manifested itself worldwide. Everywhere we find traces that point to a turning of man toward the inner reality of the psyche, toward his true and only foundation of creative fantasy—while rationalism and materialism speed to their downfall in the hands of crazy power-devils and state leaders. But the power of rationalism lives not only in such people; its demonic power still lives in us all. Wherever planning is done only rationally under the compulsion of so-called outer facts (I would rather call it compulsion neurosis!), a destructive devil is at work. Whenever we think we must alter outer nature or manipulate human beings or change them technically, we work for the destruction of our soul and our own life.

The great breakthrough, which put an end to the dualism of psyche and matter, was achieved by Jung in his work on synchronicity. It is by no means a chance event that synchronicity has to do with the problem of time, because time is, for the physicist also, an unresolved problem. Mirror-symmetry versus asymmetry, time-reversibility versus directed linear time (according to the second thermodynamic law), are still problems discussed in microphysics. It is just at this point that Jung's investigations in the realm of the objective psyche come to meet the physicists—in that marginal realm of the psychoid archetype, where activated or excited archetypes simultaneously manifest themselves in inner and outer reality, either in direct identity or in a symbolic identity of meaning. Time then appears no longer as an empty frame of reference, in which events take place, but as a *qualitatively characterized stream of events.* In his investigation of synchronistic phenomena, Jung made a further important distinction, namely between the regular eternal or timeless aspect of the principle of synchronicity (which he called acausal, or a priori, orderedness) and irregularly occurring spontaneous synchronistic events. The latter point to an active, even arbitrary, ordering of the transcendental background of existence, or to, as he puts it, a continuous creation. In another context, Jung termed this background of existence the *unus mundus,* which I think is one of the most important discoveries he made. *Unus mundus* is an expression from medieval philosophy which meant that when God created the world, He first made, like a good architect, a plan in His head—He imagined the world in a plan, and only then did He realize it concretely. So at a certain moment, the world existed—but not yet concretely. It existed only as an image in the mind of God, and it had only potential reality. That is what the medieval philosophers called the *unus mundus* and identified with Sophia, or the Wisdom of God. The *unus mundus* is, in Jung's definition, a potential matrix; it is what Jung, speaking informally, called the background of existence. According to Jung's idea, some manifested aspects of acausal orderedness could be further explored by an investigation of the natural numbers.

Spontaneous synchronistic events, however, cannot be predicted but can only be explained *after* the event; they are inevitably linked with the individual who experiences the meaning. In this connection, I would now like to return to Zosimos and his distinction between *kairikai baphai*—demonic, astrologically conditioned synchronistic events—and synchronistic transformatior.s connected with the divine spirit or the Self. I have seen that synchronistic events occur mainly in two kinds of situations. First, they happen when an individual is pressed by the unconscious toward a creative discovery or some progress in his becoming conscious. Second, synchronistic events tend to occur in the beginning of a psychotic episode. Schizoid people who are in danger of gliding into such an episode often experience a whole series of synchronistic signs—miracles, in their view, which reinforce their falling into the unconscious. These signs resemble the demonic *kairikai baphai* which Zosimos rejected. In such a case, a reflective concentration of the ego on the Self is missing. Then the shadow of the Self manifests itself as a chaotic multitude of demons, i.e., autonomous complexes. This is generally coupled with that strange concretism, so typical of schizophrenic thinking. Apparently the positive aspect of the Self in the objective psyche can only manifest when the individual ego concentrates upon the Self and tries to realize its messages creatively. If it does not do this, the same unconscious contents show their tendency toward self-manifestation in poltergeist phenomena and meaningless spooky events. The latter have no meaning, but perhaps *could* have a meaning if only the ego would look for it. The gods, as Jung writes, want to manifest themselves creatively. In my opinion, this is a problem which modern parapsychology should investigate. Today, the above-mentioned black tide of mud of occultism has come to the surface in the cult of Satan and black magic, which is countered by a rather helpless interest in exorcism. In spite of all disadvantages, this seems to me to contain a glimmer of hope. A new form of alchemy, namely, active imagination as Jung discovered it, may spring up, promising increased insight into the unitary essence of psyche and matter. Only through this can the individual be freed from all sorts of states of possession.

But there still remains the question of whether or not this can also help our general collective situation. I would therefore, in conclusion, like to repeat the story about an experience of Richard Wilhelm, which Jung told my friend Barbara Hannah to repeat in every lecture. It is the famous story of the rainmaker: In Kiaochou came a great drought so that men and animals died in the hundreds. In despair, the citizens called for an old rainmaker who lived in the mountains nearby. Richard Wilhelm saw how the rainmaker was brought into town in a sedan chair, a tiny little gray-bearded man. He asked to be left alone outside the town in a little hut, and after three days it rained, and even snowed! Richard Wilhelm succeeded in being allowed to interview the old man and asked him how he made the rain. But he answered, "I haven't made the rain, of course not." And then, after a pause, he added, "You see it was like this—throughout the drought the whole of nature and all the men and women here were deeply disturbed. They were no longer in Tao. When I arrived here I became also disturbed. It was so bad that it took me three days to bring myself again into order." And then he added, with a smile, "Then naturally it rained."

If we define the collective unconscious as Jung did, as an omnipresent continuum of an unextended presence or an unextended-everywhere, then something that happens at one point, which touches the collective unconscious, has happened everywhere simultaneously. What Jung called an omnipresence he also termed elsewhere a relativity of space-time in the deeper layers of the collective unconscious. This archetypal realm is eternal, i.e., outside time; and also everywhere, i.e., outside space. In a letter that has not come out yet in English, Jung even said:

> We might have to give up thinking in terms of space and time when we deal with the reality of archetypes. It could be that the psyche is an unextended intensity, not a body moving in time. One could assume that the psyche arises gradually from the smallest extension to an infinite intensity, and thus robs bodies of

their reality when the psychic intensity transcends the speed of light. Our brain might be the place of transformation, where the relatively infinite tensions or intensities of the psyche are tuned down to perceptible frequencies and extensions. But in itself the psyche would have no dimension in space and time at all.[1]

Jung called this idea a pure speculation. But it seems to me that it might give us a key to explain some discoveries which were made since he wrote this. With this idea we might understand the story of the rainmaker a bit better. The rainmaker was able to touch that psychic center of highest intensity in the collective psyche—the Tao—and this restoration of Tao manifested itself simultaneously everywhere. The rainmaker of Kiaochou was the only man who took his own inner psychic disorder seriously; this unintentionally saved the whole country. It seems to me one of the greatest merits of Jung, that he did not leave us an intellectually closed system or doctrine, but that he opened so many doors, through which we can perceive an enormous amount of new, creative possibilities for insight.

To clarify these creative possibilities, we would have to have a group of physicists who are willing to take on a deep Jungian analysis—not because we want to rule them or influence them—simply that they learn. And then we would have to have a few Jungian analysts who would take the trouble to study physics. I think that's what first would have to be done, so that both knew really deeply the other subject.

Then the next point, Jung thought, was to investigate synchronicity further, because synchronistic events are obviously the meeting point. In a synchronistic event something happens materially and psychically, coincides, and is united by a common meaning. It was Jung's idea that synchronistic events were always known, only they were called, in past times, signs of the gods, or in Christian times they were called miracles—or evil miracles of the devil—numinous events. Therefore there are already methods to investigate them, namely, the divination methods.

Now, in the higher civilizations, all divination methods which are a bit more advanced use the natural integers. The natural integers are not the negative/positive, complex/hypercomplex, rational/irrational numbers, but simply the natural numbers: one, two, three, four, five, six, seven, eight, nine, ten, etc. That's the natural integers. As you know, Western mathematicians are interested in the natural numbers only as a class, only interested in making logical deductions that apply to a whole class of them; they are not interested in the individual number as a qualitative number. The famous Poincaré said, "The problem is, the natural integers are all exceptions!" Especially the first ten. They are all different and therefore there are very few theorems, that is, logical generalizations, to be deduced from them. But there has always been another view of number: number symbolism. This studied the individual qualities of the numbers. But this was simply wild mythological speculation. These symbolists discarded the mathematical qualities, and the mathematicians discarded the symbolic qualities. So we have two streams of science. And there is nothing in between. The only man who seems to have seen a bit deeper is the German mathematician Hermann Weyl, who has written a very profound book on the philosophy of mathematics and natural sciences. He pointed out that the natural numbers have completely individual mathematical qualities; and that, he said, must account also for their magical importance. For the first time, he tried to unite these two streams.

Jung's idea was that one should study the individuality of these numbers—be interested in what each has that the others have not, rather than what they have in common. He made a note three inches square, on which he wrote: one, the all; two, the only even prime number; three, the first uneven prime number, the sum of one and two, the first triangular number; four, the first quadrangular number, the first square number; and so on. Then he said he couldn't do it; he felt too old. That was about two years before his death. He gave me that little paper—he said, "I give it to you." I never found out whether he thought *I* should do it, or if he thought I should keep it and hand it over if ever I should meet somebody I thought would be suitable to do such a study. After his death, I preferred to assume the latter because I felt I was much too hopeless to do anything myself. Then, as I didn't meet anybody for a long time, my conscience began to bite me, and that's why I have now written this rather unreadable book *Number and Time,* making at least a little attempt. I have tried the first four integers, as you know; I counted to four and tried to assemble the qualities of each in psychology, mythology, physics, and mathematics; and it is, to me at least, quite clear that they *really have the same function*—that if you compare the role of three in mathematics and physics, there is a similar function in psychological and symbolic manifestation. Then I discovered, to my amazement, that Chinese mathematics were completely built on this idea of the quality of numbers.

I found a wonderful story, and I forgot somehow to put it in my book—I still am angry with myself about that. It shows in a nutshell how the Chinese do not think of number as a quantity. There were once eleven generals, and they had to vote if they should attack or retreat. They voted, and eight were for attack and three were for going back. Therefore, they retreated. The three had won out because three is the number of harmony; three is a better number, qualitatively, than eight. So the people who hit the three won out. Imagine the slap in the face to our quantitative thinking! Think if the American presidential vote should be taken that way!—if you would, for instance, fix a number and say the party which gets closest to that number has won! But that's Chinese thinking. There you see another world of number. And all populations—not only the Chinese with the *I Ching*—but all populations of the world who have developed divination methods to explore synchronicity use this kind of number. That is one way Jung hinted one should study further.

I think the other way could be now the task of parapsychology. The parapsychologists could pick up the idea of synchronicity and go into it. In Germany, Bender has done that a little bit. He has taken to the idea of synchronicity and has, with a colleague, investigated the dream-series of an actress and all the synchronistic events which happened. They came to the conclusion that synchronicity really explains it better than telepathy and all the other parapsychological conceptualizations. But specific experimental setups I haven't yet found. I myself tried to make a more modest little start—to go into a modest little corner—not attack the big problem, because I did not feel up to it, but I wanted to see if I could find in mythology and fairy tales (because there I know the field), if there are not number sequences in tales, which might reveal certain structures—because Jung thought that number is the most primitive aspect of an archetype, altogether the most primitive aspect of what he called "spirit," which is the activated archetype. He said, if you strip an object of everything, its color, its size, its consistency, what remains is its how-manyness, its number. That is the most primitive thing, the primordial thing of the psyche and the mind, its most primordial manifestation, and therefore there must be a relationship between number and archetypal images. Now, there are many systems; as I mentioned, the Mayan and the Chinese and the Babylonian gods all belonged to a certain calendar number, to a certain day; that is a clear relationship between time, number, and archetypal image. But that is, to me, not sufficient. I have a feeling that one could find out more. I have made *endless* charts, and then I have been discouraged and left it. I have left it a year, and now my dreams say I should not leave it, that it's still there, that I've only attacked it from the wrong angle. So now I have to pick it up again and try from another angle. I don't know, I'm just groping . . . that's all I can say.

Another question for the science of the future is how the feminine element will manifest more in science. I have no general answer, but I can give a concrete example where I have experienced it. I have a pupil who studied agricultural engineering. He was sent to a little valley in the mountains with the task of exploring whether this valley had the right to continue to exist. See already the arrogance of the patriarchal logos at the university! One decides that this valley might not be paying financially, and therefore the people have, so to speak, no right to exist there—that's patriarchal logos. They gave my pupil such an amount of statistics—how many men, how many women, how many farms, how many average earnings, how many taxes—enormous statistics, and said he must work it out with that.

Now, he did that because he wanted his paper for the exam; he did first the statistical part. Then he quoted, from Jung's *The*

Undiscovered Self, the big attack against statistics, that they give only a mental abstract image of reality. And then he went to this valley and talked in every village to the people; especially he assembled all the young farmers and asked them if they wanted to stay, and why, and why not. He photographed them, and he asked the teachers in the school to let the children write papers about whether they wanted to stay or not, and why, and if they liked their valley. And he put all this together and made a color picture book for the second part of his paper. It came out that the people in an average—oh, I should now not talk statistics!—but in many villages, out of nineteen peasants, seventeen wanted to stay. They all had fantasies about how they could be helped. They said, if you help us with money to repair such and such a sawmill, we can subsist. So, at the end of his paper, he gave absolute, concrete, financial propositions how those people could be helped and not be displaced, and so forth. His professor was so amazed over this that he said, "Well, that is a new idea. We know that statistical procedures are nonsense, but we just had no alternative."

Well, what happened, to make a long story short, was that the government of one of our cantons, Uri, the central canton, who have always been unruly people and have the bull as their totem animal and still feel themselves to be very much the nucleus of Switzerland, suddenly picked this young man—through certain connections—and said he should do the whole land planning of Uri! Now, Bern had already spent a lot of money on that land planning because they were sure they would get it. You can imagine the political battle! The young man then did the land planning of the whole of Uri in the exact same way as he had done the valley, talked to all the people, and he made a completely different land planning, namely, we had the idea to plan not only for a boom but also for an economic depression. We made a double plan: how shall we look at it if there is a depression, how shall we look at it if there is a boom. Everything we took with a yes and a no. We tried everywhere to find the middle way and to leave leeway for free decisions, and so on. Then Bern blocked us and it looked hopeless. And at that moment, the young man, who is a Protestant, dreamt that the Black Madonna of Einsiedeln came to him and said, "I have a secret island, an eight-pointed star, covered with bushes, and in this island you can always find protection; and I will see that you get this plan through; go to Mr. B." So I said, "Well, up you go to B!"

He went to B. I had already, long before we began the whole plan, given the young man a special book by a certain man who had written beautifully about the mythology of Uri, its fairy tales and sagas. I said, if you want to do planning for that land you must first read its sagas, that's the most important thing; then you know something about the psyche of the land. So he arrived at B's. Mr. B was not home, but his wife was at home. They started a conversation, and Mrs. B was a terrific admirer of that book—they hit it off like that! Until Mr. B came, the young man sat just comfortably with Mrs. B, and everything went all right. Well, again to make a long story short, the plan went through. On the seventeenth of September the whole land voted for his plan. And Bern was left scratching its head! The Black Madonna did it!

You see, the Black Madonna is an earth mother. And it's obvious, if you plan the land, you plan, so to speak, on the belly of the earth mother. So she came and had her say. She pushed the plan through because she preferred it.

So it is in a tiny little spot in Switzerland that this miracle happened. But still that was a victory of the feminine archetype. And it was irrational; it was the exceptions of the irrational; it was the exceptions of the psyche of the people, of not only planning materialistically, but of looking at the *feelings* of the people, how they felt and what they wanted. And also not to always have this bigger, better, and so on, success outlook, this materialistic outlook; but to say, What shall we do if *bad* times come? How shall we get through if there is a depression? To be feminine is also to be closer to the earth, to be more realistic, not to fly away with plans and ideas.

So I think somehow a change of attitude along those lines is in my mind. But on the big scale I can't predict.

Note

1. Here Jung is considering the psyche as mass in motion, as he hints in cw 8, para. 441. According to the theory of relativity,

beyond the speed of light bodies would be robbed of their reality, matter would be imaginary. Imaginary matter, in turn, could be information or meaning. (See Marie-Louise von Franz, *Number and Time*, p. 210.)—Ed.

The Idea of the Macro- and Microcosmos in the Light of Jungian Psychology

The title of this paper, which seeks to combine such widely separated subjects as alchemical symbolism and modern psychology of the unconscious, might perhaps cause surprise. For the benefit of those unacquainted with the work of Jung, I would therefore like to make one point in advance, which is that modern psychology of the unconscious, as a branch of medicine, is a late descendant of that scientific spirit which, at an earlier date, manifested itself in alchemy, so that when we modern psychologists take an interest in alchemical symbolism, we are actually looking back to the historical roots of our own approach. Moreover, we largely concern ourselves with the same subject, that unknown, living factor which the alchemists thought to be the animating power in matter and which for want of a better name we now call the unconscious. In doing so we must leave the question of its relationship to matter open. Actually it is quite possible that it is a question of the self-same reality which, looked at from within and from without is described by depth psychology and by physics respectively.

In the oldest yet known alchemical texts the idea is already developed that the formation of the Philosopher's Stone represents an analogy to the creation of the world. Specific traces of an analogy between metallurgy and the creation of the world exist even as far back as Babylonian thought.[1] The minerals about to be smelted in the furnace are called Ku-bu in the Babylonian texts of the library of Assurbanipal. The translation of this word is disputed and may mean either embryo or foetus.[2] Either the ores are Ku-bu, or they were heated in the smelting furnace together with such Ku-bus. The monstrous body of the primal goddess Tiamat is also called Ku-bu after she has been killed by Marduk, when he uses it for the creation of the world. Ku-bu therefore also indicates the primal substance of the universe, so that an analogy exists between the embryonic primal substance of the world and the ore used in the earliest metallurgy.

The same analogy emerges again in the oldest specifically alchemical texts, i.e., the Greek documents of the third century A.D. and is more clearly developed there in relation to the approximately contemporaneous so-called Hermetic scriptures (third century A.D.). Thus, for instance, it is said in the *Corpus Hermeticum,* lib. 8.5,[3] that man is formed after the image of the cosmos κατ' εἰκόνα τοῦ κόσμου γενόμενος and later it is said that the cosmos is a son, and man a grandson, of God.[4] In this way they are all formed after the same likeness. In the compilation of the older Greek texts, most of which are attributed to Democritus, the following is quoted from Olympiodorus:[5]

> Hermes calls man the small cosmos (μικρὸν κόσμον) because he too is endowed with all that the cosmos possesses. The great cosmos has land and water animals. Man has fleas, lice and worms. The great cosmos has rivers, wells and oceans, so equally man has his intestines. The macrocosmos has the dwellers in the air, man has mosquitoes. The macrocosmos has breath which ascends as wind, man has the same. The macrocosmos has the sun and moon, man has his two eyes; the right eye corresponds to the sun, the left to the moon. The macrocosmos has mountains and hills, man has his bones. The macrocosmos has the heavens, man has his head. The heavens have the twelve signs of the zodiac, from the Ram as the head to the Fishes for feet. This is the cosmic image (replica = μίμημα) so often mentioned by the alchemists, of which Zosimos also speaks in his book περὶ ἀρετῆς. It is also the

basic earth of the cosmos. We must therefore mollify (λειῶσαι) and project (ἐπιβαλεῖν)—i.e., carry out the basic alchemical operation on—man himself for, says Zosimos, I have brought evidence out of the cosmic analogy that it is the egg. And in the text called "The Pyramid" Hermes uses the egg symbolically when he says that the substance of silver and chrysokolla is the egg. Earlier he also calls the egg the golden-haired cosmos, for he says that in reality the cock is "a man cursed by the sun.". . . .[6]

This absolutely fundamental text certainly requires a little elucidation. First, a simple parallel is drawn between the structure of man and that of the universe which requires no explanation. It is maintained, however, that this is the idea of the cosmos of the alchemists *and* the earth or basic substance of the cosmos itself. Accordingly, the parallel itself is not only an idea it is also a substance, indeed it is man who is the material to be worked on in the alchemical opus. But this does not appear to be the actual empirical man, the alchemist himself, for instance, but a "substance" which is somehow also man. The whole range of similes is actually used to describe this human substance, that he is a cosmic egg, the cock (in the egg) or the mole (in the earth) or the "man cursed by the sun." No doubt the alchemist in his capacity of worker would, psychologically, be the ego. The cosmos-accursed-man appears, however, to be also identical with him, but is somehow not the same thing either. It is probably a sort of Anthropos in the Gnostic meaning of the term. The text connects him with Adam, the first man, who, according to contemporary doctrine was, like the universe, created from the four elements. Therefore his name signifies virginal earth, fiery earth, carnal earth, red earth, and bloody earth. According to the above mentioned alchemist Zosimos of Panopolis there existed a Gnostic doctrine in Egypt in the third century A.D. concerning this Adam, which Jung has already published and commented on in his book *Psychology and Alchemy*,[7] so that I need only summarize it briefly here.

The first man, Thoth or Adam, is a divine man; his name is called virginal earth, carnal earth, fiery or bloody earth; and the four letters of his name are associated with the four elements and the four points of the compass. His first name means "Light."

In Paradise the so-called powers of destiny and the elements persuade him that he should incarnate in the outer, physical, mortal Adam, who is composed of the four elements. By this means he becomes Man, enslaved and suffering, but he only appears to suffer, turns back to his Father who dwells in the realm of light, drawing to himself all those enlightened men who belong to him. At the same time he throws his mortal body to the evil powers as an offering.

According to Zosimos' interpretation the alchemical work is clearly concerned with this Primal Being, who also resembles the cock (sun-bird) concealed in the egg, which must be hatched out. Therefore Zosimos even calls the work ὀρνιθογονία, the begetting of the bird. From these texts we chiefly perceive the following facts, man is an image (replica—μίμημα) of the cosmos, but this is not just an analogy, for *the parallel itself is something concrete*. It is, so to say, a substance, the earth of the Universe, which is also called the primal matter of the Cosmos. This primal matter is, as other texts declare, characterized by opposites; masculine-feminine, or it consists of chrysokolla and silver, etc. It is the Anthropos, the egg, the cock (in the egg), the mole, a "man cursed by the sun," and a carnal substance. This analogy, seen as matter, is latent as the "Divine Man" within every single human creature. We must keep sight of the problem of how a parallel, that is something which appears to us to be an abstract conception (i.e., a content of consciousness) can at the same time be something concrete, a kind of cosmic primal substance. But first I would like to discuss a few more passages from old texts.

We have already seen that an analogy can be perceived between the first man Adam, the primal substance of the world (this recalls Tiamat's body Ku-bu) and the basic material of the Lapis, which was described among other things as an egg. Therefore a text attributes the four elements to the egg.[8] "They called the egg τετράστοιχον, because it is an image of the Universe and contains the four elements in itself. They also called it the stone which the moon rolls, the stone which is no stone, the alabaster stone that is found in the brain. It is also called the living creature of the philosophers." Another text says of the stone, "They call it the ore-bearing stone, the stone in the brain, the Egyptian stone or replica of the Cosmos, μίμημα κόσμου."⁹ We hear still more concerning this same egg from Olympiodorus, namely that it is also the dragon biting its own tail, which is full of dots (stars) whose order corresponds to that of the celestial stars; it exists *before* the four elements and is the most universal, the Mediator, the Divine, the Egg, the immutable, infinite and at the same time the finite origin.¹⁰

Just as the raw material of the alchemists represents an analogy to the primal substance of Creation, so equally the alchemistic work forms a similar parallel. Thus Zosimos¹¹ says that as the demiurgic Nous (the world-soul) has separated Heaven and Earth,¹² so too in the work must body and soul be separated. The question arises here as to whether he is referring to the world-soul or the individual soul. The first view is supported by the following passage, where he says: "For those who wish to save and purify the *divine soul which is bound in the four elements*, or who seek to rescue the divine Pneuma from out of the body, a symbol of chemistry may be deduced from the Cosmogony, for then the following analogy holds good; as the sun is the heavenly blossom of fire and the right eye of the Universe, so also is the ore, when through the purification it is brought to its flowering, an earthly sun, a king upon earth, as is the sun in the heavens."¹³ This passage supports the view that the "soul" is here referred to in a cosmic sense. There are, however, also some subjective aspects, as we shall soon see.

The meaning of the analogy varies from pure parallelism to an even more precisely determined relationship between the macro- and microcosmic aspects of the Opus. A direct connection, which goes further than the conception of pure analogy, is to be found in the idea, appearing since the earliest times, that the magically correct moment, καιρός, for the chemical operation should be taken into account. This idea is already present in the previously referred to Babylonian text which says, "When you get ready to make the plan of the stove of Ku-bu, you must seek for a favorable day in a favorable month, and then you will set up the plan of the stove. . . ."¹⁴ Sacrifices, libations, and purification ceremonies are also mentioned. The "favorable day" accords with the basic tenet of nearly all magic, to take the time into account. Here, since we are dealing with Babylon, we might think more specifically of an astrological connection.

The magically propitious moment is called καιρός in Greek and plays a very important role in the work of Zosimos and other early alchemists. With Zosimos this goes so far that he speaks technically of καιρικαὶ βάφαι meaning tinctures subject to the καιρός. This text is important, for before Zosimos advances the above-quoted doctrine of the Anthropos, he speaks in the same treatise of the secret, spherical, twofold primal substance as the "round element," which in exoteric language means Ocean, origin of the gods, but whose esoteric name is not knowable.[15] This round element comprises the knowledge of the divine water. The so-called καιρικαὶ βάφαι, meaning καιρός tinctures, would, however, have made his book on the furnaces ridiculous, Zosimos continues, since certain people would have been favored by their Daimon and would have obtained καιρὸς tinctures, so that they then made fun of Zosimos. But, says Zosimos, one could not bring them to reason until their own Daimon ('ίδιος δαίμων) "transforming itself according to the Heimarmene, should bring them to misfortune." Such people are unreasoning followers of the Heimarmene (the compulsion of the stars), in contradistinction to those who, following the Divine Man, overcome this compulsion.

The text clearly shows that in this context καρικαὶ βάφαι carries the meaning of a transformation of metals engendered through a propitious astrological constellation. According to Zosimos however, such effects come about through the cooperation of the individual Daimon who is subject to the compulsion of the stars, and is therefore not to be relied upon in the end. For this reason one should raise oneself above such astrologically and demonically restricted lucky results and strive for the higher power of the gnosis of the "Divine Man."

Through this relationship to the καιρός and to the astrologically definable moment a relationship to the emotional situation of the alchemist is also indirectly implied, since through his Daimon he himself stands in relation to the astrological constellations. For which reason certain temperamentally introverted alchemists tended from the first to take the positive influencing of the individual psychic state as the starting point of the alchemical opus. For they correctly perceived that this is precisely the point of the unification of the inner and outer events in the great cosmic pattern, the place where man could most easily set to work with his influence in a direct manner. Zosimos carries this insight so far that he even rejects the astrological connection in favor of the inner gnosis, i.e., growth of consciousness, for the former brings constraint, while the latter makes freedom possible. The following text, for instance, makes this clear. Zosimos says to his spiritual friend Theosebeia:

> Do not hasten around in order to seek God, O Woman, but rather sit thyself down at home, and God the All-Seeing will come to thee, and not only a locally bound demon. When thou hast seated thyself bodily seat thyself also in regard to the emotions (πάζεσι) inordinate desire, lust, anger, grief and the twelve thousand demons of the dead. And when thou hast so attuned thyself (διευθύ-'νουσα), then call the Divine unto thyself. . . . And when thou so laborest thou wilt also achieve the real and natural καιρικαί. Do this until thou hast perfected thy soul all round. When thou perceivest, however, that it is perfected, then relinquish the natural aspect of the substance (κατάπτησον) and hasten down to the Poimandres, immerse thyself in the krater (κρατήρ), and hasten upward to thine own kind.[16]

This relates, as Jung shows in *Psychology and Alchemy*, to the doctrine of the Hermetic sect of Poimandres, according to which God dispatched a vessel filled with νοῦς (awareness, enlightenment) to earth, in order that the souls which immersed themselves therein should be enlightened. The hastening upward to one's own kind means the return once more to Paradise, to the Divine Man. This is a final stage of an inner transformation which begins with the so-called real καιρικαὶ βάφαι, i.e., material transformations, but which finally leads far beyond it. This quotation of Zosimos', which is also transmitted in other versions,[17] refers especially to the already mentioned idea that the work on one's own individual psychic condition is of essential importance to the Opus, and this throws a new light on the previously referred to quotation concerning the separation of body and soul. It shows that this separation is also to be understood as an inner psychic event, a microcosmic happening, a mystical mortification and spiritualization, the "mors voluntaria" as a much later writer calls it.[18] A similar interpretation is to be found again and again in certain alchemists.

To summarize the foregoing, we can accordingly speak of the following aspects of the micro- and macrocosmic ideas in alchemy; four analogous things are set up, God, the Universe, Man, and the Stone. The comparison is always made to the same symbolic image, which is that God created the universe and man after His own image and that man creates the Lapis after the same pattern, the God-image which he carries within himself. This parallel is, however, also a *material* reality, not a mental perception. It really exists in the form of the Anthropos-image, in the Divine Man, the egg, mole, etc. In addition to this analogy is also a relationship between the astrological constellations in the cosmos and the alchemical work on the one hand, and between the inner psychic condition and the alchemical work on the other. The latter is the place where the individual has definite freedom, and where perhaps the most intimate relationship between alchemy and the psyche of empirical man exists.

A further train of thought which seems to arise more indirectly out of the texts followed these reflections: man himself in his own body is composed of the same elements as the macrocosmos and consequently by becoming aware of his own physical being he can reach the mystery of living matter. This understanding is not, however, obtained from "without," through dissecting corpses, for instance, but through meditative introspection, through sinking down into the endosomatic psychic feelings and sensations, so to speak. As Eastern yoga arrived at an inner psychic pattern of physical processes, so also did alchemy. A fine example of this is offered, for instance, by the following text of Morienus, which probably dates from the eighth century A.D.:[19]

> This stone is that thing which is found more in thee (than in any
> other way) created by God, and thou art its "prima materia" and
> out of thee will it be drawn, and wherever thou mayest ever be, so
> will it ever remain with thee. And as man is composed of the four

elements, so also is the stone, and so it originates in man and thou
art its "prima materia" by virtue of the process, and out of thee
will it be extracted, to wit, through the separation; in thee it
abides inseparably on account of the science. Otherwise expressed the thing works secretly in thee, that is to say in the Mercurius of the philosophers. Thou art its "prima materia," in thee
it is enclosed and thou guardest it in secret and out of thee will it
be extracted, since it will be redeemed and reduced to its essence
by thee. While without thee it cannot be completed, and without
it thou canst not live, thus the end of the beginning is called to
mind, and vice versa.[20]

The old idea that the Lapis is to be found in the brain also
indicates an inner psychosomatic origin whereby the site of the
soul and of consciousness was projected into the brain as still
often happens today.

The Arab mystic and alchemist of the tenth century, Mohammed ibn Umail, known in the West as Senior, also arrived at
similar formulations. According to his statement God created
all things from water.[21] This water is the Archē of the world
(caput mundi) and of the microcosmos.[22] It is the one living thing
that does not die so long as the world lasts, and which revives all
dead things. It brings the hidden colors to light and hides away
the manifest ones. Every man needs this water, *which is within
him, and without which he cannot exist.* It is also the "red egg"
between Heaven and Earth which contains all the four elements
and by Hermes is called a microcosmos.[23]

In another part of his "Starry Earth and Silvery Water" Mohammed ibn Umail explains further that the water is that which
could transform the things from their potential into their real
state of being. Thus it is clear that his term "water" describes a
mystical, divine, world-creating principle. In man this water becomes semen and therefore the primal substance of the origin of
man.[24] The water (semen) coagulates in woman, who serves as
vessel to the masculine substance, and thus becomes a completed child which steps forth into the world. All this, Senior
proceeds, is the description of the preparation of the stone.

In such texts that unknown substance about which the alchemists concern themselves is, as it were, brought physically

closer to man, being as it were a mystery bound up in his body. When one makes an overall comparison of numerous alchemistic texts it is clear that the relation of micro- and macrocosmos occurs *especially in two phases of the work*. Firstly, right at the beginning, with the description of the raw material, I will merely call to mind the examples of the cosmic egg and the water, and secondly, in the last phases of the work, when at the end of one of the oldest texts the "Art" is compared to the rotation of the heavens.

In "Komarios and Cleopatra," a text that might date back even to the first century A.D., the soul is described calling to the body: "Wake up out of the underworld and arise from the grave, clothe thyself in spirituality and godliness, for the voice of Resurrection has reached thee, and the elixir of life is brought to thee. Spirit, soul and body will then become one, and of one unchangeable divine substance." The text then turns to the mystery of the "whirlwind," which is the body and at the same time the art, which resembles the wheel which is above it, meaning the celestial pole with its constellations. It becomes clear that this text establishes an identity with the upper heaven, and that this lower heaven is also an elixir permeating all bodies.

In other texts the substance in the retort is directly equated with the dead Osiris in his lead coffin, and the treatment of the metals is called ταρίχευσις, mummification.[25] This is of importance for our subject because *in the final stage of the work a unification of spirit and body takes place, and above and beyond this a union with the macrocosmos,* for the final product is an all-permeating breath-body-substance. All this probably goes back to the chemicomagical procedure of embalming in the Egyptian ritual of the dead, insofar as this could be interpreted as the preparation of an indestructible body and, at the same time, as the becoming one of the dead, as Osiris, with the Universal God.[26] This idea of the human being becoming one with the cosmos, mostly projected into the time after death, runs right through the whole of alchemistic tradition, and is still clearly expressed by the alchemist and pupil of Paracelsus, Gerhard Dorn, for instance. For him alchemy consists of the following basic process: extraction of the soul from the body and uniting it with the spirit (unio mentalis). This, says Dorn, is what all Christian mystics understood as the separation from the body, the *mors voluntaria* and the surrendering of the instinctual desires to the spiritual part of the soul. As the final result, however, the separated body lies there lifeless. So Dorn outlines a *unio corporalis,* which goes further than the Christian idea, in which the body is again reincluded in the inner unification. This comes about through an alchemical procedure in the retort. At the same time there results a further unification of the soul-spirit-body triad (already combined into one) with the *unus mundus,* the one world, by which Dorn meant the potential totality of the macrocosmos which existed in God's mind before the Creation.[27]

This idea also explains the previously mentioned Morienus text, according to which "Beginning and end clasp hands." At the close a return to the state of unity with the primal substance takes place on a higher, that is a more spiritually conscious, level.

If we do not wish to collect these data as historical items only, or as curiosities in the history of ideas, then naturally the question arises as to their possible validity today, and concerning the feasibility of a modern interpretation of these concepts. Here we cannot avoid referring to the parallel discoveries of the modern psychology of the unconscious and especially to those of C. G. Jung, who was himself the first to place the above-quoted alchemistic documents in the forefront of scientific discussion. He endeavored, *cum grano salis,* to do the same as the alchemists, to undertake a purely empirical introspection, as unprejudiced as possible by a religious or philosophical attitude, into the unconscious psychic processes of modern man. Condensed and reduced to the most essential, he came to the following results:

The psychic reactions in man, including his intellectual functions, are influenced and energized in the background by the so-called complexes, the emotionally toned clusters of ideas and mental images which group themselves around a central "nucleus." Certain of these complexes appear to be acquired through particular life experiences, many however seem to be structurally inborn in every human being, as is shown by the similarity of emotions and feelings, and associations of ideas which arise without any outer influence in people of the most varied times and places.

These general, one could almost say normal complexes, which function as dynamic "nuclei" in the human psyche, are called archetypes by Jung. Among other things, they engender similar or analogous symbolic images in the souls of people of the most diverse races and cultures. As, in spite of all individual differences, man everywhere has an upright posture, two eyes, a nose, and so forth, so equally he appears to possess fundamental structural elements in his psychic makeup which constitute the relative similarity of his psychic functioning. Jung calls this basic layer of the human psyche the collective unconscious. Its contents are, on the one hand, the cause of psychic symptoms of disintegration, as may be seen in schizophrenia, but on the other hand they are also the therapeutic healing factors par excellence, since they act as liberators of the instinctual reactions similarly to the "patterns of behavior" in the animal world.

During this period of his discoveries Jung left the question of the relation of these archetypes to the bodily processes open, and proceeded next to the study of the phenomenology of the psyche from the hypothesis that it is a entity existing for itself, whose nature we do not, however, understand. The fact, though, that there are psychogenic illnesses and psychogenic cures of physical pathological symptoms permits us from the start to conjecture a connection with the bodily somatic processes, about which, however, we know just as little or as much as does psychosomatic medicine as a whole; that is, we know that a connection *does* exist, but we cannot yet give an accurate causal description of its details or of the laws governing its functioning. It was almost to be expected that this psychophysical aspect of the unconscious should be discovered within the framework of scientific psychology. Nevertheless another aspect which was wholly unexpected and surprising came to Jung's notice through the treatment of the unconscious problems of his patients, namely the fact that with the intensive constellation of an archetypal complex, events were observed in the outer vicinity of the individual concerned which appeared to stand in a meaningful connection to the inner processes which were reflected in symbolic images. For such meaningful "chance" coincidences of inner and outer occurrences Jung coined the term "synchronistic" phenomena.[28] It is a question here of a combination of events through a realized similarity of meaning and not through casual conditioning. It is probable that by καιρικαί βάφαι Zosimos meant just such synchronistic occurrences.

The statement that the connection of two events is meaningful is however, an anthropomorphic interpretation.[29] But we cannot see, at least today, what precisely this meaning may be in itself. Chinese philosophy also arrived at the same conception of something rational lying hidden in the objects themselves. This also accords with the later Peripatetic doctrine of the *nous*, world consciousness, which was treated as a part of natural science. And Dorn says too: "Indeed the form, *which is the intellect of man*, is the beginning, the middle, and the end of the process, and this form will be made manifest through the yellow color, by which it is plainly indicated that man is the greater and the essential form of the whole alchemical opus."[30] This corresponds with the idea of a meaningful disposition of events in the universe, which is similar to human consciousness. When causally unconnected outer-world happenings coincide to produce patterns of events which affect man as being "meaningful," this actually presupposes that a knowledge or latent consciousness exists, not only in the collective unconscious and its archetypes, but that these can also appear outside of man. This presupposes an *a priori* psychophysical "orderedness," the archetype being the inner psychic aspect of this order.[31]

What these alchemists describe as the image of God, the egg, water, the primal Divine Man, and the beginning and end stages, corresponds exactly to the empirically demonstrable fact of the collective unconscious within ourselves, or it is still symbolized by the same images in the dreams of modern people. The unconscious does not, however, appear to consist of a chaotic accumulation of archetypal "nuclei," but it exhibits a structure which crystallizes around a center that Jung has named the Self. This central content of the collective unconscious manifests itself empirically in various God-images and symbols, such as the Oriental mandala, the *dorje*, or in the West the Philosopher's Stone. This content also shows more outstandingly than others that "meaningful disposition," that factor similar to consciousness in inorganic, material, outer-world events. The anthropomorphic meaning of outer-world happenings is, however, not only a formal factor, but also a reality which, alas, we are not yet any closer to defining, but can only describe.

By way of example I wish to give a brief psychological interpretation of the previously mentioned Morienus text, in order to point out the psychological parallels. "This stone is that thing which more than elsewhere is found in thee." The Self is in the unconscious psyche of man as the most powerful manifest operative factor. "It is created by God," the Self is an *imago Dei*. "And thou art its *prima materia*." Human individuation is the starting point of those experiences which lead to the coming to consciousness of the Self. "Out of thee will it be extracted." When we make an unconscious content conscious, we draw it up or extract it out of ourselves. "And wherever thou shalt be, so shall it remain inseparably with thee." He to whom such a content becomes conscious through experience is forever united with the impersonal center; it is a transforming event which remains unforgettably with the individual. "That is what the alchemists call the *fixatio*." Religious and traditional symbolic concepts and dogmas serve, moreover, as instruments by the use of which the content may be brought over and integrated into consciousness. "And as man is put together out of four elements, so also is the stone." The Self as well as consciousness exhibits a quaternary structure.[32] "And thou art its *prima materia*, by virtue of the process, and out of thee will it be extracted, to wit through the separation, and in thee it abides inseparably on account of the science." Here the earlier ideas are repeated and varied. As Jung says, the end of the text shows a repetition of the original condition.[33] That is exactly what happens in the psychic process of becoming conscious, in that there, too, the primal unconscious predisposition to wholeness develops into the conscious experience.

All the symbols which I have mentioned—the egg, the stone, the Divine Man, Adam, and so on—are symbols of the Self, and from these, according to Zosimos, the *correctly* understood καιρικαὶ βαφαί emanate as meaningful synchronistic events.

Should the Jungian idea of synchronicity prove to be a serviceable hypothesis for science, we would unexpectedly witness a rehabilitation of the concept of the correspondence between macro- and microcosmos in modern empirical science. Furthermore this idea appears (in modern psychology) not only as a concept but also as the manifestation of a concrete living principle which cannot be described either as dead matter, nor as "only" psychic (with the implication of not being connected with matter). It is a power which brings forth *acts of creation in time.* In this principle, still entirely unknown to us, the macro- and microcosmos actually merge into a total psychomaterial or human-cosmic unitarian reality[34] in that the remotest so-called chance events happening in the universe manifest themselves in meaningful connection with the inner psychic constellations in individual human beings.

Notes

1. Mircea Eliade, "Symbolisme et rituels metallurgiques babiloniens," in *Studien zur analytischen Psychologie C. G. Jungs* (Zurich, 1955).
2. Ibid., II, pp. 425–29. It is not clear whether the ores are so named or whether, in their capacity of having magical effects, the embryos were added to them.
3. W. Scott (ed.), *Hermetica* (Oxford, 1924–1936), I, p. 176.
4. Ibid., p. 197.
5. M. Berthelot, *Collection des anciens alchimistes grecs,* vol. 1 (Paris, 1887–1888), p. 100: "Sur l'art sacré," § 51–52.
6. In one version of the text it is not the cock but the mole.
7. C. G. Jung, *Psychology and Alchemy,* vol. 12 of *Collected Works* (cw), p. 348f.
8. Berthelot, *Collection,* vol. 1, p. 20 (I.4.I).
9. Ibid., p. 10.
10. Ibid., p. 80.
11. Ibid., p. 135.
12. Zosimos knows the Bible and refers here to Genesis.
13. Zosimos, "Book of Sophe," in Berthelot, *Collection,* vol. 1, p. 213.

14. Eliade, "Symbolisme," p. 43; the text comes from the library of Assurbanipal.
15. Berthelot, *Collection*, vol. 1, p. 228.
16. Ibid., p. 244.
17. Ibid., p. 84.
18. Gerhard Dorn, a pupil of Paracelsus; cf. page 180.
19. *Artis Auriferae, quam Chemiam vocant* (Basel, 1593), II, p. 322; cf. C. G. Jung in *Aion*, cw 9/ii, pp. 166, 168.
20. Interpreted by Jung in *Aion*, cw 9/ii, pp. 168–69.
21. Senior, "De Chemia" (ed. Stapleton), *Memoirs of the Asiatic Society of Bengal* (Calcutta, 1933), p. 174.
22. Ibid., p. 75.
23. Ibid.
24. Ibid., p. 181.
25. Cf. the error of E. v. Lippmann in J. Ruska, *Tabula Smaragdina* (Heidelberg, 1926), pp. 18–19.
26. Cf. Günther Roeder, *Urkunden zur Religion des alten Ägypten* (Jena, 1923), passim.
27. Cf. C. G. Jung, *Mysterium Coniunctionis* (Zurich, 1963), p. 533f.
28. C. G. Jung, "Synchronicity: An Acausal Connecting Principle," in *Structure and Dynamics of the Psyche*, cw 8, pp. 418ff.
29. Ibid., p. 485.
30. *Theatrum Chemicum* (1622), quoted by Jung in *Psychology and Alchemy*, cw 12, p. 248.
31. C. G. Jung and Wolfgang Pauli, *The Interpretation of Nature and the Psyche* (New York: Pantheon Books, 1955).
32. I cannot produce evidence of this here but must refer to Jung's works in general: cf. C. G. Jung "On the Nature of the Psyche," in *The Structure and Dynamics of the Psyche*, cw 8, pp. 159–234.
33. Jung, *Aion*, cw 9/ii, p. 169.
34. Erich Neumann coined this term for the Jungian *unus mundus* concept.

Some Historical Aspects of C. G. Jung's Synchronicity Hypothesis

I n 1952 C. G. Jung, together with Wolfgang Pauli, published a paper in which they proposed to introduce into the natural sciences a new basic hypothesis, which Jung called "the synchronicity principle." It is an additional concept which completes the hitherto valid three hypotheses to form a quaternio.

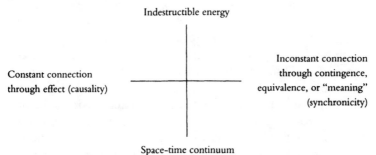

Indestructible energy

Constant connection through effect (causality)

Inconstant connection through contingence, equivalence, or "meaning" (synchronicity)

Space-time continuum

This new concept is so mind-blowing that it has mostly provoked consternation. It might therefore be helpful to cast an eye on some historical forerunners of this idea. What Jung calls contingence in this schema refers to an accidental but meaningful coming together of an outer and an inner event. He had observed that individuals chiefly experience such coincidences when an archetype is especially intensively constellated in their unconscious. In such cases, it appears as though the archetypal pattern appears not only in the individual himself but is also manifesting in his environment, even though there is no causal relationship between what is inwardly experienced and what is outwardly perceived and such a relationship is often even logically inconceivable. Therefore Jung, in his main work on synchronicity, calls synchronistic events "acts of creation in time," which implies nothing less than that creation is continually in progress in nature as a *creatio continua*.[2] These "acts of creation in time," however, are not total "leaps" of nature (as, for example, the sudden appearance on a lifeless planet of a blue dog); rather these new creations take place in each case only as a special instance within a "general acausal orderedness," that is, as a case of formal equivalence of psychic and physical processes. The recognizable form of an *a priori* psychic orderedness is the archetype.[3]

This rather abstract definition may be illustrated by an example. I once received the following communication (which I have received permission to make public) from a young Jewish doctor, an internist stationed in Hawaii. He had intended to spend a day off preparing himself for his nephew's *bar mitzvah*. Since he was completely unacquainted with the ceremony, he began to read some of the sacred texts, but he became bored and reached instead for my book *Individuation in Fairy Tales*. In this book I interpret a Spanish fairy tale in which the hero's task is to catch hold, at the right moment, of a white parrot that guards the source of life. Whoever tries to catch hold of it at the wrong moment is turned into stone, petrified. The hero succeeds in catching the bird, and the white parrot later becomes the protective spirit of the hero and his family. In Jungian terminology, it is a symbol of the center that encompasses the wholeness of the psyche that Jung calls the Self. The negative petrifying aspect of the parrot is related to the danger that threatens all religions—but especially religions of the Book—that their insights will be learned and repeated only in a parrotlike manner. In such a case, religion, instead of having a healing effect, has a petrifying one.

So the spiritual content of religion must be "grasped" in the right way for its positive impact to be reached. This interpretation directly touched the young doctor, since he had just been intending to learn the sacred Jewish texts and formulas by heart in a soulless, parrotlike manner.

At this moment he heard a cawing and chattering outside his window. He looked out, and there in a bush opposite the window sat a fat white parrot! It had a broken golden chain on its foot, having escaped from its owner. It is true that an escaped parrot can survive better in Hawaii than in Europe, but it is still far from normal to find them just flying around! It is scarcely conceivable that reading the fairy tale about the parrot had attracted it causally, and it is likewise inconceivable that the parrot had brought about the reading of the fairy tale. Thus a causal relationship is highly improbable. Therefore, we are led to understand such an event as a meaningful coincidence. That the symbol of the magical bird is a very widely appearing archetypal image is something I cannot document here; I must refer the reader to my book.[4] But that a repressed religious problem—and thus an archetype—was touched here in the young doctor is obvious. This example is very useful in explaining why Jung speaks of equivalence rather than meaning when no experiencing subject is included in an incident. If no observer were present, there would be in this story only two equivalent parrots, one inside and one outside. Meaning reveals itself only when an observer is present. It is experienced as a kind of miracle, but the scientists would mostly push it aside as a meaningless chance event.

Let us therefore turn to the historical aspect of the hypothesis of synchronicity. First we must consider the evolution of the concept of causality. The strict modern scientific concept of causality gradually evolved over the course of time from a way of looking at things in which magic, religious miracles, and scientifically provable effects were completely mixed up together. Only with the beginning of modern science were the magical and religious elements gradually eliminated as so-called superstition. Yet today fringe areas are still found in all the sciences where controversy continues over whether certain points are strictly valid scientifically or not. This is most prevalent in the many forms of paramedicine, the principles of which are viewed by some as scientifically—causally—proven and by others as purely placebo techniques. In physics, the assumption of the existence of hidden parameters or phantom particles is a similar case.

Actually we are today in the process of reclaiming from the wastebasket of history much that comes from the realms of magic and religion, having seen that, though what we have there may not be knowledge that is valid for the hard sciences, it does often contain insights that are accurate from the psychological point of view.

Let us take, for example, an ancient magical method for "repressing wrath and attaining victory and favor." This is a formula taken from Hellenistic magical papyruses found in Egypt: "Speak thus to the sun seven times. . . . Accept my greeting, thou who art set above the east and above the world, whom all gods accompany as spearbearers, in thy good hour, on thy good day, thou good daimon of the world, thou wreath of all the inhabited earth, thou who goest up out of the abyss, thou who art daily born as a youth and goest down as an old man. I ask, Lord, let me not come to harm, nor suffer from intrigues, nor receive harmful potions, nor fall into misfortune and poverty!"[5]

When we consider that, from a psychological perspective, the sun is a symbol of the consciousness principle and of the clarity of consciousness, then it no longer seems so absurd at all to invoke it in oneself to counteract chaotic affects and difficult situations in the external world.

In the same writings, we find another magical formula, a "method for bringing the beloved":

Inscribe with a bronze stylus on an unfired shard: Hecate, Hecate, three-formed one, complete are the magical signs of that [form]: thee I conjure by the great name of [magical word] and by the power of [magical word]; for I conjure thee, thee; thou who, in the form of a hawk, keepest the fire . . . that [person's name] be burned, that thou drivest her, [person's name], unto me, for I hold in my right hand the two serpents and the victory of Iaô Sabaôth, and by the great name [magical word], . . . so that she love me fervently, being burned, devoured by the fire of her love for me, yea, being tormented by it to the utmost. . . .[6]

Here too, this conjuring is not meaningless when considered from a psychological viewpoint. The magician invokes Hecate, the goddess of the underworld: that is, his own unconscious, which in a man is feminine. In addition, he invokes the fire, which is in the power of a hawk. Fire is the symbol of passion, and the hawk as a bird of prey is an image of desire. When magical actions such as these, which strongly constellate the archetype, are performed, then sometimes, *but not always,* synchronistic phenomena occur. For this reason, magic has not died out to this day!

In antiquity, astrological thought played an even more dominant role than magic. The most important alchemist of the end of the third century A.D., Zosimos of Panopolis, developed an interesting theory regarding astrology. He speaks of two types of chemical transformations, first of the so-called *kairikai baphai,* and second of "authentic transformations of metal." The first are produced by the *kairos,* that is, the god of the appropriate moment. He could be called the Greek god of the synchronicity principle. According to Zosimos, he is behind all astrological influences that bear on alchemical activity. However, Zosimos denounces this type of alchemy as misleading and deceptive and warns his student Theosebeia to turn instead to the cosmic *nous* (cosmic mind) in order to achieve the "proper" transformations.

This brings us to the necessity of dealing with a further element in the definition of synchronicity that I have hitherto passed over; it is connected with the problem of meaning. Meaning was understood by Jung not as something partial—for example, the meaning of a sentence—but rather as the meaningful coherence of being as whole. The closest thing to this is his view of the Chinese concept *Tao,* which he often explicitly refers to. This concept comes closest in the West to the *logos* fire of Heraklitos and then, later, to late antiquity's concept of *nous* as a cosmic intelligence, as it is described, for example, in the *Corpus Hermeticum.*[7]

In antiquity, this cosmic mind was understood as the "sympathy of all things." In a Hippocratic text *(De Alimento),* this meaning is described in the following terms:

[It is] a flowing together, a breathing together *[conflatio, symp-noia]*, everything sensing together. Everything with regard to the wholeness, with regard to the part, but the parts [present] in each part with intent on the effect. The great principle *[arché]* extends into the furthest part, and out of the furthest part it reaches back into the great principle: one nature, being and not-being.[8]

Views of this kind from antiquity disappeared from Europe with the rise of early Christian religion, but along with all the rest of the knowledge of ancient natural science, it was preserved in the regions of Arabic culture. There, religious Arabic mysticism added a few new elements, especially ones connected with the adept's creative and visionary use of spiritual imagination.

Henri Corbin has left us with a profound exposé of the philosophical worldview of certain Islamic mystics. According to the view of the mystic Suhrawardi (d. 1191), there exists between the visible world and the Platonic world of so-called intelligences (and souls of the divine spheres) a third intermediate world, the earth *hurqalya,* which is the world of autonomous archetypal images that the visionary perceives by means of his creative imagination.[9]

In this spiritual earth exist the original forms of that which will later become real in the visible world. This imaginary earth is not a material one, but rather a subtle *mundus archetypus.*[10] Everything that the mystic beholds there requires a symbolic interpretation. The visionary meets there psychic events that have essentially a symbolic meaning and that point to the divine secrets that lie above it.[11]

Thus between the Platonic ideas and the coarse material world lies an intermediary imaginal psychoid realm. This makes it possible for a point of view that was only implicitly present in ancient magic and alchemy now to develop a greater significance: the concept according to which the archetypal world has a relationship with the inner soul of man and can be reached and influenced through certain forms of religious yogic meditation. This is a kind of creative imagination, as described principally by the mystic Ibn 'Arabi (1165–1240).[12]

This Islamic tradition was transmitted to the West mainly by the Peripatetic, physician, and alchemist Ibn Sina (980–1037), known as Avicenna. We know that his *Liber de Anima seu Liber Sextus de Naturalibus* was translated into Latin after 1150 by Gundissalinus and had a lasting influence on Christian scholastic philosophy and theology.[13] Avicenna strongly advocated the doctrine of an *imaginatio* that had magical-creative effects. Since archetypal "forms" exist in the soul, matter can be influenced by them, and indeed not only within the body, but also—and this is the crucial point—outside the body, "as is the case with the evil eye or the imagination; indeed, if the soul resembles the principles in its constancy and sublimity, then matter in the external world obeys it and is influenced by it, and whatever is formed in the soul will be found in the matter of the external world; and this occurs because the human soul is not imprisoned in matter but rather rules it."[14]

This idea of Avicenna's had an enduring influence especially on Albertus Magnus[15] (1206–1280) and Thomas Aquinas.[16] Both of these thinkers also used it in explaining the alchemical transformation of metals. Such transformation does not take place, according to their view, in the usual causal-mechanistic way, but rather magically through the influence of the creative imagination of the alchemist. Albertus particularly stresses an important factor already mentioned by Avicenna: this material creativity of the soul is connected with its affective states. Jung cites the following passage from a text attributed to Albertus:

> I discovered an instructive account in Avicenna's *Liber Sextus Naturalium*, which says that a certain power to alter things indwells in the human soul and subordinates the other things to her, particularly when she is swept into a great excess of love or hate or the like. When therefore the soul of a man falls into a great excess of any passion, it can be proved by experiment that it binds things and alters them in the way it wants, and for a long time I did not believe it, but after I had read the nigromantic books and others of the kind on signs and magic, I found that the emotionality of the human soul is the chief cause of all these things, whether because, on account of her great emotion, she alters her bodily substance and the other things towards which she strives, or because, on account of her dignity, the other, lower things are subject to her, or because the appropriate hour or astrological situation or

another power coincides with so inordinate an emotion, and we believe that what this power does is then done by the soul. . . . Whoever would learn the secret of doing and undoing these things must know that everyone can influence everything magically if he falls into a great excess . . . and he must do it at that hour when the excess befalls him, and operate with the things which the soul prescribes. For the soul is then so desirous of the matter she would accomplish that of her own accord she seizes on the more significant and better astrological hour which also rules over the things suited to that matter. . . . Thus it is the soul who desires a thing more intensely, who makes things more effective and more like what comes forth. . . . Such is the manner of production with everything the soul intensely desires. . . .[17]

For Albertus, the "true" alchemy belongs not to the ordinary natural sciences, but to magic; its operations can only be carried out by a *magister* and are effected through the above-described psychic states, which are also connected with astrological influences. Thomas Aquinas followed his master Albertus in these views; he also says that the ordinary alchemy only appears to alter the metals, whereas the authentic alchemy is an occult art that is connected with the influence of the stars.[18]

Let us pause for a moment and look at our initial example in the light of these ancient and medieval notions. According to them, it would have been the "moving, desiring power of the soul" or of the imagination of the young doctor at a favorable astrological moment that would have made the parrot arrive. What we call synchronistic events today would have been explained in those days by a kind of psychomagical causality.

We find references to what we call synchronicity today not only in the medieval doctrine of the *imaginatio* but also in connection with a broader area of medieval theories of the soul. This is the area connected with the idea of the *nous poietikos,* an Aristotelian concept developed by the Arabs that dominated medieval scholasticism. In Islamic mysticism, the *nous poietikos* is the radiant creative energy of the divine spirit, which is comparable to light. It is, as Henri Corbin appropriately expresses it, a theophany, a mode of appearance of the divinity. This creative divine light also illuminates and inspires the mind of chosen theologians, prophets, and mystics. For Avicenna, the *intelligentia agens* is a cosmic reality.[19] Its light dwells in the planetary spheres and is ultimately the source outside the soul for all human knowledge.[20] When the human soul raises itself into ecstasy, the sacred power of this light streams into it and brings the gift of prophecy. The doctrine of the *nous poietikos* belongs to the realm of physics, because it is a divine intelligence that is located in the external world; nevertheless our soul can participate in it.

Thomas Aquinas now makes a decisive step by dividing the concept of the *nous poietikos* in two. He identifies one part with God or the *Sapientia Dei,* but the other with a natural light within the soul, a *lumen naturale* in man.[21] This contributed to the split between the profane sciences and religious belief that became manifest in the Renaissance. At that time, more and more scientists began to develop the theory of information that came from the "natural light." This led to an open conflict with traditional theological views.

Along with the *nous poietikos,* there was another "theophany" that played a crucial role in the medieval period. This was the figure of the *Sapientia Dei.* In the late writings of the Old Testament, which were influenced by Gnosticism (Proverbs 8:22ff., the proverb collection Ecclesiasticus or the Wisdom of Jesus ben Sira 24, and the apocryphal Wisdom of Solomon), the wisdom of God appears as a creative *pneuma,* feminine in nature.

This divine hypostasis "played" before God as the beloved and as the "mistress of work" as he accomplished the creation. She is a parallel figure to the Semitic goddess of love and mother goddess of the Near East. She has an Eros quality, for she is a "human-friendly" *(philanthropon)* spirit. Thus she is especially suited for reconciling the opposites contained in the Old Testament image of God.[22]

Whereas the *nous poietikos* hypostasizes the supernatural intelligence of the divine creative force, the *Sapientia Dei* represents more the *sympnoia,* the psychic total interconnectedness of the universe through a spirit of love. This feminine creative spirit of God's love, personified by Fatima, plays a major role in Islamic mysticism.[23] The poet Jalaluddin Rumi says of her: "Woman is a ray of the divine light; she is not that being that sensual desire craves as its object. She is a creator, it must be said, not a creature."

In the Christian world, she was identified with Mary. In this figure, man experienced the "sigh of God's compassion" for his creation.[24] In the eleventh and twelfth centuries, this personification gained ever greater importance in scholasticism as well. Yet even before this, a solitary thinker must be mentioned—John Scot Erigena (800–877). He describes the creation process (basing himself on Pseudo-Dionysus the Areopagite) as a transition of the excellence of God from a nothingness that lies beyond all being and nonbeing, into forms innumerable.[25] This excellence is initially a seminal force "that still is mute in the secrets of nature."[26] Then God created the world through His wisdom, "through which He knows himself."[27] It is the same as the primary causes, which are not only in God but are God Himself.[28]

The *Sapientia Dei* is a kind of primordial unity, a *single-formed* image that proliferates itself into numberless primordial forms, which at the same time nonetheless remain within the primordial unity. (Today we would call these the archetypes.) According to John Scot Erigena, these primordial forms possess their own consciousness. He calls them also *ideae* or *prototypa*.[29] Other theologians, for example, Hugh of St. Victor, call the *Sapientia* the *exemplar* of the universe or also the *archetypus mundus,* the design in the mind of God according to which He created the visible world.[30]

Since God created the world "according to measure, number, and weight" (Wisdom of Solomon 11:21), the *Sapientia Dei* was equated with a mathematical order of the creation.[31] Also for these theologians, the *Sapientia* has an Eros-like significance. This finds its clearest expression in Thomas Aquinas's theory of prophecy. In his view, there are two kinds of knowledge of truth. First, there is a speculative knowledge that consists of divine secrets being revealed to someone. The second is an "affective knowledge," which the love of God calls up in man.[32] This is a *donum sapientiae*.[33] The *Sapientia* contains higher mysteries than mere belief.[34] As a feminine figure, it has more to do with feeling, a factor that we must also take into account in connection with Jung's idea of synchronicity, because the experience of meaning is not only a result of thought but also something connected with feeling.

In addition, the *Sapientia Dei* has to do with a mathematical order of the whole of being. This order was in part arithmetically conceived, based on the image of numerical relations, or also geometrically, as an unending circle "whose center is everywhere and whose periphery is nowhere." (For the story of this famous sentence, the reader is referred to Dieter Mahnke's work, *Unendliche Sphäre und Allmittelpunkt* ("Unending Sphere and All-Pervasive Center").[35]

Before investigating the further historical development of this mathematical image of God, I would like to take up a further aspect of Jung's synchronicity principle. Here I will cite Jung at length:

> The question now arises whether our definition of synchronicity with reference to the equivalence of psychic and physical processes is capable of expansion, or rather, requires expansion. This requirement seems to force itself on us when we consider the above, wider conception of synchronicity as an "acausal orderedness." Into this category come all "acts of creation," *a priori* factors such as the properties of natural numbers, the discontinuities of modern physics, etc. Consequently we would have to include constant and experimentally reproducible phenomena within the scope of our expanded concept, though this does not seem to accord with the nature of the phenomena included in synchronicity narrowly understood. The latter are mostly individual cases which cannot be repeated experimentally. . . .
>
> [Nevertheless it seems] that even in individual cases that have no common denominator and rank as "curiosities" there are certain regularities and therefore constant factors, from which we must conclude that our narrower conception of synchronicity is probably too narrow and really needs expanding. I incline in fact to the view that synchronicity in the narrow sense is only a particular instance of general acausal orderedness—that, namely, of the equivalence of psychic and physical processes where the observer is in the fortunate position of being able to recognize the *tertium comparationis*. But as soon as he perceives the archetypal background he is tempted to trace the assimilation of mutually inde-

pendent psychic and physical processes back to a (causal) effect of
the archetype, and thus to overlook the fact that they are merely
contingent. This danger is avoided if one regards synchronicity as
a special instance of general acausal orderedness. In this way we
also avoid multiplying our principles of explanation illegitimately, for the archetype *is* the introspectively recognizable form
of *a priori* psychic orderedness. If an external synchronistic process now associates itself with it, it falls into the same basic pattern—in other words, it too is "ordered." This form of orderedness differs from that of the properties of natural numbers or the
discontinuities of physics in that the latter have existed from eternity and occur regularly, whereas the forms of psychic orderedness are *acts of creation in time*. That, incidentally, is precisely why
I have stressed the element of time as being characteristic of these
phenomena and called them *synchronistic*.[36]

Today it is not only half-life[37] that is considered as an acausal
orderedness. The astrophysicist Hubert Reeves[38] discusses the
suggestion that the Einstein-Podolsky-Rosen paradox,[39] the fossil radiation,[40] and Foucault's pendulum are also evidence of
acausal orderedness. In the area of psychology, it would be principally the natural integers that would point to it; and in the intermediate realm between the mental and material sciences,
there is my discovery that the numerical structure of the *I Ching*
agrees with that of the genetic codes.[41]

The medieval notion of *Sapientia Dei* as a preliminary mathematical design of the world in the mind of God represents a
groping attempt to understand acausal orderedness. The philosophers of that time tried to approach it by drawing mandala
models of this world order. In this, John Scot Erigena particularly had a major influence. From him, a direct lineage leads to
Ramon Lull and from him to Giordano Bruno and other Renaissance philosophers.[42] Whereas Lull tried to make a kind of computer of theological ideas out of his mandala of the divine, the
Italian philosophers stressed more the magical and Eros character of their circular divine models.[43]

Thus Marsilio Ficino says in his *Symposium*: "All the power of
magic consists of love. The working of magic is a certain attraction of one thing for another through natural similarity. All the

parts of this world, like the limbs of a living being, are dependent upon the *one* love, and are bound to one another by natural affinity . . . and that is the real magic."[44] Ficino constructed, among other things, a mandala-shaped talisman for the purpose of magically attracting this positive cosmic divine love. Giordano Bruno went the furthest in this direction. He devised numerous magical mandalas which "were meant to make an impression on the memory and transform a man into a religious personality."[45] His text *Against the Magicians* is filled with such mandalas drawn by Bruno. In other places in his work,[46] Bruno compares this love that runs like a current through everything with a lightning bolt *(fulgur)* or a light and also calls it the "world soul" or the "spirit of the universe."[47]

In Germany at this time, Agrippa von Nettesheim (who had a lasting influence on Ficino, Bruno, and Pico della Mirandola) and Paracelsus should be mentioned as also having penetrated deep into the realm of magic.[48]

In the following centuries, the tradition of devising such mathematical models of the cosmos flourished uninterruptedly. Athanasius Kircher, Fludd, and Kepler are particularly worthy of mention.[49] The last great thinker in this mold was Leibniz with his cosmic model of an acausal *harmonia praestabilita* (preestablished harmony).[50] Since Jung gives a detailed account of Leibniz, I refer the reader to his remarks.[51] It seems to have been a "meaningful coincidence" that Leibniz became acquainted with the *I Ching* through Father Bouvet just as he was working on this problem.[52] This was the starting point for the great influx of Oriental spirituality on the Western mind, the high point of which we are experiencing at present. The great contribution of Leibniz was that he once and for all cleared away the tainted—that is, magical—notion of causality.

What fundamentally distinguishes Jung's idea of synchronicity from preestablished harmony is the fact that in the Leibniz approach a constant connection is postulated, whereas according to Jung, from the empirical viewpoint, synchronistic events arise only inconstantly, sporadically, and arbitrarily, since ultimately they are dependent upon an excited archetypal situation in the observer.[53] With the loss of the idea of a continuous material connection, the magical aspect and with it the whole notion of the manipulability of phenomena is definitively laid to rest. Precisely insofar as synchronistic events are "acts of creation," they are not predictable and thus are not susceptible to scientific investigation—unless the scientific method is fundamentally changed. Jung discovered, however, that a certain predictability is possible for "acausal orderedness," which stands behind synchronistic events, through numerical divination methods. This means that the natural numbers are somehow connected with acausal orderedness. It also appears that there exists something like a time-related "play of archetypes." With a numerical divination method, such as the *I Ching,* in some way we are looking at a cosmic clock and seeing from it just how the acausal orderedness stands at a particular moment. Therefore Jung defined the natural number as "an *archetype of order* which has become conscious."[54] What acausal orderedness is in itself eludes our knowledge, but if we were to make something conscious out of it, the most primitive and archaic expression of it would be number.

Perspectives

At this point I would like to sketch quite briefly how this line of thought might be pursued further. Since Jung's death, on the whole, two steps have been undertaken. The anthropologist Dr. Hansueli Etter has, in my judgment, made a successful attempt to apply the idea of synchronicity to evolutionary theory;[55] and Michel Cazenave, in his outstanding book *La Science et l'âme du monde,* has advanced the state of the contemporary discussion of the basic principles and attempted to put across the idea that there actually is such a thing as an *anima mundi,* that is, that the Jungian "collective unconscious" not only exists in humans but represents something like a psychic aspect of the universe as a whole.[56] I myself have undertaken a third step, namely, to move in the direction of a return, already called for by Werner Heisenberg, to a certain Pythagoreanism.[57] In 1931 a revolutionary discovery was made in the realm of mathematics, of which until now too few of the consequences have been elicited. This was the rigorous proof by Kurt Gödel that the entire edifice of mathematics is built upon the given properties of natural numbers and the fact that the latter are irrational and remain so. Gödel also called for a return to Platonism, which is after all in some way Pythagoreanism.

I have tried to show that natural numbers have not only a quantitative but also a qualitative aspect, and that the latter is connected with the problem of time. According to this view, the natural number series consists not only of quantitatively lined-up units, but is at the same time also a continuum consisting always of the same primordial unit manifesting itself *in time* in a succession of qualitative changes. These qualitative numbers are counted backward. Characteristically, all numerical divination methods make use of a retrograde counting method, as is probably familiar to most of us from the *I Ching*.[58] Belatedly, I discovered that the older Chinese mathematics calculates almost entirely with "temporal numbers" and thus represents a mathematics of the synchronicity principle. My attempt to penetrate into the fundamental problems of mathematics has until now been nearly entirely ignored. However, I am convinced that the next steps of creative scientific thinking will go further in this direction—it is in this direction that the "temporal play" of the archetypes points.

What creates a great problem for the acceptance of the synchronicity hypothesis is the fact that it breaks with age-old habitual patterns of thought. It is true that the omnipotence of causality has been breached in such a way as to cast doubt on the simple-minded clockwork fantasy of a deterministic universe, but in addition the hidden omnipotence of the surviving magical thought mode is also being done away with. This amounts to a checkmate for the power drive of the scientific intellect. What the new hypothesis of Jung has to recommend it, is the fact that it introduces a creative element and a factor of meaning into the hard sciences of nature. But with this, the feelings and ethical values of the observer also must be taken into account by scientific inquiry. This aspect is something that, much to our detriment, has until now been excluded by science.

Notes

1. C. G. Jung, letter to John R. Smythies, 29 February 1952, *Letters*, vol. 2, p. 46.
2. C. G. Jung, "Synchronicity: An Acausal Connecting Principle," in *The Structure and Dynamics of the Psyche*, vol. 8 of *Collected Works* (CW), pp. 417ff.
3. Ibid., p. 516.
4. Marie-Louise von Franz, *Individuation in Fairy Tales*, rev. ed. (Boston: Shambhala Publications, 1990).
5. Karl Preisendanz, *Papyri Graecae Magicae*, vol. 2 (Stuttgart, 1974), p. 170.
6. Ibid., p. 169f.
7. Walter Scott (ed.), *Corpus Hermeticum* (Oxford, 1924–1936).
8. *De Alimento*, cited in Jung, CW 8, p. 490. The extract here is based on Jung's literal translation into German.
9. Henri Corbin, *Spiritual Body and Celestial Earth* (Princeton: Princeton University Press, 1977).
10. Ibid., pp. 118ff.
11. Ibid., pp. 128ff.
12. Cf. Henri Corbin, *L'Imagination créatrice dans le soufisme d'Ibn 'Arabi* (Paris, 1958).
13. Cf. Albert Zimmerman and Walter de Gruyter (eds.), *Albert der Grosse: Seine Zeit, sein Werk, seine Wirkung* (Berlin & New York, 1981), passim.
16. For new information, cf. Tommaso d'Aquino, Nel suo Settimo centenario, Le Fonti del Pensiero di S. Tommaso, Atti del Congresso Internazionale (Naples: Ed. Domenicane Italiane), passim.
17. Jung, CW 8, p. 448. For further material, see Marie-Louise von Franz, *Aurora Consurgens* (New York: Pantheon Books, 1966).
18. For more information, see von Franz, *Aurora Consurgens*, pp. 256, 257.
19. Cf. Etienne Gilson, "Pourquoi St. Thomas a critiqué St. Augustin," *Archives d'histoire doctrinale et littéraire du Moyen Age*, vol. 1. (1926–1927), pp. 5ff.
20. Cf. ibid., pp. 38–49, and Etienne Gilson, "Les Sources gréco-arabes de l'augustinisme avicennisant," *Archives d'histoire*, vol. 4 (1929), p. 106.

21. Cf. St. Thomas, Opus Tertium 29; Gilson, "Pourquoi St. Thomas," p. 41f; and "Les Sources gréco-arabes," p. 107.
22. For further details, see C. G. Jung, "Answer to Job," CW 11.
23. Cf. Corbin, *L'Imagination créatrice*, p. 121.
24. Ibid., p. 122.
25. John Scotus Erigena, *De Divisione Naturae*, III, 19, Migne, Patrologia Latina, vol. 122.
26. Ibid., I, 5.
27. Ibid., II, 31.
28. Ibid., III, 8.
29. Cf. W. Preger, *Geschichte der deutschen Mystik im Mittelalter*, new ed. (Aalen, 1962).
30. Explanatory note to the Gospel of John, cited by Preger, *Geschichte*, p. 328.
31. Cf. Augustine, De Genesi ad litteram, *Opera Omnia*, 1, IV, chaps. 3 and 8. For further details, cf. Marie-Louise von Franz, *Number and Time* (Evanston, Ill.: Northwestern University Press, 1974), p. 49ff.
32. Thomas Aquinas, Summa II, 171–73, De Veritate 12, 7–8; cf. Victor White, "St. Thomas' Conception of Revelation," *Dominican Studies* (St. Giles & Oxford: Blackfriar Publications), vol. 1, no. 1 (January 1948): 5.
33. Aquinas, Summa I, Quaest. 64, art. 1.
34. For further details, cf. von Franz, *Aurora Consurgens*, p. 173f.
35. Dieter Mahnke, *Unendliche Sphäre und Allmittelpunkt*, new ed. (Stuttgart & Bad Cannstatt, 1966), esp. 2, pp. 189ff.
36. Jung, CW 8, pp. 516–17.
37. That period of time after which half of the radioactive atoms originally present are spent; its half-life is a value that is characteristic of any radioactive nucleus.
38. Hubert Reeves, "Incursion dans le monde acausal," in Reeves et al., *La Synchronicité, l'âme et la science* (Paris, 1984); cf. also R. A. Wilson, "Die neue Physik und C. G. Jung," in *Sphinx* magazine (Basel), April–May 1986.
39. The Einstein-Podolsky-Rosen paradox refers to two particles behaving in corresponding ways even though there is no possibility of communication between them.
40. "Fossil radiation" refers to the cosmic background radiation that some physicists think is left over from the Big Bang.
41. Marie-Louise von Franz, *Number and Time*, p. 104f. This dis-

covery has been described in detail by Martin Schönenberger in his *Verborgener Schlüssel zum Leben* (Frankfurt, 1977).

42. Cf. Frances A. Yates, "Lull and Bruno," *Collected Essays,* vol. 1 (London, 1982).
43. Cf. Frances A. Yates, *Giordano Bruno and the Hermetic Tradition* (London, 1964).
44. Cf. ibid., p. 127.
45. Ibid., chap. 12.
46. Ibid., pp. 313ff.
47. Ibid., p. 309.
48. Cf. Yates, *Giordano Bruno.*
49. In general, see Paolo Rossi, *Clavis Universalis,* Arti Mnemonische e Logica Combinatoria da Lullo a Leibniz (Milan & Naples, 1960).
50. Cf. G. W. Leibniz, *Grundwahrheiten der Philosophie und Monadologie,* ed. J. C. Horn (Frankfurt, 1962).
51. Jung, cw 8, pp. 498ff.
52. For more details, see von Franz, *Number and Time,* pp. 99ff.
53. Cf. Jung, *Letters,* vol. 1, p. 46.
54. Jung, cw 8, p. 456.
55. In Reeves et al., *La Synchronicité, l'âme et la science.*
56. Michel Cazenave, *La Science et l'âme du monde* (Paris, 1983).
57. In von Franz, *Number and Time.*
58. Cf. Marie-Louise von Franz, *On Divination and Synchronicity* (Toronto: Inner City, 1980), passim.

Ϲⱨε SɣⲛⲥⱨⲢⲟⲛⲓⲥⲓⲧɣ
PⲢⲓⲛⲥⲓⲡⳑε ⲟⳅ C. Ꮐ. JⲩⲛꞬ

Although C. G. Jung had observed earlier through his daily work with dreams that dream motifs tend to coincide relatively often with real situations with similar meanings or even with identical real situations, he expressed himself on this subject for the first time officially in 1929 in his foreword to *The Secret of the Golden Flower*[1] by Richard Wilhelm, and in 1930 in the second edition of his commemorative speech for the anniversary of the death of Richard Wilhelm.[2] There he speaks of the Chinese scientific principle, which is based on an idea that is entirely different from our causality hypothesis, which is particularly important in connection with the *I Ching, the Book of Changes.* Time in this Far Eastern worldview is not, as with us, a linear vector and an empty framework for concrete events, but a continuum which contains basic conditions that manifest relatively simultaneously in different places in a parallelism of events that cannot be explained causally. According to Jung, the collective unconscious, as we call it, is "an omnipresent continuum, an extensive ubiquity. When something happens at point A that touches the collective unconscious or draws it into sympathy, then it has happened everywhere. . . ."[3]

Time, from this point of view, is "a stream of energy filled with qualities."[4] Jung decided to treat this subject systematically only in 1951[5] and to publish a work on it together with the physicist Wolfgang Pauli.[6]

The First Description of Synchronicity

A synchronistic event can, for example, consist either of something being foreseen in a dream, i.e., inner, psychically perceived scenes that in the external world take place somewhat later (only rarely precisely simultaneously); or of several external-world and inner-world events that are connected through their meaning or are coincident in some improbable fashion; as, for example, when through a salesgirl's error, someone receives a black dress rather than the colored one ordered, just on the day of the death of a close relative. As well as the examples that he observed himself, Jung calls our attention to the collection by Wilhelm von Scholz, *Der Zufall und das Schicksal*,[7] which presents the most amazing yet well-substantiated examples of occurrences of this nature. The experiments of J. B. Rhine, in which cards not yet dealt or the number resulting from a throw of dice has to be guessed in advance, can be regarded in this context as also showing the meaningful coming together of an inner idea and an outer happening. In the case of such inner anticipations of outer events, a causal connection becomes utterly unthinkable, since we can neither conceive that an event that has not yet happened can have an effect on our psyche, nor accept that a psychic representation could bring about an external event (for example, as though Swedenborg's vision of the Stockholm Fire could have made it happen).[8] "Since one cannot perceive something nonexistent, it must be assumed that it does exist in some form, so that it can indeed be perceived. The explanation lies in the supposition that parallel to the (future) objective event, a similar or identical subjective (i.e., psychic) configuration already exists, which, for its part, cannot be explained by any kind of anticipatory causal action."[9]

Before continuing our consideration of synchronicity, we must have a closer look at its complementary opposite, the causality principle. We know today through the results of modern nuclear physics that strict causality is only an interpretive mode of our intellect, that in nature there are only probabilities (in the sense of the probability calculus), and that therefore, logically, accidents or chance occurrences must also exist. Among these countless accidents, which we tend to characterize as "blind" chance, we are struck by those meaningful coincidences that seem to the experiencer not to be "mere chance," but rather "meaningful," "marvelous," or "as though ordained by Providence." In this category belong all "signs and wonders," all *numina* (divine signs), and all oracular occurrences, which have been observed in all times and places, in primitive as well as higher cultures. Naturally such coincidental events all have their own causal connections; only the coincidence itself is to be understood acausally.

Jung's Astrological Experiment

Jung, following the example of J. B. Rhine, now attempted to take a combination of events of this sort that seemed to lend itself to verification and to understand it in terms of statistics— namely, the coincidence of classic astrological marriage aspects (sun-moon, Mars-Venus, etc.) of married couples as compared with those of random pairs of unmarried individuals.[10] In his first attempt, he obtained an incredibly significant result. However, this result, from a statistical point of view, was itself nothing more than a very improbable chance combination, even though (by "chance"?) it was strikingly in agreement with traditional astrological expectations.[11] The result was as unexpected as if we were to take three boxes, two filled with 9,999 black ants and one white ant each, and one box filled with 2,999 black ants and one white one, and then through a small hole in each of the three boxes the three white ants were to come out first! Although the experiment had no power of statistical proof whatsoever, the result does appear to be just like a premeditated "arrangement."[12] It looked as if the synchronicity principle wanted to play havoc with statistics! Now, such a positive result seems only to turn up when the experimentor has a lively, affectively intensified interest in the experiment; through involving many test persons or through frequent repetition of the experiment, this emotional factor disappears, and the experiment then yields only correspondingly negative results.[13] But when interest, curiosity, expectation, and hopefulness are aroused, a predominance of the unconscious takes place, that is, a constellation of its archetypes.[14] Insofar as we are able to evaluate the situation today, synchronistic events always arise in connection with an activated archetype.[15]

The Archetypes of the Collective Unconscious

By "archetype," Jung understood, as we know, an inherited psychic behavior pattern that is common to the whole human species. It is not a question here of inherited ideas, but rather of the mentally expressed instincts, that is, of forms not contents.[16] The archetype is an unobservable general structure, which only in individual cases, when aroused, manifests in the inner perception of mythical images and ideas or in the expression of ritual gestures, all of which are accompanied by strong emotion.[17] Archetypes thus represent a psychic field of probability in that they delineate average instinctual unconscious activity in terms of types; the archetype is "the introspectively recognizable form of *a priori* psychic orderedness."[18] Since the archetypes are collective, it is not only in individuals that they can, in their activated state, be localized, for what appears to be going on in the collective unconscious of a single individual can never be said with certainty not to be taking place in other individuals or living beings or things or situations. For example, when the Stockholm Fire arose as an image in Swedenborg's vision, the corresponding blaze was actually raging in that city. Therefore, Jung characterized the archetype as "psychoid," because in its unobservable basic being, it cannot be differentiated from the equally unobservable objects of microphysics, and is thus no longer susceptible of being described as purely psychic.[19]

Physics and Psychology

As in the worldview of quantum physics, effects of the observer on the observed system can no longer be ignored; the result is the infiltration of a subjective psychic factor into the physical picture of the world, in the same way, complementarily, there arose also in depth psychology the view that in the description of the deepest layers of the collective unconscious, we approach something unobservable that cannot be distinguished from matter.[20] On this level, a certain latent physical energy manifests, in correspondence to which we must also ascribe a latent psyche to matter.[21] It is in this intermediary realm that parapsychological events are constellated.[22] Jung suspected that all forms of telepathy, precognition, and the like, and also psychokinesis were based on the same principle, that is, the identity of a subjective and an objective configuration that seem to fall together in time (hence the concept of synchronicity). Thus synchronicity phenomena go hand in hand with a strange relativization—indeed even an invalidation—of the usual space-time relationship and causal connection, because the latter after all presupposes the existence of space and time and is dependent on the observation of bodies in motion. Causality, or the probability concept of physics, is bound up with a way of viewing the energic aspect of nature in which kinetic energy contains measurable factors that at first seem to be incommensurable with the psychic reality. But modern depth psychology also makes use of an energy concept, which, however, rests on more archaic foundations. This concept is used to designate psychic intensity, which, though it is not measurable with instruments, can indeed be gauged by feeling.[23]

> While psychological data are essentially qualitative, they also have a sort of latent physical energy, since psychic phenomena exhibit a certain quantitative aspect. Could these quantities be measured the psyche would be bound to appear as having motion in space, something to which the energy formula would be applicable.[24] Therefore, since mass and energy are of the same nature, mass and velocity would be adequate concepts for characterizing the psyche so far as it has any observable effects in space: in other words, it must have an aspect under which it would appear as mass in motion. If one is unwilling to postulate a pre-established harmony of physical and psychic events, then they can only be in a state of interaction. But the latter hypothesis requires a psyche that touches matter at some point, and, conversely, a matter with

a latent psyche, a postulate not so very far removed from certain formulations of modern physics (Eddington, Jeans, and others). In this connection I would remind the reader of the existence of parapsychic phenomena whose reality value can only be appreciated by those who have had occasion to satisfy themselves by personal observation.

If these reflections are justified, they must have weighty consequences with regard to the nature of the psyche, since as an objective fact it would then be intimately connected not only with physiological and biological phenomena but with physical events too—and, so it would appear, most intimately of all with those that pertain to the realm of atomic physics.[25]

As physics is a mental reconstruction of material processes, perhaps a physical reconstruction of psychic processes is possible in nature itself. "It presumably happens as constantly as the psyche perceives the physical world," Jung writes.[26] In a letter to John R. Smythies, Jung goes a step further in his statements on this problem, though he explicitly emphasizes that for the moment it is a matter of speculation.[27] Jung refers prefactorily to the relativization of space and time in parapsychological events and continues:

It might be that psyche should be understood as *unextended intensity* and not as a body moving with time. One might assume the psyche gradually rising from a minute extensity to infinite intensity, transcending for instance the velocity of light and thus irrealizing the body. . . . All this is certainly highly speculative, in fact unwarrantably adventurous. But psi-phenomena are equally disconcerting and lay claim to an unusually high jump. Yet any hypothesis is warrantable inasmuch as it explains observable facts and is consistent with itself. In the light of this view the brain might be a transformer station, in which the relatively infinite tension or intensity of the psyche proper is transformed into perceptible frequencies or "extensions." . . . As in the psychic world there are no bodies moving through space, there is also no time. The archetypal world is "eternal," i.e., outside time, and it is everywhere, as there is no space under psychic, that is archetypal conditions. Where an archetype prevails, we can expect synchronistic phenomena. . . .[28]

Elsewhere Jung stresses that "in nature, there is a background of acausality, freedom, and meaningfulness, which behave in a manner complementary to constraint, mechanicalness, and meaninglessness."[29] In synchronistic events, "one and the same (transcendental) meaning might manifest itself simultaneously in the human psyche and in the arrangement of an external and independent event."[30] The meaning connected with synchronistic phenomena never evinces its dubious character of being a chance occurrence. If it did that, these events would not be what they are, that is, acausal, undetermined, and meaningful.

A More Precise Definition of Synchronicity

It can be said in summary that a synchronistic phenomenon consists of two parts: (1) An unconscious image comes directly (that is, directly corresponding to the real situation that will occur later) or in symbolic form (that is, referring to the real situation through a symbolic meaning) into consciousness, as a dream image, an idea, or a premonition. (2) With this mental representation coincides an external state of affairs equivalent in meaning.[31] Since the perception of the latter is also a psychic event, we require a more precise formulation: There is a coincidence of two psychic states: (1) The normal, causally explainable state of our perception of the outer world; (2) the state represented by a critical experience that gives the impression of an overlay or interruption of the normal state by an archetypally conditioned constellation. These two states of affairs are often not completely simultaneous (that would be "synchronous"), but rather synchronistic, in that an event that frequently becomes verifiable somewhat later is seen in the inner mental representation as already present.[32] It is also conceivable that equivalent events of this type often take place in the absence of an observer who could perceive their meaning. Jung suggests speaking in such cases of "equivalence" or "conformity." Thus, the factor of meaning is an inalienable part of the synchronicity phenomenon. What this meaning factor might consist of largely eludes our cognitive capacity.[33]

Forerunners of Jung's Synchronicity Hypothesis

The idea of a cosmic meaning has appeared in many variations in the intellectual history of mankind.[34] The idea is particularly prevalent in China in the form of the concept of the Tao, which refers to the meaningful holistic interconnectedness of all being. Chinese thought altogether is to a great extent synchronistic: Every moment was for the Chinese an accidental but meaningful configuration of things and not the result of a nexus of causal chains. Everything that happens in a given moment inevitably participates in the unique quality of this moment, including the psychological state of the observer. The causal outlook, on the other hand, tells us the story of how D arose from C and C from B and B from A and so on. With their synchronistic outlook, the Chinese asked how it comes about that A', B', C', D' all come together at a particular point in time, presuming that the situation itself presents a readable, intelligible "image." This is the basic approach not only of the Taoists, but also of all the classical Chinese sciences.[35]

In the West, among the forerunners of the idea of synchronicity is the Hippocratic "sympathy of all things," a breathing-together or flowing-together of all things, even the smallest in the cosmos. Theophrastus (371–288 B.C.) sees in this "common bond" of all things the divine principle itself. Philo of Alexandria (25 B.C.–A.D. 42) sees in this sympathy a "necessity and friendship that joins the universe together" (necessity anticipates our causality, friendship anticipates synchronicity). The monad of the alchemist Zosimos (third century) has a similar meaning of the unity of all being.

During the scholastic period, it was primarily Albertus Magnus who advocated similar ideas (inspired by the *Liber sextus* of the Persian mystic Ibn Sina). According to his view, the psyche possesses the power *(virtus)* to alter external material things when it enters into an extreme emotional state and when a favorable astrological aspect also coincides with this. This is the basis of all magic and all supernatural occurrences.

In the Renaissance, Pico della Mirandola, Marsilio Ficino,

Agrippa von Nettesheim, and others picked up the thread again, as did Johannes Kepler and Robert Fludd.

Leibniz's idea of a preestablished harmony—an acausal coordination of all things, especially of soul and body, established by God—appears against this background. Arthur Schopenhauer gives this idea, which he adopted from Leibniz, a more deterministic coloring by ascribing this coordination or synchronized interconnectedness of all events to the will of the world ground. Jung, in describing these forerunners in detail, emphasizes that his own view differs from that of Leibniz in only one point, namely, that for Jung himself, the synchronistic interconnectedness of events is not a general rule. In empirical reality, observable synchronistic events occur only sporadically and irregularly. According to Jung, synchronicity is very specifically the principle of the unique case. However, as he suggests, all reality may consist of such.[36] In contrast to this, our statistical methods create only an abstract mental schema of reality in our imagination. If, for example, we determine statistically that the stones in a pile weigh one kilogram on the average, it may be that we would be able to draw no stones or hardly any stones of just this weight from the pile. Actual reality consists in fact of a sum of completely individual exceptions.

The "Absolute Knowledge" in the Collective Unconscious

Agrippa von Nettesheim, Leibniz, and others postulated that in that world ground which causes the integral order of all things, a kind of foreknowledge of all events is also present.[37] Jung, through the inspiration especially of the work of Driesch,[38] comes to the same conclusion. "Whether we like it or not, we find ourselves in this embarrassing position as soon as we begin seriously to reflect on the teleological processes in biology or to investigate the compensatory function of the unconscious, not to speak of trying to explain the phenomenon of synchronicity. Final causes, twist them as we will, postulate a *foreknowledge of some kind.*"[39]

This is certainly not knowledge that is in any way connected with the ego; thus it is not conscious knowledge as we know it, but an unconscious knowledge subsisting or present on its own, which I would like to call absolute knowledge. "It is not cognition," Jung writes, "but, as Leibniz so excellently calls it, a 'perceiving' which consists—or to be more cautious, seems to consist—of images, of subjectless "simulacra.' "[40] The realm of these structures is (according to Jung) the collective unconscious. This "absolute knowledge" in the collective unconscious, which characterizes synchronistic phenomena, reinforces postulation of a kind of self-subsisting meaning, that is, meaning subsisting in nature,[41] but it is not identical with it.[42] As concerns this "absolute knowledge"—that is, this knowledge or ability to know that is not dependent on sense perceptions and the cerebral processing of them—medical and zoological research have brought a few surprises to light. Jung himself mentioned the observations of Jantz and Beringer, made in cases of profound syncope following acute brain injury.[43] It was shown that an injured subject could make clear observations of the phenomenal world with closed eyes and had intense psychic experiences. Jung adduced the similar case of one of his own female patients, who, uninjured but in a deep faint, nevertheless was able to develop clear perceptions of the phenomenal world. Such experiences, as he stressed, seem to indicate "that in swoon states, where by all human standards there is every guarantee that conscious activity and sense perception are suspended, consciousness, reproducible ideas, acts of judgment, and perceptions can still continue to exist."[44] The feeling of being suspended in the air that often accompanies this is an indication of a shift in the localization of consciousness in the sense of a separation from the cerebral cortex or cerebrum. It is possible that in such cases the sympathetic system begins to function as a surrogate nervous substrate. It has indeed been proven that insects, which have only a ganglionic nervous system, exhibit indubitable "intelligent" behavior (Jung alludes to Karl von Frisch's research on bees). However, even in this area, the question of the interaction between psyche and soma remains, and Jung's general idea was that the relationship between the two is one that can be represented statistically. Only in cases of ESP (extrasensory perception), which cancel out time, space, and causality, can we speak with certainty of a synchronistic relationship. The mind-body relationship remains opaque in many respects.[45] Outside of this area, we can, however, say with a fair degree of certainty that synchronistic events are rare and sporadic. In counterdistinction to the idea of preestablished harmony, we are as much impressed by the disharmony of things as we are surprised by their occasional harmony.[46]

Synchronistic phenomena can be produced experimentally with relative regularity in the intuitive, "magical" procedures, where, though they are subjectively convincing, they can hardly, or only with great difficulty, be verified objectively and cannot be evaluated statistically. (Jung mentioned this also in other contexts and claimed that the probability calculus would have to be reexamined first.)

In addition, the synchronicity hypothesis could perhaps be considered as an explanatory principle for certain aspects of biological morphogenesis.[47] This idea was particularly taken up by Wolfgang Pauli, who urged biologists to investigate it.

Acausal Orderedness

Another phenomenon that fits together with the idea of synchronicity, and which (like absolute knowledge), in contrast to "meaning," is empirically determinable, but which could be an indication of the existence of that transcendental meaning, is the phenomenon of half-life in the decay of radium and other like phenomena. Sir James Jeans writes about this in *Physics and Philosophy:* "Radioactive break-up appeared to be an effect without a cause, and suggested that the ultimate laws of nature were not even causal."[48] Jung chose for this and, as we shall see later, other similar (including psychic) phenomena the term *acausal orderedness*. This is not the same as "meaning": "Even an organic being is, in spite of the meaningful design implicit within it, not necessarily meaningful in the total nexus. . . . Without the reflecting consciousness of man the world is a gigantic meaningless machine, for in our experience, man is the only creature who is capable of ascertaining any meaning at all."[49] Acausal orderedness, in counterdistinction to meaning, is concerned with a class of empirically determinable general facts. On the one hand, discontinuities in physics, for example, the orderedness of energy quanta, provide evidence for such an orderedness in the realm of physics. The simplest example in the psychic realm is provided by the "just-so" properties of the natural integers. They too are a causeless orderedness, a psychic one. For example, it is absolutely evident that six is the sum of its divisors, even though this cannot be logically deduced from antecedent principles. In counterdistinction to the synchronistic events we have been describing up till now, such examples of acausal orderedness are of an entirely constant, general nature. Thus Jung comes in the end to the following conclusions:

> The question now arises whether our definition of synchronicity with reference to the equivalence of psychic and physical processes is capable of expansion, or rather, requires expansion. This requirement seems to force itself on us when we consider the above, wider conception of synchronicity as an "acausal orderedness." Into this category come all "acts of creation," *a priori* factors such as the properties of natural numbers, the discontinuities of modern physics, etc. Consequently, we would have to include constant and experimentally reproducible phenomena within the scope of our expanded concept, though this does not seem to accord with the nature of the phenomena included in synchronicity narrowly understood. . . . I incline in fact to the view that synchronicity in the narrow sense is only a particular instance of general acausal orderedness—that, namely, of the equivalence of psychic and physical processes where the observer is in the fortunate position of being able to recognize the *tertium comparationis*. . . . This form of orderedness differs from that of the properties of natural numbers or the discontinuities of physics in that the latter have existed from eternity and occur regularly, whereas the forms of psychic orderedness are *acts of creation in time*. . . .[50] We must regard them as *creative acts*, as continuous creation of a pattern that exists from all eternity, repeats itself sporadically, and is not derivable from any known antecedents. . . . [From this point of view] we must take the contingent partly as a universal factor existing from all eternity, and partly as the sum of countless individual acts of creation occurring in time.[51]

The Significance of Natural Numbers

As shown by Rhine's experiments and Jung's own astrological experiment, the natural integers seem to have a quite special connection with the synchronicity principle. This is why the Western as well as the Eastern arts of divination are especially inclined to use number combinations in order to "read" a situation holistically and intuitively. The affinity of numbers with the occurrence of synchronistic events induced Paul Kammerer[52] to compile an entire collection of incidents in which integers coincidentally crop up together aperiodically—as when, for example, on the same day a person's streetcar ticket has the same number as his theater ticket and in a phone call he is given the same number. Kammerer explained such phenomena through attraction, imitation, or "lawful seriality." This, Jung critically notes, amounts to a pseudocausal, not statistically provable, explanation.[53]

Arthur Koestler[54] also refers to Kammerer, but without responding to Jung's critique. The relationship of numbers to the synchronicity principle must, according to Jung, be sought in another fashion, namely, through an investigation of mantic procedures that are based on numbers and counting. Among these procedures, famous today is the *I Ching,* the Chinese *Book of Changes,* whose divinatory messages are derived from the combination of the first odd number (1 = yang) and the first even number (2 = yin). Leibniz, the Western discoverer of binary arithmetic, alludes to this. Jung asserts:

> The sequence of natural numbers turns out to be unexpectedly more than a mere stringing together of identical units: it contains the whole of mathematics and everything yet to be discovered in this field. Number, therefore, is in one sense an unpredictable entity, [and it is certainly not a matter of chance that counting is the most widespread method for dealing with chance]. . . . [Thus] I cannot refrain from pointing out that not only were they [number and synchronicity] always brought into connection with one another, but that both possess numinosity and mystery as their common characteristics. . . . Number helps more than anything else to bring order into the chaos of appearances. It is the predestined instrument for creating order, or for apprehending an al-

ready existing, but still unknown, regular arrangement or "orderedness." It may well be the most primitive element of order in the human mind, seeing that the numbers 1 to 4 occur with the greatest frequency and have the widest incidence. In other words, primitive patters of order are mostly triads or tetrads. That numbers have an archetypal foundation is not, by the way, a conjecture of mine, but of certain mathematicians. . . . Hence it is not such an audacious conclusion after all if we define number psychologically as an *archetype of order* which has become conscious.[55]

The numbers are probably the most primordial archetypes that there are; they represent the actual matrix of the archetypes.[56] A compilation of their "biological" properties would be the best way to gain a better understanding of these basic essential principles of physics and the objective psyche.[57]

Number, as it were, lies behind the psychic realm as a dynamic ordering principle, the primal element of that which Jung called spirit.[58] As an archetype, number becomes not only a psychic factor, but more generally, a world-structuring factor. In other words, numbers point to a background of reality in which psyche and matter are no longer distinguishable. Jung was particularly impressed, for example, by the fact that the Fibonacci number series corresponded to laws for the growth of plants, as well as by what Eugene Wigner called "the unreasonable effectiveness of mathematics in the natural sciences."[59] This seemed to him emphatically to suggest that one and the same ordering principle underlies both living matter and the human psyche—"ergo a property of matter (or of 'energy' . . .) in general and consequently also of moving bodies in general, the psychic 'movement' included."[60] Nonetheless this principle does not seem to turn up with any regularity; rather, synchronicity points to an indeterminable "clearly arbitrary ordering principle." In relation to the primary coincidence of psychic and physical events, these irregular synchronicity phenomena are something secondary. That being the case, the numbers appear to constitute the actual bridge between regular acausal orderedness and irregular synchronicity phenomena.[61]

Unus Mundus and Creatio Continua

The cosmic background which is neither matter nor psyche is what Jung called the *unus mundus*. This term is derived from scholastic philosophy, where it refers to the potential archetypal world plan existing in the mind of God before he began the creation. In the *unus mundus,* all opposites are still unified, even those of one and many or mind and matter. In scholasticism the *unus mundus* was especially associated with the numbers. Jung asserts that even though synchronicity is, practically speaking, a rare phenomenon, it nevertheless implies a general factor "or principle in the universe, i.e., in the Unus Mundus, where there is no incommensurability between so-called matter and so-called psyche. . . . In this connection," he continues, "I always come upon the enigma of the *natural number.* I have a distinct feeling that Number is a key to the mystery, since it is just as much discovered as it is invented. It is quantity as well as meaning."[62] The *unus mundus* is like a primordial background that sporadically manifests in synchronistic phenomena as a *creatio continua*, "as the continuous creation of a pattern that exists from all eternity, repeats itself sporadically, and is not derivable from any known antecedents. We must of course guard against thinking of every event whose cause is unknown as "causeless." This . . . is admissible only when a cause is not even thinkable."[63] This is especially the case when space and time lose their meaning or appear relativized, in which case a causal connection also becomes unthinkable. Another danger of misinterpreting the synchronicity principle is regressing to a magical-causal approach, which is characteristic of all primitive cultures and from which we have been freed by our precise scientific thinking only through the greatest effort. It would be such a regression, for example, to regard an archetype as the cause of synchronistic events.[64]

Koestler accuses Jung of doing this, although Jung explicitly rejects this approach. In concluding his work on synchronicity, Jung in collaboration with Pauli proposed the following quaternity of hypotheses as a more completely satisfactory explanation of nature than previously existing ones.[65]

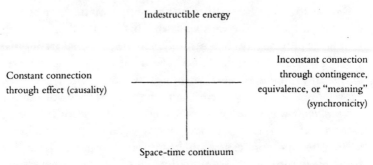

Indestructible energy

Constant connection
through effect (causality)

Inconstant connection
through contingence,
equivalence, or "meaning"
(synchronicity)

Space-time continuum

Through such a model, microphysics, depth psychology, and parapsychology can be brought closer together, meeting in the view of the archetypes as psychophysical nature constants and creative world-structuring factors. The relative multitude of these archetypes seems at the most profound level to be resolved into a unity in the *unus mundus*.[66]

This last situation is suggested by the mandala structures of the collective unconscious.[67] According to Jung, the mandala is the psychic equivalent and synchronistic phenomena are the parapsychological equivalent of the *unus mundus*.

Undoubtedly the idea of the *unus mundus* is founded on the assumption that the multiplicity of the empirical world rests on an underlying unity, and that not two or more fundamentally different worlds exist side by side or are mingled with one another. Rather, everything divided and different belongs to one and the same world, which is not the world of sense but a postulate whose probability is vouched for by the fact that until now no one has been able to discover a world in which the known laws of nature are invalid. . . .

. . . Microphysics is feeling its way into the unknown side of matter, just as complex psychology is pushing forward into the unknown side of the psyche. Both lines of investigation have yielded findings which can be conceived only by means of antinomies, and both have developed concepts which display remarkable analogies.[68]

Should these trends become stronger in the future, the hypothesis of the unity of the object of both fields of research would gain in probability. Of course, there is little or no hope that the unified cosmic background could ever be demonstrable, "but today we know this much beyond all doubt—that empirical appearance rests on a transcendental background." The latter is "as much physical as psychic and therefore neither, but rather a third thing, a neutral nature which can at most be grasped in hints since in essence it is transcendental."[69]

Other Authors, Schools, and Critics

Pauli, who published his work on Kepler along with Jung's essay, examines Jung's synchronicity principle sympathetically, not in the work on Kepler but in a later essay, "Naturwissenchaftliche und erkenntistheoretische Aspekte der Ideen vom Unbewussten" (Scientific and Epistemological Aspects of Ideas of the Unconscious).[70] He emphasized its possible significance for the concept of biological evolution. He also accepts the archetypal significance of numbers, stressing that other mathematical "primal intuitions," such as those of the continuum and of the infinity of the number series, might be archetypal. Another physicist who particularly espoused the idea of synchronicity is J. T. Fraser, the editor of *The Voices of Time*.[71] Also in his later comprehensive work *Time, Passion, and Knowledge*, Fraser considers Jung's idea of synchronicity several times in a sympathetic fashion.[72]

Various of Jung's students have presented synchronicity, such as Aniela Jaffé in her book *Themen bei C. G. Jung* (Themes of C. G. Jung) as well as in *The Myth of Meaning in the Work of C. G. Jung*.[73] Also important is Jaffé's essay "C. G. Jung und die Parapsychologie" (C. G. Jung and Parapsychology).[74] A good presentation of Jung's views is given in two essays by Michael Fordham.[75] Jung's student C. A. Meier, who often deals with the theme of synchronicity, advocates a point of view that diverges from that of Jung in one essential point, where he comes closer to Leibniz's approach: namely, he postulates that there is a regular relationship of synchronicity in the mind-body relationship.[76] The "place" where the two come together is a kind of "subtle body." He suggests that along with a special synchronicity theory, a more general synchronicity theory has also to be developed. Jung responds to this suggestion that for the moment it is only a speculation, but affirms that in case it should be confirmed, the view of synchronicity as a relatively rare phenomenon would have to be corrected.[77] He did not, however, believe that Meier's view would prove true; he conceived of the relationship of psyche and soma primarily as an *interactio,* and as a relationship of synchronicity only by way of exception.

M. Rhally, a student of C. A. Meier, has written on precognition in the synchronistic sense.[78] C. T. Frey-Wehrlin reports on the case of a precognitive dream.[79] The independent psychiatrist L. C. Kling has given an account of archetypal symbolism and synchronicity in world events.[80]

A critical treatment is afforded by K. Friedrichs,[81] who wants to replace the word *synchronicity* with *coincidence,* because he does not see the relationship with time that Jung stresses. He also accuses Jung of not making sufficient use of the idea of a psychoid integral order of nature (which is in fact contradicted by his own presentation). In the second part of his article, Friedrichs speaks primarily of the problem of morphogenesis and a possible role of synchronicity in evolution. This had already been suggested by Pauli. In the same journal with Friedrichs's article, a critical treatment of Jung's synchronicity hypothesis by Peter Urban also appears.[82] Urban understands Jung's hypothesis much better than Friedrichs but correctly points out that many individual questions remain to be resolved that will require collaboration in many disciplines. He asserts, in presumed counterdistinction to Jung, that synchronicity, causality, and finality could coexist as hypotheses, which is something Jung would doubtless not have contested. Urban further opines that Jung insufficiently emphasized that synchronicity is a generic principle. He also accepts E. Ringger's "magical causality," which Jung rejected. Finally, Urban proposes establishing a time-emotion relationship. One feels that all three critics—Meier, Urban, and Friedrichs— are disturbed by the spontaneity and irregularity of synchronistic phenomena and that they would prefer to return to something like the Leibnizian notion of preestablished harmony. Jung's reservations in this regard have already been mentioned.

As I see it, we already have in "acausal orderedness" and the *unus mundus* concept what these critics are looking for, for it remains precisely the specific quality of synchronicity that it occurs only sporadically and arbitrarily.

As Urban comes more from the philosophical side, so does the comprehensive work of Ernst Anrich, *Physik und Tiefenpsychologie* (Physics and Depth Psychology).[83] Anrich gives a detailed exposition of the meeting points between the two fields and complements this with a valuable presentation on the possible quantitative and qualitative aspects of numbers as they appear in physics. Though he presents synchronicity, he does so without drawing further conclusions from it or acknowledging the key position that, in my opinion, it occupies. Mary Gammon has done a valuable study in which she connects the idea of synchronicity with Einstein's relativity theory.[84]

Jung characterized synchronistic events as parapsychological phenomena. In accordance with this, it is primarily parapsychologists who have taken a closer interest in his ideas. Hans Bender has examined them more closely as a possible explanation for certain telepathic phenomena. Together with J. Mischo, he investigated a dream series of an actress comprised of more than a thousand dreams in regard to meaningful coincidences with real situations and came to the following conclusion: "The coincidences between dreams and real situations seem to belong to the operative type 'attraction of related phenomena.' Many, it seems, can be better grasped through the model of synchronicity (the extraordinary quality is in the event itself) than through the model of psi-abilities, in which the future event is regarded only as the object of an extrasensory perception. The two views are not mutually exclusive, but can complement each other."[85]

In the current attempts at reconciliation between physicists and parapsychologists, Jung is mentioned from time to time, as for example, at the "Quantum Physics and Parapsychology" congress in Geneva in 1974. There he was mentioned by C. T. K. Chari and N. Whiteman, as well as by Arthur Koestler. Also, in *Psychic Exploration,* a book edited by Edgar Mitchell,

Jung is alluded to in various connections; however, the idea of synchronicity does not come under discussion.[86]

Despite his attacks on Jung, which are based on misunderstandings, Koestler's book *The Roots of Coincidence* has actually contributed to the diffusion of the synchronicity hypothesis.[87] Although Jung himself explicitly rejected this, Koestler accuses him of construing the archetype as a cause for synchronistic happenings. Koestler then presents his own position of a "Janus-faced holon,"[88] which as Nathan Schwartz-Salant rightly noted, is nothing more than a copy of Jung's idea of the archetype.[89] In his essay "Physik und Synchronizität" (Physics and Synchronicity), on the other hand, Koestler gives a more accurate presentation of Jung's view.[90] He also advocated the synchronicity hypothesis at the "Quantum Physics and Parapsychology" congress mentioned above.

Friedberg Karger mentions Jung's work in his essay "Paraphysik und Physik" (Paraphysics and Physics);[91] however, he finds that the synchronicity hypothesis has no relevance for the physicist, since it cannot be evaluated statistically. Sven Krohn,[92] on the other hand, is open to it, and W. von Lucadou and K. Kornwachs[93] have even devised a mathematical model into which Jung's model, according to them, could fit. As mentioned, Jung stressed the affinity of the archetypal natural numbers with the synchronicity principle. In my book *Number and Time*,[94] and in my article "Time and Synchronicity in Analytical Psychology" (see page 293), I have attempted to look into the mathematical foundations of the problem; that is, I have attempted to substantiate the relationship of numbers to the unconscious of the mathematician by using their own testimony, and also to elaborate the qualitative aspect of the representation of number. For example, in ancient China, number was something purely qualitative and inalienably bound up with time. It denoted *ensembles* colored by a moment in time; that is, it was a symbol for rhythmic-temporal configurations. In this connection, I discovered that the number system of the *I Ching* exactly coincides with that of the DNA and RNA codes. What biochemistry discovered in the West as "information carriers" has long been known among the Chinese as a numeric order basic to psychophysical situations. The rest of *Number and Time* is concerned with differentiating the role of number in the probability calculus from its contrasting role in divination and game techniques, where numbers appear as indicators of archetypal psychic probabilities or qualitative "expectation catalogs," that is, means of relating with acausal orderedness. Finally, I attempt to amplify the *unus mundus* concept through the use of mythological material.

Peter Urban reacted positively to this book.[95] He only raises the doubt that in one of my examples we have a case of a submental thought process rather than a creative insight. He also repeats his view that the points of view of causality and finality should be applied in a unified manner.

He accepts the *unus mundus* model.

My work was also positively received by physicist Edward Russel. He amplifies my idea of a "one-continuum" that moves through the entire number series with the notion of a "general wave equation" that could solve any problem of physics that can be construed as a harmonic "oscillator." This is one of the most fundamental structures of modern physics. The Sinologist Manfred Porkert has called attention to the significance of Jung's synchronicity hypothesis for an understanding of Chinese scientific thought.[96] The Chinese image of *ch'i*, which refers to both psychic and physical energy as one, becomes in this perspective an energy concept that we in the West are now beginning to approach again on what is in some ways a more sophisticated level.

Notes

1. Richard Wilhelm, *The Secret of the Golden Flower* (1931), with foreword and commentary by C. G. Jung, trans. Cary F. Baynes, rev. ed. (San Diego: Harcourt Brace Jovanovich, 1962).
2. See C. G. Jung, "Richard Wilhelm: In Memoriam," in *The Spirit in Man, Art, and Literature,* vol. 15 of *Collected Works* (cw).
3. C. G. Jung, letter to Oeri, 4 January 1929, *Letters,* vol. 1 (Princeton: Princeton University Press, 1976), p. 58.

4. C. G. Jung, letter to Dr. B. Baur, 29 January 1934, *Letters,* vol. 1 (Princeton: Princeton University Press, 1973), p. 139.
5. However, Jung's historical presentation of the Christ symbol in *Aion* and "Answer to Job" already anticipates the idea of synchronicity; these works were written in the same year as the work on synchronicity.
6. C. G. Jung and Wolfgang Pauli, *The Interpretation of Nature and the Psyche* (New York: Pantheon Books, Bollingen Series LI, 1955).
7. Wilhelm von Scholz, *Der Zufall und das Schicksal* (Berlin: Deutsche Buchgemeinschaft, 1924).
8. In dice experiments, telekinesis might perhaps be considered if it had an energic action, as has yet to be proven.
9. Jung, letter to J. B. Rhine, 9 August 1954, *Letters,* vol. 2, p. 181.
10. Cf. also Jung's important letter to Hans Bender, 6 March 1958, concerning the Rhine experiments, *Letters,* vol. 2, pp. 420–21.
11. Cf. Jung, "Synchronicity: An Acausal Connecting Principle," in *The Structure and Dynamics of the Psyche,* cw 8, p. 480.
12. Ibid., p. 453.
13. Ibid., pp. 477ff.
14. Jung, letter to Stephen I. Abrams, 5 March 1959, *Letters,* vol. 2, p. 490.
15. Jung, cw 8, p. 494; also *Letters,* vol. 2, pp. 373ff., 398ff., 498.
16. Jung, letter to Valentine Brooke, 16 November 1959, *Letters,* vol. 2, p. 521; letter to Elisabeth Herbrich, 30 May 1960, *Letters,* vol. 2, p. 559.
17. Jung, letter to Stephen I. Abrams, 5 March 1959, *Letters,* vol. 2, p. 490.
18. Jung, cw 8, p. 516.
19. Jung, "On the Nature of the Psyche," cw 8, p. 225.
20. For more about the relationship between microphysics and the psychology of the collective unconscious, see cw 8, pp. 208ff.
21. Ibid., pp. 229ff.
22. Cf. also Jung, letter to J. B. Rhine, 25 September 1953, *Letters,* vol. 2, p. 126f., and letter to Stephen I. Abrams, 21 October 1957, *Letters,* vol. 2, pp. 398ff.; see also vol. 1, p. 420f.
23. Cf. Jung, cw 8, p. 228.
24. Cf. Jung's view on materializations in his letter to Laurence J.

Bendit, 12 November 1945, *Letters,* vol. 1, pp. 389ff. In it Jung considers possible the extension of the psychic reality into matter and calls upon scientists to create a new science of parapsychology for such problems. Cf. also Jung's letter to Gebhard Frei, 17 January 1949, *Letters,* vol. 1, p. 522.

25. Jung, cw 8, p. 234.
26. C. G. Jung, "Analytical Psychology and Education: Three Lectures," in *The Development of Personality,* cw 17.
27. Jung, letter to John R. Smythies, 29 February 1952, *Letters,* vol. 2, p. 45f.
28. Ibid.
29. Jung, "Ein Astrologisches Experiment," *Zeitschrift für Parapsychologie und Grenzgebiete der Psychologie* (1957), p. 87.
30. Jung, cw 8, p. 482.
31. Ibid., pp. 426ff.
32. Ibid., p. 423.
33. Ibid., pp. 478, 460.
34. Cf. ibid., pp. 461ff., 485.
35. Cf. Jung's introduction to Richard Wilhelm, *The I Ching or Book of Changes,* trans. Cary F. Baynes, which is not identical with the introduction translated in the German edition of the *Collected Works.* Cf. also Jung's letter to Pascual Jordan, 10 November 1934, *Letters,* vol. 1, p. 176f.
36. Cf. Jung, cw 8, pp. 474–75; also letter to N., 25 October 1935, *Letters,* vol. 1, pp. 200–201, and letter to Hans Bender, 12 February 1958, *Letters,* vol. 2, pp. 414ff.
37. Cf. Jung, cw 8, p. 500.
38. H. Driesch, *Die Seele als elementarer Naturfaktor* (Leipzig, 1903).
39. Jung, cw 8, p. 493.
40. Ibid.
41. Ibid., p. 502.
42. Jung, letter to S. Wieser, 7 June 1951, *Letters,* vol. 2, p. 18f.
43. C. G. Jung, "Das Syndrom des Schwebeerlebnisses unmittelbar nach Kopfverletzungen," *Der Nervenarzt* 17 (1944): 181–210.
44. Jung, cw 8, p. 509; cf. also letter to Mrs. Eckstein, *Letters,* vol. 1, p. 76.
45. Cf. Jung, "The Soul and Death," cw 8, p. 409.
46. Jung, "Synchronicity," cw 8, pp. 510–511.
47. Ibid., pp. 511–512.

48. James Jeans, *Physics and Philosophy* (Cambridge, 1942), p. 215. Cited in Jung, CW 8, p. 513.
49. Jung, letter to Erich Neumann, 10 March 1959, *Letters*, vol. 2, p. 494.
50. Because time plays an essential role, Jung chose the term *synchronistic*. Cf. also letter to André Barbault, 26 May 1954, *Letters*, vol. 2, p. 176.
51. Jung, CW 8, pp. 516ff.
52. Paul Kammerer, *Das Gesetz der Serie* (Stuttgart & Berlin, 1919).
53. Jung, CW 8, p. 565f.
54. Arthur Koestler, *The Roots of Coincidence* (London: Hutchinson, 1972).
55. Jung, CW 8, p. 456.
56. Jung, letter to Patrick Evans, 1 September 1956, *Letters*, vol. 2, p. 327.
57. Jung, letter to Fritz Lerch, 10 September 1956, *Letters*, vol. 2, p. 54f.
58. Cf. the proceedings of a discussion in connection with W. Nowacki's lecture "Die Idee einer Struktur der Wirklichkeit" (The idea of a structure of reality), 7 December 1957, C. G. Jung Institute, Zurich. Cited with permission of F. Riklin.
59. E. Wigner, *Symmetries and Reflections* (Bloomington: Indiana University Press, 1967).
60. Jung, letter to E. L. Grant Watson, 9 February 1956, *Letters*, vol. 2, p. 288.
61. Ibid., p. 288f.; also letter to Stephen I. Abrams, 21 October 1957, *Letters*, vol. 2, p. 400.
62. Ibid., vol. 2, p. 398f.
63. Jung, CW 8, p. 518. This is clearest in the case of precognition. Of course, the synchronicity principle might also be considered as an explanation in cases where causality is thinkable, but then it cannot be proven with certainty.
64. Jung, CW 8, p. 494.
65. Ibid., pp. 492ff.; Jung, letter to N., 7 September 1935, *Letters*, vol. 1, pp. 197–98.
66. Jung, letter to R. F. C. Hull, 27 December 1958, *Letters*, vol. 2, pp. 469ff.
67. Jung, letter to Karl Schmid, 11 June 1958, *Letters*, vol. 2, pp. 445ff.
68. Jung, *Mysterium Coniunctionis*, CW 14, p. 537.

69. Ibid.
70. See the article by Wolfgang Pauli in *Aufsätze und Vorträge über Physik und Erkenntnistheorie* (Braunschweig, 1961), pp. 113–29.
71. J. T. Fraser (ed.), *The Voices of Time: A Comparative Survey of Man's Views of Time as Experienced by the Sciences and by the Humanities* (New York: Braziller, 1966; 2nd ed., Amherst: University of Massachusetts Press, 1981).
72. J. T. Fraser, *Time, Passion, and Knowledge* (New York: Braziller, 1975).
73. Aniela Jaffé, *Themen bei C. G. Jung* (Zurich: Daimon Verlag, 1985); Aniela Jaffé, *The Myth of Meaning in the Work of C. G. Jung* (Zurich: Daimon Verlag, 1984).
74. Aniela Jaffé, "C. G. Jung und die Parapsychologie," *Zeitschrift für Parapsychologie und Grenzgebiete der Psychologie* 4 (1960): 8–23.
75. Michael Fordham, *New Developments in Analytical Psychology* (London, 1957); and Michael Fordham, *The Objective Psyche* (London, 1958).
76. C. A. Meier, *Zeitgemässe Probleme der Traumforschung*, Kultur- und Staatswissenschaftliche Schriften 75, Zurich School of Technology (ETH), 1950.
77. See Jung, cw 8, para. 938, n. 70.
78. M. Rhally, "Varieties of Paranormal Cognition," in *Spectrum Psychologiae: Festschrift zum 60. Geburtstag von C. A. Meier* (Zurich, 1965), pp. 253–66.
79. C. T. Frey-Wehrlin, "Ein prophetischer Traum," ibid.
80. L. C. Kling, "Archetypische Symbolik und Synchronizitäten im Weltgeschehen," *Verborgene Welt* 6 (1955): 273ff.
81. K. Friedrichs, Über Koinzidenz und Synchronizität," *Grenzgebiete der Wissenschaft* 16 (1967).
82. Peter Urban, Philosophische Aspekte der Synchronizitätstheorie," *Grenzgebiete der Wissenschaft* 17 (1968).
83. Ernst Anrich, *Moderne Physik und Tiefenpsychologie* (Stuttgart, 1963).
84. M. R. Gammon, "Window into Eternity: Archetype and Relativity," *Journal of Analytical Psychology* 18 (1973): 11–24.
85. H. Bender and J. Mischo, "Präkognition in Traumserien," *Zeitschrift für Parapsychologie und Grenzgebiete der Psychologie* 4 (1960–1961): 114–200; H. Bender, "Von sinnvollen Zufällen," *Zeitschrift für Parapsychologie und Grenzgebiete der Psy-*

chologie 15 (1973): 203–12; H. Bender, *Verborgene Wirklichkeit* (Freiburg: Olten, 1973).

86. Edgar Mitchell (ed.), *Psychic Exploration* (New York: Putnam, 1974).

87. Arthur Koestler, *The Roots of Coincidence* (London: Hutchinson, 1972).

88. Ibid., pp. 112ff.

89. Nathan Schwartz-Salant, "A Psychologist's View," *Quadrant* 8 (1975): 65–69.

90. Arthur Koestler, "Physik und Synchronizität, *Zeitschrift für Parapsychologie und Grenzgebiete der Psychologie* 15 (1973): 1–14.

91. Friedberg Karger, "Paraphysik und Physik," ibid., pp. 148–58.

92. Sven Krohn, "Einige philosophische und theoretische Implikationen der Parapsychologie," *Grenzgebiete der Wissenschaft* 16 (1967): 19–26.

93. W. von Lucadou and K. Kornwachs, "Grundzüge einer Theorie paranormaler Phänomene," *Zeitschrift für Parapsychologie und Grenzgebiete der Psychologie* 17 (1975): 73–87.

94. Marie-Louise von Franz, *Number and Time* (Evanston, Ill.: Northwestern University Press, 1974).

95. Peter Urban, "Philosophische Aspekte der Synchronizitätstheorie, *Grenzgebiete der Wisenschaft* 17 (1968): 347–57.

96. Manfred Porkert, "Wissenschaftliches Denken im alten China," *Antaios* 2, no. 6 (1961): 532–51.

A Contribution to the
Discussion of C. G. Jung's
Synchronicity Hypothesis

S
ince the publication of my article "The Synchronicity
Principle of C. G. Jung" (see page 203), the discussion on
synchronicity has developed further, with both rejection
and acceptance becoming ever more widespread.[1]

For Western thought since Descartes, "scientific explanation"
has amounted to causal validation: *D* is caused by *C*, *C* by *B*, *B*
by *A*. Even our language is structured so that we have to use
seemingly roundabout expressions if we wish to elucidate an
acausal nexus of meaning. No wonder, then, that discussion of
Jung's hypothesis of a synchronicity principle has produced numerous misunderstandings.[2] This has not been the case with
East Asians, a number of whom have assured me that they
thought synchronistically naturally, and tended to have more
intellectual difficulties with our strict concept of causality.

Although Jung made the only explicit foray into the realm of
parapsychology of his career with his proposal of a synchronicity principle, it is precisely a number of parapsychologists
who appear to be having difficulties with this new way of thinking. In my opinion, this arises from the fact that many parapsychologists are currently making an intensive effort to achieve
acceptability for their field by founding it on a "hard" scientific
method, that is, on quantitative methods and causal thinking,

whereas just what Jung's hypothesis proposes is an about-face away from what until now has been considered the only "scientific" way of thinking. Interestingly enough, nowadays physicists are the ones who are showing understanding of the Jungian hypothesis, because in their field causal thinking has run into its limits.[3]

The psychiatrist and psychoanalyst Jule Eisenbud has asserted that synchronicity is nothing else than what has hitherto been referred to as "psi."[4] To this it must be added that the synchronicity hypothesis does not *causally* "explain" psi-phenomena, but as compared with results obtained hitherto by research, it places them in a new, broader context, that is, in the realm of archetypes, a field in which detailed biological and psychological studies have already been made. These studies, however, unfortunately seem to be largely unknown to parapsychologists. There is a kind of "explanation" here that is definitely not causal but is rather, as Hans Bender tells us, "descriptive."[5] With regard to this, only new studies can help, studies that investigate individual cases in depth and breadth; whereas quantitative interpretations, no matter how many cases they account for, if they do not investigate their psychological background, can basically have little of new substance to teach us.

Another tendency to reject the synchronicity hypothesis is found among many who attempt to *postulate* a psychological or neurological causal explanation without producing any proof for it based on facts. Barbara Honegger,[6] for example, makes the supposition that synchronistic events arise from the same source as dreams, namely, a neurological substrate in the brain (the inferior parietal lobule [IPL]). It might be noted in this regard that the brain-dependency of certain psychic abilities of an individual (sleeping, waking up, etc.) has not been proven at all;[7] thus the localizations mentioned are extremely questionable. Moreover, precisely with synchronistic events, a causal relationship of this type seems completely absurd. If I foresee in a dream in Zurich the crash in Holland of a particular airplane identified as, let us say, XA_3-137, and the next day in Holland a plane with just this identification really is smashed to bits,[8] it would be rather absurd to suppose that my "neurological substrate" had arranged this crash (which according to the newspaper was caused by the weather).

Jule Eisenbud[9] falls into a similar trap when he tries to rescue causality by supposing that synchronistic events are "brought about" by the latent psi-powers of the observer.[10] This completely contradicts the rest of our experience of the collective unconscious. According to the Jungian view, the collective unconscious is not at all an expression of personal wishes and goals, but is a neutral entity, psychic in nature, that exists in an absolutely transpersonal way. Ascribing the arrangement of synchronistic events to the observer's unconscious would thus be nothing other than a regression to primitive-magical thinking, in accordance with which it was earlier supposed that, for example, an eclipse could be "caused" by the malevolence of a sorcerer. Jung even explicitly warned against taking the archetypes (or the collective unconscious) or psi-powers to be the *causal agency* of synchronistic events.

The philosopher Stephen E. Braude judges the synchronicity hypothesis particularly harshly.[11] One of his primary objections is that a "meaning" for a synchronistic event presupposes an observer. But this is a more than self-evident triviality: everything, including space, time, and causal connection, does not exist or exists only hypothetically if not perceived by an observer. Our consciousness is the "actualizer" of all existence—a truth that today every physicist will confirm. In this regard it is true that a synchronistic phenomenon and its meaning are not different from any other object of scientific investigation. But from this Braude jumps to the conclusion that synchronistic events and their meaning are produced by the observer! This would be like saying that before we were aware of black holes in space, they absolutely did not exist, but that now our psyche has produced these holes! This is a Hinduistic way of thinking that Jung did not agree with. He "believed" in an existence independent of our consciousness, which, however (as Kant proved), we will never be able to know "in itself," that is, independently of our structure of consciousness. Thus our consciousness does have cosmogonic significance, but that goes for *everything* existing, and not just the meaning of synchronistic events.

Braude's second major objection is also of a general meta-physical nature.[12] In agreement with John Beloff, he asserts that the mentioned connection of meaning in synchronistic events would only make sense in a cosmology in which nature was a kind of artifact or artwork or arranged drama;[13] and that, more-over, it would then also once again constitute a causal explanation *(prima causa)*. But this, Braude says, would be "crude anthropomorphic theology."[14] But this is what Braude himself projects on the argument. What lies behind synchronistic events is not a Judeo-Christian *Deus faber (prima causa)*, but an *acausal orderedness* (a concept in Jung's essay on synchronicity that Braude overlooks altogether) and a knowledge that Jung calls "absolute knowledge." And this seems to be a kind of cosmic background, which is something also posited by many physicists today, which has very little to do with a theological "God." One *can* also postulate a *Deus faber* behind these events, but that would go beyond all possibility of proof.

The Chinese see a primal ground underlying synchronistic phenomena—the Tao. The Indians see nature not as an artifact but as an emanative form of appearance of the divine (Brahma).

Thus Jung confined himself out of prudence to speaking of a transcendent cosmic background *(unus mundus)* so as not to prejudice further research into the synchronicity principle.

A further question of Braude's, which can be taken more seriously, is the problem of how we can correctly "read" the meaning of synchronistic events objectively, i.e., context-independently, rather than just reading something into them subjectively. I have gone into this problem in detail in my essay "Meaning and Order" (see page 267).

Jung himself affirmed that we can of course read meaning into an event where it does not exist at all.[15] What Jung proposes as the counterweight to such subjective fantasizing is a technique of "disciplined imagination" or "necessary statements," which he has discovered in connection with mythological, that is, archetypal images and situations. Just as I cannot say with regard to the natural number four that it is an odd number, in the same way I also cannot say, for example, about an (archetypal) king figure in myths and fairy tales that he represents the instinctual

man, but must conclude that he represents "the exemplary individual who guarantees a (mostly religio-) social collective-
conscious order." This latter notion can be documented by numerous cases; the former idea cannot. Thus in regard to archetypal phenomena there is a "logic" of assertion, which Jung calls
"necessary statements."[16] Since synchronistic events tend to occur when an archetype is constellated, the same "mythological
logic" must be applied to the reading of their meaning as to all
other archetypal phenomena. It is comprehensible that Braude
would not know this; in the same way, the objections of many
parapsychologists arise from their having read nothing else of
Jung's besides his essay on synchronicity. But this is a late work
of Jung's, which presupposes all his earlier research. Hans
Bender is one of the few to have grasped this side of the problem
correctly.[17] Nonetheless, Charles T. Tart has also at least partially taken in Jung's new paradigm. Also Wilhelm Gauger and
Alan Vaughan seem to grasp the synchronicity hypothesis accurately.[18] Tart attempts in his essay[19] to elaborate certain distinctions: (1) physical causality; (2) psychological causality
(both of these are well known); (3) state-specific causality, i.e.,
a causal connection that is only recognizable in certain states of
mind; (4) paranormal causality, i.e., correlation through still
unclarified psi-powers; (5) being-specific synchronistic causality, i.e., causal relations that, because of our being structured in
a human way, remain definitively unknowable; (6) absolute synchronicity, i.e., definable but perhaps not empirically useful.
Here it is necessary to warn, as certain physicists also do, not to
play with "hidden parameters," which are "not yet recognized." From the psychological point of view, they are no more
than a projection of the unconscious, and it would be simpler
and cleaner just to say: these are things that we *do not know about.*
But Tart is surely right that many *apparent* coincidences could
prove later to be causally conditioned. That is why Jung proposed using the expression "synchronicity" provisionally only in
those cases where a causal connection is *unthinkable,* which of
course presupposes a clarification of the concept of causality.
Many researchers accuse Jung of presenting a naive idea of causality, because he rejected a *temporally retroactive* causality such as

found in the Aristotelian idea of a *causa finalis* (Beloff). (Here we should also mention Rupert Sheldrake's principle of formative causation through a "morphogenetic field.")[20] Jung never advocated (though Braude tries to foist it off on him) the notion refuted by Hume that there is a kind of material "glue" between cause and effect, and Braude neglects to mention that present-day philosophers are in complete disagreement about the definition of causality. Jung just presumed the same thing that nearly all physicists do today: that causality implies a provable interaction within the space-time continuum. All other formulations represent for Jung an overstretching of the concept of causality that amounts to a *contradictio in adjecto*.

A balanced view of the situation, in my opinion, is offered by John Beloff in his article "Psi-phenomena: Causal versus Acausal Interpretation."[21] Only he cannot accept Arthur Koestler's declaration that psi-phenomena will forever remain unpredictable and unrepeatable.[22] He believes that psi-phenomena and other phenomena related to individual persons have a causal basis, even if for the moment this cannot yet be described as interactive. Thus perhaps a final cause might be considered. Jung rejected the Aristotelian concept of a final cause, because it represents an inner contradiction, that is, an overstretching, of the causality concept.[23] But in other respects Beloff is right, in my opinion, to assert that person-related paranormal phenomena *could* have an indirect cause, just as, according to Jung, a synchronistic explanation can only be considered seriously in cases where a causal explanation seems absurd. If an interaction between concrete factors is not provable, then indeed contemporary physicists also generally speak of an acausal connection. The astrophysicist Hubert Reeves, in his very precise essay "Incursion dans le monde a-causal,"[24] points to four newly discovered states of affairs that are currently considered acausal and that correspond to Jung's notion of *acausal orderedness*. (As we know, acausal orderedness is the more general category under which synchronistic events are subsumed as special cases.) The newly discovered acausal phenomena mentioned by Reeves, along with (1) the law of half-lives in radioactive decay (already mentioned by Jung), are (2) the unpredictability of the behavior of an individual atom in quantum mechanics; (3) the "fossil glow" in the cosmic background; (4) the pendulum of Foucault, which seems to be regulated in accordance with the entire mass of the universe rather than just that of our planet; and (5) the Einstein-Podolsky-Rosen (EPR) paradox, which prohibits localizing a property of an atom and therefore seems to suggest a kind of unity and inseparability of all particles in the universe.[25] For all these phenomena, any causal explanation falls short,[26] and therefore we are better able to speak of an acausal orderedness encompassing the whole of existence.

The EPR paradox may also provide confirmation for another concept of Jung's, the hypothesis of an absolute knowledge that seems to be diffused throughout the totality of existence[27] and "lights up" at particular points in the objective meaning of synchronistic events. At the Conference of Cordova in 1979, where the discussion was devoted to the relationship of Mind and Matter,[28] various speakers referred to such an absolute knowledge using expressions such as *protoconscience* (protoconsciousness),[29] *conscience de l'univers* (consciousness of the universe),[30] *sous-conscient universel* (universal subconscious), "information of a cosmic infrapsychism" (Costa de Beauregard), *inconscient universel* (universal unconscious), *inconscient createur* (creative unconscious), and so on.

Here we begin to see certain convergences of the various fields of science, all of which seem to suggest the existence of some such meaningfulness—*resembling but not the same as our ego-consciousness*—in the cosmic background. Psychologists of the Jungian school have long been familiar with this idea, since it comes into play in every treatment of any depth; indeed the actual process of healing consists for the most part in developing a proper orientation toward this *luminositas* of one's own psychic background.[31] That an omniscience of this kind, resembling consciousness, could exist in nature is sometimes hinted at in dreams by the motif of many luminosities in the sky or water and so on, as Jung showed in his essay and as I have also reported.[32] Jung conjectured that this was a "subjectless knowledge composed of images"—similar to the knowledge of the monads described by Leibniz.[33] It is *preconceptual* and is more like a "knowledge cloud" than any precise knowledge of the kind produced by our consciousness. In another connection, Jung also referred to this knowledge of the collective unconscious or psychophysical cosmic background as a *"luminosity,"*[34] that is, a "diffuse consciousness," which, however, is not or hardly at all connected with the ego-consciousness. In our everyday experience, this presents itself in such a way that our unconscious seems "somehow" to know everything, but also somehow not to know anything precisely. Making partial aspects of this omniscience conscious by means of dream interpretation or deciphering the meaning of synchronistic events is the daily task of psychotherapists.[35] Thus for them it is a gratifying experience to learn that present-day physicists have encountered a parallel phenomenon in their field.

Another area where the synchronicity hypothesis is under discussion is that of contemporary evolutionary theory. Hitherto it was presumed that the gene mutations underlying evolution were based on *pure accident* (J.-L. Monod), but Wolfgang Pauli has already shown that the time period of biological evolution has been *too short* for this. In his valuable work, the anthropologist Dr. Hansueli Etter has taken up this problem and, through the example of the human scapula, in my opinion has shown convincingly that "accumulations of meaningful coincidences," that is, synchronistic events, should be considered as a far more likely explanation for the leaplike mutation phenomena in evolution that are frequently bunched together in short periods of time.[36] Michel Cazenave promises to present further amplifications from the field of biology.[37] Sheldrake's new paradigm, mentioned above, of the "morphogenetic field" should also be mentioned here, even though this "field" is similar to what Jung understood by an archetype. Unfortunately, once again, Sheldrake makes out of this the *cause* of biological events.

In this connection, we must once more call attention to Jung's careful formulations:

> I incline in fact to the view that synchronicity in the narrow sense is only a particular instance of general acausal orderedness—that, namely, of the equivalence of psychic and physical processes where the observer is in the fortunate position of being able to

recognize the *tertium comparationis*. But as soon as he perceives the archetypal background he is tempted to trace the assimilation of mutually independent psychic and physical processes back to a (causal) effect of the archetype, and thus to overlook the fact that they are merely contingent. This danger is avoided if one regards synchronicity *as a special instance of general acausal orderedness*. In this way we also avoid multiplying our principles of explanation illegitimately, *for the archetype is the introspectively recognizable form of a priori psychic orderedness*. If an external synchronistic process now associates itself with it, it falls into the same basic pattern. . . .

[But if causeless events do exist,] then we must regard them as *creative acts*, as the continuous creation of a pattern that exists from all eternity, repeats itself sporadically, and is not derivable from any known antecedents.[38]

An archetypal arrangement "appears" or becomes "visible" in a synchronistic event; it does not cause it. It is a *creatio,* and that means the spontaneous arising of something entirely new *ex nihilo* that is not causally predetermined.

But then must we really, as Koestler thinks, renounce experimental study of such *creationes,* because of their irregularity and unrepeatability? Jung's "astrological experiment" has shown that statistical methods are hardly applicable, because the synchronicity principle can "play tricks on them" in the sense that in small samples positive or negative results can appear synchronistically, whereas very large samples seem to efface synchronistic irregularities. Since synchronistic events seem to be irregular, they cannot be grasped statistically; nevertheless acausal orderedness can be investigated experimentally, because it is something general and regular. At the end of his life, Jung worked out a proposal for further work in this direction. In order to understand this, however, we must take a closer look at another remark made by Jung in a letter to Pauli. There he writes:[39]

With regard to Jordan's[40] reference to parapsychological phenomena, clairvoyance in space is of course one of the most obvious phenomena that demonstrate the relative nonexistence of our empirical space picture. In order to supplement this argument, he would also have to adduce clairvoyance in time, which would demonstrate the relativity of our time picture. Jordan naturally sees these phenomena from the standpoint of a physicist, whereas I start from that of the psychologist, namely, from the fact of the collective unconscious, . . . which represents a layer of the psyche in which individual differences of consciousness are more or less obliterated. . . . [*Thus*] *all perception in the unconscious takes place as though in a single person.*[41] Jordan says that senders and receivers in the same conscious space simultaneously observe the same object. One could invert this proposition and say that in unconscious "space" senders and receivers are the same perceiving subject. . . . Jordan's view, carried to its logical conclusion, would lead to the assumption of an absolutely unconscious space in which an infinity of observers observe the same object. The psychological version would be: *in the unconscious there is only one observer who observes an infinity of objects.*[42]

If we consider the last sentence empirically, it would mean that if an individual encounters something archetypal (that is, an aspect of the collective unconscious), *one* observer in the collective unconscious would have to have one "knowledge" or one "apprehension" concerning this event. Now, traditionally, divination methods (especially numerical ones) are a means of finding out, through synchronistic coincidences (with dice, casting lots, distribution of plant stalks, reading grains), what the unconscious (the *one* observer) "thinks" about such an event.[43] Therefore, Jung suggested investigating cases where it could be supposed that the archetypal layer of the unconscious is constellated—following a serious accident, for instance, or in the midst of a conflict or divorce situation—by having people engage in a divinatory procedure: throwing the *I Ching,* laying the Tarot cards, consulting the Mexican divination calendar, having a transit horoscope or a geomantic reading done. If Jung's hypothesis is accurate, the results of all these procedures should converge. However, unfortunately, up till now no results of any such experiment have been published.[44] An institute under the leadership of a professional in Jungian psychology should, in my opinion, undertake this matter.[45] Naturally it would be necessary to substantiate why, of all things, numerically articulated divinatory systems should constitute the appropriate vehicle for this attempt. I have tried to do this in my book *On Divination and Synchronicity: The Psychology of Meaningful Chance*. Here I must refer the reader to this book, since such an exposition would far exceed the scope of this essay. The book is concerned with reflections on the foundations of mathematics—an area in which a number of researchers are currently at work.[46] (The concept of time would also require its own treatment.)[47] The synchronicity principle, as Beloff and Braude have accurately observed, is a principle of a higher order that calls into question the entire deterministic worldview of science up till now. However, as I have tried to indicate, this calling-into-question is taking place today in a number of other scientific fields as well—in mathematics, physics, biology, and astrophysics. The latest astrophysical discoveries seem to show that even the "big bang" is a dubious hypothesis.

To a certain extent, Jung's proposal is extremely audacious. However, it seems to me worthwhile for a number of parapsychologists to devote themselves to researching it *sine ira et studio,* because in this idea, a new view of things has made its appearance, one toward which today more than a few physicists and biologists are converging, groping their way forward along different paths. Therefore, it would be good if parapsychologists would not feel it necessary to take a rigid view of it as part of a vain attempt to make their still-unexplained psi-phenomena fit into a fundamentally already outdated scientific worldview.

Notes

1. I would like to extend warm thanks to Dr. Eberhard Bauer, editor of *Zeitschrift für Parapsychologie und Grenzgebiete der Psychologie,* who provided me with photocopies of many of the critiques and commentaries of parapsychologists mentioned in the text.
2. Here I am presuming the reader's acquaintance with Jung's essay "Synchronicity: An Acausal Connecting Principle," in *The Structure and Dynamics of the Psyche,* vol. 8 of *Collected Works* (cw), pp. 417–519.
3. See, e.g., David Bohm, "Discussion," in Michel Cazenave (ed.), *Science et conscience* (Paris: Editions Stock, 1980), p. 268;

and esp. Olivier Costa de Beauregard, *La Physique moderne et les pouvoirs de l'esprit* (Paris: Le Hameau, 1981).

4. Jule Eisenbud, cited in Alan Vaughan, "Synchronicity, Causality, and Consciousness as Creator," in W. G. Roll (ed.), *Research in Parapsychology 1979* (Metuchen, N.J., and London: Scarecrow, 1980), p. 21.

5. Hans Bender, "Transcultural Uniformity of Poltergeist Patterns as Suggestive of an 'Archetypal Arrangement,' " in Roll (ed.), *Research in Parapsychology 1979*. Cf. C. G. Jung's remarks in an interview, "On the Future of Parapsychology: A Symposium," in *International Journal of Psychology* 4, no. 2 (1962): 5–16 (the full text is available only in mimeograph). Stephen E. Braude, in *ESP and Psychokinesis: A Philosophical Examination* (Philadelphia: Temple University Press, 1979), p. 241, declares in brief, on the other hand, that any explanation *must* (!) be a causal explanation, which is purely prejudice. This is all the more bizarre since *explanare* means "broaden," "even out," and not causally "prove."

6. Barbara Honegger, "Spontaneous Waking-State Psi as Interhemispheric Verbal Communication: Is There Another System?" in Roll (ed.), *Research in Parapsychology 1979*, pp. 19–21.

7. Cf. Sir John Eccles, *The Human Psyche* (Berlin, Heidelberg & New York: Springer, 1980), esp. pp. 47f., 49, 53, 97f., 240; and Karl Pribram, "Esprit, cerveau et conscience," in Cazenave (ed.), *Science et conscience*, pp. 393–408 and esp. 171 (discussion); cf. also Willis Harman, "Les Implications pour la science et la societé des découvertes récentes dans le champs de la recherche psychologique et physique," ibid., pp. 431–40, esp. 435ff.

8. This example is based on a case recorded in my practice.

9. Jule Eisenbud, "Synchronicity, Psychodynamics and Psi," in Roll (ed.), *Research in Parapsychology 1979*, pp. 25–26. Eisenbud also accuses Jung of ignoring the role of the observer, which is not accurate at all. Jung speaks quite clearly about this in his essay.

10. Stephen Braude also says, in his *ESP and Psychokinesis*, p. 241, that unconscious desires of the observer could causally produce such events.

11. Stephen E. Braude, "The Synchronicity Confusion," in Roll (ed.), *Research in Parapsychology 1979*, pp. 26–28.

A Contribution to the Discussion • 241

12. Braude, *ESP and Psychokinesis*.
13. Ibid., p. 233.
14. Ibid., p. 238.
15. C. G. Jung, letter to Erich Neumann, 10 March 1959, *Letters*, vol. 2, p. 495.
16. For example, see the chapter "Meaning and Order," pp. 267ff. in this volume, passim.
17. Hans Bender, "Von sinnvollen Zufällen," *Zeitschrift für Parapsychologie und Grenzgebiete der Psychologie* 15 (1973): 203–12, reprinted in Hans Bender, *Zukunftsvisionen, Kriegsprophezeiungen, Sterbeerlebnisse: Aufsätze zur Parapsychologie II* (Munich: Piper, 1983); Hans Bender, "Transcultural Uniformity," in Roll (ed.), *Research in Parapsychologie 1979;* and esp. Hans Bender, "Meaningful Coincidences in the Light of the Jung-Pauli Theory of Synchronicity and Parapsychology," in B. Shapin and L. Coly (eds.), *The Philosophy of Parapsychology* (New York: Parapsychology Foundation, 1977), pp. 66–81.
18. Cf. Wilhelm Gauger, "Zum Phänomen des sinnvollen Zufalls," *Zeitschrift für Parapsychologie und Grenzgebiete der Psychologie* 21 (1979): 77–97; reprinted in W. Gauger, *"Y"—Paranormale Welt, Wirklichkeit und Literatur* (Berlin: Henssel, 1980), pp. 154–87; cf. also Alan Vaughan, *Incredible Coincidence: The Baffling World of Synchronicity* (Philadelphia: Lippincott, 1979). However, Vaughan suggests that a kind of cosmic consciousness "produces" synchronistic phenomena, which does not seem to me to be proven.
19. Charles T. Tart, "Causality and Synchronicity: Steps toward Clarification," *Journal of the American Society for Psychical Research* 75 (1981): 121–41.
20. Rupert A. Sheldrake, *A New Science of Life: The Hypothesis of Formative Causation* (London: Blond & Briggs, 1981).
21. John Beloff, "Psi-phenomena: Causal versus Acausal Interpretation," *Journal of the American Society for Psychical Research* 49 (1977): 573–82.
22. Arthur Koestler, "Speculations on Problems Beyond Our Present Understanding," in A. Hardy, A. Harvie, and A. Koestler, *The Challenge of Chance* (London: Hutchinson, 1973), pp. 205–47.
23. Private correspondence.
24. Hubert Reeves, "Incursion dans le monde acausal" (Foray

into the acausal world), *Cahiers de Psychologie Junghienne,* no. 29 (2nd trimester, 1981): 1ff.

25. For more on the so-called EPR paradox, cf. also Bernard d'Espagnat, *À la Recherche du reel: Le Regard d'un physicien* (Paris: Gauthier-Villars, 1980), pp. 26ff.
26. For an evaluation of this material in relation to the synchronicity hypothesis, cf. the excellent work of Michel Cazenave, "À la Recherche de la synchronicité," *Cahiers de Psychologie Junghienne,* no. 29 (2nd trimester, 1981): 8ff.
27. For a discussion, cf. d'Espagnat, *À la Recherche du réel,* p. 117, n. 27.
28. The conference proceedings were published as *Science et conscience,* ed. Michel Cazenave (Paris: Editions Stock, 1980); cf. also D. S. Kothari, "Reality and Physics, Some Aspects," in *Proceedings of the International Conference and Winter School on Frontiers of Theoretical Physics* (January 6–12, 13–21, 1977), ed. Anluck, Kothari, and Ananda. (New Delhi: Macmillan, 1978), pp. 199ff. I would like to express my thanks to Dr. Wilhelm Just for bringing this article to my attention.
29. R. Frétigny, "Embryologie de la connaissance," in Cazenave (ed.), *Science et conscience,* pp. 197–209.
30. David Bohm, "Discussion," in Cazenave (ed.), *Science et conscience,* p. 235.
31. Cf. Jean Shinoda Bolen, *The Tao of Psychology: Synchronicity and the Self* (San Francisco: Harper & Row, 1979).
32. Marie-Louise von Franz, *Number and Time* (Evanston, Ill.: Northwestern University Press, 1974).
33. Cf. C. G. Jung, "Synchronicity: An Acausal Connecting Principle," cw 8, para. 921, pp. 550ff.
34. Cf. C. G. Jung, "On the Nature of the Psyche," cw 8, paras. 387ff., pp. 188ff.
35. Cf. P. Solié, "Ouverture sur l'unité du monde," in *Synchronicité: Cahiers de Psychologie Junghienne* 28, (1st trimester, 1981); cf also Bolen, *The Tao of Psychology,* passim.
36. Title: "Zur entwicklungsgeschichtlichen Bedeutung von biologischen Form-Functionsbeziehung am Beispiel des Schulterblattes bei höheren Primaten" (On the evolutionary significance of the biological form-function relationship as exemplified by the scapula in higher primates).
37. Michel Cazenave et al., *La Synchronicité, l'ame et la science* (Paris: Editions Poiesis, 1984).

38. Jung, "Synchronicity," cw 8, pp. 516ff.
39. C. G. Jung, letter to Wolfgang Pauli of 29 October 1934, *Letters,* vol. 1, pp. 174–76.
40. This refers to the physicist Pascual Jordan (1903–1980); cf. his "Positivistische Bemerkungen über die parapsychischen Erscheinungen" (Positivistic comments on parapsychic phenomena), *Zentralblatt für Psychotherapie und ihre Grenzgebiete* 9 (1936): 1–17.
41. Emphasis mine.
42. Emphasis mine.
43. For more details, see Marie-Louise von Franz, *On Divination and Synchronicity: The Psychology of Meaningful Chance* (Toronto: Inner City, 1980).
44. Cf. J. F. Zavala, "Quelques aspect de la synchronicité en relation avec le calendrier divinatoire mexicain *Tonalamatl,*" in Cazenave (ed.), *Science et conscience,* pp. 253–65.
45. A small group did indeed tackle this problem as early as 1961; however, no results have been published.
46. Cf. E. Russel, "Psychological Modes," unpublished manuscript (March 1982); and U. Gantenbein, "Katastrophen," degree thesis, Zurich School of Technology (ETH): 1978/1979 (multigraphed), pp. 94ff.
47. Cf. "Time: Rhythm and Repose" on page 65 of the present book.

Some Reflections
on Synchronicity

Since the beginning of our century, the currents of research in physics and in depth psychology have increasingly converged, without there having been (at least for a long time) an exchange of opinions. It has been the *object* of the two sciences—the atomic and subatomic world, on the one hand, and the "objective psyche" (that is, the collective unconscious),[1] on the other—that has imposed on researchers the need to create similar hypotheses. I shall present the most important of these.

1. Configurations of Energy

Today physicists are no longer trying to find "building blocks" in matter, but rather are trying to understand these as transient configurations of universal energy. In a parallel way, Jung has observed that the final observable "entities" in the psyche, the archetypes, seem not to be static structures, but rather systems of psychic energy or a "mode of various relationships of energy,"[2] manifestations of a general psychic energy.[3]

2. The Indivisibility of the Whole

The notion of complementarity introduced by Niels Bohr to provide a better explanation for the paradoxical relationship be-

tween waves and particles in nuclear physics can also be applied
to the relationship of conscious and unconscious states of a psychic content. This fact was discovered by Jung, but it was particularly elaborated by Wolfgang Pauli.[4]

Bernard d'Espagnat pointed out that inseparability in the
world of particles, proved by scientific experimentation (suggested by the Einstein-Podolsky-Rosen paradox), confirms
Bohr's idea of the "indivisibility of the whole."[5] According to
this, particles that have been united and have then separated behave as though one "knew" the state of the other, even at a great
distance, which seems to exclude the idea of an interaction. Even
if the possibility of interaction occurring at speeds faster than
the speed of light (which is often discussed) were admitted, the
fact of the indivisibility of the whole, as d'Espagnat stresses,
would remain.

Jung also observed that the total dimension of the objective
psyche is ultimately *one;* he called this unitary aspect of the psyche the Self.[6]

3. Causality

In mechanics and quantum theory (and in particular in the
theory of the S-matrix), the notion of causality becomes quite
relativized in comparison with the traditional conception of it—
it is reduced to a statistical probability.[7] However, what is even
more important is that phenomena have been discovered that
defy causal explanation altogether. I shall mention them here
and refer the reader for details to the excellent article "Incursion
dans le monde acausal" by Hubert Reeves.[8] They are the law of
half-life in radioactive decay, the Einstein-Podolsky-Rosen paradox, which I have already mentioned, Foucault's problem of
the pendulum, and the "fossil radiation" from the beginning of
the universe, which has recently been observed by astrophysicists. All these phenomena cannot be explained by an appropriate cause, but seem rather to manifest a global, *a priori* order of
the cosmic totality.

Jung, for his part, was led to postulate an ultimate unity of the
objective psyche and to propose the existence of a global order

of this unity. Even though relatively separable archetypal structures exist, they are all in a contaminated (overlapping) state and are interdependent.[9] Thus they form a single total acausal order. Another aspect of a total acausal order in the psychic world, as again pointed out by Jung,[10] is the immediate mental representation of the existence of positive whole numbers with all the individual particularities connected with them, which also do not admit of a causal explanation.

4. Predilection for Quaternary Structures

The "world" of Einstein-Minkowski possesses a quadridimensional structure. According to modern physics, four fundamental forces can be distinguished in the universe.[11] Jung independently observed that mandalas, which are symbols of the "psychic totality," when normal, have a quaternary structure. Moreover, our field of consciousness is based on four fundamental functions: thought, intuition, sensation (function of perception), and feeling (function of evaluation). Any complete conscious realization takes place through the cooperation of these four functions.

5. Relativity of the Space-Time Dimension

In the world of particles, the dimension of space becomes a problem, because, in the experiment suggested by the Einstein-Podolsky-Rosen paradox, "objects, even if they occupy regions of space very distant from one another, are not really separate."[12] In the same way, at the time of certain synchronistic incidents (see below, pages 249–50), especially in the case of telepathy, space seems to disappear.

Today, time has also become a problem.[13] David Bohm and others point out that time can no longer be represented by a simple vector.[14] According to Bohm, an electron, for example, is a "set of enfolded ensembles" (see below, page 252), and it is only at certain instants that it manifests as localized—which also entails that linear time does not exist.[15] Bohm proposes conceiving of time as multidimensional and thinks it consists of "actual occasions" rather than of a continuum.[16] He also thinks it has a qualitative or creative aspect.[17] The implicate or "enfolded" order of the universe would, by contrast, be outside of time, "but it is present at every instant."

Jung pointed out, in a parallel way of thought, that the objective psyche seems also to exist partially beyond the spatio-temporal dimension.[18] Synchronistic incidents (see below) are in fact, as Michel Cazenave points out,[19] irruptions of nontime into time. As I have shown in *Number and Time,* in all mythological images, time is conceived as an emanation or creation of the Self, that is, of the global wholeness of being.

With the emergence of all these surprising analogies, it becomes conceivable that the dimension of universal matter and that of the objective psyche are one. Nonetheless, up to this point I have pointed to analogies and not identities in the discoveries of the two sciences. Only with the creation of the synchronicity hypothesis, based on the observation of countless synchronistic incidents, does the idea impose itself upon us that the two worlds of matter and the psyche might be not only two dimensions with similar laws but might even constitute a *psychophysical whole.* That would mean that the physicist and the psychologist in fact observe the same world via two different channels. This world, if it is observed from the outside, presents itself as "material"; if observed by introspection, as "psychic." In itself, it is probably neither psychic nor material, but altogether transcendent.[20]

By "synchronistic incident," Jung means the meaningful coincidence[21] of an external material event with the emergence of an inner symbol or psychic event, without these two events having any causal relationship between them, or even a conceivable causal connection.[22] The two events are linked only by their common meaning. Since any observation of an external fact is also a psychic event, Jung specifies:

> Synchronistic events rest on the *simultaneous occurrence of two different psychic states.* One of them is the normal, probable state (i.e., the one that is causally explicable), and the other, the critical experience, is the one that cannot be derived causally from the first. . . . In all these cases, whether it is a question of spatial or of tem-

poral ESP, we find a simultaneity of the normal or ordinary state with another state or experience which is not causally derivable from it, and whose objective existence can only be verified afterwards. . . . They are experienced as psychic images *in the present,* as though the objective event already existed. An unexpected content which is directly or indirectly connected with some objective external event coincides with the ordinary psychic state: this is what I call synchronicity, and I maintain that we are dealing with exactly the same category of events whether their objectivity appears separated from my consciousness in space or in time.[23]

This meaningful coincidence of psychic events (visions or dreams of a symbolic event) with the perception of "external or material" events reveals, in a point-instant in time, a unity of matter and the psyche. These phenomena are sporadic and irregular and seem, as far as our knowledge goes, to manifest only when an archetype is constellated in the collective unconscious. In opposition to Jung, C. A. Meier has postulated that the connection of the psyche with the body might be a regular synchronistic phenomenon, and Michel Cazenave mentions the new discoveries of psychopharmacologists that seem to show an intimate relationship between the psyche and the body.[24]

For me, these relationships seem rather to indicate a causal relationship, an *interaction* between psyche and matter. Only the processes involved in "miraculous" cures, which are unpredictable, can, in my opinion, be understood as synchronistic incidents. The facts to which Cazenave calls our attention seem rather to confirm another hypothesis of Jung's, put forward in 1952 in a letter addressed to John R. Smythies. Smythies had written him that he believed in the existence of a subtle body that had its place between the body and the conscious psyche. Jung replied:

Concerning your own proposition I have already told you how much I welcome your idea of a perceptual, i.e., "subtle" body. Your view is rather confirmed, as it seems to me, by the peculiar fact that on the one hand consciousness has so exceedingly little direct information of the body from within, and that on the other hand the unconscious (i.e., dreams and other products of the "unconscious") refers very rarely to the body and, if it does, it is always in the most roundabout way, i.e., through highly "symbolized" images. For a long time I have considered this fact as negative evidence for the existence of a subtle body or at least for a curious gap between mind and body. Of a psyche dwelling in its own body one should expect at least that it would be immediately and thoroughly informed of any change of conditions therein. Its not being the case demands some explanation.

Jung then mentions the relativity of space and time in ESP phenomena, and continues:

The obviously arbitrary behaviour of time and space under ESP conditions seemingly necessitates such a postulate. On the other hand one might ask the question whether we can as hitherto go on thinking in terms of space and time, while modern physics begins to relinquish these terms in favour of a time-space continuum, in which space is no more space and time no more time. The question is, in short: shouldn't we give up the time-space categories altogether when we are dealing with psychic existence? It might be that psyche should be understood as *unextended intensity* and not as a body moving with time. One might assume the psyche gradually rising from minute extensity to infinite intensity, transcending for instance the velocity of light and thus irrealizing the body. . . .

You will certainly object to the paradox of "unextended intensity" as being a *contradictio in adiecto*. I quite agree. Energy is mass and mass is extended. At all events, a body with a speed higher than that of light vanishes from sight and one may have all sorts of doubts about what would happen to such a body otherwise. Surely there would be no means to make sure of its whereabouts or of its existence at all. Its time would be unobservable likewise.

All this is certainly highly speculative, in fact unwarrantably adventurous. But Ψ-phenomena are equally disconcerting and lay claim to an unusually high jump. Yet any hypothesis is warrantable inasmuch as it explains observable facts and is consistent in itself. In the light of this view the brain might be a transformer station, in which the relatively infinite tension or intensity of the psyche proper is transformed into perceptible frequencies or "extensions." Conversely, the fading of introspective perception of the body explains itself as due to a gradual "psychification," i.e., intensification at the expense of extension. Psyche = highest intensity in the smallest space.[25]

This idea of an ultimate unity of physical energy and psychic energy, which would be distinguished only by their frequencies or intensities, could very well explain the psychosomatic relationships referred to by Cazenave, but then these relationships would be of the order of an *interaction* and would not represent synchronistic events. Only sporadic coincidences that do not admit of causal explanation, such as "miraculous" cures, seem to me to belong to the dimension of synchronicity.

The possible existence of an intermediary or subtle body can be clearly apprehended in the term *psychoid*, which Jung uses to characterize the fact that the archetypes of the objective psyche sometimes seem to cross over into the realm of matter.[26] The archetypes are indefinite and can only be perceived and defined approximately. "Although associated by causal processes, or 'carried' by them, they continually go beyond their frame of reference, an infringement to which I would give the name *'transgressivity,'* because the archetypes are *not found exclusively in the psychic sphere, but can occur just as much in circumstances that are not psychic.*"[27]

This seems to confirm once more the possibility of a *unus mundus* and an ultimate unity of physical and psychic energy.

It seems to me that we encounter a very striking example of the concept of a psychophysical wholeness, the manifestation of a single basic energy, in the theory proposed by David Bohm.[28] In his view, everything is in flux and everything *is* this flux, which is a view shared by many other physicists. All objects, events, entities, conditions, structures, and so forth, are finally no more than forms abstracted from this global flux.[29] Their ultimate background is the unknowable totality of this universal flux, which Bohm calls the *holomovement*.[30] Also existing inseparably from this holomovement is our flow of thought, which is partially determined by our memory, but which also passes through creative moments when a very intense energy which Bohm calls an "intelligent energy"[31] creates new mental realizations, which we call "insights." These creative moments reshape our whole being, and may even be imprinted in the furrows in our brains.[32] The holomovement (total flow) contains in its material dimension, as well as in our consciousness, two fundamental orders. One is an "explication" or unfolding (the explicate order), and the other is an "enfolding" or "implication" (the implicate order).

These terms of Bohm's can be applied quite well to the ideas put forward by Jung in his area of research. For example, in that case the archetypes can be understood as dynamic, unobservable structures, specimens of the implicate order. If, on the other hand, an archetype manifests as an archetypal dream image, it has unfolded and become more "explicated." If we go on to interpret this image using Jung's hermeneutic technique (which calls for associative amplification of the dream image), the image would "explicate" and unfold still further. If we then forget this conscious realization, it is not stored just as it was in our memory, but it is reworked in the unconscious according to certain *schemata* (see Susanne Langer and Bartlett);[33] in undergoing this, it becomes enfolded once more, that is, it becomes once again more of a hologram than a grouping of thoughts, feelings, or distinct, discursive intuitions.

Bohm says of the holomovement that it is indefinable and unmeasurable—in fact, unknowable;[34] and this is also true for the holomovement of the Self (the totality of the objective psyche). Jung nevertheless attempted to show, in his analysis in *Aion* of a small temporal segment of about four thousand years of this movement[35] where he sketches the millennial changes in the manifestations of the collective psyche, that there exists a movement within the Self, a cyclical inner movement of rejuvenation, which nevertheless returns to the same point on a higher level of consciousness—that is, it is a spiral-shaped movement.[36] However, this spiral would clearly itself be a very small, specialized, and limited part of the whole—the psychic holomovement being quite certainly unknowable.

The Jungian concept of a single energy that manifests itself in lower frequencies as matter and in more intense frequencies as psyche in many ways resembles the Chinese idea of *ch'i*.

According to Tho-tzu, *ch'i* "is a 'seamless' continuum of matter, gaseous in nature, a universal material energy that pervades all, of which the two principal configurations are yin and yang. . . . It tends to undergo partial condensation and rarefaction."[37]

Jung, on the other hand, puts the emphasis on the *psychic and spiritual* aspect of this energy, which only partly condenses and appears in materially extended forms.

David Bohm also presupposes the existence of an "ocean of energy" as the background of the universe, a background that is neither material nor psychic, but altogether transcendent. "Finally we can say that there is a ground that is the ground of matter on the one hand and of the depths of consciousness on the other . . . , the same ground, but of a higher dimension, because it can be encompassed by neither one nor the other of these aspects."[38] According to Bohm, this background even transcends everything he describes as part of the explicate or implicate orders. Ultimately, it corresponds exactly to what Jung calls the *unus mundus,* which is situated beyond the objective psyche and matter and which also is situated outside space-time.[39]

Another dimension where perhaps more than a simple analogy exists between the concepts of physics and of Jungian psychology is that of "absolute knowledge." In 1963, Costa de Beauregard, taking information theory as his point of departure, postulated the existence of an "infrapsychism" coextensive with the quadridimensional world of Einstein-Minkowski. This infrapsychism contained a knowledge or information characterized as an "overview of the whole."[40] This same idea of a "cosmic knowledge" is suggested, as Cazenave has already pointed out,[41] by the experiment carried out in connection with the Einstein-Podolsky-Rosen paradox, because this experiment leads to the supposition that particle B "knows" instantly and without any communication (slower than the speed of light at least!) what change has been undergone by particle A, with which it was initially connected (the change being imposed on particle A by the very fact of being observed).[42] Finally, this same cosmic knowledge appears in the half-life law of radioactive decay. Each atom that decays "knows" in relation to the whole to which it belongs when it must do so. Thus there is here not only a total acausal *order,* but this knowledge also possesses "knowledge" of a nature that calls for closer investigation.

For his part, Jung showed that what we call the collective psyche possesses a knowledge that he calls "absolute knowledge," in virtue of the way in which it differs completely from our conscious knowledge. Citing Leibniz, Jung describes this knowledge as representations "which consist—or to be more cautious, seems to consist—of images, of subjectless 'simulacra.' "[43]

There are today a certain number of physicists who admit something like a "universal mind," but there are divergences of opinion on the question of whether this mind is conscious or unconscious.[44] Jung calls it a "luminosity" to distinguish it from the clearer and more definite light of our consciousness.[45] He also calls it elsewhere a "cloud of cognition."[46] This cognition seems to be an awareness, which on the one hand encompasses a far vaster field of information than ours, but on the other lacks precise focus and detail. We might compare this "absolute knowledge" of the unconscious universe to (though this is only a metaphor) that cosmic background "fossil radiation,"[47] a "luminous" continuum of millimetric waves which are nevertheless distinct from the "luminescence" of the stars and suns, which would correspond in my comparison to the images of a more or less conscious ego.

In all the modern concepts of "proto-consciousness,"[48] "universal mind," and so on, much clarification as to its function and the "knowledge" that it is supposed to possess is still necessary. It seems certain to me that this knowledge is of a very different nature from our conscious knowledge. David Bohm also speaks of an "intelligent energy" existing in the implicate order that pushes us from time to time to creative discoveries; but he is not clear about whether or not this intelligence is of the same nature as ours. He only says that it is preconceptual—which certainly brings it close to Jung's "absolute knowledge."

In any case, true symbols are not invented by consciousness but are spontaneously revealed by the unconscious. Archetypal dream images and the images of the great myths and religions, for example, still have about them a little of the "cloudy" nature of absolute knowledge in that they always seem to contain more than we can assimilate consciously, even by means of elaborate interpretations. They always retain an ineffable and mysterious quality that seems to reveal to us more than we can really know. If this were not the case, they would not be symbols but only signs or linguistic metaphors. The "meaning" of a synchronistic incident only reveals itself on the condition that we understand the event symbolically and not just intellectually.[49] Physicists are in general mistrustful of mythological images and for this reason use mathematical symbols exclusively. Nonetheless, today they are almost all in agreement that the mathematics they currently employ is inadequate for formal expression of the most recent discoveries.[50] All the same, along with most mathematicians, they quite often try to ignore the ingenious and revolutionary proof of Kurt Gödel, who in 1931 showed by means of an impeccable and strictly logical argument that the ultimate basis of all mathematics is the series of natural integers (1, 2, 3, etc.) and that this basis is *irrational*. It can be neither deduced from nor subsumed under any mathematical or logical principles whatsoever.[51] The whole-number series represents a domain of *natural facts* that should be explored as such, that is, in the same way we study animals or metals. It offers an infinitude of possible insights that are yet to be discovered. What, then, is the consequence of Gödel's discovery? Gödel himself came to the conclusion that mathematicians should return to a Platonic conception of number (which also means Pythagorean). Werner Heisenberg made the same proposal independently of Gödel: that mathematicians should return to the study of numbers in a Pythagorean context. David Bohm, for his part, insists that contemporary mathematics is no longer adequate.[52] He calls for the invention or discovery of new algebras—not algebras of the holomovement, because this is ungraspable, but new subalgebras for certain so-called "unified" problems.[53] He indicates that "ultimately, of course, yet more general sorts of mathematization . . . may prove to be relevant."[54]

Though he could not know of these recent developments, Jung stumbled on the same problem concerning whole numbers, because he had observed that nearly all divinatory techniques that are based on the idea of synchronicity employ the first whole numbers to establish their predictions. Thus Jung advanced the idea that *number is an archetype of order that is in the process of becoming conscious*. It is the most primitive manifestation or the most "seminal" of all manifestations of archetypes or archetypal processes. [55]

Since today we see processes everywhere rather than structures or static orders, I have also proposed seeing numbers in this perspective—as *rhythmic configurations of psychic energy*. [56] Physicists nowadays sometimes speak of a "protoconsciousness" in inorganic matter. I would propose saying that this protoconsciousness consists in "knowing how to count." (That would be a first step toward greater precision of focus of the luminosity of the "absolute knowledge," a first individuation of the "fossil radiation" of the diffuse knowledge of the *unus mundus*.) From what we know today, the most elementary particles, such as quarks, protons, mesons, and baryons, "know how to count." They combine in hexagons, triplets, octuplets, and so forth. Particles would not know how to count as we do, but would be more like a primitive shepherd, who, without knowing how to count beyond three, can tell in the twinkling of an eye whether his herd of 137 animals is complete or not. As Kreitner postulates, man possesses an unconscious "numerical sense," and this is probably the sense that subatomic particles possess. Starting with numbers in the subatomic dimension, it would be a long road before reaching the first unicellular living beings with its genetic programing, which is also numerical. But there seem to exist *periodic recurrences* of the first simple numbers. It seems to me particularly significant that, for example, the Chinese oracle *I Ching* follows the same numerical order as the genetic code. I first published this finding in 1968 and 1974, but others made the same discovery shortly afterward. The idea was "in the air," an example of synchronicity!

In trying to study numbers as irrational facts of nature, like strange *animalia*, it seemed necessary to me no longer to conceive of them as static structures but as rhythmical configurations of psychic energy and—as I would add today—of psychophysical energy. As a numerical equivalent of the *unus mundus*, I proposed the term *one-continuum*, in which all numbers (including unity) would be configurations of rhythm.

A second aspect seems to me important to study in this connection: the relationship of number with time. The ancient Chinese did not consider numbers as indicators of quantities (they knew this, too, but did not attach any importance to it). For them, numbers were more *indicators of the qualities of the temporal phases of the Whole.*[58] "Numbers served primarily to represent the various circumstantial forms of unity, or rather, of the Whole."[59]

In this qualitative and temporal perspective on numbers, as with the quantitative perspective, there is the problem of continuity-discontinuity. (What I have called the one-continuum is for the Chinese the number eleven, the number of the Tao, because it is the "one of ten.") Between one and two, there is the "leap" from odd to even; between two and three, the leap to the first prime number; the transition to four is a leap to the first square; and so on. Thus the integer series represents a discontinuity, but, as I have shown, it is also a one-continuum.

Bohm in his own field points out that the partial holomovement of enfolding and unfolding is not continuous, and that the notion of continuum can only be applied to the implicate order of the Whole.[60] I would even say that the mathematics of continua can be utilized, without alteration and without passing over infinite values, only to symbolize the *unus mundus*. All the phenomena that we can currently observe have a discontinuous quality, discontinuity or "discrimination" being the essence of ego-consciousness.

But let us return to synchronistic incidents and to the numerical divinatory techniques that explore their "meaning."

Jung stressed that "meaning" is a transcendental notion that we are not able to define consciously,[61] and he cites Lao-tzu and Chuang-tzu on the impossibility of conceptualizing or naming the Tao. The "meaning" of a synchronistic phenomenon visibly participates in the nature of this "absolute knowledge" of the unconscious, which is nevertheless only a "cloud of cognition" for our conscious intelligence. The realization of "meaning" is therefore not a simple acquisition of information or of knowledge, but rather a living experience that touches the heart just as much as the mind. It seems to us to be an illumination characterized by great clarity as well as something ineffable—a lightning flash, to use Leibniz's expression (which he uses for the creative acts of the divine Monad). Discursive thought reveals only very little of this realization of meaning, because "meaning," in the context in which Jung uses it, is not at all the same thing as the order of discursive thought that is based on a mathematico-logical order. Realization of meaning is a "quantum leap" in the psyche.

The "meaning" of a synchronistic event, however, is not identical with "absolute knowledge," because it has added to it the realization of temporal localization arising from a conscious individual at a certain moment in his life. Such a realization, coinciding with the act of creation (which is what synchronistic phenomena are) is a *psychic event,* an experience whose essence has a healing effect or, on the other hand, a destructive one. If it brings healing, it is because even the greatest pain becomes bearable when we glimpse its meaning. The meaning links us with the numinous—the meaning of the Whole, the Tao—and, so to speak, puts us once again in our proper place in the Whole. It gives us a feeling of "that which is just as it is"; it brings a reconciliation with life *and* death, joy *and* sorrow, conflict *and* peace. It is not nirvana, a spiritual "beyond," but rather a complete acceptance of "what is." For Jung, individuation and realization of the meaning of life are identical—since individuation means to find *one's own* meaning, which is nothing other than *one's own* connection with the universal Meaning. This is clearly something other than what is referred to today by terms such as *information, superintelligence, cosmic* or *universal mind*—because feeling, emotion, the Whole of the person, is included. This sudden and illuminating connection that strikes us in the encounter with a synchronistic event represents, as Jung well described, a momentary unification of two psychic states: the normal state of our consciousness, which moves in a flow of discursive thought and in a process of continuous perception that creates our idea of the world called "material" and "external"; and of a profound level where the "meaning" of the Whole resides in the sphere of "absolute knowledge." This is why any divinatory technique that operates with the synchronicity principle (for example, the *I Ching*) recommends that we first empty the field of our consciousness so that we may, so to speak, open the door to an irruption from the dimension of "meaning." That is why the Chinese philosophers insist that if we are entirely and always connected with the Tao, we no longer have to consult the *I Ching*. In fact, at the end of his life, Jung stopped using the *I Ching*, because, as he told me one day, he always "knew" in advance what the answer would be.

Like any idea, the idea of "meaning" has an opposite, which is that of nonsense, an absurd chaos. There exist chains of causality that seem to us to have no meaning at all (like Yves Tinguely's machines), and there also exist arbitrary or chance coincidences that have no meaning. Therefore, as Jung stressed, we must be careful not to see meaningful coincidences where really none exist. I have shown in "Meaning and Order" (see pages 267ff.) that this is a danger for schizophrenics.

But how is it possible to read messages of meaning in synchronistic events without falling into absurd superstitious or magical ideas? The ancient alchemists distinguished between an *imaginatio vera* and an *imaginatio phantastica*, which Jung amplifies by emphasizing the contrast between "necessary amplification" or "disciplined imagination" and arbitrary association.[62] The latter is carried out by the ego, whereas the former develops through openness to the message of an archetypal structure, which "imposes" appropriate associations on us. This process is demonstrated most simply by the archetypal structures of the whole numbers. The conclusion that six is a perfect number ($1 \times 2 \times 3 = 1 + 2 + 3$) imposes itself on our conscious mind whether we like it or not. Now, it would seem that similar laws exist for mythical thought. In his book *Hero with a Thousand Faces*, Joseph Campbell elicited clearly the "categories" or submythologems that are regularly part of the structure of a heroic myth.[63] If a tale begins with a sterile or aged couple who wish to have a child, *it is impossible* for the tale not to continue with the motif of a child born *supernaturally*, or of a prodigal or semidivine or monstrous child. There are no exceptions! Or else: if a figure in a tale shows symptoms of inflation vis-à-vis the numinous, that being will always be humiliated or punished or destroyed—here too, there are no exceptions. In the context of a dream, this "imaginal logic" is more difficult to discover, but it has often happened to me that an analysand has skipped over a minor episode within a dream and that I noticed this, because I noticed a "gap" in the internal "logic" of the dream. There is still much to be discovered in this connection. Nevertheless, it seems to me that logical-mathematical laws (originating in the archetype of order that the numbers are) are certainly not the only ones that exist, but there are also special logical laws for the connections between associations in myths and dreams. (This phenomenon could perhaps be ascribed to the specialization of the two hemispheres of the brain.) The "right" thought in the mythical context is the one that follows the "necessary implications," that is, the one that leads closest to the realization of the "meaning."

From the historical point of view, these two logics (mathematical logic and mythological or imaginal logic) have not always been separate the way they are today. In Pythagorean arithmetic, numbers and mythological images were intimately bound up together. The same is true in the system of the *I Ching*. It is only the progressive "demythification" of modern mathematics that has brought us to this situation where the sciences based on formal mathematics are opposed to the humanities. Jung's synchronicity concept is so shocking, because it unifies these two domains on a higher level. As Hubert Reeves quite correctly pointed out, with statistical mathematics as it is practiced today, there is no way of working with synchronicity.[64] If it happens to work by chance (!), that does no more than prove the independence of the synchronicity principle.[65]

In my view, Chinese mathematics is more apt to provide us with an instrument that will permit us to work with this elusive principle. But how could we go about studying synchronicity, which is essentially so irregular and consists of unpredictable creative acts, *experimentally*?

Numerical divination techniques do not claim to be able to predict synchronistic incidents as such; rather they claim to be able to predict the *general quality* of temporal phases in which synchronistic events might take place. Thus perhaps a possibility remains, a possibility that Jung only began to work out at the end of his life and was not able to complete before he died. He had brought together a group of his students who were supposed to undertake the following project: to find individuals in a relatively critical situation (after an accident, in the midst of divorce proceedings, etc.), in which one might suspect that an archetype would be activated; then to work out a transit horoscope, consult the *I Ching,* the Tarot, the Mexican calendar,[66] a geomantic divination system, dreams before and after the accident, and so forth—and then determine whether the results of these techniques converged or not. This would have been a reversal of, or a procedure complementary to, classical experiments of modern science. In such experiments, the same types of events are repeated to see if measured values coincide. Here, by contrast, one incident is considered using a multitude of different techniques.

Michel Cazenave cites a remark made by Jung in a letter addressed to Wolfgang Pauli on the subject of the unconscious.[67] If one puts oneself in the position of a human observer, the situation is that of "an absolutely unconscious space in which an infinity of observers observe the same object." If, on the other hand, one tries to approach matters from the point of view of the Self (archetype of the Totality), "there is only one observer [situated in the collective unconscious] who observes an infinity of objects."

The first position is the situation that is normal for science, where, for example, a great number of psychologists (enveloped though they all are in the same collective unconscious) observe an identical psychological phenomenon. This leads them to a similar description of the phenomenon. The complementary procedure I described above would consist in studying an incident (accident) by the convergence—if one occurs—of a multitude of methods, with the help of which we could try to find out what the Self "thought" of this particular accident.

Unfortunately, the group selected by Jung did not continue its study. What is needed is an institution with enough resources in both students and funds to resume this project.

The generally rather vague formulations of divinatory techniques resemble these "clouds of cognition" that, according to Jung, constitute "absolute knowledge." However, they only produce fragments, never the whole meaning, which remains unknowable. With regard to the life of an individual, we will probably never know where it comes from, where it will go after its death, and what, therefore, is the global meaning of its existence. Nevertheless, with the methods mentioned, and especially the interpretation of dreams, we can gain a glimpse of some *substructures* of the total meaning. For example, we can see for what reason an individual married thus-and-such a woman or for what reason he had an accident (though it might appear to have been merely a matter of chance). In the earliest childhood dreams, we often find the symbolic pattern of a whole part of the life of an individual. But these are only a kind of lightning flash that momentarily lights up a part of the nocturnal landscape, the realization of a partial meaning that lets us guess at the existence of a much vaster meaning, which, however, cannot be grasped by our conscious ego.

With the notion of synchronicity, psychology in some sense transcends itself as pure science. But as Jung pointed out, every science does this in its fringe areas. At such a point, "science" becomes part of our individuation process itself and no longer a partial preoccupation of our conscious intelligence.

On the basis of these reflections, I do not think it is possible to introduce the notion of synchronicity into the body of the sciences such as they are today. With this notion, we find ourselves on the threshold of a radical transformation toward what the sciences could become, a transformation that will not do away with them but will put them in their "appropriate place" in a much vaster vision of reality. Ultimately, general acceptance of this concept will depend on the universal Self and its creative acts of synchronicity. In other words, it will depend on whether the notions of synchronicity and of individuation are within the creative plan for the general evolution of the sciences in the West. What seems certain to me is the fact that the quest for meaning is a problem that is much more vital to us than the quest for partial information. "Without the reflecting consciousness of man," Jung writes, "the world is a gigantic meaningless machine, for in our experience man is the only creature who is capable of ascertaining any meaning at all."[69]

Notes

1. Jung calls the collective psychic dimension the "collective unconscious" or "objective psyche." In the present context, I prefer the latter expression because it implies that we are dealing with an independent (nonsubjective) reality in the sense given to the term by Bernard d'Espagnat in *A la Recherche du réel: Le Regard d'un physicien* (Paris: Gauthiers-Villars, 1980).
2. Cf. Paul Kugler, "Remarques sur les rapports de la théorie des archétypes et du structuralisme," *Cahiers de Psychologie Junghienne*, no. 29 (2nd trimester, 1981). For physics, see Fritjof Capra, *The Tao of Physics* (Boston: Shambhala Publications, 1991), and Gary Zukav, *The Dancing Wu Li Masters: An Overview of the New Physics* (New York: Bantam, 1984).
3. Cf. C. G. Jung, "On Psychic Energy," in *The Structure and Dynamics of the Psyche*, vol. 8 of *Collected Works* (CW), pp. 3–66.
4. Cf. Wolfgang Pauli, *Aufsätze und Vorträge über Physik und Erkenntnistheorie* (Braunschweig: Vieweg, 1961).
5. D'Espagnat, *A la Recherche du réel*, pp. 19, 40ff., 45.
6. Cf. C. G. Jung, *Mysterium Coniunctionis*, CW 14, para. 776, p. 554. This unitary aspect of the objective psyche manifests itself through the symbols of the mandala or the cosmic man (*purusha-atman*, the Gnostic *anthropos*, the Chinese *panku*, etc.).
7. Cf. Paul Dirac, "Grundprobleme der Physik," a lecture delivered at the conference for Nobel Prize winners in Lindau, 1971. I am indebted to Dr. Hermann Strobel for bringing this article to my attention.
8. Hubert Reeves, "Incursion dans le monde acausal," *Cahiers de Psychologie Junghienne* 29 (2nd trimester, 1981): 11–19.
9. Cf. Marie-Louise von Franz, *Number and Time* (Evanston, Ill.: Northwestern University Press, 1974), pp. 139ff.
10. Jung, CW 8, p. 582.
11. Cf. von Franz, *Number and Time*, pp. 113ff.: nuclear and electromagnetic forces, weak interaction, and gravitation.
12. D'Espagnat, *A la Recherche du réel*, p. 49.
13. Cf. Olivier Costa de Beauregard, "Cosmos et conscience,"

in Michel Cazenave (ed.), *Science et conscience* (Paris: Editions Stock, 1980), pp. 68ff.

14. Ilya Prigogine proposes replacing it with an operator, in *La Nouvelle Alliance* (Paris: Gallimard, 1979), p. 256.

15. David Bohm, *Wholeness and the Implicate Order* (London, 1980), p. 183.

16. Ibid., p. 212.

17. Ibid.

18. Jung, cw 8, p. 506.

19. Michel Cazenave et al., *La Synchronicité, l'âme et la science* (Paris, 1984), pp. 21–68.

20. Jung, cw 14, paras. 711ff, pp. 499ff.

21. This need not necessarily be a "synchronous" coincidence, that is, within a tolerance of a second or even one or two hours.

22. Jung, cw 8, pp. 425ff.

23. Ibid., p. 445.

24. Cf. Cazenave et al., *La Synchronicité*.

25. C. G. Jung, letter to John R. Smythies, 29 February 1952, *Letters*, vol. 2, p. 43f.; see also Cazenave et al., *La Synchronicité*.

26. Jung, letter to John R. Smythies, 29 February 1952, *Letters*, vol. 2, pp. 44–45; see also the extract and commentary by Cazenave in *La Synchronicité*.

27. Jung, "Synchronicity," cw 8, p. 515. Emphasis mine.

28. Cf. Bohm, *Wholeness and the Implicate Order*, passim, and David Bohm, "Ordre involué-evolué de l'univers et de la conscience" ("The Enfolding-Unfolding Universe and Consciousness"), in Cazenave (ed.), *Science et conscience*, pp. 99ff.

29. Bohm, *Wholeness*, pp. 47ff.

30. Ibid., p. 49.

31. Ibid., p. 51.

32. Ibid., p. 149.

33. Cf. G. J. Whitrow, *The Natural Philosophy of Time* (Oxford, 1980), pp. 111ff.

34. Bohm, *Wholeness*, p. 151.

35. C. G. Jung, *Aion*, CW 9/ii.

36. Ibid., chap. 14.

37. Cited by T. Izutsu, "Matière et conscience dans le philosophies orientales," in Cazenave (ed.), *Science et conscience*, pp. 353ff., 365.

38. David Bohm, "Issues in Physics, Psychology and Metaphysics: A Conversation with John Welwood," *Journal of Transpersonal Psychology* 12, no. 1 (1980): 25ff. Cf. also David Bohm, "Insight, Knowledge, Science and Human Values," in *Education and Human Values*, ed. Douglas Sloan (New York & London: Teachers College Press, Columbia University, 1980). I am indebted to Dr. Wilhelm Just for his kindness in bringing these articles to my attention.
39. See also Bohm, "Ordre involué-evolué," in Cazenave (ed.), *Science et conscience*, p. 108 and esp. p. 119.
40. Olivier Costa de Beauregard, *La Second Principe et la science du temps* (Paris: Le Seuil, 1963), pp. 14, 75, 80, 121, 159.
41. Cazenave et al., *La Synchronicité*, passim.
42. Bohm, *Wholeness*, p. 72.
43. Jung, "Synchronicity," cw 8, p. 495.
44. Cf. the remarks of Willis Harman in Cazenave (ed.), *Science et conscience*, p. 437; and of Ullman, ibid., p. 235.
45. Jung, "On the Nature of the Psyche," cw 8, pp. 190ff.
46. C. G. Jung, *Memories, Dreams, Reflections* (New York: Vintage Books, 1965), p. 308.
47. See Reeves, "Incursion dans le monde acausal," passim, for the definition of this notion.
48. Cf. R. Frétigny, "Embryologie de la connaissance," in Cazenave (ed.), *Science et conscience*, p. 201.
49. See the example of the *Cetonia aurata* in Jung, "Synchronicity," cw 8, paras. 843ff., pp. 437ff.
50. See Bohm, *Wholeness;* and Paul Dirac, *Grundprobleme der Physik* (Lindau, 1971).
51. See Marie-Louise von Franz, "Meaning and Order," pages 269ff. of the present volume.
52. Bohm, *Wholeness*, pp. 160ff.
53. Ibid., p. 164.
54. Ibid., p. 165.
55. For these questions, see von Franz, *Number and Time*, passim.
56. This is my idea; it is derived from Jung's thought but was not formulated by Jung himself.
57. Von Franz, *Number and Time*.
58. Marcel Granet, *La Pensée chinoise* (Paris, 1948), p. 236; and von Franz, *Number and Time*.
59. Granet, *La Pensée chinoise*.
60. Cazenave (ed.), *Science et conscience*, p. 113; see also p. 107.

61. Cf. also George Elie Humbert, "Une Pratique du sens," in Cazenave (ed.), *Science et conscience*, pp. 217ff.
62. Jung, *Memories, Dreams, Reflections*, p. 310.
63. Joseph Campbell, *Hero with a Thousand Faces*, 2nd ed. (Princeton: Princeton University Press, 1968).
64. Reeves, "Incursion dans le monde acausal," p. 19.
65. It seems to me that Reeves has misunderstood Jung's astrological argument, which he rejects. Jung demonstrates that statistics do not function in this domain but, on the contrary, they are "tricked" by synchronicity. Thus, in the last analysis, he confirms Reeves's own opinion.
66. On this, see José Zavala in Cazenave (ed.), *Science et conscience*, p. 253.
67. Jung, letter to Wolfgang Pauli, *Letters*, vol. 1, pp. 174ff.; cf. Cazenave, *Science et conscience*, p. 253.
68. Jung, letter to Erich Neumann, 10 March 1959, *Letters*, vol. 2, p. 494.

Meaning and Order

I n his book on synchronicity, C. G. Jung introduces two new concepts into depth psychology concerning the world of so-called chance. One is the concept of "acausal orderedness" and the other that of "synchronistic events." The former means a regular omnipresent just-so-ness, such as, for instance, the specific speed of light, the quantization of energy, the time-rate of radioactive decay, or any other constant in nature. Because we cannot indicate a cause (for these regularities), we generally express this just-so-ness by a number, which is, however, based on an arbitrarily chosen length of space-time. One could theoretically also call a quantum of energy 1, and then add on 2, 3, 4, etc., but it would be completely impracticable because of the smallness of h. Such acausal orderedness exists not only in the realm of physics; we find it also in the human mind or psyche. The simplest example is that of the natural integers, because there too we find a just-so-ness in the form of statements we *have* to make about a number. Jung calls this "the method of the necessary statement."[1] An example would be the statement that 6 is a so-called perfect number, because $1 + 2 + 3$ is identical with $1 \times 2 \times 3$. This is an obvious just-so-ness, for which we cannot indicate a "cause" which "produces" this result. We could only say it is so because 6 is the sum of 1, 2 and 3, but this would be a mere tautology.

In the field of dream interpretation this method of necessary statements is the same as that which Jung more frequently calls "amplification." In it we also do not proceed arbitrarily, letting our imagination run free, but we use what Jung calls "disciplined imagination" to find the associations to a symbolic image. For instance, we cannot say that Circe in *The Odyssey* is a benevolent mother figure, because the very context refutes this. In the realm of the natural integers, statements of connections, such as 2 + 2 = 4, seem to be even more cogently "necessary" statements than those about mythological images. Hence their connection with logic and mathematical reasoning. Modern mathematicians tried to make their discipline as logically watertight as possible against psychological implications, because they regarded the latter as purely subjective,[2] while they thought that mathematical logic concerns a purely objective, true, nonpsychological reality.[3] It deals with a truth which serves all observers.[4] For Gottlob Frege, for instance, the statement: $1 + 1 = 2 = 6/3 = \sqrt{4}$ are all absolutely identical! They are seen as the result of a formulated *relation*, and it is the latter that counts. Even if I say in mathematics that a number is 4, I imply "nothing else than four." Numbers themselves cannot be defined, they are "logically simple."[5]

In the year 1931, Kurt Gödel dashed all these former attempts to constitute some ultimate, safe foundations for mathematics.[6] He showed "that any logical system within which arithmetics can be developed is essentially incomplete. In other words, given any consistent set of arithmetical axioms there are true arithmetical axioms which are not derivable from the set.[7] Gödel's proof is too complicated to explain here. In short: he arithmetized all formal statements of mathematics into unique, specific numbers. Then he showed that "arithmetic is incomplete in the transparent sense that there is at least always one arithmetical truth which cannot be derived from the arithmetical axioms and yet can be established by metamathematical argument outside the system . . . contrary to previous assumptions, the 'vast' continent of arithmetical truth cannot be brought into systematic order by way of specifying once and for all a fixed set of axioms from which all true arithmetical statements would be derivable." However, our creative reasoning could always establish new mathematical propositions by "informal" meta-mathematical reasoning.[8] In other words, the natural integers, the basis of arithmetics, are a partly irrational basis for our rational reasoning.

Concerning the series of natural numbers which are the foundation of all mathematics, Weyl therefore remarks that to our surprise it has an aspect of obscurity, though we believe it to be only a construct of our mind.

This element of obscurity in numbers (meaning that they are not logically diaphanous) is based, in Jung's view, on the fact that they are archetypal symbols.[9] They are also individuals and have an aspect of just-so-ness which one can ignore, as mathematicians mostly do, but which exists in our minds all the same. Viewed from this angle, most former mathematicians were something like the theologians of the number-gods. They shared their resistance against psychology with the "other" theologians! They argue along the "necessary statements" induced by the archetypes but ignore the concomitant psychological experiences which they consider to be purely subjective.

Jung goes one step further and calls number an "archetype of order which has become conscious."[10] It is thus *the* predestined instrument for creating order, or for apprehending an already existing, but still unknown, regular arrangement or "orderedness."

Since the times of Archimedes and later, particularly to a much greater degree, since Galileo, physics has concentrated on exploring the *measurable* aspects of the outer, so-called natural reality, and thus on its mathematization. And it works! The mathematical forms of order which the mind of a physicist manipulates coincide "miraculously" with experimental measurements. The absolute differential calculus, for instance, which was born in the fantasy of the mathematician Riemann, became later *the* mathematical tool for Einstein's theory of relativity and its applications.[11] This led Eugène Wigner to speak of an "unreasonable effectiveness of mathematics in science."[12]

Nowadays physicists have become mainly interested in the concept of order; they are also fully realizing that it is inseparably related to the functioning of their own mind. Their equations are no longer perceived to be an objectively accurate reflection of material reality, but only a structurally accurate relationship-connection. Like the mathematicians, physicists also do not look out much for numbers but mostly use algebra and topology as their tools, because these are the logical abstractions drawn from number *relations* and less irrational than the number individuals themselves. They mostly express relationships which are true for *all numbers*. (For instance, if $a + b = c$, then $a = c - b$.) Seen from this angle, algebra is a kind of group psychology of numbers and topology is concerned with their possible spatialization by viewing them as arrangements of points and their connections in a manifold.

However, an archetypal representation also always contains meaning. Thus if we assume that number is an archetype of order which has become conscious, then it possesses a preconscious, latent, psychic reality which would be indefinable. Only when it becomes conscious do we feel motivated to call one: unity, *the* unity, the All-oneness, individuality, nonduality, counting unit, etc., or do we have to say about 2 that it is the halved, the doubled, duality, distinctness, non-uniqueness, etc. Our mind is in no way free to speculate randomly about a specific number; what we say about it is determined and limited by the conception of oneness, twoness and their implications.[13]

Among these "necessary statements" which are engendered by number, only one part is what one calls the statements of mathematical logic. (The latter uses, for its operations, for instance, only the statement: One is a counting unit—and ignores the others). We could say that mathematics deals with the "acausal orderedness" in our own mind, which is based on number; and physics, among other themes, deals with the "acausal orderedness" in nature, such as the speed of light and the rate of radioactive decay, which could also be designated by number. But do they have meaning? Jung writes:

> The concept of "order" is not identical with the concept of "meaning." Even an organic being is, in spite of the meaningful

design implicit within it, not necessarily meaningful in the total nexus. For instance, if the world had come to an end at the Oligocene period, it would have had no meaning for man. Without the reflecting consciousness of man the world is a gigantic meaningless machine, for in our experience man is the only creature who is capable of ascertaining any meaning at all.[14]

Jung uses here the term "order" as a subterm of "meaning," order being a partial fact, a meaningful design, for instance, which can be found in all mathematically or biologically organized phenomena; but "meaning," on the contrary, rather concerns a holon, or rather *the* holon, the Unitas (in the sense of the gnostics of Princeton), and simultaneously it concerns that *one* individual who realizes it. This does not imply that man creates the meaning;[25] he only realizes it or lifts it into consciousness, but it is already latently existent in nature itself, independent of our conscious realization.[16]

As I mentioned in the beginning, Jung subdivides the principle of synchronicity into two subterms: acausal orderedness, which concerns "all . . . *a priori* factors such as the properties of natural numbers (and) the discontinuities of modern physics,"[17] and, secondly, *synchronistic events* as a particular instance of general acausal orderedness, "namely, of the equivalence of psychic and physical processes where the observer is in the fortunate position of being able to recognize the *tertium comparationis*,"[18] namely, its meaning.[19] Synchronistic events are "acts of creation in time,"[20] but they are *not caused* by any archetype, they merely let its latent meaning become visible. Thus the contingent would be "partly . . . a universal factor existing from all eternity—a just-so order—partly . . . the sum of countless individual acts of creation occurring in time."[21] Although these acts probably occur all the time in nature, they become *meaningful* coincidences only when an individual experiences them.

In the case which Jung reports as an example in his paper, for instance, his patient dreamt of a scarab and most surprisingly a *Cetonia aurata* flew into the room when the dream was told. If nobody had seen the meaning, there would have been only a *similarity* between the outer and inner events; only if one knows that in Egypt the scarab is a symbol of the reborn Sun-god rising in the morning, i.e., a rebirth of consciousness, does the event become meaningful, and it had in fact a healing impact on the dreamer. Thus synchronistic events constitute moments in which a "cosmic" or "greater" meaning becomes gradually conscious in an individual; generally it is a shaking experience. One is moved because one feels like a primitive, that a higher force, a ghost or god, aims at you, often by playing a trick on you. But such an interpretation regresses to the level of magical causal thinking, which Jung sought to avoid. The archetype does not magically cause such events but becomes manifest in them without any antecedents seeming to exist. As Jung points out, such events can also occur without anybody seeing their meaning, but it is latently present there all the same. But there also exists a "danger that meaning will be read into things where actually there is nothing of the sort,"[22] or that one misinterprets the meaning. Let me give an example:

A man who suffered from a psychotic idea that he was the savior of the world attacked his wife with an ax in order to "exorcise the devil out of her." She called for help. At the very moment when a policeman and a psychiatrist entered the house the only lamp, which lit up the passage where they all stood, exploded. They were plunged into darkness, covered with glass splinters. The sick man exclaimed: "See . . . this is like it was at the crucifixion of Christ! The sun has eclipsed." He felt confirmed that he *was* the savior. But if we amplify this symbolism correctly with "necessary statements," i.e., with "disciplined imagination," there appears a completely different meaning: a lightbulb is *not* the sun, that symbol of a numinous source of cosmic consciousness; it only symbolizes a "little light" made by man, i.e., his ego-consciousness. So the event means a "blackout" of that man's ego-consciousness, the disruption of his ego, which is exactly what happens in the beginning of a psychotic episode. When I saw the man and his wife two days later, *I* saw the meaning and was able to show it to them, which had a positive, sobering effect on the poor man. The correct interpretation of a synchronistic event is essential and can only be done by a sober and disciplined mind which keeps to the necessary statements and does not run off into arbitrary assumptions.

Another amusing example of misinterpreting the meaning of a synchronistic event can be found in old annals of the T'ang period in China.[23] Once after an earthquake a new lake was formed and in its middle a mountain arose. The wife of the emperor, called Wu Tse-t'ien, said that this was a lucky sign and named the mountain "Mountain of Luck." But a citizen of the capital wrote her a letter, saying: "Your servant has learned that cold and heat become disturbed when the breath of Heaven and mankind is not in harmony, and that hills and mountains arise when the breath of the earth is disturbed. Your majesty as a woman takes over the role of the male principle Yang on the throne. . . . That means to exchange the strong for the weak. . . . Your majesty should practice penance and fear in order to answer to the admonition of Heaven. Otherwise I fear that there will be misfortune." The Empress got furious and banished the poor outspoken citizen from court.

Now, her interpretation of "lucky mountain" was purely arbitrary. The citizen, on the contrary, used the classical Chinese archetypal associations: for Kên—the mountain—is male, and Tui—the lake—is female, as we know from the *I Ching*. The animus-possessed Empress was overpowering her weak husband, and the outer event was a meaningful coincidence. This coincidence has no thinkable causal connection: the volcano did not arise because of the wrong attitude of the Empress (to assume that would be magical thinking), nor did the Empress behave in such an overpowering manner because of the volcano. The connection of the two events lies purely in the meaning of the coincidence. In old China one thought that all unusual events in the Empire were thus revealing the psychological situation at the Emperor's court. The citizen was "in Tao," to use Chinese language, and thus he saw the true meaning of the event.

We all know from the *I Ching* that "the kind man discovers Tao and calls it kind. The wise man discovers it and calls it wise. The people use it day by day and are not aware of it." "The Tao of the universe is kindness and wisdom, but essentially the Tao is also beyond kindness and wisdom."[24] The sages of ancient times "put themselves in accord with Tao," in order to build the oracle.[25] And the same holds true in order to understand it.

274 · PSYCHE AND MATTER

Here we can see again, as I have already mentioned before, that in contrast to order "meaning" has to do with the ultimate, the whole of existence, in other words it points to a connection with what we call the Self.

Viewed naively and more superficially: synchronistic events seem to be meaningful coincidences between one inner and one or more outer events. But, as Jung pointed out, the awareness of the coinciding outer events is ultimately also a different psychological condition. Therefore a synchronistic event is, in fact, this: "One (psychic state) is the normal, probable state (i.e., the one that is causally explicable), and the other, the critical experience, is the one that cannot be derived causally from the first."[26] It is a content of "immediate knowledge" or "immediate existence" which suddenly irrupts into the ordinary state of mind, generally accompanied by a strong emotion which causes an *abaissement du niveau mental* and makes the irruption of that other abnormal state of awareness possible.[27]

In the unconscious there seems to be an *a priori* knowledge or immediate presence of events which has no cause and which from time to time irrupts into our "normal" state.[28] Jung stresses: "Synchronicity in space can equally well be conceived as perception in time, but remarkably enough it is not so easy to understand synchronicity in time as spatial, for we cannot imagine any space in which future events are objectively present and could be experienced as such through a reduction of this spatial distance."[29]

We know now, through Einstein, that space and time are somehow inseparable entities; there seems, however, to be a difference in that the annihilation of time or even its reversal in the psyche is more easily possible than the annihilation of space. We must therefore look at time a bit more closely from a psychological angle. Measured time, or clock time, as we know, is only a Western culturally specific way of thought. Psychologically time is rather to be seen as the flow or stream of inner and outer events. As I tried to show in my paper two years ago, the archetypal image of that time-stream of events is always associated with each culture's highest god-image, or image of the Self. Time is, so to speak, engendered by the internal motion of the

Self archetype. So, for instance, Tao is the nameless, still void, but also "the begetter of all begetting" and, in this latter aspect, it is called "change," says the *I Ching*.[30] "It is something that sets in motion and maintains the interplay of forces." Tao brings this about without ever becoming manifest."[31]

In the Aztec religion the highest god, Omote'otl, is the Lord of Time. In the *Bhagavad Gita* the Indian highest god, Vishnu, calls himself "Time" and so is Shiva called by his adorers. Only in the Judeo-Christian religion is God timeless and only creates (not emanates) time. He is the unmovable mover, outside time-space. But even here time is closely linked with the idea of the supreme godhead and its creative activity.

Now if synchronistic events are what they seem to be, they point to the fact of a continuous creation going all along with the stream of time, and that would also imply that meaning (in the sense of concerning the unitas or the holon) uses time as a vehicle of its realization in man. "Time," says G. J. Whitrow, "is the mediator between the possible and the actual."[32] This is just another aspect of the concept of "continuous creation." It needs a flow of outer and inner events to actualize the latent meaning of archetypal patterns in the form of sporadic synchronistic events. Each time such an event takes place, the Holon of existence is changed. What I call holon or unitas, using a word of the so-called gnostics of Princeton, is the same as that which Jung calls the *unus mundus,* the one world, which transcends the duality of psyche and matter.

The mandala, Jung pointed out, is the inner psychic counterpart of the *unus mundus* and synchronistic phenomena the parapsychological equivalent of it.[33] How these two factors can be combined in so-called divinatory double mandalas I have tried to show in my book *Number and Time* and cannot discuss here; but I would like to probe a bit deeper into the experience of meaning as it is conveyed to us by synchronistic events. As Jung already remarked, synchronistic events sometimes appear like something arbitrary or like something having a purpose. That is why they were understood in the past as the action of a god or a ghost, a saint or devil, who wanted to demonstrate something by it. Only in China was the Tao not viewed as being personal, but besides the Tao the ancient Chinese also knew a so-called "Will of Heaven," which could be benevolent or annoyed, like a human being.

Our Western civilizations seems to have believed predominantly in a personal god to whom they have attributed, at least in the past, personal, even anthropoid, psychological reactions. Synchronistic events were seen as miracles performed by God or the Devil. But even in our Western world the highly personal God, Yahweh, and the Christian God were imagined to be a sphere, which is a symbol of mathematical order, not of some partial order but of a total order, a world-formula, so to speak.

Why should God not reveal Himself also in mathematics? as Novalis asks. The history of this symbolic idea is very old.[34] It began with Empedokles, who called God "an infinite sphere which enjoys its eternal circling." For Parmenides too the true Existence is circular and infinite. For Plato the totality of the world of ideas is irrepresentable, but its replica in matter, the universe, is a geometrical sphere. But the more explicit description of God as a perfect but infinite sphere stems from Plotinus.[35] For Plotinus's god is one *omnipresence* in the multiplicity of concrete things. Plotinus illustrates this with a threefold sphere.

The outer one is the cosmic sphere of the many things, the middle sphere is subdivided by the radii into the different ideas (νοητὰ) and represents the world soul; and finally the central sphere represents the *compact oneness* of all ideas; this central sphere is without movement. Its center is "the soul's most genuine nature, the idea of its inner unity, uniformity, and totality."[36] This image, however, is only an incomplete schema, compared to what is really meant, for there is absolutely no difference between the smallest and the bigger spheres. In other words, there is no real extension at all; one could just as well call it a single point.

The next important continuer is Salomon ben Gebirol (ca. 1020–1070), whose main work was translated into Latin as *Fons vitae (Source of Life)*. Gebirol calls the godhead for the first time a *"sphaera intelligibilis"*—a spiritual sphere. His book was translated into Latin in 1150 in Spain and influenced Wilhelm of Auvergne (d. 1249), John Duns Scotus, Albert the Great, and many others. Another continuation of this tradition is the so-called theology of Pseudo-Aristotle, which originally was a Syrian-Arab excerpt of the last three of Plotinus's *Enneads,* where God is seen mainly as the nondimensional center, but also as the all-embracing circular periphery of all Existence.[37] God emanates into all things and remains simultaneously a unity without any subdivision into space and time.[38] And last there is an anonymous *Liber XXIV philosophorum* (twelfth century), which sums this up in the famous sentence: *"Deus est sphaera infinita, cuius centrum est ubique circumferentia nusquam"* (God is an infinite sphere whose center is everywhere and whose circumference is nowhere). And this famous sentence went on to be quoted by Alanus de Insulis (d. 1203) as a saying of Hermes, because another title of the treatise was *Liber Termegisti de regulis theologiae.*[39]

The next most famous theologian who took up this symbolism was Meister Eckhart. "God is an immeasurable and unmeasured circle which embraces the widest mind of man in the form of a point which is—compared to God's incomprehensible measurelessness—so small that one cannot even name it."[40] Christ as the Incarnation of God is the squaring of the circle, because "Christ is quadrangular" and because the squaring of the circle can be only an infinite approximation. We find similar ideas in the works of mystics like Ruysbroek and Tauler and Seuse. Eckhart added certain new aspects to the old symbolism: namely, that in God all is equal; there is no plus or minus: *"Deus est sphaera intellectualis infinita, cuis tot sunt circumferentiae quot sunt puncta,"* or, *"cuius centrum est ubique et circumferentia nusquam,"* or, *"qui totus est in sui minimo."*

But it is the mathematician-mystic Nicolas of Kues (Cusanus) who most often made use of this simile of the godhead.[41] In this "sphere" the straight and the curved become one in an infinite process of approximation,[42] whereby God is more the curved, his creation more the straight aspect. Thus the infinite sphere is also, in a way, a straight line *(infinita circularis est recta)*. The circumference is the Holy Ghost.

From here we come to Johannes Kepler, who, however, wanted God to be more the center of the sphere than the surface, Christ the surface (the becoming visible of the center), and the Holy Ghost the radii. Kepler's model of the planetary spheres is a "play of nature" which imitates God's "play," and the human mind must imitate this spherical play in its search for the truth.[43]

Copernicus also was inspired by the sphere of Cusanus,[44] and Valentin Weigel later postulates that because the center of the sphere is everywhere, it is also at the bottom of the human soul.[45] In the center "I am God and God is in me, I am the heavens and the heavens are in me."[46]

I skip such intermediary adherers of this idea as Johannes Reuchlin, Pascal, Bovillus Zozzi, Boehme, and Henri More,[47] and come to Leibniz, who taught that from all monads (souls) God is the most primary monad, *"le centre primitif"* from which all others are fulgurated (produced by an act of lightning). He continues: *"Une fort bien dit qu'il est comme un centre partout mais son circumférence n'est nulle part"* (All monads, and thus also our own psyches, are all psychic centers which express the infinite circumference of the cosmos).[48] These centers are not only passive "collecting" points but active centers which radiate forth a spontaneous individual representation of the universe.

I shall skip a few more philosophers to end up with the German philosopher J. G. Fichte, who saw this image of the infinite sphere as a symbol of the creative absolute Ego in our psyche, in contrast to our accidental ego,[49] and these egos are all united by universal love into the great All-Sphere, where God and man are one. From there—as you see—the step to Jung's interpretation of the sphere as a symbol of the Self is not a big one.

In modern mathematics one could compare this old *sphera intelligibilis* with the nondimensional point and space as conceived as an infinite manifold. (The so-called Hilbert space, on the contrary, contains already *one* limitation because its vectors are an infinite series of real numbers whose quadratic sums are convergent.)[50]

This geometrical symbol has been, one could say, the god of the mathematicians, and in it prevails the intuition of all-embracing cosmic order, which has also a meaning though the latter is interpreted slightly differently throughout the ages.

This geometrical God-image, the mandala, is as a whole a relatively *static* symbol of order, even if it can include an internal rotating movement. As a whole it is represented as standing still. And what is more important, it is something completely *impersonal*. One can admire a mandala or be moved by its harmony, but one cannot talk to it or quarrel with it. That is why in most existing religions the Godhead is also represented by a personal being. Krishna can speak to man, as we see in the *Bhagavad Gita,* though he is inhumanly terrible in his true form. The Judeo-Christian God is a person. The advantage of a personal God-image, Jung says, "lies in making possible a much better objectification of the *vis-à-vis.*" Its "emotional quality confers life and effectuality" upon it. "Hate and love, fear and reverence enter the scene of confrontation and raise it to a drama. What has merely been 'displayed' becomes 'acted.' The whole man enters the fray with his total reality."[51] This implies again that meaning is more total, more a "holon," than order, and also that there is no meaning except for *me,* for that very individual who is "hit" by it. The realization of order suggests a wise adaptation to it, but entails a kind of stoic or epicurean fatalism which, as Raymond Ruyer points out, is the average attitude nowadays among leading American physicists. But there is no *feeling* confrontation. Meaning, on the contrary, implies feeling reactions and ethical decisions; it contains a personal nuance.

Originally, as we saw in the example of the sphere, meaning and order were combined; only with the development of modern science did they become separate. The tearing apart of order and meaning also becomes visible in another symbol, in the idea of a cosmic machine, i.e., the idea that the universe is like an enormous machine, preferably conceived as a clock. The first clocks were mostly used in monasteries and cathedrals, and one attributed to them a kind of religious meaning. Nicolas Cusanus, for instance, says in his *Vision of God* (1453): "Let then the concept of the clock represent eternity's Self, then the motion of the clock representeth succession. Eternity therefore enfoldeth and unfoldeth succession, since the concept of the clock which is eternity doth alike enfold and unfold all things."[52] One sees here a close relation of the clock to the idea of the divine sphere.

Only in post-Cartesian sciences and philosophies did the symbol of the clock as an image of the universe become the image of a soulless, autonomous mechanism which stupidly ticks on into all eternity toward its entropy-death. This mechanistic view prevailed until some thirty years ago. Man forgot that no clock can exist without a clockmaker, a purposeful intelligence behind it. If we look at the symbolism of machines, how it appears in dreams and unconscious phantasies, it generally points to the existence of such a purposeful intelligence working behind it in the unconscious. Such a dream, for instance, is the world-clock vision which Jung published in *Psychology and Alchemy*. Another dream is the following: "I am in a deep cellar, together with a boy and a man. The boy has been given an electric installation for Christmas: a large copper pot is suspended from the ceiling and electric wires from all directions make it vibrate. After some time there are no more wires; the pot now vibrates from atmospheric electric oscillations."[53]

For us this is a symbol of the Self. In a letter, Jung comments on this dream:[54] what is so peculiar is the symbolization of the Self as an apparatus. A "machine" is always something *thought up,* deliberately put together for a definite purpose. The Tantrists say that things represent *the distinctness of God's thoughts.* The machine is a microcosm that Paracelsus called the "star in man." I always have the feeling that these symbols touch upon the great secrets, the *magnalia Dei* (great things of God).

Distinctness is *the* characteristic of order. If the modern physicists mainly search for order in matter, they really look out for distinctness in the chaotic dance of subatomic particles. Let us look closer, therefore, at the problem of distinctness. For us it is an achievement of consciousness. The archetypes in the collective unconscious have no distinctness; they contain or are only a latent preformed order. Jung saw them surrounded by a "diffuse cloud of cognition."[55] Only when an archetype becomes conscious in us does it manifest in a more distinct image, but in fact never in *one* image alone but in a large amount of images. The archetype of the Great Mother, for instance, can become manifest in the mother goddesses, Paradise, the Kingdom of God, the Heavenly Jerusalem, the Church, city, country, heaven, earth, the woods, the sea, the still waters, matter, and the moon; they all can be mother symbols. Also all places of fertility, such as the cornucopia, the plowed field, and the garden. It can also be associated with a rock, a cave, a tree, a spring, a deep well, various vessels such as the baptismal font, the Grail, or with flowers such as the rose or the lotus, and various animals such as the cow, the hare, the bear, etc.[56] In this way what we think to be a distinct archetype is empirically only graspable by a whole bundle of archetypal images. And this is true for all archetypes such as the hero (think of Campbell's *Hero with a Thousand Faces!*), the life tree, the divine child, etc. If we attribute meaning to an archetype it is therefore something very indistinct. Jung says quite rightly that what "that factor which appears to us as 'meaning' may be in itself we have no possibility of knowing."[57] The Chinese equivalent of cosmic meaning is their concept of Tao.[58]

> Incommensurable, impalpable,
> Yet latent in it are forms;
> Impalpable, incommensurable,
> Yet within it are entities.
> Shadowy it is and dim.
>
> —*Tao Tê Ching*, chap. 21[59]

Tao does not manifest in the world of the senses, but it is somehow its organizer.

> Because the eyes gazes but can catch no glimpse of it,
> It is called elusive.
> Because the ear listens but cannot hear it,
> It is called the rarefied.
> Because the hand feels for it but cannot find it,

It is called the infinitesimal. . . .
These are called the shapeless shapes,
Forms without form, Value semblances.

— *Tao Tē Ching,* chap. 14

Now, if number is an archetype, as I tried to show before, it shares this ungraspable vagueness with everything else in the unconscious. It becomes "number" in the usual distinct sense of the word only when its latent orderedness has become conscious. We effect this by trying to make those "necessary statements" about each number which I mentioned before. Then number reaches the state of definite distinctness in our mind and even becomes the foundation of mathematical logic, but it does not lose completely its obscurity, as Hermann Weyl saw correctly, or as he once remarked jokingly: "God exists because mathematics is consistent; but the Devil too exists because we cannot prove this consistency."[60]

Now we have to turn to the question of how the archetypes of number relate to the other archetypes which we generally discover at the bottom of mythological images and collective ideas. Are they something different or not? If we look at different cultural traditions, we see that the first numbers were frequently associated with certain archetypal images. The number 1, for instance, with the supreme Godhead, the total *unus mundus,* and the singled-out individual, etc. The most impressive system of such combinations is the *I Ching.* It uses number, as it says, because "the language of communication with suprahuman intelligences was believed to be based on number."[61] There Heaven is the ultimate unity, the Creative is 1; Earth, the feminine, the receptive, is 2; Heaven encompassing the Earth (1 encompassing 2) is also 3. However, Heaven is not just Heaven; it is round, the prince, the father, jade, metal, cold, ice, deep, red, a good horse, an old horse, a lean horse, a wild horse, fruit. The Receptive is earth, mother, cloth, a kettle, frugality; it is level, it is a cow, a calf, a large wagon, the multitude, a shaft, various kinds of soil; it is black.[62] We have here the same "cloud of cognition" or bundled images we saw before in the example of the mother. In spite of this vagueness, we feel that there is a kind of meaning in this bundle of images, of which the number association appears to be just one among others.

But number, when it is conscious, seems especially to be "order." What more special kind or order is it then? Western mathematics chose an order of quantity and of the logical relations of number sets; the Chinese, on the other hand, chose a *temporal* order, an active dynamic form of order. Thus a commentary to the *I Ching* says: "The Changes have no consciousness, no action; they are quiescent and do not move. But if they are stimulated, they penetrate all situations."[63] The *I Ching* "serves for exploring the laws of number and thus for knowing the future."[64] They use number as *a time-phase indicator* of dynamic processes. Jung too saw in numbers such a time factor, for he says: "The first ten numbers represent—if they represent anything at all—an abstract cosmogony derived from the monad."[65] This means, for instance, that the All-One-God or Unitas comes necessarily before the Two-God, etc.

Now, the Chinese used number especially to express qualitative time-phases. For them there are oneness moments, so to speak, times of duality, times of fourfoldness. The whole *I Ching* is nothing more than a most impressive symbolic system of such a play or order of possible archetypal moments, expressed in the form of numerical permutations of lines. This makes use of something we know but tend to forget: Archetypes are not only relatively permanent structures in the unconscious psyche, they are dynamisms; and if they are dynamisms, i.e., if they are in movement, they enter time. We can actually observe such time-phases in the constellation of an archetype. In most cases when any archetype constellates, it first manifests as *one* archetypal image in a dream. When it moves toward the threshold of consciousness it generally appears doubled, as two identical or nearly identical images, two people, two dogs, two trees. We take this as a sign that the unconscious content is beginning to reach the threshold of consciousness. That would be the two-phase of its "time." Three groups of beings symbolize that that very archetype is actively possessing the ego, forcing upon it actions or thoughts. That is why fate gods are so often triadic. When the same content appears in its four-phase it has reached

284 · PSYCHE AND MATTER

its best possibility for being realized in our consciousness (namely, through the four functions).

Seen from this angle, number is not only quantity but has also a *temporal* quality. One would be the quality of origin, beginning point; two the quality of polarization or symmetry; three of directed action, movement; four of confinement, consolidation; and so forth.

Fritjof Capra has asked me the relevant question: why are we so interested in number and not so much in geometrical or topological structures? This is, I think, because synchronicity seems more connected with time than with space. For, as Jung pointed out, "it is not easy to understand synchronicity in time as spatial, for we cannot imagine any space in which future events are objectively present and could be experienced as such through a reduction of this spatial distance."⁶⁶

Let us look at an example. I dream that a friend in the United States dies. Twenty-four hours later this actually happens. It is thinkable that the dream image of the friend's death exists in my unconscious psyche (which is outside time and space) and that the synchronistic event takes place in the U.S. after my dream (here we could speculate about a contractability or relativization of time). However, it is more difficult to think that the friend already died somewhere near me, and that I perceived it there at the time of the dream, and that he then died farther away, in the U.S. (that would be a contractibility of space). This difficulty is the reason why Jung was more interested in number as time-phase indicators than in topological structures. Since Einstein, however, we know that time and space are inseparable as an observable factor. It seems to me that the difference of arithmetic and topology resembles that between music and the visual arts. Number has more to do with rhythm and with processes in time, the visual arts more with the mysteries of space. But a combination of the elements of order and of meaning probably exists in both temporal and spatial structures. Time, seen not as a vector or empty frame of reference, as the physicists see it, but in the Chinese way as a succession of *qualitatively* distinct phases in which a specific amount of inner and outer events coincide, would be something slightly different from space, being more closely connected with the unconscious psyche than the latter. Spatialization seems to be a concept derived from the experience of time, not vice versa.[67] Perhaps the fact that time-inversion (operation T) resists being reduced into perfect symmetry has to do with this fact (while operation P, spatial mirror inversion, and operation C are more frequent and less absurd than is operation T.)[68]

In his paper on S-matrix theory[69] which Dr. Capra had the kindness to send me, he points out that in S-matrix theory physicists abandon "the idea of fundamental building blocks of matter and accept no fundamental entities whatsoever."[70] The universe is rather "seen as a dynamic web of interrelated events."[71] Each network of events which we observe "in an experiment is nevertheless structured according to definite rules. These are the conservation laws. Only those reactions can occur in which a well defined set of quantum numbers is conserved."[72]

Only those reactions would be possible which show a *flow*[73] of quantum numbers exhibiting the patterns associated with quarks, i.e., the "twoness" characteristic of mesons and the "threeness" characteristic of baryons together with the various flavors that can combine to form the quantum numbers of the observed hadrons."[74] As a layperson in physics I cannot judge the implications of this, but it seems to me that in this more dynamic view of the reality of matter we could find a rapprochement to Jung's dynamic view of the archetypes in the unconscious psyche. Physics and psychology indicate that not only topological structures but numbers also appear as qualities of matter—just as they appear as a quality of psychic contents. The only difference, it seems to me, would lie in an interpretation of this quality only in terms of order or also, as we do in psychology, in terms of meaning. Up until now most physicists certainly do not associate consciously any meaning with order. The "twoness" of mesons is only a fact without "meaning," if I understand them rightly.

We therefore touch here upon the differences between the two fields of science. Let me amplify this difference in the language of some modern physicists. According to Ruyer's book *La Gnose de Princeton*, some modern physicists see reality in the following way: We have a direct consciousness of ourselves consisting of a certain amount of direct information. This is not our body, but our "I." But if we look at another being or object we can in fact not truly see it because we see only its body, its outer appearance, which we call matter, and not its "inwardness," which is its true nature.[75] The corporeal existence is only an illusion, or a by-product of our sense perception. We have two modes for acquiring information: by observation and by participation.[76] The latter consists in participating in trans-spatial "themes," as they put it. This is very similar to Jung's idea of a collective unconscious, which is, by his definition, partly trans-spatial and trans-temporal; its themes are what we call the archetypes.[77] God, for instance, is a participable, more than an observable.[78] Ruyer also calls some of the themes superindividual domains and part of a Universal Consciousness. In contrast to "observables," participables are postulated to be outside space.[79] But the very "participables" have a timeless aspect which causes time, as Ruyer formulates, to be more than a functioning of spatial structures; they give time a direction in the sense of time's arrow and a *meaning*. Science "reveals" the world of participation but it sees it only in its observable "other" side.[80] The universe makes "meaning" manifest by its very existence, form and life.[81]

In such modern speculative ideas of some physicists we come very close to each other. For Jungian psychology is mostly an attempt to describe participables, or man, as a holon of meaning, in contrast to certain schools of psychiatry which look at man only as an "observable," not allowing any empathy or communication of meaning. Aniela Jaffé rightly called Jung's myth "the myth of meaning." But there are still also great differences, because although the physicists in question believe in God as a superdomanial ultimate intelligence with which we can play, so to speak, by making scientific experiments, this intelligence or cosmic mind does not, or rather only partially, comes to meet us in our soul. That is why these physicists mostly do not believe in incarnation and in Christ. For Jung, on the contrary, the dramatic encounter of man with the personified God-image in his psyche is *the* essential meaning of man's existence.

The Princeton physicists imagine God as a cosmic domanial supra-intelligence far transcending the intelligence of man, so it seems not concerned with details. We also would say: yes, the Self is a supra-*intelligence* far transcending that of man (Jung calls it "absolute subjectless knowledge, consisting of images"), but it is the intelligence of the collective unconscious. It is vast but not focused. On this planet at least man has probably the most focused consciousness; he can experience definite realizations of meaning which are more "real" than these latent "clouds of cognition" in the unconscious. Jung writes:

> Since a creation without the reflecting consciousness of man has no discernible meaning, the hypothesis of a latent meaning endows man with a cosmogonic significance, a true *raison d'être*. If . . . the latent meaning is attributed to the Creator as part of a conscious plan of creation, the question arises: Why should the Creator stage-manage this whole phenomenal world since he already knows what he can reflect himself in, and why should he reflect himself at all since he is already conscious of himself? Why should he create alongside his own omniscience a second, inferior consciousness—millions of dreary little mirrors when he knows in advance just what the image they reflect will look like?
> . . . He is just as unconscious as man or even more unconscious, since according to the myth of the *incarnatio* he actually felt obliged to become man and offer himself as a sacrifice.[82]

The God of modern physicists resembles more the God-image of Hinduism, or generally of the Far East, and has been, as Ruyer points out, actually influenced by it. Jung's view stands closer to Western Christianity, though he thought it incomplete and in need of a further unfolding of its myth. This does not mean that one is more "true" than the other; what one believes in this respect is more a matter of temperament.

> To Western man, the meaninglessness of a merely static universe is unbearable. He must assume that it has meaning. The Oriental does not need to make this assumption; rather he himself embodies it. Whereas the Occidental feels the need to complete the meaning of the world, the Oriental strives for the fulfillment of meaning in man, stripping the world and existence from himself.[83]

Jung, as you can see from this quotation, sees it as the task of man to complete the meaning of nature by his efforts to become conscious. *"Quod natura relinquit imperfectum, ars perficit,"* as the old alchemists said. He was not at all sure that meaning would prevail. At the end of his life he wrote in his *Memories, Dreams, Reflections:*

> The importance of consciousness is so great that one cannot help suspecting the element of *meaning* to be concealed somewhere within all the monstrous, apparently senseless biological turmoil, and that the road to its manifestation was ultimately found on the level of warm-blooded vertebrates possessed of a differentiated brain—found as if by chance, unintended and unforeseen, and yet somehow sensed, felt and groped for out of some dark urge.[84]

> The world into which we are born is brutal and cruel, and at the same time of divine beauty. Which element we think outweighs the other, whether meaninglessness or meaning, is a matter of temperament. If meaningless were absolutely preponderant, the meaningfulness of life would vanish to an increasing degree with each step in our development. But that is—or seems to me—not the case. Probably, as in all metaphysical questions, both are true: Life is—or has—meaning and meaninglessness. I cherish the anxious hope that meaning will preponderate and win the battle.[85]

Here Jung reaches out into realms which lead far away from a strictly scientific outlook. He did it quite consciously because the meaningful but rather vague language of myth is in his view more appropriate for the description of psychological facts. Only so can it include the vagueness of meaning and the feeling function. This, I think, will always keep psychology separate from physics. If we try, all the same, to meet, it is for the reason that in its fringes, where psychology reaches over to other fields of science, there should exist—if possible—no fundamental contradictions. A psychology which does not keep pace with the findings of the other sciences seems to me no good. I think that Jungian psychology meets nuclear physics on a fringe via the concept of order, especially closely in the view that number is an archetype as well as a property of material phenomena, be it quantum numbers or patterns of particle interactions. Capra writes: "When the particles are arranged according to their values of their quantum numbers they are seen to fall into very neat patterns, hexagonal and triangular patterns, known as octets and decuplets."[86] Very similar patterns appear in the archetypal structures produced by the unconscious psyche, but in contrast to the aspect of order alone we have in psychology also to search for their "meaning." Number, it seems to me, unites both: order and meaning, and is therefore, together with its topological spatializations into "patterns," a possible meeting point for the two fields of science. In dealing with "particibles," however, psychology has to transcend the hitherto delineated limits of science, because it cannot exclude "meaning" and the feeling function from its way of describing its object. That seems to be the specific value but also the limitation of psychology. The search for order appeals to the function of sensation, thinking and also sometimes intuition. But to include feeling values and thus the "whole," the vagueness of "meaning" forces us to go beyond science and leads us back to the older way of mankind for expressing itself: to myth. That inevitably leads to antinomies and an obscuring of scientific clarity. It makes understandable why the "theologians of number" do not like us and why the gnostics of Princeton feel that we are occultists. But because we have to deal with the human individual as a whole, we are forced into this outlook. To me this is something positive because I would regret it if physics as it is were to swallow up psychology or vice versa—it seems more fruitful to me that each field keep its own field of thought and action but that they exchange their views in those fringe areas where we can creatively meet.

Notes

1. C. G. Jung, *Memories, Dreams, Reflections* (New York: Vintage Books, 1963), p. 310.
2. Cf., for instance, Gottlob Frege, *Grundgesetze der Arithmetik* (reprint) (Hildesheim: Olms, 1962), pp. vii, xivff.
3. Ibid., pp. xvii, xviii.
4. Gottlob Frege, *Funktion, Begriff, Bedeutung* (Vandenhoeck, 1975), pp. 17–18, 44–45; cf. also p. 83.
5. Ibid., p. 67.

6. See Hermann Weyl, *Philosophy of Mathematics and Natural Science* (Princeton: Princeton University Press, 1945).

7. Quoted from E. Nagel and J. R. Newman, "Goedel's Proof," *Scientific American*, June 1956, p. 81. I owe the knowledge of this article to the kindness of Dr. Wilhelm Just.

8. Ibid., p. 86.

9. Jung, *Memories, Dreams, Reflections*, p. 310.

10. Cf. C. G. Jung, "Synchronicity: An Acausal Connecting Principle," in *The Structure and Dynamics of the Psyche*, cw 8, para. 870.

11. Cf. T. Danzig, *Number: The Language of Science* (New York: Macmillan, 1954), p. 234.

12. Eugène Wigner, *Symmetries and Reflections* (Cambridge, Mass.: MIT Press, 1970).

13. Jung, *Memories, Dreams, Reflections*, pp. 310ff.

14. C. G. Jung, *Letters* (Princeton: Princeton University Press, 1976), vol. 2, p. 494.

15. As Aniela Jaffé erroneously asserted.

16. Jung, *Letters*, vol. 2, p. 495.

17. Jung, "Synchronicity," cw 8, para. 965.

18. Ibid.

19. My addition.

20. Jung, "Synchronicity," cw 8, para. 965.

21. Ibid., para. 968.

22. Jung, *Letters*, vol. 2, p. 495.

23. Liu Guan-ying, "Die ungewöhnlichen Naturerscheinungen in den T'ang Annalen und ihre Deutung," in *Symbolon*, ed. I. Schwabe (Basel, 1961), II, pp. 32ff.

24. Richard Wilhelm, *The I Ching or Book of Changes*, trans. Cary Baynes (London: Routledge & Kegan Paul, n.d.), II, p. 321.

25. Ibid., p. 281.

26. Jung, "Synchronicity," cw 8, para. 855.

27. Cf. ibid., para. 856.

28. Ibid.

29. Ibid., para. 855.

30. Wilhelm, *I Ching*, p. 322.

31. Ibid., p. 320.

32. G. J. Whitrow, *The Natural Philosophy of Time* (London, 1961), pp. 295–96.

33. C. G. Jung, *Mysterium Coniunctionis*, cw 14, para. 662.

34. I base the following representation on D. Mahnke, *Unendliche Sphäre und Allmittelpunkt* (Stuttgart, 1966).
35. Ibid., pp. 230–35, 215ff.
36. Ibid., p. 273.
37. Ibid., p. 199.
38. Ibid., p. 202.
39. Ibid., p. 175.
40. Ibid., p. 167.
41. Ibid., p. 141.
42. Mahnke, *Unendliche Sphäre*, pp. 141ff.
43. Ibid., p. 139.
44. Ibid., p. 127.
45. Ibid., p. 125.
46. Ibid.
47. Mahnke, *Unendliche Sphäre*, pp. 18ff.
48. Ibid., p. 17.
49. Ibid., pp. 8, 10.
50. Cf. Marie-Louise von Franz, *Number and Time* (Evanston, Ill.: Northwestern University Press, 1974), p. 122.
51. Jung, *Memories, Dreams, Reflections*, p. 337.
52. Cf. F. C. Haber, "The Darwinian Revolution in the Concept of Time," in J. T. Fraser and N. Lawrence (eds.), *The Study of Time* I (Heidelberg & New York: Springer, 1972), p. 383.
53. Jung, *Letters*, vol. 1, p. 325.
54. Ibid., p. 326.
55. Jung, *Memories, Dreams, Reflections*, p. 308.
56. C. G. Jung, *Psychiatric Studies*, cw 1, p. 81.
57. Jung, "Synchronicity," cw 8, para. 916.
58. Ibid., para. 917.
59. Quoted ibid., para. 921.
60. Quoted in Morris Kline, "Les Fondements des mathématiques," *La Recherche*, no. 54 (March 1975): 207.
61. Wilhelm, *I Ching*, I, p. 282.
62. Ibid., pp. 295–96.
63. Ibid., p. 339.
64. Ibid., p. 323.
65. Jung, *Memories, Dreams, Reflections*, pp. 310–11.
66. Jung, "Synchronicity," cw 8, para. 855.
67. This is the view of the *I Ching:* Heaven as Spirit has time as its field of action; Earth as a derived principle has space as its field of realization.

68. M. Ruyer, *La Gnose de Princeton* (Paris, 1974), pp. 120–21.
69. Fritjof Capra, "Quark Physics without Quarks: A Review of Recent Developments in S-Matrix Theory" (reprint), submitted to *The American Journal of Physics*.
70. Ruyer, *La Gnose*, p. 29.
71. Ibid., pp. 121–22.
72. Ibid., p. 10.
73. My emphasis.
74. Ruyer, *La Gnose*, p. 17.
75. Ibid., p. 34.
76. Cf. ibid., pp. 123ff.
77. Ruyer compares them too with the pattern of behavior of animals. Ibid., p. 124.
78. Ibid., p. 129.
79. Ibid., p. 128.
80. Ibid., p. 130.
81. Ibid., pp. 131–32.
82. Jung, *Letters*, vol. 2, pp. 495–96.
83. Quoted in Jung, *Memories, Dreams, Reflections*, p. 317.
84. Ibid., pp. 338–39.
85. Ibid., pp. 358–59.
86. Capra, "Quark Physics without Quarks," p. 7.

Time and Synchronicity
In Analytical Psychology

S tudies of the concept of time, entropy, and information theory have resulted in some recent suggestions that topics in psychology be incorporated in the domain of inquiry of physics.[1] Earlier, C. G. Jung in his exploration of the unconscious and of the psychoid layers[2] of the human psyche also came upon certain problems where what we call "psyche" seems to fuse with what we usually call "matter" and where the applicability of the concept of time itself becomes questionable. It may, thus, be useful to give a brief report of his relatively secure, pertinent discoveries and list, as well, some open questions, reflections, doubts and proposed ways of research which might elucidate the obscure relation between psyche, matter, and time.

1. The Unconscious Psyche and Its Structures

The greatest and most revolutionary finding of modern psychology is the discovery of the unconscious by Sigmund Freud, that is, that realm of the psyche which manifests itself relatively independently of the structure of our conscious mind. It is a well-known fact that an impulse, wish, thought, fantasy, or the like, can be temporarily unconscious (i.e., forgotten). This fact would justify the use of an adjective "unconscious" but would not allow us to hypostatize a noun "the unconscious" as a self-subsisting entity. Further observation, however, has shown that unconscious or forgotten contents[3] often undergo specific transformations during their unconscious phase of existence. For example, they can become more emotionally important, automatic, stereotyped, or more mythological and archaic in form, or they can become associated with material which originally did not belong to them and thus they reappear in consciousness in a different condition. This fact forces us to conclude that the unconscious is a psychism sui generis[4] which seems to work differently from our conscious mind. Following William James, Jung and Pauli compared this concept with the concept of field in physics,[5] and Niels Bohr pointed out that the relationship between conscious and unconscious is a complementary one.[6]

In the wakened state this psychism sui generis or the unconscious[7] in the human personality mainly manifests itself by interrupting the continuity of our conscious mental operations, e.g., by the invasion of fantasies, speech mistakes, involuntary gestures, auditions, visions, or even hallucinations, and during sleep in the form of dreams.

In studying dream life as our major source of information about the unconscious area of the psyche, Jung found that a number of recurrent dream motifs strikingly resemble mythological themes and motifs as studied by the science of comparative religion.[8] Whenever such motives appear in the dream they also bring up or constellate strong dynamic and emotional reactions in the dreamer. They tend to produce passionate impulses such as sudden conversions, "holy" convictions, fanatical actions, obstinate thoughts, and so on. In a positive sense, they can also bring about a passionate and creative pursuit of a theme. *Jung called the* (probably inborn) *unconscious, structural dispositions which cause the abovementioned reactions "archetypes."*[9] Their products in dreams and semiconscious states, i.e., the mythological fantasies, thoughts, symbolic actions, etc., he calls "archetypal."[10]

These archetypes actually coincide to a great extent with what zoologists call patterns of behavior, and the Jungian archetypes could, in a way, just as well be called patterns of human behavior. [11] There is, however, a difference in that the zoologist can only study these patterns in the outwardly carried-out instinctual actions of an animal, while in our psychological studies of man we can also observe "from within" the accompanying subjective processes such as typical, recurring fantasies, representations, feelings and emotions.

The next most important discovery of depth psychology lies in the fact that these archetypal patterns of mental behavior contain not only an imaginative but also a definitely cognitive element which can influence the conscious mind in the form of sudden "flashes of insight"—as I will demonstrate later. [12] Jung calls the cognitive element of the archetype "luminosity" in order to distinguish it from the conscious daylight mind or ego-consciousness. [13]

The patterns of behavior in animals often include spatial as well as temporal elements in their radius of activity. Animals, for instance, have specific territories, migration routes, mating places, i.e., spatial relations, whereas other patterns imply a sort of "knowledge" of future states of evolution, i.e., temporal factors. [14] It is thus not surprising that Jung independently discovered similar facts while studying the archetypes or human patterns of psychological behavior.

2. Time in the Conscious and Time in the Unconscious

Physicists studying cybernetics have observed that what we call consciousness seems to consist of an intrapsychic flux or train of ideas, [15] which flows "parallel to" (or is even possibly explicable by) the "arrow" of time. While M. S. Watanabe [16] convincingly argues that this sense of time is a fact sui generis, others like Grünbaum tend to believe that entropy is the cause of this time sense in man. [17] Olivier Costa de Beauregard stresses that whatever its origin is, it runs parallel to the arrow of time in physics: *"le flux intérieur de la vie physique est lié de manière essentielle à un flux d'information entrante."* [18] For the psychologist, this statement (that the train of ideas runs parallel with the arrow of time) is acceptable only as it applies to our conscious psyche, or to the concentrated "attention to life," as Bergson calls it.[19]

As soon, however, as we study the functioning of the unconscious psyche, the validity of this statement becomes questionable. It is generally admitted that people who have not succeeded in building up a concentrated state of consciousness or a sharply focused "attention to life," such as certain primitive groups or children, lack the ability of consciously "counting time." They rather live in a relatively and vaguely perceived stream where only a few emotionally important events are perceived and recorded, which then act as signposts in an indistinct flux of life.[20]

When the psychologist explores the phenomena which come immediately from the unconscious, such as visions, obsessive fantasies, and above all dreams, the regularity, "speed," and distinct discernibility of time become uncertain[21] or even questionable. It is as if in a dream one would rather experience a pictorially represented cluster of events perceived simultaneously, while the conscious mind when recording these dream events later would automatically put them into an order which we perceive as a logical time sequence. This seems to lend some support to the idea of a block universe with which the unconscious would be coextensive.[22] It seems that the conscious conception of time as an arrow and "flux" seems to become curiously relative (or possibly nonexistent) in the unconscious.[23]

Beyond the observation of dream material, this seems to be confirmed by the myths of all times if, as we said, such myths are admitted as archetypal in substance. In most mythologies and primitive religious systems there is the representation of a primordial time or an *illud tempus,* as Mircea Eliade calls it,[24] an "other" time beyond our actual time in which miraculous primordial mythological and symbolic events took place, or even still take place. This primordial time dimension has either now disappeared or continues to exist beside our usual time but can be reached only in exceptional unconscious mental conditions, such as in the dream state, coma, ecstasy, or intoxication. This primordial time is often described not as a time but as a creative *durée* in the sense of Bergson, or as an eternity meaning an actual extension of time without progress.[25] The Australian aborigines call this mythical time *aljira,* a word which also means "dream," for it is, according to them, the time-space continuum in which dream events occur. In other words, this mythical idea of a primordial time as the time dimension of dream events, visions, etc., seems to coincide with what modern depth psychology would now call the unconscious, for contact with this dimension is only possible by becoming unconscious.[26]

The testimonies concerning the relative "timelessness" of the unconscious do not come only from primitives; we find the same in all mystical experiences characterized by a feeling of oneness with the universe[27] and of timelessness.[28] This feeling of timelessness is inherent in the experience of the deeper layers of the unconscious, which Jung calls the collective unconscious because its structure is substantially the same in everyone. People who have had such experiences often claim that they can then also foreknow future events. The ordinary time experience with its subdivisions of past, present, and future fades.[29] This is the "mystical" experience generally sought for in many Eastern religious movements. The feeling of oneness with all things is probably founded upon the cluster nature or contamination of unconscious contents.

We also find this same phenomenon of a timeless simultaneity in the appearance of unconscious products in the history of scientific discoveries. We may mention the famous example of Henri Poincaré[30] and a similar testimony from a letter of Karl-Friedrich Gauss to Olbers that he found the proof of an arithmetical theorem in this way: "Finally . . . I succeeded, not on account of my painful efforts, but by the Grace of God. Like a sudden flash of lightning the riddle happened to be solved. I myself cannot say what was the conducting thread which connected what I previously knew with what made my success possible."[31] Jacques H. Hadamard[32] and B. L. van der Waerden[33] have collected many more examples of such mathematical "illuminations" and Harold Ruegg[34] of similar experiences in other fields of scientific activity. The always recurring and important factor for our theme is the simultaneity with which the complete solution is intuitively perceived and which can be checked later by discursive reasoning. This, in our opinion, is due to the fact that the solution presented itself as a sort of ordered Gestalt,[35] or, in Jungian terms, as an archetypal pattern or image and still carries with it some of the relative timelessness of the unconscious. These examples also demonstrate the cognitive element in archetypal patterns which was mentioned above.[36]

Similar evidence of a fading time sense in semiunconscious conditions can also be found in states of pathological overexcitement, intoxication and the disturbance provoked by prolonged isolation,[37] with their slowing of intellectual activity and accompanying intensification of dream life. All these factors seem to suggest that the time flux, as a subjective psychological experience, is bound to the functioning of our conscious mind but becomes relative (or possibly even nonexistent) in the unconscious. Thus Costa de Beauregard's suggestion to consider the unconscious as timeless and coextensive with the Minkowski-Einsteinian "block universe" appears to the psychologist a new and more precise formulation of the age-old archetypal idea of an "other time."

3. Meaningful Coincidences of Consciously Perceived External Events with Archetypal Unconscious Processes

In the course of observing the effects of activated archetypes or patterns of psychological reactions in his patients, Jung again and again encountered cases where rare outer chance events tended to coincide meaningfully with archetypal dream images. Such cases seem to occur only when an archetype is activated producing highly charged conscious or unconscious emotions. The following may serve as an illustration:[38] A woman with a very strong power complex, and a "devouring" attitude toward people, dreamt of seeing three tigers seated threateningly in front of her. Her analyst pointed out the meaning of the dream and through causal arguments tried to make her understand the devouring attitude which she thus displayed. Later in the day the patient and her friend, while strolling along Lake Zurich, noticed a crowd gazing at three tigers in a barn—most unusual inhabitants for a Swiss barn!

Taken separately, the causal background of the two events seems clear. The power display in the woman probably brought about her tiger dream as a warning illustration of what was constellated in her. The three real tigers were in that barn because a circus was spending the night in town. But the highly improbable coincidence of the inner and outer three tigers in this woman's life seems to have no common cause, and therefore it inevitably struck her as "more than mere chance" and somehow as "meaningful."

At first sight there is no reason for concern about such events even if they prove highly impressive to the person who meets them, for the coincidence may be looked upon as mere chance. Jung, however, became impressed by the relative frequency of such occurrences[39] and named them synchronistic events. Synchronicity may be defined as simultaneity *plus connection by meaning,* in contrast to synchronous events, which only coincide in time. Before following up his argument further, we must recall that our laws of nature are statistical and thus valid only if applied to large aggregates. This implies that there must be a considerable number of exceptions which we call chance. Further, experimental approach postulates the necessity of repeatability and thus rules out a priori all unique and even rare events.[40]

We may now define chance coincidences as relating to the independence of the coinciding events from any common causal bond, and we can subdivide them in two categories, namely meaningful or meaningless coincidences.[41] A synchronistic event is thus a meaningful coincidence of an external event with an inner motif from dreams, fantasies, or thoughts. It must concern two or more elements which cannot for an observer be connected causally, but only by their "meaning." What the factor "meaning" consists of transcends scientific comprehensibility for us at the moment, but the psychologist can show that it is conditioned by emotional and preconscious cognitive processes of a "Gestalt" or pattern nature. These processes sometimes seem already to have established an "order" or "system" before they come above the threshold of consciousness.[42]

They seem to depend on the activation of an archetypal pattern. In other words, the archetype sometimes preconsciously organizes our train of ideas.[43]

Meaningful coincidences are by no means rare and have therefore attracted not only Jung's but other people's attention, such as in more recent times, Paul Kammerer,[44] Wilhelm von Scholz,[45] W. Stekel,[46] J. W. Dunne,[47] and several parapsychologists.[48] J. B. Rhine was the first to attack the problem with statistical methods,[49] whereas the others only collected more or less well-documented examples similar to the one I mentioned above.

4. Philosophical Attempts to Formulate the Idea of Synchronicity[50]

The idea that *all* events in nature are somehow connected by meaning (which is a purely anthropomorphic term) appears first in Western philosophy in the concept of the *Logos* of Heraclitus and in the idea of an *oulomeliē* (all-harmony) or of a "sympathy" of all things in Hippocrates, Philo (25 B.C.–A.D. 42) and Theophrastus. This "sympathy" was conceived as the reason why similar external and internal events occur simultaneously even though the simultaneity lacks a causal basis. Philo and Theophrastus both postulate God as *prima causa* of this whole principle of correspondence in the universe. This idea survived in vague form throughout the Middle Ages and was still maintained by Pico della Mirandola, Agrippa of Nettesheim, Robert Fludd, and Paracelsus.[51] It also occurs in most alchemistic and astrological treatises of these times. The "cause" of this correspondence is for many of these authors either God or the World Soul. For instance, according to Agrippa this World Soul, being a spirit that penetrates all things, is responsible for the "foreknowledge" in animals. Even Johannes Kepler still believed in an *anima terrae* that was responsible for similar phenomena.[52]

The only one who perceived of the emotional factor as being relevant in the occurrence of such phenomena was Albert the Great. He emphasized that such "magical occurrences," as he called them, can take place only when the right astrological constellation dominates and the person involved finds himself in an *excessive affect.*[53] This statement is interesting in so far as excessive affects are normally only constellated by an archetype and Jung observed the occurrence of synchronistic events only when an archetype was activated.[54] Albert's idea is not really his own but borrowed from Ibn Sina (Avicenna).[55]

None of these above-mentioned medieval authors, however, succeeded in freeing themselves from some vague idea of a magical causality which is characteristic of all primitive thinking. Only the great Arab philosopher Ibn 'Arabi tried to give a purely acausal description of such events, though he still postulates the idea of God as prima causa. For him the whole universe is a theophany, created by an act of God's primordial imagination which goes on incessantly. This same divine imagination works within man and renews from moment to moment man's idea of the cosmos.[56] This is why certain real and intelligent inner imaginative activity (not a vain fantasy) in man can "click" with the outer facts. The Creation recurs from moment to moment in a pre-eternal and continuous movement by which the pre-eternal and post-eternal God manifests in all beings. There is no interval between these constant acts of creation because the moment of the disappearance of a thing is the same moment that its similar replica comes into existence. In its hidden form God remains in His *hecceitas*[57] but in His manifestation He assumes existential determination.[58] This happens by a continuous activation of the Divine Names.[59] The continuity lies in these Divine Names, while on the side of the actual phenomena there is only an acausal connection of things. There are only similarities from moment to moment, but no actual empirical continuity and identity.[60] Whatever "view" man has of this Creation is also created by the same God who shows Himself to man from within in His different Names or *ipseities.*[61] This philosophical idea is, as far as I know, the most remarkable attempt in the Middle Ages to abolish the idea of causality, but it is still obliged to postulate a common prima causa of all things.

Inspired by Kant's reflections in *The Dream of a Spirit-Seer*, Schopenhauer has also made an attempt to account for synchronicity in his book *On the Apparent Design in the Fate of the Individual*. He pictured a double pattern of events like the lines of longitudes and latitudes. The longitudinal lines he imagined as representing the causal connections of events, the latitudinal lines as representing cross-connections of acausal meaningful coincidences. He thought that

> both kinds of connections exist simultaneously, and the self-same event, although a link in two totally different chains, nevertheless falls into place in both, so that the fate of one individual invariably fits the fate of the other, and each is the hero of his own drama while simultaneously figuring in a drama foreign to him—this is something that surpasses our powers of comprehension, and can only be conceived as possible by virtue of the most wonderful pre-established harmony.[62]

Concerning the cross-connections, Schopenhauer considered the pole as being the origin in which all longitudinal lines converge. The pole is "the one subject of the great Dream of life," namely the transcendental Will or *prima causa* from which all causal chains radiate like meridian lines from the poles; and the parallels stand to one another in a meaningful relationship of simultaneity.

In Jung's view, however, we have no proof that there is only one *prima causa* and not a multiplicity of them. Moreover, the idea of an absolute determinism with which Schopenhauer still reckons has collapsed. Schopenhauer's postulate of synchronistic events being regular occurrences and the fact that he assigns a cause to them come from his wish to fit synchronistic phenomena into a deterministic idea of the world: but this goes far beyond what we can actually see or prove.[63]

Another remarkable attempt to integrate synchronicity into an image of reality is that of Gottfried Wilhelm Leibniz, who could be called the originator of the idea of psychophysical parallelism. He thought of body and soul as two synchronized clocks. His monads, or souls, as he put it, had "no windows" (i.e., no causal interconnections), but were "synchronized" in a "pre-established harmony."[64] Against this view Jung raises an objection which actually can and must be applied to all the above-mentioned attempts at explanation:[65]

> The synchronicity principle thus becomes the absolute rule in all cases where an inner event occurs simultaneously with an outside

one. As against this, however, it must be borne in mind that the synchronistic phenomena which can be verified empirically, far from constituting a rule, are so exceptional that most people doubt their existence. They certainly occur much more frequently in reality than one thinks or can prove, but we still do not know whether they occur so frequently and so regularly in any field of experience that we could speak of them as conforming to law. We only know that there must be an underlying principle which might possibly explain all such [related] phenomena.[66]

Instead of postulating a pre-established harmony of all things, Jung proposes to explain synchronistic events by the existence of a formal factor, namely by what he termed an *equivalence of meaning*. In his reflections he assumed that the same living reality expresses itself, but not causally, in the psychic as well as in the physical state. Jung called this hypothetical underlying "same reality" *unus mundus*.[67] The *unus mundus* is to be understood as an entity which consists of formal structures, systems or images, and of a knowledge which is prior to consciousness. He calls this knowledge absolute knowledge because it is detached from consciousness.[68] We face here again, according to his hypothesis, a certain preconscious orderedness of some of our conscious representations.[69]

5. Reflections on Synchronistic Events as Subspecies of a Possibly More General Principle of Acausal Orderedness

According to Jung, synchronistic events should be taken as "just-so" facts, as irreducible contingencies. Then he raises the question[70] of whether the principle of equivalence of psychical and physical processes, which according to his experience appear in synchronistic events, might not require some conceptual expansion. There exist two well-known examples of acausal orderedness, namely the discontinuities of physics and the individual mathematical properties of natural numbers.[71] Curiosities, like the tiger story described above, are perhaps only a rare subspecies of a more general principle of acausal orderedness or "of all equivalences of psychic and physical processes wherever

the observer is capable of recognizing the *tertium comparationis*."
Since Jung wrote this in 1952, it seems to me that the advance of
natural science has done much to make this idea of a general
acausal orderedness a feasible principle of explanation. Needham even goes so far as to say that "perhaps we might characterize the only two components required for the understanding of
the universe in terms of modern science as Organization[72] on the
one hand and Energy on the other."[73]

In collaboration with Pauli, Jung proposed a schematic representation of explanatory principles, as shown in the diagram.

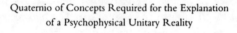

Quaternio of Concepts Required for the Explanation
of a Psychophysical Unitary Reality

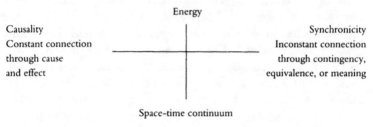

Energy

Causality		Synchronicity
Constant connection		Inconstant connection
through cause		through contingency,
and effect		equivalence, or meaning

Space-time continuum

The principle of contingency or equivalence would be in no way
replacing causality but would be seen as complementary to
causal determination.[74]

In physics causality has become only a relatively valid principle and we now only look for "statistical laws with primary
probabilities" as Pauli puts it.[75] One could also call these primary probabilities, lists of expectation values. In a similar way
we could call the archetype a list of expectation values or "primary probability" for certain psychological (including mental)
reactions. Just as expectation values in quantum theory cannot
be measured to any desired arbitrary accuracy if, at the same
time, we wish to measure their complementary parameters, so
a unique manifestation in a list of psychological expectation values also eludes accurate observation if one insists on a sequence
of temporal repetition.[76] Niels Bohr's idea that the conscious
and the unconscious psyche are a complementary pair of entities
refers to this problem. The archetype above all represents psy-

chic probability,[77] but curiously enough sometimes it not only underlies psychic but also psychophysical equivalences. Therefore Jung attributes a psychoid quality to the archetype or a certain "transgressiveness"[78] because it reaches out into areas of experience which we normally call material.

Normally and usually the archetype is only an introspectively recognizable form of an a priori psychic orderedness, but if an external synchronistic process associates itself with it, the external process also falls into the same basic pattern, i.e., it too is ordered. This form of orderedness differs from that of the mathematical properties of natural numbers or the discontinuities of psychics in that both occur regularly, whereas the forms of psychic orderedness when coinciding with outer events are acts of creation in time.[79] They represent creative acts within a pattern that itself exists from all eternity but repeats itself sporadically and is not derivable from any known antecedents.[80] Synchronistic events would thus be a relatively rare and special class of natural events, while the contingent would have to be understood partly as a universal fact existing from all eternity and partly as the sum of countless individual acts of creation occurring in time.[81] These acts of creation are essentially unpredictable[82] and thus, at least seen from the point of view of depth psychology, they give time a specific and unpredictable turn[83] by interrupting the continuity of the time arrow. Psychology thus arrives from a different angle at the idea of a *creatio continua*—an idea which A. N. Whitehead and M. Čapek also postulate when they talk of a movement of nature[84] advancing creatively forward.

It has also lately been postulated that the physical concept of information is identical with a phenomenon of reversal of entropy.[85] The psychologist must add a few remarks here: it does not seem convincing to me that information is *eo ipso* identical with a *pouvoir d'organisation*[86] which undoes entropy. I can watch disorder without doing anything about it unless I am emotionally stimulated to put it into order,[87] and the emotional stimulus rising from within to establish order[88] comes, as the psychologist can prove, from preconsciously activated patterns of mental behavior, that is, from the archetypes. It is only *there,* if anywhere, that we might discover instances or sources of negentropy.[89]

6. The Problem of a Methodical Approach to Synchronicity

Before discussing the problem of how to grasp the subspecies, the relatively rare and random phenomena of synchronistic events, it seems to me more important or rather more feasible to search first for a mathematical approach to the more general factor: the equivalence of meaning between a psychic and physical process, wherever the observer has the chance to recognize the *tertium comparationis*.[90] The question would then be: can we in some way quantify the psychological experience of "meaning"?[91]

As Jung noticed,[92] up till now psychologists can only approximately determine intensities of reactions. They do this with the "feeling function" which replaces the exact measurement in physics. But "the psychic intensities and their graduated differences point to quantitative processes. While psychological data are essentially qualitative, they also have a sort of latent physical energy." If these quantities could be measured, mass and velocity would be adequate concepts to use in describing the psyche insofar as it has any observable effects in time and space. It looks as if the most intimate connections of psychic processes with material phenomena belong to the realm of microphysics. But how can we get closer to this connection?

It seems to me that this would not be possible with the mathematical means we now have at our disposal, because our present use of numerical elements and their abstractions is purely quantitative and thus no more appropriate an instrument for exploring meaning than a black-and-white film would be for reproducing color. But this predominantly quantitative use of the natural numbers is a specialty of the Western mental outlook. In China, numbers were rarely used in this way but were seen above all as qualitative instruments of order. According to Granet[93] the Chinese did not use numbers as quantities but as polyvalent emblems or symbols which served to express the quality of certain clusters of facts and their intrinsic hierarchic orderedness. Numbers, in their view, possess a descriptive power and thus serve as an ordering fact for *"des ensembles concrets qu'ils paraissent spécifier par le seul fait qu'ils les situent dans le Temps et l'Espace"*[94] (clusters of concrete objects, which they seem to qualify through positioning them in space and time). In Chinese thought there is an equivalence between the essence of a thing and its position in space-time. This equivalence can only be expressed by number,[95] for numbers characterize arrangements rather than quantities,[96] but these qualitatively characterized arrangements (like our natural laws) also represent "regular connections of things."[97] Moreover, Chinese thought has been altogether more interested in synchronicity than in causality,[98] i.e., they observed the coincidence of events in space and time realizing that they meant something more than chance. Namely they signify peculiar interdependence of objective events among themselves, as well as the subjective (psychic) state of the observer or observers.[99] Jung says:

> Just as causality describes the sequence of events, so synchronicity to the Chinese mind deals with the coincidence of events. The causal point of view tells us a dramatic story about how *D* came into existence. It took its origin from *C*, which existed before *D*, and *C* in its turn had a father *B*, etc. The synchronistic view, on the other hand, tries to produce an equally meaningful picture of coincidence. How does it happen that *A' B' C' D'*, etc., appear all in the same moment and in the same place? It happens in the first place because the physical events *A'* and *B'* are of the same quality as the psychic events *C'* and *D'* *and further because they are the exponents of one and the same momentary situation.*[100] The situation is assumed to represent a legible or understandable picture.

Using binary numerals, but with the above-explained qualitative idea of numbers in mind, the Chinese invented the technique of the *I Ching (Book of Changes),* in order to grasp by means of numbers the equivalence of physical and psychic systems. What Costa de Beauregard says about the modern experimental physicist standing before the cosmos like a dice player, whose empirical information comes ultimately from what his successive "throws of the dice" reveal to him about a universe whose laws are essentially contingent,[101] has already been observed by the Chinese, for they have long tried to gather information about synchronicity by just such a "throw of dice."

According to Wang-Fu-Chih (1619–1692), the whole of existence is a continuum which is ordered in itself. It has no manifest appearance and thus cannot be observed immediately by sense perceptions, but its inherent dynamism manifests in images whose structure participates in that of the continuum. This idea of an irrepresentable continuum containing latent pictorial structures forms an exact parallel to Jung's concept of an *unus mundus*. The images in Wang-Fu-Chih's continuum form the sixty-four basic symbolic situations of the *I Ching*. Because they are ordered and therefore participate in the world of numbers, they can be grasped through a numerical procedure, which only works if handled truthfully.[102]

In no way do I want to suggest that we should adopt ideas or techniques bound into the specific cultural development of the East. What I am suggesting is that our arithmetical concepts, especially our theory of numbers, might have to be expanded by studying the qualitative ordering aspect of number in collaboration with depth psychology before we can use any numerical method in comprehending synchronistic phenomena.

7. Conclusions

Synchronistic events are, according to Jung, meaningful coincidences of external and internal events. They seem to happen at random, and to be contingent to the principles of causal explanation. Possibly they are a subspecies of a more general principle of acausal orderedness. The only existing primitive attempts to grasp synchronicity are the divinatory methods of East and West. Most of them use numbers as the basis for understanding synchronistic events.

According to Jung,[103] number is an instrument of our mind to bring order into the chaos of appearances, a given instrument for either creating order or apprehending an already existing regular arrangement or "orderedness." It is a more primitive mental element than concept. Psychologically we could define number as *an archetype of order which has become conscious.* Jung considers it an archetype because, as the arithmetical revelations mentioned in section 2 demonstrate, the unconscious often uses number as an ordering factor much in the same way as consciousness does. [104] Thus numerical orders, like all other archetypal structures, can be pre-existent to consciousness and then they rather condition than are conditioned by it. Number forms an ideal *tertium comparationis* between what we usually call psyche and matter, for countable quantity is a characteristic of material phenomena *and* an irreducible *idée force* behind our mental mathematical reasoning. The latter consists of the "indisputability" which we experience when contemplating arrangements based on natural numbers. [105] Thus number is a basic element in our thought processes, on the one side, and, on the other, it appears as the objective "quantity" of material objects which seem to exist independently outside our psyche. If we do not want to agree with the Neopythagoreanism of D'Arcy Thompson, who attributes a world-creating faculty to number and thus sees it as the cause or causes of existence, [106] Jung proposes looking at the natural numbers rather as manifestations of the *unus mundus* or of that one reality which does not "cause" the coincidences of physical and psychic structures *but rather manifests in them.* This actually happens in every act of conscious realization[107] concerning external or internal facts. Thus, studying the "meaning" aspect of each individual natural number might best bring us closer to a comprehension of a more generally existing phenomenon of acausal orderedness, i.e., synchronicity, and to representing it in numerical lists of expectation values.

The curiosities of the more special synchronistic events, however, seem to me for the moment essentially unpredictable. Apparently they point to a basic creative factor which manifests itself at random within the flux of time. Mythologically it has always been thought that these events also "undo" time, i.e., represent instances of negentropy (or interrupt the mathematical density of time). I would not dare to assert this, however, because it does not seem to me that we have yet penetrated deep enough into the conditions which surround synchronistic events. [108] C. G. Jung's idea of synchronicity is only intended as a working hypothesis which might help to solve some of the riddles of meaningful noncausal coincidences without abandoning causal thinking. [109] Our time concept, however, would have to be revised if we are to include not only the conception of a countable-uncountable infinity but also the interruption of it by essentially unpredictable acts of a *creatio continua*—acts which do not happen completely at random but within a certain set of structural patterns which are in some way linked with the natural integers.

1. In *Le Second Principe et la Science du Temps* (Paris: Editions du Seuil, 1963), p. 130, Olivier Costa de Beauregard tries to integrate the study of cybernetics into the field of general epistemological problems in physics and concludes that physics is being forced to enter into an active dialogue with the science of psychology in order to build up a more comprehensive science. Though using a different approach, he actually reiterates a postulate of Wolfgang Pauli, who, being familiar with the concepts of C. G. Jung's depth psychology, expressed the hope that we might now be able to create a new abstract *neutral* language in which certain psychological and physical discoveries could find their common expression, *Aufsätze und Vorträge über Physik und Erkenntnistheorie* (Braunschweig: Vieweg, 1961), p. 121. In his contribution to the symposium *The Unity of Knowledge,* ed. Lewis Leary (New York: Doubleday, 1955), Niels Bohr proposed to introduce his concept of complementarity into psychology, i.e., he prepared to look at the conscious and the unconscious psyche as a complementary pair of opposites. Cf. also Max Knoll, "Transformations of Science in our Age," in *Man and Time: Papers from the Eranos Yearbooks* (New York: Pantheon, 1957), p. 264, and Ernst Anrich, *Moderne Physik und Tiefenpsychologie* (Munich: Klett, 1963).
2. Jung calls "psychoid" those areas of the unconscious where psychic phenomena fuse with or transgress into matter (see below). This psychoid area corresponds closely with what P. Vignon and Costa de Beauregard call *infrapsychisme* (*Le Second Principe,* p. 80).
3. A "content" in psychology is a thought, wish, impulse,

phantasy, etc., that is, any relatively definite self-identical entity in the field of a psychic structure.

4. *Cf.* C. G. Jung, *The Structure and Dynamics of the Psyche*, vol. 8 of *Collected Works* (CW) (New York: Pantheon, 1960), p. 186.
5. *Cf. Pauli, Aufsätze*, p. 113. See also William James, *Varieties of Religious Experience* (New York, 1902), lecture 10.
6. Leary (ed.), *The Unity of Knowledge.* Cf. Pascual Jordan, *Verdrängung und Komplementarität* (Hamburg: Strom Verlag, 1947).
7. Jung, in contrast to others, prefers the term *unconscious* to *subconscious*, for we do not know enough about it to introduce terms which imply a localization or evaluation.
8. See, for instance, G. van der Leeuw: *Religion in Essence and Manifestation* (London, 1938), where such recurrent motives are discussed in each chapter.
9. Freud calls these motives "archaic remnants" or "vestiges" in contrast to Jung's "archetypal images."
10. The archetype is in itself irrepresentable and can only be abstractly described, in contrast to its products: images, symbolic gestures, thought forms, etc. Pauli presents an excellent survey of the development of Jung's idea of the archetype in his *Aufsätze*, p. 119.
11. Cf. Jung, CW 8, p. 201. No instinct is amorphous, for it bears in itself the complete pattern of a situation, e.g., the instinct of a leaf-cutting ant includes in its pattern the image of the ant, leaf, cutting, transport, fungi-garden, etc. Without *all* these elements the instinct cannot function. Such an image is an a priori type. The human instincts function in a similar way and also include patterns, i.e., the archetypal images.
12. As Henri Poincaré, *Science and Method* (New York: Dover, 1952), chap. 3, points out, however, such "flashes of insight" are only fruitful if they meet a prepared and trained mind.
13. Cf. Jung, CW 8, p. 199. The consciousness of a psychic content is always only relatively conscious, just as its unconscious is also only relative. A dream, for instance, is not a completely unconscious phenomenon insofar as it is recorded. Cf. Jung, CW 8, p. 187, and Pauli, *Aufsätze*, p. 116.

As Pauli stresses, a dream is also a psychophysical fact insofar as it is accompanied by processes in the brain.

14. Cf. Adolf Portmann, "Time in the Life of the Organism,"
in *Man and Time*, p. 310. Cf. also p. 318: "Just as the adult
animal acts 'instinctively,' so the plasm of the species 'instinctively' regulates the temporal sequence of formative
processes."

15. It would perhaps be better to say "train of representations."

16. M. S. Watanabe, "Le Concept du temps en physique moderne et la durée pure de Bergson," *Revue de metaphysique et
de morale* 56 (1951): 128.

17. Cf. Costa de Beauregard, *Le Second Principe*, p. 114.

18. I would not dare to give a decided opinion on this question
with the few facts we have now at hand, but, I tend to agree
rather with Professor Watanabe that the "time sense" is not
necessarily "caused" by the law of entropy.

19. Cf. Costa de Beauregard, *Le Second Principe*, p. 115: "In
brief, granting that the universe of the relativists must be
considered at every moment as spread out in all its temporal
extent, we would propose the following metaphor: In Min-
kowskian space-time, Bergson's 'attention to life' can be
compared to one's attention to reading a book, the successive 'three-dimensional space-like states' playing the same
part as the successive pages of the book. And just as an effort
to understand the book requires us to read its pages in the
order in which they were written, effective participation in
the 'text' of the four-dimensional cosmos requires that the
'attention to life' continually peruse the three-dimensional
states of the universe in their order of increasing probability." (Notes 19, 21, 22, 82, 85, and 87 have been translated
from the French by Prof. David Park.)

20. This does not a priori decide the old philosophical question
of whether time is only a category of our conscious mind
(Kant) or whether it also has an objective existence. It only
means that accurate *awareness* of what we today call time
seems to be dependent on the functioning of our conscious
mind.

21. Cf. also Costa de Beauregard, *Le Second Principe*, p. 124:
"Similarly, even if it is the nature of consciousness always to
explore the temporal dimension of the cosmos in the same
direction, without any gaps, and trailing after it a long wake

of memory gained from the information that it has acquired, the subconscious mind, which is neither logical nor methodical, has no reason to be subject to the same law. Would one not have to say of the subconscious that it coexists with the temporal extent of the cosmos?"

22. Costa de Beauregard says: "It has thus become impossible to conceive the time of the material universe as an advancing front. The time of the material universe, like its space, is an extension, and the parameter that explores this 'fourth dimension' is a coordinate just like those which parametrize ordinary space." *Le Second Principe*, p. 123. The unconscious would be coextensive with the "étendue actuelle," p. 124.

23. Cf. Jung, CW 8, p. 231.

24. Mircea Eliade, *The Myth of the Eternal Return* (New York: Pantheon, 1954). Also see G. van der Leeuw, "Primordial Time and Final Time," in *Man and Time*, p. 324.

25. Cf. ibid., p. 326.

26. Cf. Jung's introduction to W. Y. Evans-Wentz, *The Tibetan Book of the Great Liberation* (Oxford: Oxford University Press, 1954), p. xiv.

27. Jung says: "Because the unconscious is the matrix mind . . . it is the birthplace of thought forms. . . . Insofar as the forms or patterns of the unconscious belong to no time in particular, being seemingly eternal, they convey a peculiar feeling of timelessness when consciously realised. . . . An introverted attitude, therefore . . . which withdraws its emphasis from the external world . . . necessarily calls forth the characteristic manifestations of the unconscious, namely, archaic thought forms imbued with 'ancestral' and 'historic' feeling and beyond them, the sense of indefiniteness, timelessness and oneness. . . . [This] derives from the general contamination of contents, which increases as consciousness dims . . . it is not unlikely that the peculiar experience of oneness derives from the subliminal awareness of all-contamination in the unconscious" (ibid., p. xlvi).

28. Cf. ibid., p. lix: "I have already explained this 'timelessness' as a quality inherent in the experience of the collective unconscious. The application of the 'yoga of self-liberation' is said to reintegrate all forgotten knowledge of the past with consciousness. The motif of ἀποκατάστασις (restoration,

restitution) occurs in many redemption myths and is also an important aspect of the psychology of the unconscious, which reveals an extraordinary amount of archaic material in the dreams. . . . In the systematic analysis of an individual the spontaneous reawakening of ancestral patterns (as a compensation) has the effect of a restoration. . . . The unconscious certainly has its 'own time' inasmuch as past, present, and future are blended together in it."

29. Cf. ibid., p. 7.
30. Poincaré, *Science and Method,* chap.3.
31. In K.-F. Gauss' *Werke,* vol. 10, p. 25, quoted in B. L. van der Waerden, *Einfall und Überlegung: Drei kleine Beiträge zur Psychologie des mathematischen Denkens* (Basel & Stuttgart, 1954), p. 1. This same passage is translated into English in Harold Ruegg, *Imagination: An Inquiry into the Sources and Conditions That Stimulate Creativity* (New York: Harper, 1963), p. 9.
32. J. H. Hadamard, *An Essay on the Psychology of Invention in the Mathematical Field* (Princeton: Princeton University Press, 1949).
33. B. L. van der Waerden, *Einfall und Überlegung.*
34. Ruegg, *Imagination.*
35. Cf. Lancelot L. Whyte, *Accent on Form* (New York: Harper, 1954), p. 155.
36. About this see Jung, cw 8, p. 231: "Archetypes, so far as we can observe and experience them at all, manifest themselves only through their ability to *organise* images and ideas and this is always an unconscious process which cannot be detected until afterwards. By assimilating ideational material whose provenance in the phenomenal world is not to be contested, they become visible and *psychic.*" Because of this cognitive element in the unconscious P. Vignon even thought of calling his "infrapsychism" a "supraconsciousness." Cf. Costa de Beauregard, *Le Second Principe,* p. 120.
37. Cf. J. P. Zubeck's experiments in the Psychological Institute of the University of Manitoba in Winnipeg.
38. Quoted with the permission of the patient.
39. Wilhelm von Scholz's *Der Zufall, eine Vorform des Schicksals* (Stuttgart: Koch-Verlag, 1924) is a collection of documented coincidences of this type.
40. The energetic impulse of a particle, for instance, is ruled by

probability only. I agree here with the argument of Costa de Beauregard (*Le Second Principe*, pp. 23, 27; cf. also pp. 45, 47) that chance must be looked on as an objective factor not only as a "chance of ignorance." Cf. also Wolfgang Pauli, "Wahrscheinlichkeit und Physik," *Dialectica* 8, no. 2 (1954): 114, who stresses that a unique realization of a very improbable event is treated from a certain point on as if it were practically impossible.

41. If I sneeze when an airplane crashes before my eyes, this is apt to be a meaningless coincidence. If, however, I have entertained hostile fantasies about that plane and then it crashes before my eyes, it will impress me as a meaningful coincidence, though here too we must assume complete causal independence.

42. We can, for instance, observe while analyzing creative scientists or artists that their dream images often anticipate in symbolic form their later conscious discoveries or inventions. Harold Ruegg (*Imagination*, p. 49) speaks of this as "the creative preconscious activity of the transliminal mind."

43. Cf. Jung, cw 8, p. 231.

44. P. Kammerer, *Das Gesetz der Serie* (Stuttgart & Berlin: Deutsche-Verlags Anstatt, 1919), quoted in Jung, cw 8, p. 426. Kammerer specialized in collecting "run" manifestations of numbers. Cf. also L. Kling, "Irrational Occurrences in Psychotherapy and Tendentious Apperception," *Journal of Existential Psychiatry* 4 no. 15 (1964).

45. Von Scholz, *Der Zufall*.

46. W. Stekel, "Die Verpflichtung des Namens," *Zeitschrift für Psychotherapie und medizinische Psychologie* 3 (1911): 110.

47. J. W. Dunne, *An Experiment with Time*, 2nd ed. (London: Black, 1938).

48. Charles Richet, Xavier Dariex, Frank Podmore, W. H. Myers, Camille Flammarion. Cf. the titles and examples in Jung, cw 8, pp. 427, 430.

49. For the literature see S. G. Soal and F. Bateman, *Modern Experiments in Telepathy* (London: Routledge & Kegan Paul, 1954), and J. B. Rhine, *The Reach of the Mind*, 1954. Cf. also Jung, cw 8, p. 432.

50. This section is mainly a shortened version of Jung's third

chapter on synchronicity except for the exposition of Ibn 'Arabi's views.

51. For details see Jung, cw 8, p. 491.

52. Cf. Wolfgang Pauli, "The Influence of Archetypal Ideas on the Scientific Theories of Kepler," in Jung and Pauli, *The Interpretation of Nature and the Psyche* (London: Routledge & Kegan Paul, 1952).

53. Albert the Great, *De mirabilibus mundi,* first printed Cologne, 1485.

54. In my practice I have found that in psychic borderline states such actual events *and* the acute awareness of synchronistic events rapidly increase, a fact which would again link up with the "excessive affect" dominant in such conditions.

55. In Ibn Sina's *De Anima* (chap. 4), the same ideas are expressed. (Cf. *Avicenne perhypatetici philosophiae medicorum facile primi:* Opera etc. Venetiis, 1508. This was the only Latin translation available to Albert the Great.)

56. Cf. Henri Corbin, *L'Imagination créatrice dans le soufism d'Ibn Arabi* (Paris: Flammarion, 1958), p. 140.

57. *Heccëitas* means here God's pure inconceivable *esse,* that is, selfsame substance in the Aristotelian sense of the word, in contrast to existence.

58. Corbin, *L'Imagination,* p. 150: "An identical, eternal *Heccëitas* assumes existential determination; and this actually happens in an instant *(al-ân)* of an indivisible moment (even though this moment is divisible in thought), that atom of time which one calls the 'present' *(amân hadir,* but not the 'nunc' which is an abstract limiting condition of past and future and is an idea of pure negativity) without the senses being able to perceive any temporal interval."

59. The Divine Names in Ibn 'Arabi's system are pure formal potentialities; they correspond very closely to Jung's concept of archetypes, but have (like the Platonic ideas) a more intellectual character.

60. Corbin, *L'Imagination,* p. 150.

61. Ibid., p. 146. "Ipsëities" are potential but continuously self-identical aspects of God's selfsame inconceivable substance. They work as intermediary agencies between God and the Creation.

62. Quoted in Jung, cw 8, p. 427 sq.

63. Cf. ibid., p. 428: ". . . Neither philosophical reflection nor

experience can provide any evidence for the regular occurrence of these two kinds of connection in which the same thing is both subject and object." Cf. also p. 429.
64. Cf. ibid., p. 498. Arnold Geulincx exposed similar ideas.
65. Only Ibn 'Arabi escapes this objection. Even Costa de Beauregard still postulates a "Grand Esprit" as Source and "first cause" within his neofinalistic views.
66. Jung, CW 8, p. 500, cf. also note 70: "I must again stress the possibility that the relation between body and soul may yet be understood as a synchronistic one. Should this conjecture ever be proved, my present view that synchronicity is a relatively rare phenomenon would have to be corrected." Cf. C. A. Meier's observations in *Zeitgemässe Probleme der Traumforschung*. Kultur- und Staatswissenschaftliche Schriften 75 (Zurich School of Technology, 1950), p. 22, and "Psychosomatic Medicine from the Jungian Point of View," *Journal of Analytical Psychology* 8, no. 2 (London: 1963): 103.
67. The *unus mundus* idea of Jung should not be confused with Erich Neumann's term *Einheitswirklichkeit*, "unitarian reality," in "Die Psyche und die Wandlung der Wirklichkeitsebenen," *Eranos Yearbook* 21 (1952): 169. The latter means a fusion of individuals, into and with their surroundings through their patterns of behavior. The *unus mundus*, on the contrary, has only a *potential* reality as a conglomerate of archetypal structures which have not yet become dualistically actualized into psychic or material (or both) phenomena. Cf. Jung, *Mysterium Coniunctionis*, vol. 14 of *Collected Works* (1963), p. 534.
68. This idea of a foreknowledge originally comes from Hans Driesch, *Die Seele als elementarer Naturfaktor* (Leipzig, 1903), p. 80. Cf. also Costa de Beauregard, *Le Second Principe*, p. 137, who postulates a "Source" of Information existing before all cosmic events. Cf. also p. 131.
69. Cf. Jung, CW 8, p. 231, and Pauli's comments ibid. Many of our representations can well be explained by sense stimuli, even if unconsciously perceived, but the archetypally ordered structures seem to have no outer causal basis. The cognitive element which is contained in these images underlies sudden intuitive creative insights.
70. Ibid., p. 526.
71. For instance, the existence of primary numbers or the num-

ber 2 being the only even primary number or 6 being a "circular" number in a decimal system. These are facts which, though seemingly logical, cannot be reduced to any other facts. They are facts of an a priori or given character similar also to the mathematical characteristics of groups, or the fact that it is impossible to solve algebraically equations of degrees greater than 4.

72. Some scientists prefer the word *system* to *organization*.

73. Joseph Needham, "Biochemical Aspects of Form and Growth," *Aspects of Form,* ed. Lancelot L. Whyte (Bloomington: Indiana University Press, 1951).

74. I.e., there exist between them and the causal processes no relations that conform to law.

75. Pauli, *Aufsätze,* p. 114.

76. The inability is related to the so-called decline effect, i.e., repetition seems to tire the emotional participation. Stimulated by the well-known experiments of J. B. Rhine, in which he tried to tackle the problem of precognition on an experimental and statistical basis, Jung also tried to attack the same problem with statistical means. His idea was that one must first find out whether two undeniable facts, which are clearly *not* causally interconnected, might tend to coincide in a frequency which lies above mathematical probability. That two people are married is an undeniable fact, and the astrological marriage constellations Sun-Moon conjunctio and Venus-Mars conjunctio are also facts which can be stated independently of whether one "believes" in astrology or not. It is highly improbable that the planets have an actual causally comprehensible influence on the marriage motivations of human beings. Should the two facts therefore coincide more frequently than chance probability would predict, they would represent synchronistic events. Jung's statistical analysis at first showed highly remarkable results, but as Jung's interest decreased, the results became increasingly less striking. A similar effect is known from Rhine's experiments. Only persons whose emotional participation is highly aroused tend to produce high scores of extrasensory perception results. Perhaps it is on account of this that ESP results evade statistical analysis, for the same experiment is not sufficiently repeatable with one and the same person. There are two reasons for this: we cannot always

voluntarily activate an intense emotional condition, and secondly, even if it is activated it tends to "cool off" by repetition. Jung's results at first were highly improbably "good" (i.e., far above mathematical probability), but this ultimately seems to have been just a synchronistic event in itself. The outcome of the complete test proved to be a highly improbable but definitely a chance result. It was, however, a meaningful chance result, that is, a synchronistic event, but not the statistically tested regularity which he had hoped for. Jung found himself forced to reflect once more critically on the epistemological basis of causality and statistical probability. He says (cw 8, p. 477): "Statistics would not even make sense without the exceptions. . . . Because the statistical method shows only the average aspects, it creates an artificial and predominantly conceptual picture of reality. This is why we need a complementary principle for a complete description and explanation of nature."

77. Ibid., p. 515.
78. Ibid.: "Although associated with causal processes and 'carried' by them, they [the archetypes] continually go beyond their frame of reference, an 'infringement' to which I would give the name 'transgressiveness,' because the archetypes are not found exclusively in the psychic area, but can occur just as much in circumstances that are not psychic. . . ."
79. Ibid., p. 517. That is, Jung continues, why he called these events synchronistic.
80. Ibid., p. 518. Jung continues: "We must of course guard against thinking of every event whose cause is unknown as 'causeless.' This is admissible only when a cause is not thinkable. But thinkability is itself an idea that needs the most rigorous criticism. Meaningful coincidences are thinkable as pure chance. But the more they multiply and the greater and more exact the correspondence is, the more their probability sinks and their unthinkability increases until they can no longer be regarded as pure chance, but, for lack of a causal explanation have to be thought of as meaningful arrangements. . . . However their inexplicability is not due to the fact that the cause is unknown, but to the fact that a cause is not even thinkable in intellectual terms. This is necessarily the case when space and time lose their meaning or have become relative, for under those circumstances

a causality which presupposes space and time for its continuance can no longer be said to exist and becomes altogether unthinkable."

81. Ibid., p. 519.

82. Cf. Costa de Beauregard, *Le Seconde Principe,* p. 137: "We do not believe like Bergson that 'what happens' (in phylogenesis or in the individual activity of living beings) is necessarily unpredictable, either by the collective consciousness of phylogenesis (if there is such a thing) or by the individual consciousness of living beings." We can confirm this for it is just *there* that the psychologist observes the occurrence of synchronistic events. What Costa de Beauregard, following Vignon, calls "infrapsychisme" coincides very closely with what Jung calls the psychoid nature of the archetypes.

83. I must add a few warning remarks here against the habit of regressive magical causal thinking. Again and again I come across a misunderstanding when Jung's idea of synchronicity is considered. The reason usually turns out to be a relapse into mankind's powerful age-old primitive habit of thinking in terms of magical causality. I have often noted talk of "synchronistic causality" or stress that the archetype *causes* the synchronistic events, instead of becoming manifest within or through a cluster of synchronistic events. In my view, words such as *telepathy* or *telekinesis* also imply the vague underlying idea of a "transmitting energy" and are thus misleading.

84. Alfred North Whitehead, *Science and the Modern World* (New York: Macmillan, 1926), p. 304, and M. Čapek, "Bergson et l'esprit de la physique contemporaine," *Bulletin de la Société Française de Philosophie,* 53 année (1959), special number, *Bergson et nous,* Paris (May 1959), p. 53.

85. Costa de Beauregard, *Le Second Principe,* p. 133: "What is accomplished in spite of the decreasing negentropy of the cosmos, and at its expense, is the accumulation of information by conscious beings incarnated in matter."

86. Ibid., p. 76.

87. Ibid., p. 79: "Action and organization, in our view, are the same." And p. 78: "We conclude that there is no essential difference between the image which represents what we perceive and the project which represents what we wish to do—that is, between the representation which follows a

physical situation and that which precedes it." Cf. H. Reichenbach, *The Direction of Time* (Berkeley: University of California Press, 1956), who also identifies these two things.

88. What Costa de Beauregard calls "conscience volitive" which is based on emotional facts in contrast to the "conscience cognitive" which is based on the observation of causality (*Le Second Principe*, p. 95).

89. As Pauli already proposed, it is barely possible that the "meaningful" mutations (that is, mutations appropriate to a situation as judged by man) postulated by a few evolutionists could be explained as synchronistic events (*Aufsätze*, p. 122). He thought of neofinalists and scientists such as B. Rensch and A. Pauly, Cf. also C. Cuénot, *Invention et finalité en biologie* (Paris, 1941); P. Vignon, *Introduction à la biologie expérimentale* (Paris, 1930), and Costa de Beauregard, *Le Second Principe*, p. 120. Pauli (*Aufsätze*, p. 124) points out that the modern idea of evolution (chance events plus selection) would only be valid if one could show that "fitting" chance formation had enough opportunity to come into existence within the known time of life on our planet. But biologists tend to sidetrack this by using vitalistic ideas, or by pointing out that unfitting mutations would certainly die. Whereas the safe results of genetics are statistical laws, rare or even unique events might also be important in biological evolution. Pauli therefore suggests (ibid., p. 127) that synchronicity might play a role in evolution.

90. The problem is reduced to the question: what is the nature of the preconscious orderedness of our representations and how does this link up with the apparent orderedness or system-quality of outer facts? The concept of causal determinism seems to be connected with a pre-conscious adaptation of our psyche to the law of entropy and the arrow of time implied by this. (Cf. Costa de Beauregard, *Le Second Principe*, p. 112.) The concept of synchronicity, on the other hand, seems to be based on a pre-conscious expression of our psyche in the form of systems, structures, or "Gestalts," defined as a simultaneously present "whole" or "order."

91. Because this has not hitherto been possible, many works on cybernetics tend to ignore the factor of meaning. But, as

Costa de Beauregard points out, we cannot simply eliminate the "résonnance psychique." *Le Second Principe*, p. 75.

92. Jung, cw 8, p. 233.

93. Marcel Granet, *La Pensée chinoise* (Paris: Albin Michel, 1948), p. 150.

94. Ibid., p. 153. Cf. also pp. 159 and 174.

95. Ibid., p. 158.

96. Cf. also ibid., p. 173. For instance, 5 in Chinese means the center of a quaternary structure.

97. "Des rapports réguliers des êtres," ibid., p. 174.

98. As Manfred Porkert points out, "Wissenschaftliches Denken im alten China—Das System der energetischen Beziehungen," in *Antaios* 2, no. 6 (1961). Jung's concept of synchronicity provides us with a clue with which we may understand some aspects of Chinese medicine and natural science which were hitherto despised as superstitions.

99. Jung, Introduction to the *I Ching* (New York: Pantheon, 1949), p. iv.

100. Author's italics.

101. Costa de Beauregard, *Le Second Principe*, p. 74.

102. Cf. Helmut Wilhelm, "The Concept of Time in the Book of Changes," in *Man and Time*, p. 219. Leibniz was familiar with this and also tried to make use of his binary calculating system for such purposes in his own way. See his correspondence with Father Bouvet. Cf. H. Wilhelm: *Leibniz and the I Ching*, Collectanea Commissionis Synodalis 16 (Peking, 1943), p. 205. Cf. also Joseph Needham, *Science and Civilization in China* (Cambridge: Cambridge University Press, 1954–59), vol. 2, p. 340.

103. Jung, cw 8, p. 456.

104. Ibid., p. 457. L. B. van der Waerden stresses *(Einfall und Überlegung,* p. 9) that we must assume on account of the occasional unconscious origin of arithmetical theorems, that the unconscious is even capable of reasoning and judging.

105. As Pauli *(Aufsätze,* p. 122) rightly stresses that the mathematical a priori intuitions belong in the class of what Jung calls archetypal representations, such as the arithmetical idea of the infinite series of integers or the geometrical continuum, for they are regularly recurrent ideas. As the internal logical consistency of the analysis cannot be formally proved from its own premises, Pauli adds that we must find

its roots outside mathematics. It seems to be a natural fact which is connected with the functioning of our mind. One finds here again a preconscious orderedness of our representations.

106. D'Arcy Thompson, *Growth and Form* (Cambridge: Cambridge University Press, 1942). Joseph Needham objects to this in his "Biochemical Aspects of Form and Growth," in Whyte, *Accent on Form* (p. 79), because these mathematical forms too often harbor secret "devils of vitalism." I would agree with him here if these "forms" are seen as "causes" but not if seen as patterns which manifest through synchronistic phenomena.

107. I would prefer this word to *information*.

108. It seems to me that if the quantitative concept of number in mathematics and cybernetics could be revised (i.e., not used only as "counting instruments") and could, in collaboration with depth psychology, be studied as aspects of preconscious qualitative elements of order in our mind (without relapsing into ideas of magical causality as the Chinese numerical concepts, for instance, partly presuppose), we might get closer to a method of grasping acausal orderedness in an accurate form. It might also be useful if biochemists would investigate how far number plays a role in this field of study. We then might get closer to the "material" aspect of the instinctual patterns of behavior and at their concomitant emotional factor.

109. It can thus also help us to avoid the danger of stumbling into the pitfall of that old Aristotelian internally contradictory idea of a *causa finalis* which has turned up again in neofinalistic theories.

BIBLIOGRAPHY

Aaronson, B. S. "Time, Stance and Existence." In *The Study of Time I*, edited by J. T. Fraser and N. Lawrence. Heidelberg & New York, 1972.

Albertus Magnus. *De mirabilibus mundi*. Cologne, 1485.

Anrich, Ernst. *Moderne Physik und Tiefenpsychologie*. Stuttgart, 1963.

Ariotti, P. E. "The Concept of Time in Western Antiquity." In *The Study of Time II*, edited by J. T. Fraser and N. Lawrence. Heidelberg & New York, 1975.

Augustinus. "De Genesi," ad litteram, in *Opera omnia*, 11 vols. 1, vol. 4, chaps. 3 and 8. Paris, 1836–1838.

Barth, Karl. "Descartes' Begründung der Erkenntnis." Dissertation, Bern, 1913.

Beadle, George, and Muriel Beadle. *The Language of Life: An Introduction to the Science of Genetics*. New York: Doubleday, 1966.

Beloff, John. "Psi Phenomena: Causal versus Acausal Interpretation." *Journal of the American Society for Psychical Research* 49 (1977): 573–82.

Bender, Hans. *Verborgene Wirklichkeit*. Freiburg, 1973.

———. "Von sinnvollen Zufallen." *Zeitschrift für Parapsychologie und Grenzgebiete der Psychologie* 4 (1960–1961).

———. "Meaningful Coincidences in the Light of the Jung-Pauli Theory of Synchronicity and Parapsychology." In *The Philosophy of Parapsychology*, edited by B. Shapin and L. Coly. New York: Parapsychology Foundation, 1977.

————. "Transcultural Uniformity of Poltergeist Patterns as Suggestive of an Archetypal Arrangement." In *Research in Parapsychology 1979*, edited by W. G. Roll. Metuchen, N. J. & London: Scarecrow, 1980.

———— and J. Mischo. "Präkognition in Traumserien." *Zeitschrift für Parapsychologie und Grenzgebiete der Psychologie* 4 (1960–1961).

Berthelot, M. *Collection des anciens alchimistes grecs.* Vol. 1. Paris, 1887–1888.

The Bhagavad Gita. Translated by A. W. Ryder. Chicago: University of Chicago Press, 1929.

Bi-Yän-Lu. *Niederschrift von der smaragdenen Felswand.* Edited by Wilhelm Gundert. Munich, 1960.

Bohm, David. "Discussion." In *Science et Conscience,* edited by Michel Cazenave. Paris, 1980.

————. *Wholeness and the Implicate Order.* London, 1980.

————. "Issues in Physics, Psychology and Metaphysics: A Conversation with John Welwood." *Journal of Transpersonal Psychology* 12, no. 1 (1980).

Böhme, G. *Zeit und Zahl: Studien zur Zeittheorie bei Platon, Aristoteles, Leibniz und Kant.* Frankfurt, 1974.

Bolen, Jean Shinoda. *The Tao of Psychology: Synchronicity and the Self.* San Francisco: Harper and Row, 1979.

Bonnet, H. *Reallexikon der ägyptischen Religionsgeschichte.* Berlin, 1952.

Brandon, S.G.F. *History, Time and Deity.* Manchester, 1965.

————. "The Deification of Time." In *The Study of Time I,* edited by J. T. Fraser and N. Lawrence. Heidelberg & New York, 1972.

Braude, Stephen E. *ESP and Psychokinesis: A Philosophical Examination.* Philadelphia: Temple University Press, 1979.

————. "The Synchronicity Confusion." In *Research in Parapsychology 1979,* edited by W. G. Roll. Metuchen, N. J. & London: Scarecrow, 1980.

Bünning, E. *Die physiologische Uhr.* 2nd ed. Berlin & New York, 1963.

Büttner, H. *Meister Eckharts Schriften.* Jena, 1934.

Campbell, Joseph. *The Hero with a Thousand Faces.* New York: Pantheon Books (Bollingen Series XVII), 1949.

Campbell, L. A. *Mithraic Iconography and Ideology.* Leiden, 1968.

Čapek, M. "Bergson et l'esprit de la physique contemporaine." *Bulletin de la Societé Française de Philosophie* 53 (May 1959).

Capelle, W. *Die Vorsokratiker*. Leipzig, 1935.

Capra, Fritjof. *The Tao of Physics: An Exploration of the Parallels between Modern Physics and Eastern Mysticism* (1975). 3rd ed. Boston: Shambhala Publications, 1991.

Carnap, Rudolf. *Physikalische Begriffsbildung*. Darmstadt: 1966.

Cazenave, Michel (ed.). *Science et Conscience*. Paris: 1980.

————. *La Science et l'âme du monde*. Paris, 1983.

————. "A la Recherche de la synchronicité." *Cahiers de Psychologie Junghienne* 29, 2nd trimester (1981).

Chang Chung-Yuan. *Creativity and Taoism*. New York: Julian Press, 1963.

Chin-te Cheng, D. "On the Mathematical Significance of the Chinese Ho-t'u and Lo-shu." *The American Mathematical Monthly* (1925).

Corbin, Henri. *L'Imagination créatrice dans le soufisme d'Ibn 'Arabi*. Paris, 1958.

————. *Spiritual Body and Celestial Earth*. Princeton: Princeton University Press, 1977.

Costa de Beauregard, Olivier. *La Physique moderne et les pouvoirs de l'esprit*. Paris, 1981.

————. "Cosmos et Conscience." In *Science et Conscience*, edited by Michel Cazenave. Paris, 1980.

————. *Le Second Principe et la science du temps*. Paris, 1963.

Cuénot, C. *Invention et finalité en biologie*. Paris, 1941.

Cumont, Franz. *Astrology and Religion among the Greeks and Romans*. New York & London: G. P. Putnam's Sons, 1912.

Da Fiori, G. *Tractatus super quattor Evangelia*, edited by E. Bonaiuti. Rome, 1930.

Danzig, Tobias. *Number: The Language of Science*. 4th ed. New York: Macmillan, 1954.

Dauer, D. W. "Nietzsche and the Concept of Time." In *The Study of Time I*, edited by J. T. Fraser and N. Lawrence. Heidelberg & New York, 1975.

Davids, Rhys. "Zur Geschichte des Radsymbols." *Eranos Jahrbuch*, 1934.

Denbigh, K. G. "Defense of the Direction of Time." In *The Study of Time I*, edited by J. T. Fraser and N. Lawrence. Heidelberg & New York, 1975.

De Solla Price, D. J. "Automata and the Origins of Mechanism and Mechanistic Philosophy." *Technology and Culture* 5 (1964).

————. "Clockwork before the Clock and Timekeepers before Timekeeping" in J. T. Fraser and N. Lawrence (eds.), *The Study of Time*, Proceedings of the First Conference for the Study of Time. Heidelberg & New York, 1972.

d'Espagnat, B. *A la recherche du réel: Le Regard d'un physicien.* Paris, 1980.

Deussen, P. *Sechzig Upanishads der Veda.* Darmstadt, 1963.

Diels, H. *Doxographi graeci.* Berlin & Leipzig, 1929.

Dirac, Paul. *Grundprobleme der Physik.* Lindau, 1971.

Dorn(eus), G. In *Theatrum Chemicum.* Ursel, 1602.

Driesch, H. *Die Seele als elementarer Naturfaktor.* Leipzig, 1903.

Dunne, J. W. *An Experiment with Time.* 2nd ed. London, 1938.

Durand, Gilbert. *Les Structures anthropologiques de l'imaginaire.* Paris, 1960.

Eibl-Eibesfeld, Irenäus. *Liebe und Hass: Zur Naturgeschichte elementarer Verhaltensweisen.* Munich, 1970.

Eigen, M., and R. Winkler. *Das Spiel: Naturgesetze steuern den Zufall.* Munich & Zurich, 1975.

Einstein, Albert. *Über die spezielle und allgemeine Relativitätstheorie.* Brunswick, 1918.

Eisenbud, Jule. "Synchronicity, Psychodynamics and psi." In *Research in Parapsychology 1979,* edited by W. G. Roll. Metuchen, N.J. & London: Scarecrow, 1980.

Eliade, Mircea. "Time and Eternity in Indian Thought." In *Man and Time: Papers from the Eranos Yearbooks.* Princeton: Princeton University Press (Bollingen Series XXX), 1957.

————. *The Myth of the Eternal Return.* Translated by Willard R. Trask. Princeton: Princeton University Press (Bollingen Series XLVI), 1954.

————. *Schmiede und Alchemisten.* Stuttgart, 1956.

Erigena, John Scotus. "De Divisione Naturae." 3, 19. *Migne Pat. Lat.,* vol. 72.

Etter, Hansueli. *La Science et l'âme du monde.* Paris, 1983.

Evans-Wentz, W. Y. *The Tibetan Book of the Dead.* London, Oxford & New York: Oxford University Press, 1954.

Fordham, Michael. *New Developments in Analytical Psychology*. London, 1957.

———. *The Objective Psyche*. London, 1958.

Franz, Marie-Louise von. *Aurora consurgens: A Document Attributed to Thomas Aquinas on the Problem of Opposites in Alchemy*. Translated by R.F.C. Hull and A.S.B. Glover. New York: Pantheon Books (Bollingen Series LXXVII), 1966.

———. *Die Behandlung in der analytischen Psychologie*. Stuttgart, 1979.

———. *Dreams*. Boston & London: Shambhala Publications, 1991.

———. *Individuation in Fairy Tales*. Rev. ed. Boston: Shambhala Publications, 1991.

———. *Number and Time: Reflections Leading toward a Unification of Depth Psychology and Physics*. Translated by Andrea Dykes. Evanston, Ill.: Northwestern University Press (Studies in Jungian Thought), 1974. Originally published as *Zahl und Zeit*. Stuttgart, 1970.

———. *On Divination and Synchronicity: The Psychology of Meaningful Chance*. Toronto: Inner City, 1980.

Fraser, J. T. (ed.). *The Voices of Time: A Comparative Survey of Man's Views of Time as Experienced by the Sciences and by the Humanities*. New York: Braziller, 1966. 2nd ed.: Amherst: University of Massachusetts Press, 1981.

———. *Of Time, Passion and Knowledge*. New York: Braziller, 1975.

——— and N. Lawrence (eds.). *The Study of Time I*. Proceedings of the First Conference of the International Society for the Study of Time. Heidelberg & New York: Springer Verlag, 1972.

——— and N. Lawrence (eds.). *The Study of Time II*. Proceedings of the Second Conference of the International Society for the Study of Time. Heidelberg & New York: Springer Verlag, 1975.

——— and N. Lawrence (eds.). *The Study of Time III*. Proceedings of the Third Conference of the International Society for the Study of Time. Heidelberg & New York: Springer Verlag, 1979.

Frege, Gottlob. *Funktion, Begriff, Bedeutung*. Vandenhoeck, 1975.

———. *Grundgesetze der Arithmetik*. Hildesheim: 1962.

Frétigny, R. "Embryologie de la connaissance." In *Science et Conscience*, edited by Michael Cazenave. Paris, 1980.

Frey-Wehrlin, C. T. "Ein prophetischer Traum." In *Spectrum Psychologiae: Festchrift zum 60. Geburtstag von C. A. Meier*. Zurich: 1965.

Friedrichs, K. "Über Koinzidenz und Synchronizität." *Grenzgebiete der Wissenschaft* 16 (1967).

Gammon, Mary R. "Window into Eternity: Archetype and Relativity." *Journal of Analytical Psychology* 18 (1973): 11–24.

Gamov, G. *Atomic Energy.* Cambridge, 1947.

Gantenbein, U. "Katastrophen." Diploma Thesis, Zurich School of Technology (ETH), 1978–1979.

Gauger, W. "Zum Phänomen des sinnvollen Zufalls." *Zeitschrift für Parapsychologie und Grenzgebiete der Psychologie* 21 (1979). Also in *"Y"-Paranormale Welt, Wirklichkeit und Literatur.* Berlin, 1980.

Gilson, Etienne. "Pourquoi St. Thomas a critiqué St. Augustin." *Archives d'histoire doctrinale et littéraire du Moyen Age,* vol. 1 (1926–1927).

———. "Les Sources gréco-arabes de l'augustinisme avicennisant." *Archives d'histoire doctrinale et littéraire,* vol. 4 (1929).

Granet, Marcel. *Das chinesisches Denken.* Munich, 1963.

———. *La Pensée chinoise.* Paris, 1948.

Green, H. B. "Temporal Stages in the Development of the Self." In *The Study of Time II,* edited by J. T. Fraser and N. Lawrence. Heidelberg & New York, 1975.

Haber, F. C. "The Darwinian Revolution in the Concept of Time." In *The Study of Time I,* edited by J. T. Fraser and N. Lawrence. Heidelberg & New York: 1972.

Hadamard, Jacques H. *An Essay on the Psychology of Invention in the Mathematical Field.* New York: Dover, 1954.

Harman, W. M. "Les Implications pour la science et la société des découvertes récentes dans le champs de la recherche psychologique et physique." In *Science et Conscience,* edited by Michael Cazenave. Paris, 1980.

Hentze, Carl. *Tod, Auferstehung, Weltordnung.* Vol. 1. Zurich, 1955.

Honegger, Barbara. "Spontaneous Waking-State psi as Interhemispheric Verbal Communication: Is There Another System?" In *Research in Parapsychology 1979,* edited by W. G. Roll. Metuchen, N.J. & London: Scarecrow, 1980.

Huber, P. M. *Die Wanderlegende von den Siebenschläfern.* Leipzig, 1910.

Ibn Sina. *Avicenna Latinus Liber de Anima seu Sextus de Naturalibus.* Edited by Simone van Riet. Louvain-Leiden, 1972.

I Ching. See Wilhelm, Richard.

Izutsu, T. "Matière et conscience dans les philosophies orientales." In *Science et Conscience,* edited by Michael Cazenave. Paris, 1980.

Jacobsohn, H. "Das göttliche Wort und der göttliche Stein im alten Ägypten." *Eranos Jahrbuch* 39 (1970).

Jaffé, Aniela. *Apparitions: An Archetypal Approach to Death Dreams and Ghosts.* Dallas: Spring Publications, 1979.

———. "C. G. Jung und die Parapsychologie." *Zeitschrift für Parapsychologie und Grenzgebiete der Psychologie* (1960).

———. *The Myth of Meaning in the Work of C. G. Jung.* New York: G. P. Putnam's Sons for the C. G. Jung Foundation for Analytical Psychology, 1971.

James, William. *The Varieties of Religious Experience: A Study in Human Nature.* New York: Mentor, 1958.

Jammer, Max. *Die Entwicklung des Modellbegriffs in den physikalischen Wissenschaften.* Studium Generale 18, no. 3. Heidelberg, 1963.

Jantz and Beringer. "Das Syndrom des Schwebeerlebnisses unmittelbar nach Kopfverletzungen." *Der Nervenarzt* (1944).

Jenny, H. *Kymatik.* Basel, 1976.

Jordan, Pascual. "Positivistische Bemerkungen über die parapsychischen Erscheinungen." *Zentralblatt für Psychotherapie und ihre Grenzgebiete* 9 (1936).

Jung, C. G. *Memories, Dreams, Reflections.* Edited by Aniela Jaffé. Translated by Richard and Clara Winston. New York: Vintage Books, 1965.

———. *The Collected Works of C. G. Jung.* 20 vols. Edited by Herbert Reed, Michael Fordham, and Gerhard Adler. Translated by R.F.C. Hull. Princeton: Princeton University Press (Bollingen Series XX).

Vol. 1: *Psychiatric Studies,* 1957.
Vol. 8: *The Structure and Dynamics of the Psyche,* 1960.
Vol. 9/i: *The Archetypes and the Collective Unconscious,* 1959.
Vol. 9/ii: *Aion: Researches into the Phenomenology of the Self,* 1959.
Vol. 11: *Psychology and Religion: West and East,* 1958.
Vol. 12: *Psychology and Alchemy,* 1953.
Vol. 14: *Mysterium Coniunctionis,* 1963.
Vol. 15: *The Spirit in Man, Art, and Literature,* 1966.
Vol. 17: *The Development of Personality,* 1954.
Vol. 18: *The Symbolic Life: Miscellaneous Writings,* 1976.

———. *Letters.* Selected and edited by Gerhard Adler with Aniela Jaffé. Vol. 1: 1906–1950. Vol. 2: 1951–1961. Princeton: Princeton University Press (Bollingen Series XCV), 1973 & 1976.

————. *Psychologie und Religion.* Olten, 1971.

————. *Psychologie und Alchemie.* Olten, 1975.

————. "Psychologische Interpretation von Kinderträumen." Unpublished monograph, edited by Liliane Frey and Rivkah Schärf. Zurich School of Technology (ETH), Winter 1938/1939.

————. "Ein Brief zur Frage der Synchronizität," *Zeitschrift für Parapsychologie und Grenzgebiete der Psychologie,* no. 1 (1961): 1ff.

———— and Wolfgang Pauli. *The Interpretation of Nature and the Psyche.* New York: Pantheon Books, 1955.

Kammerer, Paul. *Das Gesetz der Serie.* Stuttgart & Berlin, 1919.

Karger, Friedberg. "Paraphysik und Physik." *Zeitschrift für Parapsychologie und Grenzgebiete der Psychologie* 15 (1973).

Kastenbaum, R. "Time, Death and Old Age." In *The Study of Time II,* edited by J. T. Fraser and N. Lawrence. Heidelberg & New York, 1975.

Kline, Morris. "Les Fondements des mathématiques." *La Recherche* 54 (March 1975).

Kling, L. C. "Archetypische Symbolik und Synchronizitäten im Weltgeschehen." *Verborgene Welt* 6 (1955).

————. "Irrational Occurrences in Psychotherapy and Tendentious Apperception." *Journal of Existential Psychiatry* 4, no. 16 (1964).

Knoll, Max. "Transformation of Science in our Age." In *Man and Time: Papers from the Eranos Yearbooks.* Princeton: Princeton University Press (Bollingen Series XXX), 1957.

Koestler, Arthur. *The Roots of Coincidence.* London, 1972.

————. "Physik und Synchronizität." *Zeitschrift für Parapsychologie und Grenzgebiete der Psychologie* 15 (1973).

————. "Speculations on Problems Beyond Our Present Understanding." In *The Challenge of Chance* by A. Hardy, A. Marvie, and A. Koestler. London, 1973.

Kothari, D. S. "Reality and Physics: Some Aspects." In *Proceedings of the International Conference and Winter School on Frontiers of Theoretical Physics.* Edited by Anluck, Kothari, and Ananda. New Delhi, 1978.

Krickeberg, W., H. Trimborn, W. Müller, and O. Zerries. *Pre-Columbian American Religions.* London: 1968.

Krohn, Sven. "Einige philosophische und theoretische Implikationen der Parapsychologie." *Grenzgebiete der Wissenschaft* 16 (1967).

Kugler, Paul K. *The Alchemy of Discourse: An Archetypal Approach to Language.* Lewisburg, Pa.: Bucknell University Press, 1982.

Lao Tsu. *Tao-te Ching.* Translated by Gia-fu Feng and Jane English. New York: Vintage Books, 1972.

Leary, Lewis (ed.). *The Unity of Knowledge.* New York: Doubleday, 1955.

Leeuw, G. van der. *Religion in Essence and Manifestation.* London, 1938.

———. "Primordial Time and Final Time." In *Man and Time: Papers from the Eranos Yearbooks.* Princeton: Princeton University Press (Bollingen Series XXX), 1957.

Leibniz, G. W. *Kleinere philosophische Schriften.* Leipzig, 1883.

———. *Grundwahrheiten der Philosophie und Monadologie.* Edited by J. C. Horn. Frankfurt, 1962.

Le Lionnais, F. "Le Temps." In *Encyclopédie essentielle.* Paris, 1959.

Léon-Portilla, Miguel. *Aztec Thought and Culture: A Study of the Ancient Nahuatl Mind,* translated by Jack Emory Davis. Norman: University of Oklahoma Press, 1963. 2nd ed., 1970.

Lévi-Strauss, Claude. *The Savage Mind.* Chicago: University of Chicago Press, 1966.

Lindsay, Jack. *The Origins of Alchemy in Graeco-Roman Egypt.* London, 1970.

Lippmann, E. *Ruska: Tabula Smaragdina.* Heidelberg, 1926.

Liu Guan-Ying. "Die ungewöhnlichen Naturerscheinungen der T'ang Annalen und ihre Deutung." In *Symbolen II.* Basel, 1961.

Lucadou, W. von, and K. Kornwachs. "Grundzüge einer Theorie paranormaler Phänomene." *Zeitschrift für Parapsychologie und Grenzgebiete der Psychologie* 17 (1975).

Lu K'uan Yü. *Ch'an and Zen Teaching.* London, 1961.

Macrobius. *Saturnalia.* Lyons, 1556.

Mahnke, D. *Unendliche Sphäre und Allmittelpunkt.* Stuttgart, 1939; reprinted 1966.

Marshack, Alexander. *The Roots of Civilization: The Cognitive Beginnings of Man's First Art, Symbol, and Notation.* New York: McGraw-Hill, 1972.

Maupoil, B. *La Géomancie à l'ancienne Côte des Esclaves.* Paris, 1943.

Meier, C. A. *Zeitgemässe Probleme der Traumforschung.* Kultur- und Staatswissenschaftliche Schriften 75. Zurich School of Technology, 1950.

————. "Psychosomatic Medicine from the Jungian Point of View." *The Journal of Analytical Psychology* 8, no. 2 (1963).

————. *Experiment und Symbol*. Olten, 1976.

Meyerhoff, H. "The Broken Center," cited in "Time and the Modern Self: A Change in Dramatic Form" by T. Ungvar. In *The Study of Time I*, edited by J. T. Fraser and N. Lawrence. Heidelberg & New York, 1972.

Mitchell, Edgar. *Psychic Exploration*. New York, 1974.

Moberly, C.A.E., and E. F. Jourdain. *An Adventure*. London, 1907; reprinted 1948.

Morienus. *Artis Auriferae quam Chemian vocant*. Basel, 1593.

Morley, S. G. *An Introduction to the Study of Mayan Hieroglyphs*. Washington, D.C., 1915.

Müller, Gerd. *Der Modellbegriff in der Mathematik*. Vol. 18 of *Studium Generale*, 1965.

Müller, W. *Indianische Welterfahrung*. Stuttgart, 1976.

Nagel, E., and J. R. Newman. "Goedel's Proof." *Scientific American* (June 1956).

Needham, Joseph. "Biochemical Aspects of Form and Growth." In *Accent on Form*, edited by L. L. Whyte. Bloomington: Indiana University Press, 1951.

————. *Time and Eastern Man*. The Henry Myers Lecture. London, 1964.

———— and Ling Wang. *Science and Civilization in China*. 7 vols. Cambridge, 1954–1959.

Neumann, Erich. "Die Psyche und die Wandlung der Wirklichkeitsebenen." *Eranos Yearbook*, 1952.

Onians, R. B. *The Origins of European Thought*. Cambridge, 1954.

Pauli, Wolfgang. "Wahrscheinlichkeit und Physik." *Dialectica* 8, no. 2 (1954).

————. *Aufsätze und Vorträge über Physik und Erkenntnistheorie*. Braunschweig, 1961.

Piaget, Jean. *Le Développement de la notion du temps chez l'enfant*. Paris, 1964.

Pierce, John Robinson. *Symbols, Signals and Noise: The Nature and Process of Communication*. New York: Harper, 1961.

Plato. *Timaeus*. Translated by Francis M. Cornford. Indianapolis & New York: Bobbs-Merrill, 1959.

Poincaré, Henri. *Science and Method*. Translated by Francis Maitland. New York: Dover, 1952.

Pöppel, E. "Oscillations as a Possible Basis for Time Perception." In *The Study of Time I*, edited by J. T. Fraser and N. Lawrence. Heidelberg & New York, 1972.

Porkert, Manfred. "Wissenschaftliches Denken im alten China: Das System der energetischen Beziehungen." *Antaios* 2, no. 6 (1961).

Portmann, Adolf. "Time in the Life of the Organism." In *Man and Time: Papers from the Eranos Yearbooks*. Princeton: Princeton University Press (Bollingen Series XXX), 1957.

Preger, W. *Geschichte der deutschen Mystik im Mittelalter*. Munich, 1874; Aalen, 1962.

Preisendanz, K. *Papyri Graecae Magicae*. 2 vols. Stuttgart, 1973 & 1974.

Pribram, Karl. "Esprit, cerveau et conscience." In *Science et conscience*, edited by Michael Cazenave. Paris, 1980.

Prigogine, Ilya. *La Nouvelle Alliance*. Paris, 1979.

Purce, J. *The Mystic Spiral: Journey of the Soul*. New York: Avon, 1974.

Quispel, G. "Zeit und Geschichte im antiken Christentum." *Eranos Yearbook* 20 (1952). Published in English as "Time and History in Patristic Literature" in *Man and Time: Papers from the Eranos Yearbooks*, vol. 3 (Princeton: Princeton University Press, 1957).

Reeves, Hubert. "Incursion dans le monde acausal." *Cahiers de Psychologie Junghienne* 29, 2nd trimester (1981).

———, M. Cazenave, P. Solié, K. Pribram, H. U. Etter, and M.-L. von Franz. *La Synchronicité, l'âme et la science*. Paris, 1984.

Reichenbach, H. *The Direction of Time*. Berkeley: University of California Press, 1956.

Rhally, M. "Varieties of Paranormal Cognition." In *Spectrum Psychologiae: Festchrift zum 60. Geburstag von C. A. Meier*. Zurich, 1965.

Richter, C. P. "Astronomical References in Biological Rhythms." In *The Study of Time II*, edited by J. T. Fraser and N. Lawrence. Heidelberg & New York, 1975.

Rivière, D. *La Physique et le temps*. Proceedings of the Schweizerische Naturforschenden Gesellschaft, 1965.

Roeder, Günther. *Urkunden zur Religion der alten Ägypter*. Jena, 1923.

Rossi, Paola. *Clavis-Universalis: Arti, Mnemoniche e Logica Combinatoria da Lullo a Leibniz*. Milan & Naples, 1960.

Rump, A. "Das Problem des Bösen im I Ging." Unpublished dissertation.

Ruyer, M. *La Gnose de Princeton.* Paris, 1974.

Sambursky, S. *Das physikalische Weltbild in der Antike.* Zurich & Stuttgart, 1965.

Saussure, L. de. *Les Origines de l'astrologie chinoise.* Paris, 1930.

———. "Origine babylonienne de l'astronomie chinoise," Archives des Sciences Physiques et Naturelles 5, vol. 5 (1923).

Schaltenbrand, G. "Cyclic States as Biological Space-Time Fields." In *The Study of Time II,* edited by J. T. Fraser and N. Lawrence. Heidelberg & New York, 1975.

Schönenberger, Martin. *Verborgener Schlüssel zum Leben.* Frankfurt, 1977.

Schwartz-Salant, Nathan. "A Psychologist's View." *Quadrant* 8 (1975).

Scott, Walter (ed.). *Corpus Hermeticum (Hermetica).* Oxford, 1924–1936. Also published as *Hermetica,* 4 vols. Boston: Shambhala Publications, 1985.

Seidenberg, Abraham. "The Ritual Origin of Counting." *Archive for History of Exact Sciences,* 2, no. 7 (1962–1966).

Senior (Mohammed ibn Umail). *De chemia Senioris antiquissimi philosophi libellus.* Frankfurt, 1566. See also *Bibliotheca chemica Curiosa,* vol. 11.

———. *Memoirs of the Asiatic Society of Bengal.* Calcutta, 1933.

Sheldrake, Rupert. *A New Science of Life: The Hypothesis of Formative Causation.* London, 1981.

Simplicius. "In Aristotelis Physicorum Libros Commentarius." See H. Diels, *Doxographi graeci.*

Soal, S. G., and F. Bateman. *Modern Experiments in Telepathy.* London, 1954.

Solié, P. "Ouverture sur l'unité du monde." In "Synchronicité," *Cahiers de Psychologie Junghienne* 28, 1st trimester (1981). Also in *Spektrum der Parapsychologie: Festschrift zum 75. Geburstag von Hans Bender.* Freiburg im Breisgau, 1983.

Stekel, W. "Die Verpflichtung des Namens." *Zeitschrift für Psychotherapie und medizinische Psychologie* 3 (1911).

Suzuki, D. T. *Studies in the Lankavatara Sutra.* London, 1930; reprinted 1957 & 1968.

Symbolon: Jahrbuch für Symbolforschung, vol. 1. Edited by I. Schwabe. Basel, 1960.

Tart, Charles T. "Causality and Synchronicity: Steps toward Clarification." *Journal of the American Society for Psychical Research* 75 (1981): 121–41.

Thompson, D'Arcy. *Growth and Form*. Cambridge, 1942.

Thorndike, Lynn. *A History of Magic and Experimental Science*. Vol. 1. New York: Macmillan, 1923.

Urban, Peter. "Philosophische Aspekte der Synchronizitätstheorie." *Grenzgebiete der Wissenschaft* 17 (1968).

Usener, Hermann. *Götternamen*. Frankfurt, 1948.

Vaughan, Alan. *Incredible Coincidence: The Baffling World of Synchronicity*. New York: Ballantine, 1989.

———. "Synchronicity, Causality and Consciousness as Creator." In *Research in Parapsychology 1979*, edited by W. G. Roll. Metuchen, N.J. & London: Scarecrow, 1980.

Vignon, P. *Introduction à la biologie expérimentale*. Paris, 1930.

Waerden, B. L. van der. *Einfall und Überlegung: Drei kleine Beiträge zur Psychologie des mathematischen Denkens*. Basel & Stuttgart, 1954.

Watanabe, M. S. "Le Concept du temps en physique moderne et la durée pure de Bergson." *Revue de metaphysique et de morale* 5, no. 56 (1951).

Wehr, Gerhard. "Beiträge zur Zeitstruktur." In *Offene Systeme*, 1st ed. Stuttgart, 1975.

Weitzenböck, Roland. *Der vierdimensionale Raum*. Basel & Stuttgart, 1958.

Wenzel, A. *Die philosophischen Grenzfragen der modernen Naturwissenschaft*. Stuttgart, 1960.

Weyl, Hermann. *Philosophy of Mathematics and Natural Science*. New York: Atheneum, 1963.

———. *Raum, Zeit, Materie*. Darmstadt, 1961.

———. *Über den Symbolismus in der Mathematik und mathematischen Physik*. Studium Generale, vol. 6 (1953).

White, Victor. "St. Thomas' Conception of Revelation." *Dominican Studies* 1, no. 1 (January 1948).

Whitehead, Alfred North. *Science and the Modern World*. New York: Macmillan, 1926.

Whitrow, G. J. "Reflections on the History of the Concept of Time."

In *The Study of Time I,* edited by J. T. Fraser and N. Lawrence. Heidelberg & New York: 1972.

————. *The Natural Philosophy of Time.* London & Edinburgh, 1961: Oxford, 1980.

Whorf, B. L. *Sprache, Denken, Wirklichkeit.* Hamburg, 1963.

Whyte, Lancelot L. *Accent on Form.* New York: Harper, 1954.

Wigner, Eugène. *Symmetries and Reflections.* Cambridge, Mass.: MIT Press, 1970.

Wilhelm, Helmut. *Leibniz and the I Ching.* Collectanea Commissionis Synodalis 16. Peking: 1943.

————. "The Concept of Time in the Book of Changes." In *Man and Time: Papers from the Eranos Yearbooks* vol. 3. Princeton: Princeton University Press (Bollingen Series XXX), 1957. See also *Eranos Jahrbuch* vol. 20 (1951).

Wilhelm, Richard. "Einführung zum I Ging." Cologne, 1984.

———— (trans.). *The Secret of the Golden Flower: A Chinese Book of Life.* New York: Harcourt Brace, 1931.

———— (trans.). *The I Ching or Book of Changes.* Rendered into English by Cary F. Baynes. Princeton: Princeton University Press (Bollingen Series XIX), 1950 (2 vols.); 1967 (1 vol.).

Wilson, R. A. "Die neue Physik und C. G. Jung." *Sphinx* (April–May 1986).

Wit, C. de. *Le Rôle et le sens du lion dans l'Égypte ancienne.* Leiden, 1951.

Yates, Frances A. *Girodano Bruno and the Hermetic Tradition.* London, 1964.

————. *Lull and Bruno.* Vol. 1 of *Collected Essays.* London, 1982.

Zavala, J. F. "Quelques aspects de la synchronicité en relation avec le calendrier divinatoire mexicain 'Tonalamatl.' " In *Science et Conscience,* edited by Michael Cazenave. Paris, 1980.

Zimmer, Heinrich. *Myths and Symbols in Indian Art and Civilization.* Princeton: Princeton University Press (Bollingen Series VI), 1972.

Zimmermann, Albert, and Walter de Gruyter (eds.). *Albert der Grosse: Seine Zeit, sein Werk, seine Wirkung.* Berlin & New York, 1981.

Printed in the United States
78453LV00007B/34